# Ethnicity and Identity

# Ethnicity and Identity

*Global Performance*

---

*Edited by*

**Ravi Chaturvedi**
**Brian Singleton**

## RAWAT PUBLICATIONS

Jaipur • New Delhi • Bangalore • Mumbai

ISBN 81-7033-916-2
© Contributors, 2005

*Published by*
Prem Rawat for *Rawat Publications*
Satyam Apts., Sector 3, Jawahar Nagar, Jaipur 302 004 (India)
Phone: 0141 265 1748 / 7006  Fax: 0141 265 1748
E-mail: info@rawatbooks.com
Website: www.rawatbooks.com

*Delhi Office*
4858/24, Ansari Road, Daryaganj,  New Delhi 110 002
Phone: 011-23263290

*Also at Bangalore and Mumbai*

Typeset by Rawat Computers, Jaipur
Printed at Chaman Enterprises, New Delhi

# Contents

# Part II
## Political Polarities and Identity Formation

# Part III
## Ethnic Issues and Challenges

# Part V
## Subjugation of Identities and Ethnic Icons

# Foreword

As I have mentioned on several occasions, I think along with many others scholars that one of the functions of a Federation like ours is not only to promote theatrical research and to be a leader in the field but to be able to do so while not forgetting the real world around us with its share of dramatic events and its unequal development. Our research, however "de pointe", is never more interesting, more profound, more convincing than when it takes into account the real world around us.

From this point of view (as such?), the topic, *Ethnicity and Identity: Global Performance,* adopted for the Jaipur conference is not only especially inspiring but absolutely compelling too. It is indeed deeply rooted in today's problematics, which is the centre of most of our 19th and 20th centuries history, which raised resistance, civil fights, wars as well as genocides (Rwanda, Ivory Coast to name but a few). This topic touches upon western as well as eastern countries, developed as well as developing countries. It is particularly appropriate for the kind of times we are living in and it will certainly help us reflect, among other things, on the tremendous changes that theatre studies have gone through over the last twenty years being at the crossroads of society, identity and culture of the past and the present. How do theatre studies relate to all the changes, which have occurred in the nations or states regarding cultures or art forms? What do theatre studies have to say to keep in touch with that "reality"? It is a question, which is central to our endeavour, and the conference held in Jaipur helped answer some of it.

This question of ethnicity and identity brings about a certain number of observations that Ravi Chaturvedi has perfectly summed up in his introductory words:

> During the last decade, everyone throughout the world, has experienced rapid changes in economic development, urbanization, and westernization in varying degrees. Industrialization and mass communication technology have dismantled the traditional social structure and changed the lifestyles of the masses. Regional imbalance in political power and economic development has further created social and cultural problems. The above picture does not reflect the face of Asia, Africa and Latin America only, but more or less prevails in the developed part of the world in some or other way also. The varied theatres of the world are proving effective evidence of such reality throughout the times. The fact can easily be underlined that, unlike the traditional societies, where cultural unity is generally expressed in local communities, the contemporary nationalities and societies, demarcated by new political boundaries, are characterized by the dichotomy of indigenous culture and imported culture, dominant group and periphery group culture, nationalism and globalization. Faced with such encounters of cultures of the world are compelled to search for a path that is suitable for them, with their own agenda and priority.
>
> The major issues include identity crisis, creation of a new national culture, conflicts derived from regional imbalance in economic development and power sharing, fear of erosion of indigenous value and problems of morals and cultures in the waves of cyber streams and globalization. However, these issues, whether nationalism, national integration, urbanization, multiculturalism, or mass culture transmitted by electronic media, are invariably related to the key issue of cultural identity and ethnicity, the identity that defines the sense of nation, community and ethnic roots is generally linked to the politics of nationalism, national integration and political contests.

What seems striking in these few introductory remarks is the deep link, which is highlighted here between interculturalism and identity:

an identity, which can be understood differently whether one speaks about *nation identity* (close to the notion of ethnicity; in this instance, the notion stresses the differences between countries, or social groups), or *cultural and artistic identity* (bringing along, on the contrary, the notion of federation of cultures, as is presently attempted by Arabic countries around the Mediterranean Sea; this latter notion tries to bring out the resemblances rather than the differences between nations).

These two notions, I am afraid, are exclusive of one another because they rely on two different visions of the world, whether one assumes, to start with, that countries identities are fundamentally different but that they share something in common (hence the Federation attempt around the notion of culture and art around the Mediterranean Sea), or that countries work at keeping their social as well as cultural specificity in order not to be swallowed by an endemic globalization. In this latter instance, "culture" is taken in its anthropological or sociological meaning, and goes way beyond its artistic dimension. In the first assumption, one is looking for common points of convergence, a common denominator beyond the nations in order to bring them closer, in the second, it is rather stressing the necessary disparities in order to highlight the differences and preserve the specificities in order for each individual not to be swallowed in one common global mass culture.

Both discourses are justified and present today – sometimes in the same country – but their relevance depends on the objectives which are carried by the researcher or the artist who holds them. Indeed, beyond the assertions, which seem self-evident, both discourses convey an ideological discourse, which carries an undisclosed agenda: assert the specificity of each culture as if the notion of identity was necessarily positive. This is debatable. However, in both cases, it is a way to acknowledge the "other" – whether outside or inside of one's own culture – and bring it closer without loosing one's own identity.

This curiosity about other cultures is not recent, no more so than the practices of adapting and borrowing. As has been said repeatedly, it is the essence of art. However, what has changed is that the notion of exchanges, borrowings is no longer given for granted and that it has become absolutely mandatory to understand the reasons for such transfers, crossings, contributions and exchanges so that they do not erase the specificity of the targeted culture.

Two attitudes can be observed towards this question: the first one acknowledges that it is beneficial to widen our mental attitudes, that it makes us more aware of our neighbours' otherness, hence better able to listen to others. The practices of artists or writers such as Montesquieu, Artaud, Stanislavski, Craig, Brecht, Grotowski and Mnouchkine, as well as the statements of Ariane Mnouchkine, Peter Brook, Elizabeth Lecompte, Reza Abdoh, Peter Sellars, Robert Wilson, Ping Chong, Laurie Anderson, Richard Foreman, Meredith Monk or Lee Breuer fall into this category.

The second type of reaction, which should not be underestimated, comes from investigators for whom interculturalism contains a threat from a ruling culture to unduly appropriate other, often "minority" cultures and traditions without offering anything in return. Carl Weber, Una Chaudhuri, Daryl Chin and most of all Rustom Bharucha to name but a few, enter in this category.

The purpose of the texts included in this book highlights these points. Either, they fall in the first or the second category but all of them encourage us to treat the intercultural phenomenon carefully, to reflect on what it implies on social, political as well as aesthetic levels. They invite us to be more lucid, prudent and re-assess our behaviour.

In other words, duality and ambiguity always exist. Any study on interculturalism must take this into account or else dissimulate an important aspect of the phenomenon. It follows that studies of theatrical interculturalism must be executed within a political context. If one insists on protecting the integrity of art outside its relationship with society, then art might miss out on the real challenges of what it represent.

We are grateful to Ravi Chaturvedi to have allowed all these exchanges to take place with such acuteness in India.

**Josette Féral**
IFTR President (1999-2003)
Theatre Department
Université du Québec à Montréal

# Preface

Most social scientists agree that ethnicity is one of the most misunderstood and misused words in the study of politics. This is not surprising, given that it is easy to be confused when the subject is that of defining ethnicity. In the positive viewpoint, ethnicity is a warm, comfortable feeling, which gives a sense of belonging to a group of people. In this definition, ethnicity is also about 'shared memories' or 'fake memories'. Leadership and trust within the ethnic groups are benefits that are otherwise absent in multi-ethnic groups. However, the hardheaded instrumental approach to the understanding of ethnic conflicts in modern times has always been under question. The theatre of the world is also not an exception in this respect, which has raised an endless series of questions under the changing socio-economic scenario during the 20th century emphasizing 'how' and 'why' ethnic conflicts in the political institutions of liberal democracy evolved after the post-colonial nation-building exercise.

Needless to say that the idea of ethnicity and identity, in the vicinity of their interrelationship, requires a thorough introspection. Several social scientists do not agree that 'ethnicity' is synonymous with 'identity'. On the contrary, the two are quite distinct. Ethnicity is a socially negotiated achievement, rather than a fact, while identity is a theoretical proposition that seeks to explain political, cultural and social behaviour based on an underlying web of contingent conditions and achievements, like ethnicity. This usage differs somewhat from the standard psychologically influenced definitions and applications that pervade the study of national identity. One element of identity studies has been to explore the various processes by which identities are created, imagined or dissolved. This process-based approach has inspired a number of scholars to explore a variety of case studies, but it has failed to address the theoretical concerns that support these classic endeavours, namely, ethnicity.

Although ethnicity is clearly defined in anthropology, sociology and political science textbooks, it remains a historically situated phenomenon whose meaning and relevance varies with both time and place. The term 'ethnicity' is a derivative of the Greek *ethnikos*, which originally meant "heathen" or "cultural strangers". In conjunction with this usage, ethnicity is a global phenomenon created by the imperial expansion of Europe and the United States with the ethnic 'other' placed in contradistinction to the globalizing European self. Ethnicity undoubtedly existed before this expansion wherever people of different languages and cultures encountered each other, but this consciousness served to localize identities, rather than to socially validate ethnicity as a universal 'fact'. Since then, ethnicity has been understood as a concrete social fact, used in everyday conversation, scientific discourse, writing and politics.

On the other hand, identity is dependent on memory and is therefore undergoing constant revision. Furthermore, just as memory and identity are mutually dependent, they "sustain certain subjective positions, social boundaries, and, of course, power". Political leadership worldwide use the language of identity, claiming an interest in protecting and enhancing national identities. This global discourse on identity is a recent one, and a testimony not to the universality of identity concerns but, rather, to the "rapid spread of hegemonic ideas about modernity and ethnicity". Recently, historians, psychologists and anthropologists have acknowledged the subjective nature of identity. Ironically, the fierce battles that continue to be waged worldwide over identity make apparent that identity is "highly selective, inscriptive rather than descriptive, serving particular interests and ideological positions". Linking identity with the concept of 'nation' further enhances the sensitivity of the issue. The German philosopher, Karl W. Deutsch defines nationalism as "a state of mind which gives 'national' messages, memories, and images a preferred status in social communication and a greater weight in the making of decisions". By emphasizing social communication as the precondition for the establishment of feelings of national identity, Deutsch places too high a premium on communication at the expense of other important variables – a criticism that scholars have lamented for years by insisting that definitions of nationalism be capable of addressing both the 19th and 20th centuries forms: the nationalism of people who possess a state and the nationalism of those who do not. With our experiences of the history, it will not be wrong to say that "nationalism is primarily a political principle, which holds that the political and the national units should be congruent". Nationalism, as a sentiment, or as a movement, can best be defined in terms of this principle. Nationalist *sentiment* is the feeling of anger aroused by the violation of this principle, or the feeling of satisfaction aroused by its fulfilment. "A nationalist *movement* is one actuated by a sentiment of this kind...nationalism is not the awakening of nations to self-consciousness; it invents nations where they do not exist." What is central to a nationalist movement is its claim to represent members of the nationality by virtue of the cultural and material interests that they share. It asks its supporters to subordinate their common interests (class, religion, party, etc.) with their fellow citizens in favour of those that they share with the members of the national group.

Having examined a number of interpretive analyses of identity and ethnicity, a definite difference can be seen between ethnic and national identity for a number of different reasons. Nation and the foundations of nationalism differ from ethnies in the following ways: (1) they entail a definite historic territory or homeland, not just some association with it, (2) they share a common economy, with territorial mobility throughout, (3) they share a public, mass education-based culture, and (4) they provide for the common legal rights and duties for all members. Accordingly, national identity represents a composite and multidimensional amalgam of processes, which develop in unequal rhythms. These include growing territorialization, the growth of a mass public culture, economic centralization and legal standardization. National identity differs from ethnicity, however, by ceding more weight to territorial, economic and legal-political processes. The process of turning an ethnie into a nation is one that is associated with the politicalization of culture, the delimitation of space and the standardization of social life.

Pointing out these notions, Josette Feral rightly emphasized in her inaugural address to the international conference of IFTR held in 2003 at Jaipur that:

> As I have just mentioned, this question of identity is central to our field as it is to any field of research and to any individual, for that matter. Indeed, while we can detect a general tendency to make national, economic, political and cultural frontiers more porous, we can detect at the same time an opposite tendency which suggests that despite this global movement toward openness, we also create endless zones of exclusion and isolation. We create new boundaries, new territories.

> This notion of "territory" has come under scrutiny in the last fifteen years, namely, in the works of Homi K. Bhabha, Arjun Appadurai, Akhil Gupta and James Ferguson. These scholars remind us how the notion of identity as well as the notion of ethnicity have long been associated with that of territory. The idea of nation sovereignty ethnic group has thus long been legitimised through the existence of a defined "territory", defined itself according to geographic borders.

> However, with today's numerous migrations of people and with the porousness of nation borders, the notion of territory is no longer self-evident. A new cartography has been instated whereby subjects are more and more "deterritorialized" that is severed from the country or culture they are originally linked to and "reterritorialised" according to new parameters more akin to the localities they live in. These localities are defined through "human sociality" rather than geographic borders.

> The synchronization of an ideal territory with an ideal state in a nationalist vision legitimising a single ethnicity creates the conditions for the wars of extermination or of ethnicity of which our century has been far from innocent. Paradoxically, while phenomena are increasingly fragmentary and while we cannot conceive of their eventual unity, at the same time, territorial nationalisms assert themselves. Indeed, one observes that while economical frontiers

may have been altered on a long scale (as in Europe or North America), political frontiers still exist. They reaffirm, rather than dissolve, themselves.

We are reminded at the same time that while boundaries may be geographic, they are more often ideological and constitute a process by which we imprison one another in a single origin, culture, religion or ideology. Through this process of identification we exclude the other from our shared space. This would seem to be the final program of the discourse of enclosure and exclusion – to clear the space.

Now, I am glad to remind all of us that theatre has always been a place of resistance against these tendencies. It has always been a place of exploration, a transitional space, a space of passage and crossing rather than a place of identification or enclosure. It has always been zone where hegemonic cultures have been requestioned and transformed, where they have been contaminated by other influence through a network of movements and exchanges. We all know, for instance, how much Indian art forms have been important to such directors as P. Brook, A. Mnouchkine, E. Barba, R. Schechner, how much oriental art forms have been borrowed and have had a major impact on today's theatre.

This book, which contains the papers presented in the sa conference, touching the various aspects of the issue in question, divided in five sections. The selection of these thirty-seven articles on of eighty-four papers presented in the conference is an effort of under lining the universality of the reflection of ideas in the world theatre.

My acknowledgements are due to all the distinguished cont butors who waited for couple of years with great patience. I a thankful for their understanding. I also submit my sincere apology those whose articles could not be included in the book, not because their quality and standard but considering the volume of the book. I a also thankful to Prof. Josette Feral for writing a very enlightenir encouraging and motivating foreword. When the editing work w turning into a nightmarish task, Dr. Brian Singleton, the co-editor the book, and Vice-President of IFTR, gladly offered his helping ha and shared a larger portion of this enormous job proving his friendsh in need. Preeti S. Kurup is another person who was also a great help this project by providing all the secretarial and editorial assistance in an always-ready-to-work manner repeating her spirits of the Conference Secretary. My loving thanks to her. Last but not least, my thanks are due to Mr. Pranit Rawat of Rawat Publications, Jaipur, without whose initiative and having confidence in me, this book would have not been a reality.

**Ravi Chaturvedi**

# Part I

Trans-Action, Encounter and
Traditional Space

# 1

# Revisiting Ancient Tradition

## The Modern Laban/Bartenieff System as Applied in Practice to Indian Classical Dance

### Ciane Fernandes

This paper makes a parallel between Indian classical dance of *Bharatanatyam* style and Laban/Bartenieff system, in order to facilitate and provide the learning of such ancient technique, as much as research the integration between tradition and innovation in the choreographic process.

After studying German dance theatre and movement analysis in New York and Germany for five years, my research has concentrated on body techniques integrating process and product, in a complete training philosophy connected to dance theatre principles. During seven months in Berlin, the intense training on *Bharatanatyam* at Rajyashree Ramesh Academy for Performing Arts, demonstrated the connection between Indian Classical dance and movement analysis of European origin. The association of both tendencies facilitated the learning of *Bharatanatyam*, and after five months it was already possible to follow classes of the second year.

The association of both German and Indian techniques also facilitated the learning process at body technique classes for actors – levels I to IV – at Federal University of Bahia, Brazil. Such association has proved to be coherent and efficient in both body training for the actor and in choreographic projects.

## Dance Theatre: Tradition and Innovation

The complexity of performing arts of India and, more specifically, of *Bharatanatyam*, is due to their historicity. They have been registered during the Vedic civilization, in the *Nâtya Úâstra* manuscript – the oldest and more complete treatise about performing arts, written 200 years before Christ.[1] Alarmél Valli explains the depth and inclusiveness of this dance:

> The greatness of *Bharata Natyam*, for me, lies in its ability to harmonise the physical, intellectual, emotional and spiritual dimensions of life, giving the dance the power to touch and to communicate at all levels. Being a composite art, it synthesises melody and rhythm, painting and sculpture, poetry and theatre. The dancer is simultaneously the musician, singing with her body... She is the sculptor, shaping and structuring space in forms both graceful and powerful. She is the painter, adding tints and hues to a line drawing... She is the poet, writing her poems with movement, gestures and expressions. Ultimately she is the seeker, whose dance becomes a transcendental, transforming experience – an ecstatic prayer that celebrates the beauty, the wonder and the mystery of life.[2]

The association of these various human aspects, is also a theme of Meyer-Dinkgraefe's comparative study relating the *Natya Sastra* to western theatre techniques and philosophies influenced by the east.[3] In his book, the professor of the Department of Theatre, Film and Television Studies at the University of Wales demonstrates that the classical Indian training of the actor is most complete, and proposes its use for the development of consciousness in the training of an "enlightened actor," of either western or eastern origin. In fact, the east-west dialogue has inspired various researches[4] and is one of the main themes of contemporary performing arts, also in regard to an intercultural and interdisciplinary analysis of the technique-performance relationship. In other words, it is an appropriate moment to join different approaches to the arts and to artistic making, from scientific and technological knowledge to cultural, historical, anthropological and aesthetic studies.

In this context, I introduce the founder and pioneer of German dance theatre, Rudolf von Laban (1879-1958). In the beginning of the 20th century, Laban proposed an aesthetic system at the same time wide and extremely detailed, overlapping objective and subjective approaches, practice and theory, kinesthetic experience and cognitive understanding, in the training of a complete "thinking-feeling-acting being":[5]

> In his complex system of movement language, later called Laban Movement Analysis – LMA, or Laban System, the languages of behavioral and performing representation are gathered under the hegemony of "movement", broken up until its most simple element... and articulated till its most complexes harmonies, organized in a proper language and symbolism structured similarly to a musical motif.[6]

Besides being a complex and multifaceted system of bodily movement, the Laban System also shares the following points with *Bharatanatyam*: the concern with systematization and recording of movement, the width of its movement possibilities, its inter-artistic quality, and aspects specific to body technique. The systematization and recording of body movement, started by the detailed *Natya Sastra* in its 5,800 verses, had in Laban a faithful supporter:

> When I undertook as the first one among dancers of today to speak of a world for which language lacks words, I was fully aware of the difficulty of this undertaking. Only a firm conviction that one has to conquer for dance the field of written and spoken expression, to open it up... to widest circles, brought me to tackle this difficult task.[7]

This modern dance pioneer created a system applicable to the *a posteriori* observation and analysis of dance, as much as to the *a priori* dance processes, as creative method and recording of improvisations. According to Claire Osborne,[8] the Laban system developed from *Tanz-Ton-Wort* (Dance-Tone-Word) improvisations, creating pieces with daily movement, abstract or pure, in a narrative, comic or more abstract form. On the other hand, Indian classical dance presents three categories: *Nritta* (pure and abstract dance); *Abhinaya* (expressive dance, usually telling stories of the Hindu literature through hand gestures, facial expressions, etc.), and *Nritya* (a combination altering the two previous ones). Therefore, both Indian classical dance theatre and German modern (Laban) and contemporary (for example Pina Bausch) dance theatre encompass a wide possible range of bodily movements, varying from facial expressions, minimal gestures – illustrative or abstract – to functional and daily movements with the whole body in the three-dimensional space.

Also, both performing art forms imply the relationship between the arts. The training of the performer proposed by Laban was in accordance to the multidisciplinary philosophy of the artists in the beginning of the 20th century, integrating the arts in movements such as Dada and Bauhaus, in the birth of the so-called "performance art". During the training in the Laban System in New York, students visit museums and choreograph out of sculptures; create sequences out of an architectural analysis of, for example, a church, or out of poems, as the beautiful Haikai; draw and do collages in personal daily report notebook, among other activities. During the day, students have practical classes dealing with whole body postures to studies of minimal gestures and expression, theoretical seminars, and learn to draw the detailed notations created by Laban and his disciples. Movement transforms itself in drawing/notation, in sculptural shapes on space and in lines in movement (in LMA, respectively called Space Harmony and Trace Forms), as in the interartistic descriptions of Valli in relation to *Bharatanatyam*. In presentations at the Laban/Bartenieff Institute of Movement Studies (New York), and in all my career following that, German dance theatre has proved to be a "complete art", as referred by Valli in regard to the Indian classical dance of her specialty. Today, though, this "completeness" is within an environment of unpredictable genetic manipulations, virtual bodies and spaces, in other words, concrete contexts of transforming tradition.[9]

This takes us to one of the major exponents of the dance of today, Pina Bausch (1940), pioneer of German contemporary dance theatre, disciple of Kurt Jooss, one of the main disciples of Laban. In 1994, Bausch and her international company travelled to India, where they had several presentations in a tour with Chandralekha, Indian contemporary choreographer trained in *Bharatanatyam*. According to Georg Lechner,[10] in spite of all the visible differences between the works of the two choreographers, both are dealing with a post-industrial, productive, disoriented and "docile" body,[11] in search of a (in-constant) beginning in dance. Still in 1994, Bausch's company received daily training in Classical Indian dance in Germany. This tour influenced Bausch technically and aesthetically, and she started to develop choreographic projects connected to different localities, travelling and experimenting with her company "in transit" in other cultures, including Brazil (2000).

Another more concrete connection between German dance theatre and *Bharatanatyam* is the specific technical correspondence between the Laban/Bartenieff System and the didactic organization of *Bharatanatyam* training. During classes on this dance of India, one can observe and apply Laban/Bartenieff principles to each exercise, clarifying them and making them more accessible, dynamic and healthy. For example, to practice the exercises created by Laban's disciple Irmgard Bartenieff[12] in the warm up helps on performing the basic *Bharatanatyam* position *Aramandi*, in which the legs are flexed with a wide external rotation, the pelvis as low as possible, without forcing the spinal curves at any point. This is exactly the work done by the Bartenieff Fundamentals,[13] developed initially for polio patients and today used by dancers all around the world. These exercises work on body movement out of deep pelvic muscle support for breathing, providing a Gradated Rotation of the femoral joint, connected to a Dynamic Alignment based on Bony Connections (Bartenieff) – imaginary lines linking important Bony Landmarks, generating simultaneous support and agility, Stability and Mobility (one of the four Laban Movement Principles).

Besides Core Support (inner muscular support) and Bony Connections, another relevant Bartenieff Principle in this comparative study is the Body Organization, which evolves in the following order of growing neuromuscular complexity: Cellular Breathing, Navel Radiation or Centre-Periphery, Spinal or Head-Tail, Homologous or Upper-Lower Body, Homo-lateral or Body Half (Right-Left), Contra-lateral or Crossed-Sides. In its ancient wisdom, *Bharatanatyam* exercises are organized in an order of growing neuromuscular complexity, as described by Bartenieff and present in her Fundamentals. Also in terms of Shape or Relationship (LMA), the learning of *Bharatanatyam* follows a growing complexity, with the majority of its exercises in Spoke-Like or Arc-Like Directional Shape (creating straight or curved lines by the flexion/extension, abduction/adduction), and evolving into Shaping (sculpting in the three-dimensional space by the use of rotation) in more advanced exercises.

Also, the relationship of the body with the space, in both techniques – in the case, actually, systems – is visible. According to Chandralekha, one of the questions of her work is "how to visualize this body-geometry [present in well-defined shapes of *Bharatanatyam*] in terms of space-geometry – the inner/outer correspondence."[14] In his

Spatial Harmony, Laban talks about an architecture of the body in movement on space, determining at least 50 scales created by pathways between geometric points on space, based on regular polyhedrons. In *Bharatanatyam* training, the exercises follow a growing order of spatial complexity, as proposed in the Laban training:[15] Dimensions of the Octahedron (Vertical, Horizontal and Sagital, each one with 2 points in opposite directions), Planes of the Icosahedron (Vertical, Horizontal e Sagital, each one with 4 points, resulting of the intersection of 2 dimensional points) and Diagonals of the Cube (8 points resulting from the intersection of 3 dimensional points). And one of the four Laban Movement Principles, besides the already mentioned Stability/ Mobility, is exactly Inner/Outer, cited by Chandralekha.

Another relevant point of technical-philosophical contact between the two systems is the concept of *rasa*. *Rasa* is a key-concept exposed in the *Natya Sastra*, but also found in many Vedic texts. It refers to water, juice, essence, tasty liquid and, in the context of the philosophy of India, to the aesthetic experience of the actor and, mostly, of the public.[16] *Rasa* can be translated to "sentiment", classified by the *Natya Sastra* in long lists of different "transitory states" with subdivisions. I compare here this concept of *rasa* to Laban's *Eukinetics*,[17] in which combinations of inner attitudes provide an expression that reaches the public. He also called these combinations of "states", with a main quality of mutability – a constant transition between "polarities". These are not taken as opposite, but rather as gradations among extremes of a specific expressive factor: flow (bound-free), weight (strong-light), time (accelerated-decelerated), and space (direct-indirect or flexible). While weight is associated to sensation, time to intuition, and space to thinking,[18] flow associates itself to emotion, and is subliminar to the other three factors. Flow is the basis of every movement, as subliminar tension and initial impulse present, for instance, in all vital functions. It can be associated to *Shape Flow* or the relationship of the body with itself, perceiving its own volume and moving out of its breathing, organs and body liquids. Bonnie Bainbridge Cohen,[19] disciple of Bartenieff, has proved the importance of the "Fluid System of the Body" – cellular and intercellular fluid, blood, lymph, cerebrospinal fluid, synovial fluid – in the expressive movement, as in the Vedic concept of *rasa*.

The next section presents two items: some main characteristics of *Bharatanatyam* according to the Laban/Bartenieff System; and a Laban

Movement Analysis of some *Bharatanatyam* exercises, in the order performed in class and learned along the years of training. This will allow the visualization of growing complexity in neuromuscular patterns and use of space.

## Laban Movement Analysis of Bharatanatyam and Some of Its Exercises

A. General principles of the dance, followed by LMA terms:

1. Separation into Major Limbs (initiate the movement: feet, hands, eyes, head, neck, waist) and Minor Limbs (follow the previous: legs, arms, face, torso...) – Bartenieff Principle of Initiation and Sequencing.

2. Initiation of movements mostly in the extremities, different and simultaneous movements of different body parts (each one with specific qualities) – Distal Initiation, Simultaneous Sequencing, creating a "high energy level"[20] in complex combinations.

3. Steps with Locomotion associated to hand gestures and facial expression – Gesture/Posture Merger and Bartenieff Principle of Weight Shift for Locomotion.

4. Basic Posture with straight spinal column and arms opened to the sides – Bartenieff Principle of Bony Connections (specially Head-Heels, Head-Tail, Scapula-Scapula, Scapula-Hand), Vertical and Horizontal dimensions, Spoke-Like Directional Shape.

5. Foot Stepping on the ground, bringing heels high up till the sit-bones and back to the floor – Strong weight and Quick time, Heels-Sitz Bones Connection, Effort Life for Body Connectivity (another Bartenieff Principle).

6. Abstract dance (*Nritta*): mostly condensing qualities combined in Awake State (space and time), Mobile State (flow and time), Rhythm State (weight and time), action drives (punch). Expressive Dance (Nritya): all combinations of effort life, especially important is phrasing (distribution of expressive emphasis, if any, or rhythm of energy in the movement phrase) and Exertion/Recuperation Movement Theme (natural tendency to recuperate of a movement by performing complementary or different expressive qualities to it).

7. Emphasis in bound flow and verticality of torso in *Bharatanatyam* – compensated by Bartenieff Fundamentals warm up (shape flow and floor work with passive weight and free flow on the ground, supported by deep breathing).

8.  Torso bending to the sides or slightly forwards are done from the waist (main limb), maintaining the relationship between arms, spine and head as in the Basic Position, in other words, without twisting at the neck nor projecting shoulders or thorax forwards or isolately in any direction – Emphasis on the Head-Tail, Scapula-Scapula and Scapula-Hand Connections, keeping spine and shoulders with a primary horizontal (side-side) emphasis or vertical (in the case of the spine), rather than sagital (forwards or backwards) emphasis.

9.  Clear Positioning of Limbs on Space – Bartenieff Principle of Spatial Intent.

10. Elbows always out or up, initiating the arm movements – Mid-Limb Initiation, Spoke-Like Directional Shape.

11. Hand Gestures – Hand-Scapula Connection, Directional (e.g. *Katakamukham* – stretched first and second fingers touching thumb, while 2 smaller fingers stretch upwards) or Shaping Movement (e.g. *Alapadma* – fingers opened as in a lotus flower).

12. The position of the sitting Budha – Tetrahedron (Cristaline Form of previous complexity to the Octahedron, Icosahedron, Cube and Dodecahedron).

B. Selected *Bharatanatyam* exercises, in the order performed in class and in the learning process (names based on Mrinalini Sarabhai[21] and Padma Subrahmanyam[22]). OBSERVE THE GROWING COMPLEXITY FROM ITEM TO ITEM. Some exercises are followed by their rhythmic syllables (e.g. "ta tai ta ha"), to facilitate their identification by the practitioners. Detailed descriptions of some of these exercises can be found in Van Zile.[23]

Obs. *Adavus* are units of pure dance; "exercises" which are gradually added to each other in complex choreographies.

*TATTADAVUS* ("tattu" = to strike flat; "tatta" = to beat): Core Support, Dynamic Alignment, Homologous (Upper/Lower), Heels-Sitz Bones Bony Connection, Gradated Rotation (hip joint), Vertical Dimension, Thigh Lift (initiated by the heels towards the sitz-bones).

*1° e 2° NATTADAVU* ("nattu" = to stretch): Hands-Scapulas Bony Connection, Heels-Sitz Bones Connection, Head-Hands (Eyes-Hands) Bony Connection, Homolateral (Left/Right), Spoke-like Directional, Horizontal Dimension.

*3° e 4° NATTADAVU*: Hands-Scapulas Bony Connection, Heels-Sitz Bones Connection, Head-Hands (Eyes-Hands) Bony

Connection, Homolateral (Left/Right), Gradated Rotation, Arc-Like Directional, Vertical Plane.

*5° NATTADAVU:* Hands-Scapulas Bony Connection, Heels-Sitz Bones Connection, Head-Hands (Eyes-Hands) Bony Connection, Homologous (Upper/Lower) and Homolateral (Left/Right), Gradated Rotation, Spoke-Like Directional, Sagital Plane and Horizontal Dimension.

*6° NATTADAVU:* Hands-Scapulas Bony Connection, Heels-Sitz Bones Connection, Head-Hands (Eyes-Hands) Bony Connection, Homolateral (Left/Right), Gradated Rotation, Spoke-Like Directional and Arch-Like Directional, Vertical and Horizontal Dimensions, Sagital Plane.

*7° NATTADAVU:* Hands-Scapulas Bony Connection, Heels-Sitz Bones Connection, Head-Hands (Eyes-Hands) Bony Connection, Homologous (Upper/Lower) and Homolateral (Left/Right), Gradated Rotation, Spoke-Like Directional and Arch-Like Directional, Vertical (door) and Sagital (wheel) Planes.

*8° NATTADAVU:* Hands-Scapulas Bony Connection, Heels-Sitz Bones Connection, Head-Hands (Eyes-Hands) Bony Connection, Homologous (Upper/Lower) and Homolateral (Left/Right), Gradated Rotation, Spoke-Like Directional and Arch-Like Directional, Sagital (wheel) and Vertical (door) Planes, Horizontal and Vertical Dimensions (for the first time including Place Low with the pelvis, while earlier the Vertical Dimension was restricted to arm movements).

*TATTI METTU ADAVU* ("tattu" = to strike; "mettu" = to beat; lifting and striking heel down): Heels-Sitz Bones Connection, Homologous (Upper/Lower), Homolateral (Right/Left), Gradated Rotation, Spoke-Like Directional, Vertical Dimension. The neurological and spatial regression of this exercise is compensated by the increase of complexity in rhythmic terms, in the new action of stepping alternately in half-point and heels (left and right), while earlier the whole sole of the feet would step on the ground at each strike.

*KUDITTU METTU ADAVU* ("tai ha tai hi") ("kudittu" – jump): Bony Connections (already cited), Homologous (Upper/Lower), Distal Initiation (hands and feet), Gradated Rotation, Spoke-Like Directional, Vertical Dimension (heels jumping up in half-point and back down); Vertical, Horizontal and Sagital Dimensions and Diagonals with the arms, torso bending into Vertical Plane from the waist.

*KHUTTHADAVU*, also called Ettadavu ("etta" = to reach out) (ta tai ta ha – dhi tai ta ha) ("khuttha" = slight jump with both feet): Bony Connections (already cited), Homologous (Upper/Lower), Homolateral (Right/Left), Contralateral (UpperRight/LowerLeft; UpperLeft/LowerRight), Gradated Rotation, Spoke-Like Directional and Arc-Like Directional, Vertical Dimension (feet during jumps or stepping down), Horizontal Dimension (arms to the sides), Horizontal (table) Plane (arms crossing towards forward middle right or left), Vertical (door) Plane (last part, arms going to Low Right and Low Left), Cube Diagonals (last part, arms going to High Forward Right and High Forward Left).

*KHUTTADAVU* – VARIATION (legs as in Khuttadavu; arms almost as in the last part of Kudittu Mettu): Bony Connections (already cited), Homologous (Upper/Lower), Homolateral (Right/Left), Contralateral (UpperRight/LowerLeft; UpperLeft/LowerRight), Gradated Rotation (arms and legs), Spoke-Like Directional and Arc-Like Directional, Vertical Plane, Cube Diagonals (last part, arms going to High Forward Right and High Forward Left).

*SARUKKALADAVU* ("sarukkal" or "skhalita" = one or both feet slip): Bony Connections, Homologous, Homolateral, Contralateral, Spoke-Like Directional and Arc-Like Directional, Horizontal Dimension, Vertical Dimension and Plane.

*MANDI ADAVU* ("mandi" = knees; down with knees opened, heels high): special emphasis on Bartenieff Movement Principles – Bony Connections, Breath Support, Kinetic Chains, Core Support and Spatial Intent for agile and rhythmic Weight Transfer on Place Low; Homologous, Homolateral, Contralateral (on the 3rd variation in the *Allarippu*, to stand up), Spoke-Like Directional and Arc-Like Directional, Horizontal Dimension, Forward Low Diagonals (arms), Sagital Plane and Vertical Dimension (2nd variation).

*MAKUTA* or *TIRMANA ADAVUS* ("dhi dhi tai") ("tirmana" = to conclude): Bony Connections, Gradated Rotation. It includes five variations:

1.  With arms in arch crossing in front of the torso: Spoke-Like Directional (legs) and Arc-Like Directional (arms), Homologous (Upper/Lower), Sagital Plane (arms), Diagonals of Cube (legs).

2.  With arms alternately forward and back, on same side as leg going forward sideways: Spoke-Like Directional (arms and legs) and Arc-Like Directional (arms coming back to centre), Homolateral (Right/Left), Sagital Dimension (arms), Diagonals of Cube (legs).

3.  With arms alternately going in the diagonal, on opposite side of leg going forward sideways: Spoke-Like Directional (arms and legs), Contralateral (UpperRight/LowerLeft; UpperLeft/ LowerRight), Diagonals of Cube (arms and legs).

4.  With arms initially in *Natyarambhe* (stretched in the Horizontal Dimension), and then alternately going Back Middle, Place High, and diagonal pull Forward Low on the opposite side while the other arm goes Forward Middle and opens gradually in the Horizontal Plane back to the side in *Natyarambhe*: Spoke-Like Directional (arms and legs), Arc-Like Directional and Shaping (Arms), Homologous, Homolateral and Contralateral, Dimensions (Octahedron; arms), Planes (Icosahedron; arms), Diagonals (Cube; arms and legs).

5.  "Ta ha ta jam ta ri ta – Jam ta ri ja ka ta ri tai": Spoke-Like Directional (arms and legs), Arc-Like Directional and Shaping (Arms and hands), Homologous (jump), Homolateral (step with one leg and arm on the same side stretch in the diagonal) and Contralateral (one arm and opposite leg in the diagonal), Dimensions (Octahedron; arms), Diagonals (Cube; arms and legs).

Obs: in all five variations, before going into the diagonal, and back to centre, the lower leg goes up into Place Middle (Vertical Dimension) from the heel (Heels-Sitz Bones Connection).

## Final Considerations

The continuation of this study can open lots of technical and performative possibilities of application in intercultural settings. For example, through LMA, one can associate distinctive forms such as *Bharatanatyam* and *Orixa* dance (from the polytheist Afro-Brazilian *Candomble* religion). The *Candomble* dances, although quite complex, are to a certain extent absorbed in popular street dances of Bahia, and their rhythm does not seem difficult to the Bahian body. On the other hand, *Bharatanatyam* is a totally foreign system, with its rigid and agile postures, stable pelvis, detailed hand gestures and facial expressions completely new and distinct of Brazilian rhythms such as *frevo* or *samba*. LMA can facilitate such difficult learning of *Bharatanatyam* by Brazilians, as well as allow the creative correlation between different dances of Gods and Goddesses. For example, both Hindu *Shiva* and Afro-Brazilian warrior-God *Ogum* can be portrayed with strong weight, bound flow and direct focus (all condensing or "masculine" qualities in LMA), with a horizontal opening emphasis, altogether representing a wide impact and presence beyond time (notice that the time factor is neither accelerated or deccelerated: it is constant, eternal, as *Shiva*, the Lord of Time or *Mahakala*).

I hope this study opens up possibilities of cultural interchange, recognizing and validating differences as learning challenges and stimuli for enhancing the body (which for Laban, as much as for Bharatamuni and *Candomble* "dancers", includes all aspects mentioned by Valli – from emotional to spiritual), expanding creative possibilities (as for Bausch and Chandralekha) much beyond post-industrial, productive, docile and disoriented limitations.

## Notes

1. See *The Natya Sastra* by Bharatamuni. Translated into English by a Board of Scholars. Sri Satguru, New Delhi, 2000.

2. "Der Stil ist der Mensch." In: *Ballet International/Tanz Aktuell*, India Special Issue (July 1997), p. 32.

3. See the book of Daniel Meyer-Dinkgraefe, *Consciousness and the Actor: A Reassessment of Western and Indian Approaches to the Actor's Emotional Involvement from the Perspective of Vedic Psychology*. Peter Lang, Frankfurt, 1996.

4. Amy Matthews, "Laban Movement Analysis and Yoga." In: *Movement News*, Spring 2002, pp. 17-20. Christine Greiner, *O Teatro Nô e o Ocidente*. São Paulo: Annablume, 2000. Eugenio Barba and Nicola Savarese, *A Arte Secreta do Ator. Dicionário de Antropologia Teatral*. Hucitec, Sao Paulo, 1995.

5. Irmgard Bartenieff, "The Roots of Laban Theory: Aesthetics and Beyond." In: I. Bartenieff, M. Davis and F. Paulay, *Four Adaptations of Effort Theory in Research in Teaching*. Dance Notation Bureau, New York, 1970, p. 11.

6. Regina Miranda, "Prefácio". In: Ciane Fernandes, *O Corpo em Movimento: O Sistema Laban/Bartenieff na Formação e Pesquisa em Artes Cênicas*. Annablume, São Paulo, 2002, pp. 17, 18, 20.

7. Rudolf Laban in Vera Maletic, *Body – Space – Expression: The Development of Rudolf Laban's Movement and Dance Concepts*. Mounton de Gruyter, Berlin, 1987, p. 51.

8. Claire Osborne, "The Innovations and Influence of Rudolf Laban on the development of Dance in Higher Education During the Weimar Period (1917-1933)." In: *Working Papers* v. 2., Laban Centre, 1989.

9. H. Ploebst. *No Wind No Word: New Choreography in the Society of the Spectacle*. Munique: K. Kieser, 2001.

10. Georg Lechner, "Pina Bausch in/and India: Invitation to an Intercultural Discourse." In: *Tanztheater Today: Thirty Years of German Dance History*. Kallmeyersche, Seelzem, 2000, pp. 84-87.

11. See the book of Michael Foucault, *Discipline and Punish: The Birth of the Prison*. 2nd ed. Vintage Books, New York, 1995.

12. See the book of Irmgard Bartenieff, *Body Movement. Coping with the Environment*. Gordon & Breach Science Publishers, Langhorne, 1980.

13. Peggy Hackney, *Making Connections: Total Body Integration Through Bartenieff Fundamentals*. Gordon and Breach Publishers, Amsterdam, 1998.

14. "Die Wirbelsäule der Freiheit: Ein Statement von Chandralekha." In: *Ballet International/Tanz Aktuell*, India Special Issue (July 1997), p. 47.

15. See the book of Rudolf Laban, *The Language of Movement. A Guidebook to Choreutics*. Lisa Ullmann, ed. Plays Inc., Boston, 1976.

16. Daniel Meyer-Dinkgraefe, ibid., p. 85.

17. Rudolf Laban, *The Mastery of Movement*, ed. Lisa Ullmann. Plymouth, Mass.: Northcote House, 1988. See also Cecily Dell, *A primer for movement description*. Dance Notation Bureau, New York, 1977.

18. Vera Maletic, ibid., pp. 203-217.

19. See the book of Bonnie Bainbridge Cohen, *Sensing, Feeling, and Action: The Experiential Anatomy of Body-Mind Centering*. Contact Editions, Northampton, 1993.

20. Judy Van Zile, "Characteristics of Nrtta in Bharata Natyam." In: George Kliger, *Bharata Natyam in Cultural Perspective*. Manohar and American Institute of Indian Studies, New Delhi, 1993, pp. 43-90.

21. Mrinalini Sarabhai, *Understanding Bharata Natyam*. Darpana, Ahmedabad, 1996, pp. 27-28.

22. In Sunil Kothari, ed. *Bharata Natyam: Indian Classical Dance Art*. Marg Publications, Mumbai, 1979, pp. 36-38.

23. See the whole article of Judy van Zile, "Characteristics of Nrtta in Bharata Natyam." In: George Kliger, *Bharata Natyam in Cultural Perspective*. Manohar American Institute of Indian Studies, New Delhi, 1993.

# 2

## The Soul of the Story

### Blending Hart, Bogart and Suzuki in a Curricular Shift for the Globalized American Actor

#### Diane Smith-Sadak

The setting is a studio at Skidmore College, September 1993. I arrive 45 minutes before the first day of this International Fall Intensive, feeling proud of my discipline. I walk into the space – a dance theatre. In the room, Tadashi Suzuki sits 8 rows back in the middle of the house with a middle-aged assistant at his side. Astonished and humbled, I see the stage is already full of the other 17 participants in the workshop. There is no sound. I see 17 variations of stretching, breathing, yoga, and tai chi. For the next week, I do not know anyone's country of origin. I do not know what languages we speak. We work with Suzuki with a rigour I have never before experienced; we speak the few lines of required memorization – both English and Japanese – in a tightly structured unison. We do not talk, or ask questions. Then he tells us – through his interpreter – that his technique is fundamentally about the voice.

It is a 93-degree day in Atlanta, Georgia, 1996. I am at Emory University with Anne Bogart and her SITI Company in a black box theatre. There are 25 of us divided into three groups working in what Anne calls "Open Viewpoints". As we take the stage to begin, we are told to "make the space awake" as we choose our starting position. Shifts occur in the room until the actors settle into a tableau. We hear a voice, "It's already started – respond to what's already in the room," and other than the music underscoring our work, that is all we hear from Anne for the next 15 minutes.

It is Sunday afternoon, May 2001. I walk into a small studio on the 3rd floor of 440 Lafayette Street in downtown Manhattan. Studio 3G. In the room there is a piano and bench, an old air conditioning unit, a stool, a couple of chairs and a cloudy wall mirror. The grimy windows look out to a shaft of no more than 2 feet between the walls of two buildings. It is time for my lesson. Richard Armstrong is not yet here, so I position the piano and "get ready". Stretch. Breathe. Touch the tiniest bit of sound to my breath. Relax my face; soften my eyes. Breathe. When Richard enters, it is invariably with the question, "How are you today?" He meets me exactly where I am, using the what and how of my answer as our place of meeting.

The work begins.

How are you?

This is not a rhetorical question. It has nothing to do with politeness. It is at the root of our work here. At the moment when that question enters into our consciousness a series of very complicated neurological firings begin. Let them go. Telling the story of "How Are You?" from the *soul of the actor* is what drives Suzuki, Bogart and Armstrong (with due homage to Hart) deeper into their training ideologies and experimentation. It is a dance between the experience of body and soul versus the codification to which the brain is longing to leap. Please resist that urge to codify too quickly.

Trans – 1. a prefix occurring in loanwords from Latin (*transcend, transfix*); on this model, used with the meanings "across," "beyond," "through," "changing thoroughly," "transverse," in combination with elements of any origin.

Action – *n.* 2. Something done or performed; act; deed 3. An act that one consciously wills and that may be characterized by mental or physical activity 4. *(pl)* habitual or usual acts; conduct....

Transaction – *n.* 3. Something that is transacted, esp. *a business agreement.* 4. An interaction of an individual with one or more other persons, esp. as influenced by their assumed relational roles.....

p. 20 and 2009. Webster's New Unabridged Dictionary, Deluxe Edition.

Barnes and Noble, Inc. by Arrangement with Random House Value Publishing, 1996.

In all elements of theatre we assume a transaction is continuously occurring. In rehearsal there is actor to actor, director to actor and designers, etc. In performance there are countless transactions backstage and onstage, but the one we claim to most carefully attend is actor to audience. Yet how often are we aware that each moment of trans-action is a cross-cultural experience leading to the Soul of a Story? We can parse the definition of culture to more infinitesimally small increments until we are left with Self, or we can go to the current macro-obsession with globalization, but it doesn't change the fact of *trans-action* one whit. There is something being passed, and how it is passed, as well as to and from whom, are at the heart of actor training if we are to progress in educating performers who take responsibility for their part in the cross-cultural communication of story. Perhaps one performance only. Simple. Direct. Immediate. It is the Soul of the Story that is born from an intimate fusion of our bodies on the boards with our history and experiences. Direct experience forces us to face obstacles – face habits – face ourselves.

I posit that the Soul of the Story lay rooted in our problems, our blocks and our fears as they connect to the body and the voice, and that the American theatre is just beginning to awaken to that fact. American actor training institutions lag even further behind. It is time to find a new developmental acting pedagogy to reconnect the over-stimulated, yet profoundly disassociated, acting students back to their own souls and their own stories. This is precisely what Rollo May said throughout his book, *The Courage To Create*, when he suggested that the artist is always pushing the edges and is forever the outsider even if it means becoming the outsider to our own training establishments. He writes:

> The creativity of the spirit *does* and *must* threaten the structure and presuppositions of our orderly, rational society and way of life. Unconscious, irrational urges are bound by their very nature to be a threat to our rationality, and the anxiety we experience thereupon is inescapable.[1]

And further,

...the creative encounter does, to some degree, change the self-world relationship. The anxiety we feel is temporary rootlessness, disorientation; it is the anxiety of nothingness.

Creative people, as I see them, are distinguished by the fact that they can live with anxiety even though a high price must be paid in terms of insecurity, sensitivity, and defenselessness for the gift of the "divine madness", to borrow the term used by the classical Greeks. They do not run away from non-being, but by encountering and wrestling with it force it into being. They knock on silence for an answering music; they pursue meaninglessness until they can force it to mean.[2]

Years later in Parker Palmer's book the *Courage To Teach*, which he titled as a tribute to Rollo May, Palmer states that:

First, the subjects we teach are as large and complex as life, so our knowledge of them is always flawed and partial. No matter how we devote ourselves to reading and research, teaching requires a command of content that always eludes our grasp. Second, the students we teach are larger than life and even more complex. To see them clearly and see them whole, and respond to them wisely in the moment, requires a fusion of Freud and Solomon that few of us achieve.

If students and subjects accounted for all the complexities of teaching, our standard ways of coping would do – keep up with our fields as best we can and learn enough techniques to stay ahead of the student psyche. But there is another reason for those complexities: we teach who we are.[3]

A starting blend of Bogart and Hart with subsequent Suzuki training *before traditional monologue and scene study* may be just the radical foundational shift the American actor needs to meet a globalized theatre and the cross-cultural transactions that globalization necessitates.

## Bogart and Suzuki: The Revitalization of American Actor Training

I was an actor trained in the "American method" – the Strasburg-derived, Stanislavskian-based principles of psychological realism. It was a good, solid foundation, but there was, as Stephen Nachmanovitch recounts in his parable of The Flute Player "something lacking".[4] There is that ancient truism from Buddhist thought, "When the student is ready, the teacher will appear". This happened to me three times and has forced me over ten years as a teacher of young actors in 2003 United States to redefine my pedagogical approach to actor training. After meeting Anne at several callbacks for her production of Clare Booth Luce's *The Women* at San Diego Repertory Theatre in 1992, it became clear to me that this was a woman on a mission. But more than that, a woman with the force of intelligence combined with the humanity and attention to each individual artist to truly transform how the American actor thinks and perceives herself as part of a whole on the stage. Anne's wonderful question that she has posed countless times in discussions and lectures all over the world, "What do you do with the meat?"[5] was a slap in the face as I re-encountered the dormant notion that the truest emotional freedom for an actor lies in physical and vocal release.

Anne Bogart speaks about the theatre – each moment, each element – being "awake".[6] Suzuki talks about "theatre you can't blow over".[7] Suzuki has gone so far as to say that his technique is designed to point out your failures, and to challenge you to approach your failures with the joy of discovery and the hope of growth.[8] And Roy Hart, influenced deeply by Carl Jung, defined the voice as "the muscle of the soul".[9] All three artists have found dynamic ways into *The Problem* in order to awaken story at its most vital level through the instrument of the actor. Defining *The Problem* will be familiar to all teachers of actors, and has certainly been recognized and experienced by all three of these artists. Primarily, there is a disassociation with the body, the voice and the instrument of feeling that manifests itself in the following ways:

- Compressed vocal range and power
- Weak, stiff and untrained bodies at younger and younger ages
- Low facial affect or, conversely, gross affect that is clearly mask-like and designed to conceal
- Increasing lack of ability to discern or define their own immediate experience, especially as related to emotions
- Intense ego-driven performance often at the sacrifice of awareness of surrounding actors or environment

Bogart, Suzuki and Hart's theories, taken together, create a *fusion* of working methodologies that reach a commonality of actor experience serving to bring about an astonishing *fission* of form; each actor becomes more of who he or she is – each culture *and* individual artist crystallized and more clearly defined. This notion is especially important in response to frequently expressed concerns by theatre artists and scholars: that we are creating a more homogeneous theatre, "globalized art" that speaks to everyone generically, and no one specifically. This does not have to be the case. Bogart, Suzuki and Hart look for individuation of the performer through ensemble awareness, empathy to group experience and the shared rigour of strong discipline.

As actors, we are constantly expected to prepare, to warm up, be ready. But with the best of teachers and directors, the rug is pulled from us as soon as we walk into the studio or on the stage. Warm up for what? Be ready for what? A piece of blocking? The crack of the shinai stick against the mat? Suzuki's directive to stomp on the floor with the sole of my foot so hard I am sure I have broken my bones (I haven't!) is done to build, among other things, a platform for my voice. Anne Bogart gives me 6 (or 7, or 9, or 13...) points of view to juggle at once, and then tells me to take the stage voraciously but not to act or make anything. Silence, an empty space, "It has already started."[10] Doing as Re-Action. Richard Armstrong will say the most wonderful paradoxical things: "We must go down to go up" or "Find the cracks between the notes and sing from there". If these are not cross-cultural experiences, I charge you to sing from your cracks, and to stomp. It is destabilizing and invigorating in the most cross-culturally alive acting experience an actor can hope to have.

Fundamentally, the act of creating theatre – telling a story, actor to audience in the moment – is a trans-action across the boundaries of culture. I have learned that from each of my mentors. The practice of an actor-in-training is identical to a traveler in culture shock: Look at the maps for a destination, make up the itinerary and travel arrangements, and pack for the journey. We arrive full of trepidation and hope; all is projection, as yet there is no real experience. But it has, indeed, already begun. Initially there is an overwhelming banquet of sensation: some pleasant, some not. Some recognizable, some for which we have no frame of reference. We have the initial euphoria of discovery that co-exists with the terror of becoming lost, followed then by the opposite anger at having to shift our comfort zone to accommodate the unfamiliar. It is after the pendulum has completed one full swing that the real work begins: the application, the integration and the transmission into our own Soul that New Thing which enriches our palette of experience, and once encountered, can never be completely erased or withdrawn. Having spent a year in South Korea (another Seoul!), I can confidently tell you that this metaphor applies as directly to *kimchi* as a dietary staple as it does to Suzuki training.

I had the great fortune of meeting Anne Bogart at the precise moment in time when she and Suzuki had formed their artistic alliance and were about to launch the first training intensives of the Saratoga International Theatre Institute at Skidmore College in the lower Adirondack mountains of New York State. Their idea, "to redefine and revitalize theatre in the United States through an emphasis on cultural exchange and collaboration"[11] struck a chord in me, and so I pursued any opportunity to work and train with them. At the beginning, I was an acolyte. It took time for me to move out from beneath the enormous implications of Suzuki's forms and Anne's Viewpoint vocabulary and make it my own, as we all must do if the forms are to remain vital. In January of 2000 at the International Theatre Institute's Conference hosted at Towson University I took my first workshop with Richard Armstrong. Until that time I knew nothing of Roy Hart, nor his work with the so-called "extended voice" – but within three days I again knew that another piece of the puzzle had been located. Since that week over three years ago, I have been training with Richard Armstrong and am now convinced that this work can constitute another "missing link" in *birthing a performer rich with both inner fire and outer form; an actor rigorous in technique, and yet vitally alive from their own unique point of view.* Suzuki, Bogart and Armstrong are all asking the same attention and the same accountability at each moment from their actors. They demand the radical confrontation with both Self and Other in order to communicate the Soul of the Story. When actors are working together with a director and other like-minded theatre makers at such a high level of artistic accountability the story will inevitably bloom and transcend any individual ego and transform moments into theatre that we can all acknowledge as being born of our Souls in a moment of grace and beauty. That is the contract that each actor and audience member make when a moment of theatre is enacted in a cross-cultural transaction.

Suzuki's training exercises, for those who may have never seen it in practice, began primarily as a series of walks and basic exercises created as a way to address particular problems in rehearsals. These forms have since become an objective diagnostic tool by which the actor can measure the state of their being at any particular moment. To quote J. Thomas Rimer's preface from *The Way of Acting*, "the method can merely be *evoked* from the outside; true understanding of it can come only as one lives through and experiences his discipline. Perhaps it must even be lived through *before* it can be grasped intellectually."[12] Borrowing in part from both Noh and Kabuki, the work focuses a great deal on the actor's relationship to the floor, most often through the sole of the foot: his now famous "stomping" exercises. So then, the soul of the story is not a metaphorical construct, but a tangible fact: the sole – or bottom – of the story. Such a vital relationship between the sole of the foot and the performer is also very much a part of all aboriginal forms of dance and storytelling. Indigenous cultures from around the world frequently have some kind of stomp as the basis for ritual and performance and these forms were created to pass down stories of community and religious history and beliefs from one generation to the next. While training in Suzuki we speak of the placement of the body (as defined by physical centre for gravity) in relationship to the foot and the floor, but what is really occurring is a conditioning of the actor's body to transmit the Soul of a Story to an audience at a level heightened beyond any one language or cultural perspective. It is Suzuki's contention that Western Culture, and American culture in particular, has lost its soul because of the many cultural and techno-logical changes that have *literally* removed us from the ground. Think of the current fashions in footwear, floor coverings, chairs, cars, sitting toilets, high-rise buildings and office cubicles and you begin to glimpse the enormity of the remove. It is my firm belief that student actors today must reinvent their relationship to the earth, and to experience for the first time these connections as individual being/performers and as a cultural whole, otherwise the actor has no story to transmit and becomes merely a cipher of someone else's vision. Where is the contem-porary United States equivalent of a stomp? Suzuki training places the actor's inner soul firmly on the ground via transmission with the sole of the foot. Through structured and unison exercises of the most rigorous forms and standards, Suzuki's method reaches our core of individuality, and asks us to Be Here Now, and to make it mean something.

Training simultaneously in both Suzuki and Bogart is required of anyone who makes theatre with the SITI Company.[13] It can be both a frustrating and absolutely joyous collision of will and impulse, of thought and intuition, of group and self. Bogart's Viewpoints are a set of perspectives on the principles of time and space that theatre makers learn to perceive and use to their greatest stage advantage. Bogart, deeply influenced by modern dancer and teacher Mary Overlie who created the original Six Viewpoints, has created a usable, action-based vocabulary for those moments that are universally experienced on the stage. Actors, directors and designers can only use the tools of Viewpoints if they are open to who they are and where they are at each moment. Not a creative invention, but the corporeal fact of Now. Bogart has said that, "in the Viewpoints work, nothing is invented – everything is a response."[14] The response is to the omnipresent question, "How are you now? And now? And now?" When you work in Viewpoints you are encouraged to embrace stereotype, to perform the obvious archetype until it morphs into something that is uniquely yours. What Bogart is encouraging is *translation* via the body. The idea here is that we neither can nor should try to avoid any facet of our own cultural surroundings or history, but to work through them (trans-act) until the new thing is achieved.

## A Third Perspective[15]

In 1896 Alfred Wolfsohn was born in Berlin, Germany. At age 19 he was a reluctant inductee into the German Army and served as a stretcher carrier in World War I which put him on the front lines of battle. During that time he became acutely aware of both the range and power of the human voice in extreme states of being: wounded, dying, fighting: grown men crying at the last for their mamas. After WWI Wolfsohn pursued what was, at first, a very traditional career as a singing teacher back in Berlin. Yet he was haunted by past wartime experience. He began to ask himself the question: if the human voice is capable of such breadth, depth and power, why is it never heard in daily life? What has been shut down?[16]

His research, which became increasingly less traditional, found the links between psychology and the human voice that are now taken for granted in the work of such established Western voice teachers as Kristen Linklater, Eileen Skinner and David Smuckler. In the 1920s however, Wolfsohn was marginalized and shunned by the singing teachers of his day.

Wolfsohn, a Jew, was forced to flee Berlin in 1939 and he found himself in London. Meanwhile, in 1925 in Johannesburg, South Africa, was born Roy Hart (neé Reuben Hartstein). Roy Hart became a college student of psychology, English, the history of music, and philosophy at the University of Johannesburg in Witwatersrand, but wanted very much to be an actor. This was deeply out of alignment with his orthodox Jewish family and traditions. At age 19 he moved to London where he received a scholarship at RADA, met Alfred Wolsohn very soon thereafter and was constantly at odds with the cross-trainings he was receiving.[17] Said Hart, "[I] was told that I had a good voice and stage personality. Yet I had known for some time that my voice was not rooted, not literally embodied; that the varied roles I was considered to perform so well were actually only figments of my imagination with no connection with my body. In personal relationships I was an aloof outsider."[18]

Roy Hart began studying with Wolfsohn and became his pupil for 12 years. After Wolfsohn's death in 1962 Hart continued the work of his mentor working further, exploring the links between body, soul, voice and psyche. This work was becoming increasingly more holistic in approach (new in the days of "bel canto", the "beautiful singing" techniques which were the modus operandi of voice teachers of the day.) By 1969 an eclectic group of people had collected themselves, for one reason or another, around Hart and lived and worked together in an intensive laboratory situation, exploring the potential of the human voice at its most extreme and applying this, at times, to both musical composition and the creation of works of theatre. The communal living style, guru-like atmosphere and extreme reaction to previous conventions of the field make perfect socio-political sense in the parallel movements of the 60s in both England and the United States at that time. In London, this was met often with skepticism if not overt hostility!

Undaunted, by 1974 the Roy Hart Theatre picked up and moved itself to France where it gained an audience and acceptance it had not experienced in England. They were awarded grants, treated with due artistic respect and created work that was extraordinary primarily in the sense that it had not been heard by Western ears before. Frequently, however, this hodge-podge group of company members – some of them performers before coming to Hart, but many of them simply souls looking for a community to belong to – would be approached by prominent artists of the day who exclaimed, "You *must* have been with the click-tribe people of Southern Africa" or, "I hadn't realized you spent time in Tibet with the Tuvan throat singers".[19] Of course, they had not. They had, in fact, rarely left their communal laboratory chateau in France. So how had these people come to make these sounds and find the beauty, the power and the artistic fidelity of ethnicities and cultures so removed from their own experience?

While some attempted to write this off to freaks in the likes of PT Barnum and the *Guinness World Book of Records* (several of the company members were examined by doctors who were convinced that surgical implants had been placed in the throats of these performers), this recurring phenomenon of 5 1/2 to 8 octave range vocalization drew the notice of great theatre artists and composers who would quietly come to the rehearsal studios and simply watch Roy and his Theatre Company work. Among them were such artists as John Cage, Peter Brook, who brought Grotowski with him, the Huxley Brothers, Harold Pinter, Jerome Robbins, Jean-Louis Berrault, Irene Worth, and composers Peter Maxwell-Davies, Henze, Stockhausen, Birtwhistle and others.[20]

In 1975 Roy Hart was killed in a car accident, along with his wife, Dorothy and company member Vivienne Young. The group continued on officially as a theatre company until it changed its name to the Roy Hart International Centre for Voice Study in 1990, where it exists today in Malérargues, Thoriras, France. The founding members of that company have spread across the globe – each taking the foundational work of Hart and continuing to develop it through each one's specific and unique lens.

Richard Armstrong, a company member from 1967 until Hart's death, is a master teacher in his recollection and reinterpretation of the work of Roy Hart. During my years of private and group study with Armstrong, I have begun to incorporate much of his work into curricula with new undergraduates and graduate students as well. The results are astonishing. From a pedagogical perspective, this work is neither a series of exercises nor a clearly defined technique. Much of the teacher/student learning is a direct, intimate encounter with the source of the voice. For the purposes of this work, it is critical that each teacher begin by asking the students to define, explain and articulate their relationship to their voices. This may include past experiences, messages they have received about their voices and current ways in which they perceive the voice as being a (dis)trusted part of their instruments. In this way, each student is first heard and listened to without judgment, without necessarily being aware that much of the work has already started. After the initial discussion, there may be little sound made for a week or more. The sound is alive in the liquidity of the body, the contact of the body on the floor, the twist of a spine, the empathetic breathing with a partner. The remainder of the process is a highly individualized integration of the body/voice/personae into a free and dynamic maker of sound. Sound without borders, sound without being hampered by standards of beauty, a voice in which there is a place for every vibration coming forth from the instrument. In short, it opens and frees beyond any single vocal technique of the singer or the actor, and is equally beneficial for those with a great deal of confidence and comfort with their instruments and those whose voices are locked in fear and self-loathing. For the performer and the teacher both, this work is an act of courage and compassion. It is an intimate meeting and trans-action.

Wolfsohn, Hart and Armstrong have all stated in variation, "The voice is the muscle of the soul."[21] This idea fuses the tangible reality of the actor's body with the intangible life inside each being. An actor's work is to embody soul. It is not enough to feel emotions, nor is it enough to train the body. Body and voice must come together through each actor and transmit to audience the fullness of his or her unique experience. Hart's ideas started in England, developed in France, and are now translated around the world. Wolfsohn and Hart were both refugees in a sense from their own countries; The Roy Hart Theatre was displaced from its home country to France and now his descendants are many and nomadic. Richard Armstrong and others are constantly creating new ways into the soul of the student as made manifest by the voice. As a companion to Viewpoint Theory and Suzuki training, an actor grows physically, vocally, culturally and spiritually. The actor is stronger in body and voice, and knows how to communicate in ways that are authentic, rigorous and awake.

## How are you now?

In the end, technique and training are as individual as the actors who engage in them and as myriad as the languages spoken across the globe. There are approximately thirty click-tongue languages still spoken in Southern Africa alone.[22] And it is the charge of each acting teacher, of each director to meet the individual performer at the place of his or her most personal and specific need. Build from the Now a theatre that is both epic and specific, that addresses the reality of a globalized network of theatre without compromising at all on cultural specificity. We can train together and remain distinct. Because of the work of practitioners like Suzuki, Hart and Bogart there is theatrical language and a theatrical culture from which we can build and play. The trans-action is occurring in the present moment and moving actor to actor, and through actor to director to audience and back again.

Compared to many other acting teachers and theorists, the body of writing by or about Suzuki, Bogart or Hart is still relatively small. Bogart and Suzuki are still in constant development of their ideas, and Hart's first generation protégé's continue to hone their own unique take on Hart's work. The Viewpoints today may be codified by the same words tomorrow, yet they do not reap the same results. Viewpoints in Korea looks and feels different than in the United States. The Suzuki of 10 years ago has marched on to become the Suzuki training of today. There is some suspicion of any acting technique as it gets removed from the originator – from Stanislavsky to Meisner we feel there is a dilution and dissipation of the original insight. Perhaps. But that is also the history of cultures over thousands of years and hundreds of generations passing along oral traditions and the ideas and practices of a community. I take what I can from Bogart, from Suzuki and from Hart and I ask the question again, "How are you?" The answer, if authentic, comes from the soul and translates between actor and audience as story, a living slice of culture.

## Case Study

I have taught courses and workshops in Viewpoints, Suzuki and Hart-influenced voice at Universities in Australia, England, India and Korea as well as in the United States. Each is unique, and each teaches me something about the ability of these forms to translate across borders. As one example, I will write briefly of my own cross-cultural case study as a Visiting Professor of Voice and Acting at the Korean National University of Arts (KNUA) in Seoul, South Korea. In 1997 I had never before travelled to Asia. I certainly did not speak Korean, and embarrassingly, I knew very, very little of the culture. What would I say to them? How and what would I teach?

KNUA is a conservatory operated under the auspices of their government whose mandate it is to train a new generation of artists that will remain in Korea and advance indigenous Korean art forms while sparking new experiments into unique 21st century Korean performing and visual art. There are six schools within KNUA: traditional Korean performance, theatre, music, film and TV, dance and visual art. Money is allocated for faculty from around the world to introduce Korean students to the aesthetics and methods of other cultures. In the Theatre Department, students must train in traditional Korean instrumental music, singing, dance, drumming and masks as they simultaneously explore the offerings of their guest teachers. The end result of this rich and demanding environment is a modern Korean theatre artist, with both a deep skill and sense of indigenous Korean performance, and thoroughly contemporary global perspectives and sensibilities. The actor leaves knowing who she is and is capable of creating work both specific to her historical culture and also vital within the contemporary Korean and global theatre community.

I was asked to "teach Linklater". Teaching Linklater through an interpreter it became clear that there were distinct limitations in bringing this work to students with whom I did not share a common language, or a common set of phonetics. But there was also an unexpected gift in the slower pace of teaching through interpreters. I was forced to clarify – to simplify – and to wait and watch each student to gauge if my ideas had reached their intended audience. I took the time to listen to my own authentic voice and make adjustments based solely upon the need to communicate. This idea is fundamental to the Roy Hart work, although I did not know this at the time. I soon turned to Suzuki and Bogart out of instinct, sensing that the students and I also needed a shared physical vocabulary. Once Viewpoint vocabulary was shared among us, it became a primary way of communicating. We had our own language. Similarly, in the stomping of Suzuki we all had an empirical diagnostic form that transcended culture and language and brought us all to the edge of our unique (and, paradoxically, universal) performance struggles. With this combined inner fire and outer form, we came back to ourselves with newly translated creative energy and craft. In facing what we did not know we found the soul, sole, Seoul of our story.

## Implications for American Actor Training

The state of American undergraduate actor training today is at a cross-roads. Many questions are being asked about the nature of a BFA versus the value of an enhanced BA within a liberal arts setting. Curricula are mired in ties to a past based upon the standards of Strasberg and Adler, the American Method and so-called realism. Often, students are trained to a slick audition package, but have little resources for a deeper artistic process once they are out on their own trying to make their way as American theatre artists and actors in the 21st century reality of cross-border theatre, ethnic fusion of styles within production, differing perspectives of new playwrights and more and more travel of actors to venues abroad.

The question is: how does an undergraduate training institution in the United States today (be it a conservatory or liberal arts setting) reinvent the training of the contemporary American actor? This paper is proposing a radical shift in which an *Alice In Wonderland* inversion of curricula takes place, leaving the scenes and monologues of our past Acting 101 days until later in the curriculum and proposing a gateway into the body and voice through the work of Roy Hart, Anne Bogart and Tadashi Suzuki, respectively.

Placing this voice and body work at the very beginning of the actor's training, before monologue work, scene study or the intro-duction of "playing an action" provides the student with tools and confidence from which to reach more height and depth in early monologue and scene work. Many educators with whom I have spoken are dubious. It is as if I am promoting a type of theatre in which the values of action, objective, character biography and sense memory play no part. That is not the case. However, if we are to open ourselves to transactions with peoples and cultures for whom the very definition of a realistic action is vastly different than our own, we *must* re-examine the value of a more universally transmutable starting point in our education of the actor/artist.

Both Roy Hart's so-called "extended voice" technique and Viewpoint training, if studied in conjunction with one another are magnified and enhanced in the young actor's instrument. Viewpoints demands direct, intimate awakening moment-to-moment. It demands physical awareness of all stimuli and a taut dynamic between impulses of self and ensemble. It requires a dance between ego and no-self. And although Bogart has taken on the voice through Viewpoints, it is my experience that a firm foundation and experience with Hart enhances an actor's ability to listen and respond within the Viewpoints from a much more integrated and mature place of deep listening and the authentic, raw *need* to make sound.

Richard Armstrong notably rejects this titled for Roy Hart and Alfred Wolfsohn's exploration of the voice. His response to the notion of training the extended voice: it is not a training, and there is nothing extended about an instrument already contained in each one of us from conception.[23]

What a first semester experience for a neophyte actor! Imagine the additional breadth and depth a student actor could bring to initial Stanislavskian principles of action, objective and tactics; how much further ahead the student actor would be *after* a semester of both Hart and Bogart in tackling parables of Maria and the Director sitting on stage together in the art of doing nothing (*An Actor Prepares*, Stanislavsky, Chapter 3). And if, after a semester of Hart of Bogart, we add to that the rigour and deep will and focus brought to the actor's body and voice through Suzuki training, we begin to prepare a student actor for the realities of 21st century theatre, a theatre unlike any that has come before.

It is certainly of great value to continue to include in a curriculum the fundamentals of Stanislavsky, Meisner, Linklater and others. But by reversing the order in which these courses are placed we are more quickly freeing the student of preconceived notions of acting from sources as diverse, yet equally potent, as television and film, community theatre experiences or high school theatre where the best-intentioned teachers and directors inadvertently reinforce bad habits and patterns that must be unlearned before any true training of an actor can begin. As college and university training programs, we have a responsibility to prepare the actor for an increase in diversity of scripts and playwrights, in performance styles, in director/actor relationships, in audiences and in venues of performance. It is perhaps too easy to say we must train the "global actor"; I am never more American than when I am in another country. But we must train actors with a facility to tap into wider and wider ranges of vocal and physical capabilities and with broadening definitions of what constitutes theatre – let alone realism or naturalism. The Soul of the Story for each human being in today's world is ever changing and expanding; can our institutions flow with such momentous change in order to keep our young artists alive and well-poised to be the mirrors and refractors of such change?

Such a shift in curriculum will not happen overnight. It is not happening overnight in my own home institution. But it is beginning, and the students are responding with enthusiasm, delight and trust in the value of the experiences. The world is simultaneously expanding and contracting, and it is contingent upon college and university faculty ensuring that actor training does not get mired in old ways of thought and being that are Ameri-centric and based in narrow definitions of what theatre can, should and will be.

Where do we go now?

## Notes

1. Rollo May, *The Courage To Create*. George J. McCleod, Ltd. Toronto, Canada, 1975, p. 71.

2. Ibid., p. 93.

3. Parker J Palmer, The *Courage To Teach: Exploring the Inner Landscape of A Teacher's Life*. 1998. Jossey-Bass Inc. San Francisco, California, p. 2.

4. Ibid., Rollo May, *The Courage To Create*, p. 2.

5. Author's Notes from the Spring 1993 Intensive at the Saratoga International Theatre Institute at Skidmore College.

6. Author's Notes from the Spring 1994 Intensive at the Saratoga International Theatre Institute at Skidmore College.

7. Author's Notes from the Fall 1993 Suzuki Intensive at the Saratoga International Theatre Institute at Skidmore College.

8. Ibid.

9. Noah Pikes, Dark *Voices: The Genesis of the Roy Hart Theatre*. 1999. Spring Journal, Inc. Woodstock, Connecticut, p. 93.

10. Author's Notes from the Spring 1993 Intensive at the Saratoga International Theatre Institute at Skidmore College.

11. SITI Company Promotional Brochure, 1995.

12. Tadashi Suzuki, *The Way of Acting*. J. Thomas Rimer, Translator. 1986, Theatre Communications Group, New York City, p. ix.

13. www.siti.org. Mission Statement.

14. Joan Herrington, *"Breathing Common Air: The SITI Company Creates Cabin Pressure"* The Drama Review: Journal of Performance Studies. Richard Schechner, Editor. MIT Press. Cambridge, Massachusetts. Summer 2002, Vol TI74, p. 156.

15. All historical information regarding Roy Hart and Alfred Wolfsohn has come to me through conversations with Richard Armstrong in various

workshops and voice lessons over the past three years. Additionally, this information is recounted in some detail in Noah Pike's book, *Dark Voices: The Genesis of the Roy Hart Theatre*. 1999. Spring Journal, Inc. Woodstock, Connecticut. ISBN 1-882670-19-1.

16. Ibid. Banff, 2001.

17. Ibid, Noah Pikes, *Dark Voices: The Genesis of the Roy Hart Theatre*, pp. 69-71.

18. www.roy-hart.com/rth *"How Voice Gave Me A Conscience"* by Roy and Dorothy Hart, 1967.

19. www.theage.com.au/2003/03/18/1047749768828.html Nicholas Wade, *"How An Ancient Click Clique Started Our Mother Tongue"*.

20. Author's notes from conversations with Richard Armstrong, 2001 – 2003.

21. www.new.towson.edu/theatremfa/artists/rarmstrong.html.

22. www.theage.com.au/2003/03/18/1047749768828.html Nicholas Wade, *"How An Ancient Click Clique Started Our Mother Tongue"*.

23. Author's notes from conversations with Richard Armstrong, 2001-2003.

# 3

# Creating the Cognitive Space of the Character

## Erik Rynell

The research I am involved in is closely related to my work as a teacher at Malmö Theatre Academy, where I am responsible for the Playwrighting Programme.

The title of my project is "Drama Without Action". The background for this, first, is the fact that action is traditionally considered the most essential element in Western drama, and second, is that the importance of action is challenged in modern and postmodern theatre. Both of these circumstances have methodological implications for the actor. The work with a traditional, action-based, mostly fictive text entails an element that has a kind of *cognitive* character. The actor engages himself in a world or a set of circumstances that differ from his own personal ones. This cognitive element is less conspicuous in relation to alternative dramatic forms, or must at least be defined in another way.

The issue, as I see it, can be expressed in the following question:

What are the epistemological implications of involving oneself in fictive acting? I will not be able to answer this question here, only point in a direction, where highly interesting aspects are to be found.

The question relies on the assumption that the working process of an actor with a fictive text involves perception and understanding of the world in a non-fictive sense. The work on a role is, first of all, a question of putting oneself into the situation of the character. This situation has primarily spatial and temporal aspects. When students at our school once worked on Chekhov's *Seagull*, one of the first exercises consisted of drawing a map of the site where the action takes place, Sorin's mansion, the lake and its surroundings. The drawings should be as accurate as possible according to details given in the play – not in order to make a correct or "authentic" depiction, but to gather knowledge as to possible relations between the action of the characters and the space.

A process of this kind is not only a matter of free imagination, Hans Georg Gadamer writes in *Truth and Method*:

For the writer, free invention is always only one side of a communication, which is conditioned, by what is pre-given as valid. He does not freely invent his plot, however much he imagines that he does. (...) The free invention of the writer is the presentation of a common truth that is binding on the writer also.[1]

An actor going into the fictional conditions of the character must give sensual form to that which in Gadamer's words is "pre-given as valid". He has to gain knowledge about something that lies outside him, which is compelling to him and to which he must adapt himself. This kind of cognition, specific to an actor is what will here be referred to as the epistemological element in acting.

The common truth presented in the text, which according to Gadamer is "binding on the writer" is of course binding on the actor as well. If there is an element of necessity involved in the acting process, this is obviously where we will find it. This process is influenced by the stage director too, although without essentially altering it.

The students' mapping of Sorin's mansion mentioned previously has a counterpart in a text by Stanislavski entitled *Griboyedov's Woe from Wit*, to be found in *Creating a Role*. In this text, which dates back to *c.* 1916-17, Stanislavski makes one of his first attempts to describe an ideal work on a text and a role. As an example he chooses the part of Chatsky in Griboyedov's comedy. I will here make a brief summary of the plot:

Full of radical ideas the young hero Chatsky returns to the place where he grew up, the house of the prominent Moscow citizen Famusov. He finds that his beloved, Famusov's daughter Sophia has forgotten him. His struggle to win her back and the struggle against the trickery of a corrupt society as represented in the house only results in attempts to declare him insane. Finally he leaves the house. *Woe from wit* has a status as a classic in Russia, and the role of Chatsky is often referred to as a *Russian Hamlet*.

According to Stanislavski the work begins with an attentive, careful reading of the dramatic text, followed by a detailed analysis, heading first of all for the plot and the "facts" laid down in the text.[2]

When the actor has come to know the play thoroughly he should make a virtual imaginative "visit" to the house of the Famusov family. He should move around imperceptibly, walk up and down the stairs, open doors, watch the life of the inmates, noticing various details of the daily life, as well as characteristics in furniture and other objects. Finally he should make imaginative contacts with the inmates themselves.

In his later writings, Stanislavski developed a working method which is perhaps more influential today and goes under the name "the method of physical actions". He now abandoned the earlier approach, finding it too cerebral, but without rejecting its underlying ideas. Instead of imaginary work in solitude, the actor, according to the late Stanislavski, meets his co-actors on the floor and explores the text together with them. The initial work on the role in this case too becomes a scrutiny into partly inevitable implications of given situations.

The aim of the actor in this procedure is to relate in a personal way to the circumstances of the character. This conforms to a basic idea in Stanislavski's work and in his teaching, the one of the "magic if". In his autobiography *My Life in Art* he tells the background to this concept. It came to him in connection with an artistic crisis, the core of which was discomfort with the element of deception involved in theatrical fiction. This is how he describes the solution to the problem:

The actor says to himself:

'All these properties, make-ups, costumes, the scenery, the public-ness of the performance, are lies. I know they are lies, I know I do not need any of them. But *if* they were true, then I would do this and this, and I would behave in this manner and this way towards this and this event.[3]

Stanislavski also found another expression for this idea in what he calls "given" or "proposed" circumstances.

A joint effect of the "magic if" and the "given circumstances" is that they render the scenic enunciation conditional. The actor no longer identifies with the person of the character; he does not claim to "be", for example, Doctor Stockman in Ibsen's *Enemy of the People*. In his action he essentially just accounts for how he himself would have responded to the conditions ascribed to Doctor Stockman. The actor's scrutiny does not have to do with the elusive character of an actually non-existing personality, but to a set of human possibilities.

Now, understanding fiction as conditional automatically becomes a way to assign to it a special logical status. Keir Elam in his *Semiotics of Theatre and Drama* devotes one chapter to this aspect on fiction.[4] He finds the logic side of fiction somewhat neglected and goes into a discussion on different means to deal with it. In this context he mentions the theory of the so-called "possible worlds". This theory had already been under debate in modal logic for some time and it had also found its way into fiction theory via writers like Eco and Dolezel, among others.

Since Elam issued this book in the eighties a lot has been written on this subject, primarily by logicians, secondly by literary scholars, but to my knowledge not very much in the field of theatre. Now, talking about Stanislavski it might seem natural to enter this field, as the concept of the "magic if" could be seen as a kind of fictional operator in the sense that has been discussed in connection with "possible worlds" theory. A fictional operator is the idea of a thought assumption, mostly invisible in the text, which turns a narrative from just being false, a lie, into being a fictive text worthy of respect for truthfulness in some sense. Stanislavski's "magic if" in fact is a rare example of such an operator expressedly in use for practical artistic purposes.

In modal logic, the theory of "possible worlds" was used to solve a problem in semantics: the fundamental one of how we can ascribe properties to objects. A classical explanation is that the property of, for example, being "green" could be defined as the adherence to the class of all green objects. This idea proved to entail some inconveniences. Saul

Kripke and other logicians therefore developed a theory with the content that a proposition which ascribes a property to something can be verified in relation to the "possible worlds" in which the proposition holds. The proposition that an object is green, according to this theory is mapped on the conditions, under which the proposition is true. Propositions about properties thus appear as essentially dependent on intra-logical considerations. "Possible worlds" theory was also introduced within fiction theory. A statement, for example, "Sherlock Holmes lives in Baker Street" which would be qualified as just a false statement by Bertrand Russell was now by some logicians considered true in view of the "possible world" created by fictive discourse. Ruth Ronen, who has issued an interesting book about possible worlds in literary theory, explains:

Discourse creates an object that exists in some logical space, allowing us to refer to it and to make true assertions about it.[5] The interpretation of fiction as a form of "possible world" lays focus on logic as a ground for scenic necessity. In fact one can talk about a kind of scenic truth in terms of circumstances, which are logically implied in what is given on stage and thus appear as analytically true. As an example one can chose Macduff's words to Macbeth in Act V, Scene 7 of the drama: "Macduff was from his mother's womb untimely ripped". Inevitable conclusion: he was not "of woman born". He was the exception to the prediction of the witches and could kill Macbeth. In fact logic works on much more basic levels in the construction of scenic fiction and thus also on the expectations of the public. The audience makes deductions about events appearing on stage, in a way quite similar to ordinary life. In this respect scenic events not only mirror reality, but are in fact subjected to identical laws.

Now, despite this, as Ronen also states,[6] there are limitations to logic as an explanation of fictive construction. First "possible worlds" in the sense given to the concept by logicians differ from possible worlds as used in fiction theory. In terms of modal logic "possible worlds" cannot contain contradictions. Fiction on the other hand can. If the colour of Emma Bovary's eyes are first described as brown and later as green this could be understood as a minor mistake on the part of the author, but it is by no means fatal for the fictive narrative.

As logic is not totally compulsive in fiction, and fictive necessity can be related to other elements, referring to logic is not enough. The idea of "possible worlds" despite introducing interesting aspects on fiction turns out to be an impasse if the aim is to explain fictional necessity.

Now, let's return to our young actor, sneaking around in the imaginative corridors of Famusov's house, peeping in through half-open doors, making observations and inhaling the atmosphere of the place, perhaps trying to make as little notice as possible in the squeaking staircase. The kind of scrutiny he is performing is not just a one of cerebral conclusions or inferences. It is first and foremost an approach with senses wide open to virtual possibilities. It is at the same time a question of capacity for imagination and a way to render creative experience from his own life, applying it to a new situation.

If there should be talk of epistemology in connection with the acting process the point of departure must not only be a limited section, like logic, but the totality of human capacity for perception and understanding.

This is the field of investigation for cognitive science, bringing together knowledge from disciplines like philosophy, cognitive psychology and computer science. In a book entitled *Conceptual Spaces, The Geometry of Thought*, Peter Gärdenfors, and Professor of Cognitive Science at Lund University makes an attempt to outline a theoretical framework for his discipline. According to the author, the book should rather be seen as a set of suggested approaches to be elaborated separately in other contexts. I have found several ideas in this book useful for mapping the kind of knowledge involved in an actor's working process.

What one might find particularly attractive in this theory is a general approach to knowledge as spatial. This in fact conforms well to Stanislavski's approach as expressed, for example, in his work on Chatski. Knowing Chatski is first of all relating to his cognitive space, on a basic level understood literally as the environment he inhabits in the situation given.

Gärdenfors takes his starting point in a questioning of intentional semantics, the theoretical basis for the idea of "possible worlds" within modal logic.[7] He criticizes this theory for making the question of meaning in language a matter of intra-logical considerations about truth-values. One of the most important aims of his book is to outline a conceptualistic analysis of natural properties. He is interested in how the basic predicates, for example, green, are established. In his opinion this issue has been neglected by logical positivists.

By "conceptualistic analysis of natural properties" Gärdenfors means an analysis, which begins in considerations about human cognition. He claims that concepts we use in language gain meaning neither by direct reference to an external reality, nor to intra-linguistic or intra-logical determinants, but to our perceptions of the world. These he sees as organised in "conceptual spaces", built up of what he calls "quality dimensions". Temperature, weight, brightness, pitch, the ordinary spatial dimensions height, width and depth are examples of such quality dimensions. According to Gärdenfors these are mentally organized in a geometrical way, which also brings a form of analyticity, i.e. of truth that is independent of empirical considerations. I will not here go further into this part of his theory, which he demonstrates in a rather technical way. I will just state that one of the aims of our young actor's visit to Famusov's house is to gather this kind of sensual experience of the objects. Stanislavski suggests that he "lifts" the objects, "pushes them around" etc to grasp their sensual qualities, as a way to so to speak scenically reconstruct their meaning.

Starting his theory in human cognition, Gärdenfors also develops a theory about semantics. He discusses meaning in natural language, but the idea he promotes could be tried on other forms of meaning production as well. Gärdenfors criticizes what he calls "mainstream contemporary linguistics dominated by the Chomskian school, where syntax is viewed as the primary study object of linguistics; semantics is added when grammar is not enough; and pragmatics is what is left over (context, deixis etc.)"

The other tradition turns the study program upside-down: actions are seen as the most basic entities; pragmatics consists of the rules for linguistic actions; semantics is conventionalised pragmatics and finally syntax adds markers to help disambiguate when context does not suffice.[8]

An interesting feature about the latter theory is that meaning is related to action. This is an idea, which is strongly supported by experience of the actor's work. In theatre we can take part of the moment when language as well as objects acquire meaning by and in action. The final task of the young imaginary visitor to Famusov's house is to make his observations, the whole space of the house, the persons he meets in it, attain meaning by means of scenic action.

Mimetic action is an old and significant way for human beings to deal with reality.

The approach described here, which is under development within cognitive science offers highly stimulating opportunities for comparisons with experiences from methodological praxis in the field of drama and acting.

## Notes

1. Hans Georg Gadamer, *Hermeneutik I, Wahrheit und Methode. Grundzüge einer philosophischen Hermeneutik*, Tübingen J.C.B. Mohr (Paul Siebeck), 1990, p. 138.

2. Constantin Stanislavsky, *Creating a Role*. Translated by Elizabeth Reynolds Hapgood, London Eyre Methuen, 1984, p. 4 ff.

3. Constantin Stanislavsky, *My Life in Art*, Translated by J.J. Robbins, London Methuen Drama, 1991, p. 466.

4. Keir Elam, *The Semiotics of Theatre and Drama*. London and New York Methuen, 1980, p. 40 ff.

5. Ruth Ronen, *Possible Worlds in Literary Theory*, Cambridge, Cambridge University Press, 1994, p. 39.

6. See for example, Ronen, 1994, p. 103.

7. Peter Gärdenfors, *Conceptual Spaces. The Geometry of Thought*. Cambridge, The MIT Press, Massachusetts, London 2000, p. 60 ff, p. 152 ff.

8. Ibid., p. 185.

# 4

## Theatresports and Live Performance in Contemporary Western Culture[1]

### Matthijs Engelberts

Given the dearth of research on theatresports, it is practically impossible to provide an exhaustive or even near-exhaustive picture of the international dissemination of this immensely popular theatrical improvisatory match.[2] The website[3] of the International Theatresports Institute (ITI) – the existence of such a (commercial) institute alone is an indication of the quantitative importance of this sort of theatre – lists the groups that have been 'licensed' by the Institute, which acts on behalf of the founder of theatresports, Keith Johnstone: 6 groups in Canada, 14 in the United States, 1 in Australia and 4 in New Zealand; 2 in South America; 1 in Hong Kong and 3 in Japan; and finally 13 in Europe, of which 6 make their home in Germany. But this is without doubt only a small (commercially interesting) fraction of the operating groups. An article in *Theater Heute* about the German theatresports championship reports the existence of over 20 groups in Germany in 1996[4] – and none of the five teams mentioned in the article as participating in the '3. Deutsche Meisterschaft im Theatersport' is on the list of the ITI. In 2002 the Dutch theatresports association, Theatersport Vereniging Amsterdam (TVA), organized its eighth International Improvisation Theatre Festival in Amsterdam, at which all teams played theatresports matches. None of the four participating teams[5] in this the eighth week-long international festival is on the ITI list – nor is TVA the only theatresports group in Amsterdam, let alone in Holland.[6] Taken together, these figures clearly indicate that it is safe to conclude that theatresports 'matches' are very frequently organized – although to date their spread has been limited almost exclusively to what are called 'economically developed' countries. Moreover, theatresports do not seem an ephemeral phenomenon: this kind of performance has existed since the 1970s, and the international dissemination has been noticeable since the 1980s.

Despite their popularity, theatresports have not attracted any serious attention from researchers: international data-bases are still silent about the phenomenon.[7] The deviant form of this improvisational theatrical contest, and the mere fact that it is improvisation,[8] the predominantly 'amateur' status of theatresports, and the fact that this theatrical form exceeds the artistic domain to which theatre is usually limited, especially in economically developed societies, may be the main reasons for this neglect. However, the widespread popularity, the exceptional nature of the phenomenon, and the often reported liveliness of the sessions demand serious enquiry into theatresports as a significant development in contemporary theatre.

Two characteristics of this improvisatory theatre are especially interesting: the live interaction which is exploited in a way that reaches far beyond what interactivity in the media can achieve in the current technical conditions; and the fact that, in addition to its artistic goal, it seems to fulfil several social functions, mainly in small-scale, short-lived communities. Complaints about 'bad' acting, which are sometimes made by professional critics who only occasionally indulge in watching theatresports, cannot be considered an appropriate, overall evaluation of this kind of theatre. It is worth noting that in ancient Greece and in medieval societies members (mostly non-professional actors) of small to medium-scale communities acted out before the other members the social and psychic nodal preoccupations of their communities in the form of more or less standard and immediately recognizable plots, sometimes in a kind of contest – a form of theatre found in non-Western societies as well. Today, communities – particularly in the 'developed world' – have changed radically, and thus the preoccupations and the stories; the locus and importance in society of acting on the live stage, and the modes of interaction have also changed; and these evolutions obviously affect specific forms of direct theatrical expression in an eminently social, live gathering, which, even in the specialized Western society, largely transcend the boundaries of the artistic. It would be unfortunate not to take account of such contemporary theatrical events, which, as I hope to show, reveal much about the current position of theatre in the arts and in society.

I would like to state clearly that my aim here is not to describe (forms, groups, nature and themes of the improvised scenes, history), nor to extensively define theatresports (although obviously it is indispensable to outline a working definition and to sketch the phenomenon tentatively). The approach in this article is rather theoretical, in the sense that I would like to examine what the success of this kind of theatrical event shows about live performing art in contemporary conditions – what it reveals about theatre today. What are some of the main reasons for the widespread success it has had; or rather, what does the particular kind of success of this form tell us about theatre, about the position in contemporary society of the live performing art called theatre? This question is certainly wide-ranging and may seem presumptuous, but on the other hand it would be quite odd if the undeniable success of theatresports would not to some extent be indicative of structural features of the field of contemporary theatrical performance. After a few preliminary remarks (I), I would like to concentrate on two of these characteristics: the live nature of performance, its 'immediacy' (II), and its distinctive social quality (III).

# I

But first, what are theatresports? In order to avoid, to the extent possible for the moment, the problems surrounding the definition of concepts like 'theatre' and 'performance', the best way to describe (at least operationally) this particular kind of event is to particularize its process, the way it takes place. Generally speaking, it is a form of improvisational theatre in which two teams compete with each other in front of an audience. Each team, usually consisting of about 4 players, challenges the other to perform a particular kind of scene in turn. Details about the scene are provided to the teams, usually by asking the audience to give suggestions about the characters, for instance, or the setting of the action (where does it take place?), or a title. After the completion of a scene by a team, costumed judges, two or three as a rule, award points to the team (for such aspects of their performance as technique and content). The second team plays its improvised scene (the same challenge but different suggestions), and the judges again award their points. The spectators are then asked to give their opinion by shouting the name of their favourite team, for instance, or by raising a card with the colour of the team, and the audience's favourite team is awarded extra points. During the performance, the spectators can throw (plastic) roses to the actor or team they particularly like, and wet sponges at the judge(s) with whom they disagree.[9] Quite often, the scenes are accompanied by an improvising musician. After a series of challenges, the team, which has the highest score, is named the winner of the 'evening'. A commentator or 'master of ceremonies' (MC) guides the audience through the performance.

Theatresports are thus improvisational theatre in that a series of (fictional) events (a 'story') that is not known before the actual performance, is enacted by actors in front of an audience. It will be clear that 'events which are not known before the performance' applies to the players as well as to the audience; the performance is *not* improvisational in the sense of having been conceived by improvising actors during *rehearsals*. That kind of theatre is what is sometimes called 'improvisation-*based*', as opposed to 'text-based', performance. In the 1960s and 1970s, one could find many different forms of this kind of theatre (of which some continue to be produced) such as – at random – the early productions of Mnouchkine's *Theatre du Soleil*, the Dutch *Werkteater*, and several kinds of political theatre and community theatre.[10] In the creative process that precedes this type of performance, improvisation is used to devise the show, but the actual performance in this kind of theatre is nearly always a shaped product that reaches a final and more or less fixed form before it is presented to the audience. Theatresports, on the contrary, are improvisational in that the performance itself is largely improvised during the play of the performers on stage. It is thus in fact a particular form of 'impro' theatre, or 'improv', which evolved into a professional public form from the late 1950s onward. Unlike theatresports, impro has attracted some attention from researchers: there are not only practical, but also other, especially historical accounts, such as a history of the 'Compass', the first professional impro theatre group, founded in Chicago in 1955 by David Shepherd and Paul Sills, who later directed 'Second City'.[11] Since theatresports are a special kind of impro theatre, a 'genre' or 'format' so to speak, it is not surprising that comedy tends to dominate theatresports, as it does most improv shows. Nor is it surprising that theatresports often can be found in combination with other types of improv: *groups* may practise different genres and thus not specialize exclusively in theatresports, and *shows* may consist of different genres, with a theatresports match before the break, for instance, and a 'long form' after the break.[12] Nevertheless, it is useful to consider theatresports *per se*. On a *theoretical* level, this form differs from other kinds of impro theatre, most noticeably because of the particular competitive element that is part of the performance, making this genre easily identifiable. Indeed impro shows commonly use audience suggestions and volunteers, but other forms of interaction are specific to theatresports, such as the roses and sponges, cheering and booing the judges, voting, and interaction led by the MC who has a central role in orchestrating the event. Furthermore, theatresports *historically* developed more or less parallel to, but separate from, other improvisational performances, such as other forms of public impro theatre and stand-up comedy, and it thus does not seem to be a direct offshoot of another specific genre of improvisational (performing) art. Moreover, on a *practical* and contemporary level, the diffusion of theatresports has been such that its popularity alone would justify an in-depth study of the phenomenon.

## II

Is it possible to understand the success of this kind of theatrical event? In what light should it be considered if we want to understand its popularity, and thus, eventually, its position in the field of performance today? The most striking feature of theatresports is probably the degree to which this form utilizes the fact that theatre is a live art: it rests, obviously, on the simultaneous presence of performers and audience in the same space. It is the 'immediacy'[13] of theatre that theatresports exploit to a remarkable extent by diversifying and intensifying the communication between live performers and their audience. The spectators cooperate with the players by consciously communicating (and being invited to communicate) verbally and nonverbally over the course of the event, and thus collaborate in creating the performance of which they are a constitutive element, not only as 'recipients' of the theatrical artefact but also as active participants who shape the performance and the event of which it is a part. The term 'interactive' nowadays suggests computer and media communication primarily, that is, what might be called communication through technical devices. The term is hardly ever used for non-media communication. However, it is clear that in theatresports, it is precisely the high level of 'non-mediatized' interactivity that forms the basis for its utilization of the immediacy of theatrical communication.

This interactivity – the different kinds of communication between the performers and the audience – can be illustrated by an examination of the details (in more or less chronological order) of a theatresports match. Roses are distributed when the audience enters the theatre (a special form of greeting the audience by the performers, one could say) and these are thrown on the stage during the performance to honour a player or a team. Before the 'contest' starts, the game is explained to the audience, and this usually involves the MC posing questions to the audience and responses from the audience. There may also be a 'warm-up' of the audience, guided by the MC that may include some kind of exchange between the spectators – shaking hands with somebody next to you whom you do not know, for instance.[14] Moist sponges are distributed, generally by throwing them into the audience to be caught. Usually everybody ends up having about the same number of sponges, which also supposes a specific kind of communication between the individual members of the audience. The 'tossing' – or establishing the order of performance – is sometimes done by using the presence of the audience, for instance "which team is the first to find the youngest member of the audience." Cheering and booing are part of the performance event; the judges wearing robes are traditionally booed as soon as they are introduced, and the teams may be cheered right from the start when they are introduced by the commentator. Moreover, volunteers from the audience are used – maybe only about once or twice every night, but this still blurs the distinction between performers and audience. And the audience, of course, is asked to give suggestions for the scenes and votes at the end of each challenge.[15] Much more frequently and radically than in the huge majority of theatrical performances (*and* of sports matches), the audience intervenes in and influences the course of the event.

*Immediacy*: The foundation of theatresports is the fact that theatrical communication is live and direct, that it does not depend on, and thus does not necessarily use, relayed communication. This feature of theatre is clearly an important one in a situation in which dramatic performance is, in economically developed societies, the major form of art and entertainment that still rests predominantly and constitutively on direct live communication, in a field which has progressively become 'mediatized', especially in the course of the twentieth century. This assertion calls for some necessarily succinct remarks – to which we will briefly return below with regard to the social functions of theatresports. Nowadays, in the domain of art and entertainment, theatre, along with dance, is the only major (i.e. widely and frequently practised) art, whether high or not, which depends on live communication – that is, communication between human beings in the same place who are in direct contact with each other. Other subsisting live arts, such as circus arts or oral delivery of poetry and narrative, on the one hand, and modern live shows of a different kind, such as beauty contests and fashion shows, on the other, can not be considered 'major' kinds of performances from a quantitative point of view – they simply do not occur as often and as widely as theatre ('live enactment'). Interestingly, the other major art that is still structurally performed live has a much more symbiotic relation with mediatized communication than theatre: music. Music has seen the *extension* of its domain as a result of the application of recording techniques appropriate for music (much like sports, which have likewise witnessed a noticeable increase of their impact due to broadcasting). Theatre on the contrary has entered into competition with the arts that arose from the recording technique – the camera – that is most suited to theatre. Film, television, and video are indeed widely regarded as *other* arts, not as the continuation of theatre. Music and sports, on the other hand, have not given birth to this kind of independent spectral double. The live aspect of theatre has accordingly become more prominent, precisely because of the absence of live communication in theatre's twin arts, cinema and television. Theatresports, in turn, highlight this distinctive feature of theatrical performance in modern society: theatresports performances bring into prominence the contemporary specificity of theatre, its current position in the artistic field, its 'live locus'.

For those who are familiar with general academic trends it will not come as a surprise that the distinction between live and mediatized events has been contested by advocates of 'deconstruction'. As regards performance, Philip Auslander in particular has tried interestingly to contest the opposition between 'liveness' and mediatization. He convincingly points out that many live performances use different forms of media, that media and live performance influence each other, and that in some cases, especially in contemporary popular music, the live performance recreates the recorded standard (whether audio or video). Moreover, Auslander is right in stressing the fact that champions of live arts tend to ascribe qualities to liveness in terms that have little to do with an overall analysis of the position of these arts in modern society; live arts are thus in some cases mythicized – and the apologists accumulate 'symbolic capital'. But Auslander's more radical claim is that "live performance cannot be shown to be [...] ontologically different from mediatized forms". Indeed Auslander repeatedly mentions the contested 'ontological characteristics'; however, the pages devoted to a sustained analysis and critique of the characteristics of the opposition are few.[16] In contrast to explicit statements such as the one quoted above, the focus seems to be not on the (attack on) the so-called 'ontological' difference, but predominantly on the valuation of the one of the terms, i.e. on the overrating of liveness. The following sentence, taken from Auslander's conclusion, is revealing in this respect. After having stated once more that "there is little basis for convincing distinctions" between live performance and mediatized forms, the author concludes: "Therefore, ontological analysis does not provide a basis for privileging live performance" (159). Two different stances toward the distinction are presented as one: the question whether there *is* a difference, and the question whether one of the terms is to be privileged. For Auslander, 'ontology' seems thus to imply a preference, as if making a distinction necessarily implies attributing greater value to one of the terms. His attack on the valuation of liveness is interesting and invigorating, but his effort to prove that there is no difference between live and non-live forms is disappointing;[17] demonstrating that live and mediatized forms influence each other, or that they can be mixed, does not prove that there is no difference between them. It is thus not surprising that, for all his repudiation of the "intrinsic characteristics of live and mediatized forms" (11), Auslander himself constantly distinguishes sharply between what is live and what is mediatized,[18] without explaining how he is able to do so if there is no basis for a distinction. I agree partly that the distinction is not "immutable", but "determined by cultural and historical contingencies" (8, 11); however, this means one would need to specify in detail for each case *on what grounds* one decides what aspect of an art or particular work is live and what is mediatized. Auslander omits this, partly because, contrary to his claim about the absence of 'intrinsic characteristics', his focus is not on the distinction itself, but on the hierarchization of the terms. As for theatresports, this kind of performance shows clearly what possibilities liveness offers to performers and audience. This intense use of the live nature of theatrical performance may or may not have originated as a reaction to the progressive mediatization of modern society; the structure of this kind of performance may or may not have influenced the ensuing development of the media – which try for instance to integrate audience response (by incorporating voting into such televised contests as *Big Brother* or *Idols*, for example). The fact remains, however, that theatresports saliently exploit the possibilities of the live situation in the contemporary context.

One can legitimately speculate whether ever before in the history of theatre the immediacy of dramatic communication has been exploited so diversely and so structurally in public performances.[19] Naturally, there have been historic forms of improvisational theatre; the standard example is the *commedia dell'arte*. However, that form did certainly not imply the same frequency, range and intensity of exchanges between stage and audience. The same holds true for contemporary improvisational theatre other than theatresports: the latter structurally offer the most possibilities for the audience to communicate (with the performers and with the spectators), to intervene, and hence to determine the course of the event. Even the participation of the audience in theatrical events like the 'happening' does not seem to me to have structurally provoked the range of communication and participation between audience and players one finds in theatresports. In non-Western forms of improvisational theatre, such as the Indian Karyala which includes dance and music, "actors and audience get involved in conversation"; the audience offers money during the performance and the actors thank them, or songs may be sung with the audience. However, during this open-air "revue" that lasts until dawn, "the spectacles performed [...] are more or less the same everywhere",[20] and the audience does not decide the course of the enacted story, nor does it judge who is the 'winner'. In fact, when one considers the three basic features of theatresports – improvisation, the competitive aspect (bout/repartee), and audience participation both in the form of suggestions and of (contributing to) designating the winner – these features may only have previously occurred simultaneously in poetry: oral poetry (which is obviously also a performing art). Indeed, the medieval French *tenson*, as broadly defined by Pierre Bec, is "the performance of a veritable poetic match [which] generally takes place in front of an audience that participates in the exchange, appreciates (or not) the contributions, and finally serves as judge."[21] In the history of theatre such forms seem not to have been documented, although there may certainly have been *isolated* cases that are more radical, mostly only in a single respect, than theatresports. Stendhal gives the example of a soldier shooting the actor playing Othello in *Racine and Shakespeare*! And it is well known that Verdi's operas provoked nationalist riots. Moreover, non-public performances such as psychodrama can lead to diversified and intense 'audience' participation. But unscripted theatre of the kind theatresports offer in public performances does not depend on exceptional circumstances for its intense bi-directional communication between the stage and the audience, nor does it call forth a limited range of reactions in the audience. It constitutively depends on a diverse range of frequent audience involvement.

If indeed theatresports highlight the locus of theatre in the modern artistic field, it is interesting to find a remarkable similarity between the ideas on theatre expressed by a contemporary author of *scripted* theatre like Sarah Kane and the principles on which the phenomenon of theatresports is grounded. Here is what Kane states about the difference between (screen) media and (live) theatre for which she has a preference:

> I decided on theatre because it's live art. The direct communication with an audience I really like. When I go to a film, it doesn't matter what I do. It makes no difference. But when you go to the theatre, and you just cough, it may alter a performance. As a member of an audience I like the fact that I can change a performance. As a writer I like the fact that no performance will ever be the same.

For Kane, the possibility of direct communication between the audience and the performers is what makes theatre interesting – in other words, the immediacy of live performance.

> It's always been the form I love most because it's live. There's always going to be a relationship between the material and the audience that you don't really get with a film. I mean with the film I wrote, *Skin*, people can walk out or change channels or whatever, it doesn't make any difference to the performance. But with *Blasted*, when people got up and walked out it was actually part of the whole experience of it. And I like that, it's a completely reciprocal relationship between the play and the audience.[22]

"A *completely reciprocal* relationship between the play and the audience": this is a description of scripted theatre, but the ideal which reverberates in these words is, it seems to me, not really attainable in scripted theatre – not even in improvisational theatre, and not even if it demands audience participation as much as do theatresports. Nonetheless the ideal voiced by Kane *does* underscore to what extent current writers of scripted theatre and performance practitioners[23] of improvisational theatre alike tend to stress the importance for theatre of the fact that, as a live art, it presents possibilities of direct communication between audience and performers that should be used. The liveness of theatre is foregrounded in theatresports and in other kinds of (scripted) contemporary performance.

It is also striking that a description of the history of theatre in the *entire* twentieth century, offered by such an influential theatre reformer as Eugenio Barba, concurs with what can be said about theatresports. In his essay 'The Essence of Theatre', Barba claims that all innovations in twentieth-century theatre spring mainly from one source, namely 'the need to feel alive and present'.

> More than anything else there was an urgent need to fight the sensation of loss – a loss of existence. The word "existence" has to be taken literally: a *capacity to be*, to feel alive and present, and to pass this *essential* quality on to the spectator [...], to engender a vital condition that permeates every level of a performance starting with the basic one: the art of the actor.[24]

The concept of a 'vital condition' that Barba describes has obviously not been formulated with a view to the kind of improvisational theatre we find in theatresports. However, it is noticeable that the terms can serve as a definition of what is ultimately at stake in theatresports: 'a capacity to feel alive and present *and to pass this essential quality on to the spectator*'. This striking parallel is, ultimately, not surprising: if theatresports indeed lay bare a significant characteristic of theatre in modern society, it would on the contrary be astonishing if they were the sole theatrical form in which the live locus of theatre is tangible. "Today, the question of the audience seems to be the most important and difficult one to face," wrote Peter Brook in 1968, in his chapter 'The Immediate Theatre'; and in this 'immediate' theatre, which he recommends, "there is only a practical difference between actor and audience, not a fundamental one."[25]

It might be questioned at this point that the parallel between these contemporary reflections on theatre and the improvisational form called theatresports only underscores that the 'art of theatre' as a whole has gone through a paradigm shift. It is well-known that in the course of the twentieth century, the live element of any kind of 'performance', *whether contemporary or not*, has indeed been brought to the fore, as opposed to a view of theatre as an art of interpretation, as execution of a dramatic text. It is true, obviously, that theatresports are a manifestation of this shift of paradigm, which has occurred both in dramatic practice and in the theory of theatre. It should be noted, however, that theatresports are not simply one of the examples of the significance of this shift. Because of their pronounced, intense use of the immediacy of the theatrical event, theatresports are an exceptional, revealing example of the shift to live performance, and as such the matches pre-eminently exemplify an important aspect of what attracts certain modern authors of scripted theatre and practitioners of performance alike in theatre today. At the same time, it is important to add that there is no noticeable revolutionary fervour in theatresports, as there has been in earlier or even contemporaneous forms of 'experimental' performance. There is for instance no rejection of the basic *pretence* of 'traditional' theatre, no refusal of the 'illusion' of the fiction, as in performance art or body art: no austere revolutionary goal to 'undo' and recreate theatre, to arrive for instance at something like a 'nonsemiotic performance', to quote a term devised for experimental theatre forms like happenings.[26] Referentiality, narrativity, even psychology, categories flouted by countless innovative currents in twentieth-century theatre, reappear in theatresports.

## III

Thus far I have presented theatresports as part of the artistic field. However, this theatrical phenomenon clearly transcends the boundaries of the artistic – probably much more so, in practice, than do other forms of performance designed to free theatre from the precinct of art, such as political theatre. Given the pronounced social nature of this improvisational form, its artistic qualities coexist with, and are in fact inextricably linked with other goals. The social potential of theatresports is indeed often stressed by the practitioners. The terms they use often recall other forms of modern improvisation that have been purposely, and usually exclusively, designed for social and psychological application, and not as a public 'show'. In fact, the social potential of theatresports is best described as being twofold. Apart from their use as a developmental, formative, social and psychic tool for the *performers*, which will be discussed below, theatresports in public performances have a marked social quality due to the heightened social awareness they produce. Indeed one could say theatresports events temporarily create a community: a 'flash'-community. The communication between the performers and the *audience*, and their collaboration in an event the course of which is decided on the spot, makes the group of performers and spectators susceptible to a noticeable increase in social cohesion. The communicative atmosphere that is produced by the multiple occasions and invitations to participate in the course of and in the outcome of the event bring about a heightened awareness of the fact that the audience and the performers are going through an experience together.[27] Theatresports thus markedly bring to the fore the social nature of theatrical performance.

Theatre, of course, always creates a form of community among the audience, to a certain extent; Marvin Carlson for instance underscores at the end of his *Performance: A Critical Introduction* that what is "important in defining the particular quality and power of 'theatrical' performance [...] is that such performance is experienced by an individual who is also part of a group, so that social relations are built into the experience itself." For him, this brings "the experience inevitably into the realm of the political and the social."[28] It seems to me disputable that (theatrical) performance is *always* 'inevitably political' simply because the audience is collective; and I would also not defend the idea that each and every theatrical performance necessarily makes the spectator experience the 'inevitably social' nature of the audience more than any other (non-theatrical) group activity (for instance, shopping...). Moreover, mediatized art or events can also create a (sense of) community, as Auslander has pointed out (55-56). Theatresports events as a specific form of theatrical performance, however, undoubtedly capitalize on the social nature of theatre that is so often postulated; and they do so to such an extent that one can say they create temporary communities. In a largely individualized contemporary 'Western' society, these events produce a flash community, an instantaneous and short-term social framework: groups of people who do not know each other yet in a group setting. There is, firstly, no individualized social control exerted by a community pre-existing the performance. In such a short-lived community composed of those who freely decide to gather and who stay together only for the performance, there is, secondly, no risk of the individual being encapsulated in a social structure experienced as 'limiting'. Moreover, the flash communities are usually rather small groups[29] of individuals – contrary to mass communication which creates undifferentiated and boundless groups, or to sports matches and concerts of pop music which tend to merge large groups of spectators – and the social framework does not blunt initiative or prescribe only a limited number of fixed roles. It is therefore not surprising that Johnstone has recourse to the concept of a "party"[30] when he describes what a successful theatresports event should be like. The use of this metaphor is obviously partly promotional, but it also indicates the importance of the intense social nature of this kind of theatrical performance. Other terms used in Johnstone's book, like "togetherness" and being welded into "one creature" (322, 331, 340), also point to the increase in social cohesion, without highlighting the sudden, free, brief, active and participatory quality of the 'community' inherent in the 'party' concept. But whatever the usefulness of these epithets, it seems possible to conclude that theatresports put to use theatre as a cohesive social force; as a way of countering the disappearance of small-scale communities[31] in modern society, but in a manner that radically rejects those aspects of (fixed) communities that have led to the process of individualization.

As we have noticed, the social function of theatresports is not limited however to the fact that it calls into being a short-term community. It is clear from the writings of Keith Johnstone, and also from the history of non-public improvisational theatre (whether one considers the psychodrama developed by Moreno in the interwar years, or the independent sociological counterpart inspired by Neva Boyd's work in the same period) that theatresports have what can be called a 'therapeutic' function – the term 'educational'[32] or 'formative' function is preferable – in that for the *players* participation can be a form of social education. Johnstone occasionally uses the epithet "therapeutic", but more often writes about improving "interpersonal skills" and "human interaction".[33] This is possible, simply, because theatre is live communication between the stage and the audience, which is generally collective and thus implies communication between the members of the audience, as we have already observed; but also *on* stage, between the enacted 'characters', and at the same time between the players as such. For these two reasons, theatre is the most eminently *social* art, and therefore it can readily be used, and has been used as a formative instrument in communication in social relations. However, this is still a very general remark, and the question in fact should point to a more specific relation. Why do theatresports, and the history of improvisational theatre in general, make this feature of theatre so apparent? Why is it that this development in theatre, the use of its potential as social formative instrument, comes to the fore in the present time? How does the form of theatre that flourishes in theatresports today blend its specialized artistic function with this specific social function?

Surely many factors could be mentioned here, among which one should probably count the growing importance of psychology and sociology in the course of the twentieth century, and, independently, the reflexive turn of the modernist spirit which radically probes the frontiers of the arts. But one of the reasons that should be taken into account is the fact that theatre is still rearranging its resources after having been chased from its more central position in the arts by screen media, such as film and television. Eugenio Barba has recently summarized the situation:

> Compared to other forms of spectacle – sport or cinema – theatre proves to be anachronistic, answering the needs of another age, out of tune with the very flow of civilization and its other means of communication. The objective of this "modern" civilization is to reach the greatest number of people in the shortest time and as economically as possible. Theatre is quite the opposite: it involves vast expense, a waste of resources, both human and material, not to mention the time needed to prepare a performance that will only be seen by a limited number of spectators.

Quite a few things can be said about this contention,[34] one of which is certainly that it seems wrong to state indiscriminately, on the basis of Barba's analysis, that theatre – live dramatic performance – is 'of another age' as such; the manifold theatrical activities, whether subsidized or unsubsidised, that attract the attention of small and large audiences and of the media in many parts of the world cannot simply be dismissed as 'anachronistic'. On the other hand, it is undeniably true that the position of live dramatic performance in the field of the arts has been significantly modified, and in many respects weakened, because of the more competitive conditions in which it operates, principally due to the rise of film and television. Again, this does not mean that theatre is not vigorous, or that it has not in some ways even extended its domain – sometimes precisely because of the new possibilities offered by the artistic developments of the twentieth century: live pop concerts have tended to become increasingly theatrical, and inversely pop stars such as Madonna use their fame to star in live theatre productions. The structural subsidizing of theatre in the Western world after World War II has also created new areas for the development of theatre. But on the whole, Barba's summary is correct in that it brings out the fact that the position of theatre has undergone changes which have resulted in a less unique and less central place for this art, mainly as a result of its separation from the arts that have arisen from the technology of the camera.

Live dramatic performance has thus been compelled to situate itself in new conditions, and together with, for instance, the self-reflexive tendency and experimentation that characterize modernism, this repositioning has led to a reassessment of the social potential of acting as a means of forming (young) people. This function has obviously been employed before in the history of theatre, for instance in Jesuit schools, and today the use of theatre in schools also exploits this function, for all the 'waste of resources' live performance generally implies. However, theatresports prominently revaluate this function of theatre, and are thus a contemporary answer – only one of the contemporary answers, to be sure – to the changing conditions of live performance in a modern, mediatized society.

It is not surprising, in these conditions, that theatresports are often not primarily a professional activity for the players (whereas other public forms of impro tend to be professional events). Professional theatre is a specialized activity, and as such it has a definite, usually limited goal: the production of shows that function in the public sphere of 'art' and 'entertainment'. Theatresports on the contrary are not solely oriented towards producing an artistic object, since the social effect of the production on the actors (and on the audience, as we have already seen) is generally a constituent part of the activity. The social effect of the act of performing can be a major goal. It should be added that this does not change the activity into (professional) education, or therapy; it is simply often *not primarily a specialized activity* any more, and thus moves away from the professional domain, which in 'developed' societies consists almost exclusively of highly specialized activities.[35] Now it may seem that this blending of artistic and social qualities occurs in all amateur theatre; but what is important is that in theatresports the social function is explicitly revaluated and stressed, for example, in the writings of one of the genre's foremost practitioners, Johnstone. Moreover, in amateur theatre it is most often not the performing itself, which is supposed to contribute to the forming of the actors, but the rehearsals, that is, the part of the process that the audience does *not* see. In 'traditional' amateur theatre, therefore, the social function is only a side effect of a performance, which can be seen as the major product and which is mostly meant to be equivalent (or as close as possible) to the specialized 'artistic' productions of professional theatre.

Theatresports matches have been played for a few decades now, and the form moreover can claim international acceptance. This success is most likely best viewed against the background of the issue of the position of theatre in the contemporary field of the arts. Theatresports take advantage of the specificity of theatre, of its immediacy, of the fact that it is 'live' art, and do so to a high and maybe unprecedented degree, thus stressing to what extent the 'live' aspect of theatrical performance has become distinctive in the domain of art. In addition, theatresports make use of the social nature of theatre, both for the audience and for the players, to such an extent that they take theatre to the border of the artistic and the social or formative fields. Theatresports are situated on the cutting edge of theatre and act as a social instrument, thus highlighting – but also turning to advantage – the fact that theatre occupies a less privileged position in the artistic field after the rise of screen media. In summary, one could say that theatresports playfully exploit theatre, and retreat from the developed, individualized, mediatized and specialized society, by energetically turning to account non-mediatized and functionally unspecialised theatrical communication in short-lived and small-scale communities. They do so 'playfully' and 'energetically': there is no pessimism or detachment, on the one hand, and there is no militancy, on the other hand, in these performances in which the spirit of negativity and withdrawal or of doctrinal struggle against 'political systems' seems to be absent.[36] Without wanting to adopt the promotional tone one sometimes finds in the writings of advocates of this improvisational form, and without wanting to deny that measured against professional standards, the acting may sometimes be found deficient, or the character of the scenes found facile; without denying, furthermore, the failures that can occur in all improvisatory art, and knowing that commercial exploitation, or even the non-professional match, can lead to a slightly spurious, forced situation, it is possible to call theatresports a jubilant art. For researchers, it may seem more important to know that theatresports are a significant form in theatre today, since they reveal much about the current position of live dramatic performance – and therefore, this form deserves to be studied.

## Notes

1. I would like to thank Marta Engelberts for valuable and stimulating discussions as well as for important comments on earlier versions of this article. Toneelsport Vereniging Amsterdam (TVA) has been instrumental in developing my knowledge of theatresports.

2. The best-written overview, without doubt, can be found in Lyn Pierse (*Theatresports Down Under: A Guide for Coaches and Players*, Sydney: Improcorp Australia (second edition, 1995), 375-400), although it is far from being complete (even for the middle of the nineties when the second edition of *Theatresports Down Under* was published). She also documents (5-16) the history of theatresports in Australia and New Zealand.

3. *www.theatresports.org*; accessed on 17, July 2002.

4. Stammen, Silvia (1996), 'Theater bis zum Abpfiff. Eindrücke von der 3. Deutschen Meisterschaft im Theatersport', *Theater Heute* 37:12, 68-69.

5. 'TVA' from Amsterdam, 'Liga de Improvisación Madrileña' from Madrid, 'Oui Be Negroes' from San Francisco and 'Slap Happy' from Toronto. There have been many international 'tournaments', such as the first International Theatresports Tournament at Expo '86 in Vancouver or the Calgary Winter Olympics '88 (Pierse 12, see note 2).

6. In 1994 there were reportedly 30 groups in the Netherlands (Veldman, Maart (1994), 'Natte sponzen en plastic rozen; beperkingen en mogelijkheden van de theatersport', *Toneel Theatraal* 115:5, 16-19); the Dutch website *www.theatersport.nl* lists more than 60 groups (accessed on 25 February 2003). The history of theatresports in the Netherlands is outlined in Besseling, André (1999), *Theater vanuit het niets; alles over improvisatietheater*, Amsterdam: IT&FB (Theorie en praktijk serie), 32-39.

7. There is not a single entry in the *MLA Bibliography*, the *International Index to the Performing Arts*, the *Arts and Humanities Citation Index* and the *Social Sciences Citation Index*, nor in *Backstage* (all databases accessed 16 February 2003; spelling theatre/theater and sport/sports), apart from a one-page

report on a German contest in *Theater Heute* (Stammen) listed in the *IIPA*. The books on theatresports listed at the end of this article are mainly practical guidebooks written by practitioners.

8. Cf. Smith & Dean: "The impression gained is that artistic improvisation is gradually becoming a serious and more common area of academic attention, though the small number of publications do not permit a clear assessment of the change." (Smith, Hazel & Roger T. Dean, *Improvisation, Hypermedia and the Arts since 1945*, Amsterdam: Harwood Academic Publishers,1997, p. 9)

9. Needless to say, this description is not prescriptive. In his book *Impro for storytellers: Theatresports and the Art of Making Things Happen*, Keith Johnstone (London: Faber and Faber 1999; earlier version: *Don't be prepared – Theatresports for Teachers*, Calgary: Loose Moose Theatre Company, 1994) condemns quite a few of these common practices, quite often rather imperatively, for instance the division of roles between the judges (325), the use of techniques other than shouting for the audience vote (4), the use of wet sponges (322), and even the frequent use of suggestions (25-27, 368).

10. 'Devised' theatre, as it has been defined – rather loosely however – by Oddey on the basis of British professional examples includes improvisation-based theatre in which the text has been created by the performers during the 'rehearsals', but also performances for which a script has been written by a writer working with the group of performers, and other kinds of theatre as well, such as primarily visual and/or site-specific performances (Oddey, Alison (1994), *Devising Theatre: A Practical and Theoretical handbook*, London: Routledge).

11. On the 'Compass', cf. Coleman, Janet (1991), *The Compass: The Improvisational Theatre that Revolutionized American Comedy*, Chicago: University of Chicago Press. Paul Sills is the son of Viola Spolin, the author of the often reprinted, mainly practical book of exercises ("theater games" 5) *Improvisation for the Theatre*, which is inspired by the social work of Neva Boyd (Spolin, Viola (1973), *Improvisation in the Theatre: A Handbook of Teaching and Directing Techniques*, London: Pitman; first edition 1963, Evanston, Illinois: Northwestern University Press). Impro has been given much publicity by the British and later also American TV show *Whose line is it anyway?* The best general overview of (the history of) modern improvisatory theatre is probably Frost & Yarrow (Frost, Anthony & Yarrow, Ralph (1990), *Improvisation in Drama*, Basingstoke: MacMillan); the best book about improvisation in the arts in general is undoubtedly Smith & Dean (see note 8).

12. As is the case in the International Improvisation Theatre Festival organized in Amsterdam by the Theatersport Vereniging Amsterdam; the name of

this group and of the festival already indicate the close connection between theatresports and impro (cf. as does the title of Johnstone's book *Impro for storytellers: Theatresports and the Art of Making Things Happen*). The 'long form' may be a 'fixed genre' (i.e. a formula that is used also by other groups) or an improvisational form that has been developed by a particular group and is not (yet) used by others.

13. 'Immediacy' here means that performer and audience are physically present at the same time and in the same space. The term is thus synonymous with 'liveness'; however, 'live' is also used for media like radio or television when an event is broadcast at the same *time* as it happens, but in the *absence* of the audience to which it is relayed by these media. In this article, 'immediacy' and 'live' both refer to the fact that performer and spectator are present, not only *nunc* but also *hic*. I deliberately avoid the less specific term 'unmediated'. The played scenes may be 'mediated' in that they do not refer directly to 'reality' but rather to representations of reality. Content and form of the scenes, and the suggestions, indeed often derive from widely known images drawn from (other) forms of communication, such as the mass media.

14. "Tell a stranger the vegetable that you most hate!" (Johnstone 3, and other examples, see note 9)

15. Some less frequent forms of communication include: spectators using flashlights to illuminate the stage, spectators being penalized by the judges, the audience speaking in one voice, or the audience 'counting out' a team or counting down before a scene (Johnstone 36, 4 + 325, 175, 326-27 + 332, see note 9).

16. Auslander, Philip (1999), *Liveness: Performance in a Mediatized Culture*, London: Routledge; 55-57 mainly. The quotation is from page 7; 'ontological characteristics' are discussed on e.g. 159.

17. At one point, the book suggests the existence of "phenomenological distinctions" (54), but the term is not specified (cf. the same omission for the 'ontological' and the 'intrinsic' differences), nor are there any examples of these 'phenomenological' distinctions! As regards the attack on the distinctions (of whatever nature) between live and non-live, the book seems unfortunately aimed more at being conspicuous than at clarifying and informing. The "speculative spirit" and "a certain tendentiousness in [the] arguments," as Auslander calls it himself (9), can hardly be considered an excuse for this attitude.

18. Madonna's concerts for instance are "mediatized performances in a live setting" (158), and mixed-media performances combine "live actors with film, video, or digital projections" (36); *Miss Saigon* is cited unambiguously as an example of a 'live performance' in which the helicopter effect is "a direct importation of cinematic or televisual realism into the theatre" (25);

Auslander also claims to offer "a detailed analysis of the relationship between live and recorded performances in the culture of rock music" (159). It is apparently possible, in the case of a musical or concert as well as for a performance that uses different media, or that recreates a recorded performance as in Madonna's case, to ascertain *that* it is live or *what* is live in it and what is mediatized (or what *resembles* mediatization – there is room for another distinction here!).

19. Apart from Frost & Yarrow (see note 11), Smith & Dean offer one of the very few solid (but brief) historical overviews. Theatresports (which are not treated in any detail by these authors) buttress their hypothesis that "[i]mprovisation, though common in earlier forms, may often have been used in quite constrained ways. Its influence and significance are therefore probably rather different from those of post 1945 improvisation." (Smith & Dean 10, see note 8)

20. Ahluwalia, Kailash (1995), *Karyala, An Impromptu Theatre of Himachal Pradesh*, New Delhi: Reliance Publishing House; quotations are from pages 49, 7, 59; cf. also 80, 107.

21. Bec, Pierre (2000), *La joute poétique. De la tenson médiévale aux débats chantés traditionnels*, Paris: Les Belles Lettres (collection Architecture du verbe), 9 (my translation). The use of improvisation is discussed 28-32; the use of suggestions in a contemporaneous Basque form of the 'poetic bout' is mentioned 40. The 'poetry slams' organized in the US since 1986 do not involve improvisation (www.poetryslam.com). The case of the *tenson* was suggested to me during the IFTR conference in Jaipur (2003) by Seth Wolitz, whose erudition, generosity and wide interests are invigorating.

22. Saunders, Graham (2002), *'Love me or kill me'. Sarah Kane and the Theatre of Extremes*, Manchester: Manchester UP (series 'Theatre: theory, practice, performance'). Quotations (Kane's words) are from pages 17 and 13.

23. Cf. performance artist Eric Bogosian's revealing terms: "Theater [...] is something we make together every time it happens. [...] Instead of being bombarded by a cathode ray tube we are speaking to ourselves." (quoted in Auslander 4, see note 16). Although Bogosian paints a very negative picture of television (and thus values live art by depreciating screen media, a point with which Auslander takes issue), the first part of his sentence is again a very adequate description of what theatresports are striving to attain!

24. Barba, Eugenio (2002), 'The Essence of Theatre', *The Drama Review*, 46:3 (fall), 12-30. Quotation on page 21, italics as in the original.

25. Brook, Peter (1968), *The Empty Space*, London: Penguin; quotations are from pages 146, 112, 150.

26. Cf. Kirby, Michael (1982), 'Nonsemiotic Performance', *Modern Drama*, 25, 105-111.

27. It is undoubtedly useful here to insist on the second part of the word theatre*sports*: a sports match can indeed lead to the intense sharing of participation in or watching an activity, which temporarily enhances social cohesion. However, the sports metaphor is hardly ever elaborated in the writings of theatresports practitioners, and there are indeed many differences between a sports match and a theatresports event. The audience does not steer the course of and co-decide the outcome of a sports match, for instance: there is far less participatory activity. Furthermore, in theatresports physical strength or skills are not foregrounded (as is the case in most sports), nor is the fact of winning as such, nor even the competitive element (in the televised singing contest *Idols*, for instance, competition is much more pronounced than in theatresports matches, or even in a theatresports championship).

28. Carlson, Marvin (1996), *Performance: A Critical Introduction*, London: Routledge, 198.

29. Major Australian cities seem to be the only areas specializing in huge audiences, e.g. the exceptional 2600 spectators in Melbourne (Pierse 381).

30. "With luck you'll feel as if you've been at a wonderful party" (Johnstone 6, cf. 60, see note 9).

31. Theatresports *create* a community, as opposed to 'community theatre' in a restricted sense (cf. van Erven), which originates in (and for) an existent (and not necessarily small-scale) community and heightens its awareness as a community by presenting (social and political) issues in which the group in question has a stake (Van Erven, Eugene (2001), *Community Theatre: Global Perspectives*, London: Routledge).

32. Pierse xv.

33. Johnstone's *Impro for Storytellers*, 6, 24 (see note 9). In *Improvisation in Drama*, the authors also state that for "Johnstone and Grotowski, the 'educational' or developmental aspect emerges from the practice of theatre activities," and "for Paul Sills and Viola Spolin, the work passes (like Grotowski's) beyond the borders of the theatre, into the para-theatrical world of self-discovery and self-actualisation" (Frost & Yarrow 56, 54). Grotowski should, by the way, be considered as a quite different case. The 'educational' aspect of theatresports and impro is also commercially exploited in corporate training.

34. Barba 20 (see note 24). Television is missing from Barba's short analysis, and sport is certainly mentioned mainly because of its contemporary entanglement with broadcasting (without the media, sports are comparable to theatre in that they often involve the same kind of "vast expense, a waste of resources, both human and material").

35. The neglect of amateur theatre by theatre research has recently been pointed out and criticized by Claire Cochrane ('The Pervasiveness of the

Commonplace: The Historian and Amateur Theatre', *Theatre Research International*, 26:3 (2001), 233-242). It is important to note that the use of theatresports in professional settings, such as commercial shows, regular education and corporate training demonstrates that theatresports are not wholly incompatible with, and not in principle opposed to, the specialized activities of the economic sphere.

36. There is thus for instance no fundamental hostility to mass media: theatresports have been televised quite often, e.g. in Australia and New Zealand (Pierse 13, viii, see note 2) and the Netherlands (Besseling 38, see note 8).

# 5

# Understanding Understanding

## Phenomenological Hermeneutics in Thomas Lehmen's Clever[1]

### Nigel Stewart

This essay is an attempt to show how phenomenological hermeneutics, as exemplified in the writings of Martin Heidegger and Hans-Georg Gadamer, can illuminate recent European dance theatre, as exemplified in the work of the German choreographer Thomas Lehmen. In particular, I will use phenomenological hermeneutics to reflect on *Clever*, a full-length sextet by myself and five other English dancers in 2001 that toured England in 2003. Interposing fragments of text and movement arising from the dancers' idiosyncratic responses to a range of set tasks, *Clever* can be identified loosely as a post-Bauschian *Tanztheater* work that blurs the genre boundaries between post-modern dance and autobiographical performance.

If phenomenology is the study of the structures of lived experience and hermeneutics the art of interpretation, then phenomenological hermeneutics is nothing less than an attempt to understand the experience of understanding itself. This, I want to argue, is what Lehmen's work does. With reference to the methods by which *Clever* was devised as well to the final *mise-en-scène*, I will not only indicate how hermeneutics can help us to "understand" the kind of hybrid work that Lehmen creates, but also how Lehmen's methods of sourcing and composing performance material are themselves hermeneutic in that they actually frame the deep structures and conditions which make understanding itself possible.

## Stage 1: "Phenomenological" Sourcing

Lehmen's choreographic method is in two stages. I want to characterize the first stage as a "phenomenological" process in which movement material is sourced and its qualities are distilled, and the second stage as more of a "hermeneutic" process in which the meaning of that movement material is disorientated and recontextualized. During the first stage Lehmen is concerned not with perpetuating a received movement style, but rather with investigating the *temporal modes of reality* to which movement is orientated and through which the performer's presence on stage can be modulated. There are three temporal modes – the 'historical', which *retains* a *past*; the 'fantastical', which *anticipates* a *future*, and the 'functional', which *attends* to the *present*.

For the sake of brevity and consistency, I will provide examples from my own work for Lehmen. During the devising of *Clever,* we were asked to originate movement from activities in the historical mode in which we consider ourselves to be "skilful" and those in which we deem ourselves to be "poor". I improvised around cooking as an instance of the former! Forefingers and thumbs twist the skin off a garlic clove, hands rapidly karate chop onions, the left arm unfurls as I lunge forward left to sizzle onions in a skillet, I *grand plié* to tear basil with my arms in fifth, I complete a forward and backward roll over my right shoulder to press out pastry, and so on!

In the "fantastical" mode, the performer is also taken up with a sense of self outside of the present moment, but by being transported towards an imaginary future world. In one such sequence called "Bubble Bird", my arms glide and my right leg thrusts in different unfoldings and elongations to various edges of my kinaesphere, where I burst imaginary bubbles until a bird flies forth.[2] In the functional mode, by contrast, the performer investigates anatomical articulations or task-based activities which encourage the body to be present *to* the present. For instance, I derived one action by finding different ways to hang off a ballet bar. With my back to the bar which I firmly grip with both hands, I slowly pluck my midriff forward, then, abruptly letting the bar go with my left hand whilst continuing to grip it with my right, I slash the left arm around to twist my torso into the bar. The task was then to develop this activity away from the bar.

In rehearsal, Lehmen insists that his dancers never lapse into stylistic generalities – least of all not the fluid floor patterns, hand-hops and spiraloid risings and fallings typical of the release techniques in which he and his dancers are mostly trained. On the contrary, Lehmen bids each dancer to *select* movements from the kind of activities I have illustrated. By then removing all that is not essential to their significance and articulation, these raw movements are distilled into essential idiosyncratic actions, which can then be composed into sequences of action, which constitute the quirky and often very funny strips of human behaviour which are, in turn, montaged by Lehmen into the final work.[3] This technique of distillation is crucial to my argument, but one example should suffice. Whereas for my "Cooking" sequence I originally devised, as I have said, a full forward then backward roll over my right shoulder, I was instructed by Lehmen to concentrate this whole move into just a counter clockwise torsion of the right arm as a result of which my right shoulder pulls my whole body into a forward lunge that stops the instant I touch the floor.

Sequences made up of such actions are *synecdochic*, not just in the sense that they represent an original activity in the way that a part stands in for the whole to which that part is intrinsic, but particularly in terms of the distinction that Susan Foster makes between metonymic and synecdochic modes of representation. According to Foster, a *metonymic* representation would *imitate*, say, an actual river by abstracting its geometric outline to "clearly indicate the size and shape" of the river; however, a *synecdochic* representation not only *replicates* "the functionally distinct parts" of that river, but renders "the river as a dynamic system" by establishing those parts in a new matrix of relations – "for example, between the flowing water and the bounded channel or between the current and a small island".[4] Likewise, I did not attempt to imitate the original activity of cooking, but to transform the structure of that activity by establishing a dynamic set of relations between its parts – for example, between twisting, chopping, frying, tearing, pressing and other ways of handling foodstuffs.

Now from what I have said so far, the first stage of Lehmen's choreographic method is true enough to the descriptive phenomenology of Husserl. In the first place, there is a similar conception of time. In so far as the dancer performs sequences in which an action in one temporal mode cuts or is dissolved into an action from another modality, choreographic time is not conceived objectively as a

one-dimensional punctilinear series of "nows", but phenomeno-
logically in the Husserlian sense of a distended three-dimensional
matrix in which the performer can play with the presencing and
absencing of herself or himself as he or she slips from a sheer atten-
tiveness *to* the present to either a preoccupation with a retained past or
the anticipation of a protensive future *within* the present.

In the second place, Lehmen's method compares in some respects
with Husserl's method of phenomenological reduction. Lehmen
obliges each dancer to avoid habitual neuromuscular patterns and to
remove raw movement from its originating context by reducing it to its
most essential feature. In the *epoché* of phenomenology, Husserl obliges
the subject to suspend her or his habit or "natural attitude" to the object
so that the subject (as the object's field of experience) can imaginatively
vary the qualities of the sensations that are experienced until he or she
apperceives those qualities that are invariant and irreducible.[5]

Yet, there are crucial respects in which Lehmen is different from
Husserl. Indeed, in as much as Lehmen's suspicion of "artistic style"
arises primarily from, as he puts it, his "interest in working with the
'artist as a person' " and his belief that his dancers should never "hav[e]
to give up their human-ness", Lehmen's work has more to do with the
phenomenological hermeneutics of Heidegger – for Heidegger was
primarily concerned with *Dasein* (*i.e.*, "there-being" or human
being-in-the-world) and how "understanding is not just theoretical
cognition but rather a basic category of human existence itself" and
therefore is "an essential, not merely contingent feature of *Dasein*".[6]

Husserl, too, refutes understanding as merely an epistemological
or cognitive process, but his understanding of understanding in terms
of the structures of our sensory experience of the objects that we understand is in fact part of his ultimate project to understand the absolute
and transcendental conditions of any and all experience. By contrast,
Heidegger claims that we fail to get to grips with experience if we
reduce an object of experience to an abstract "throng of sensations" –
for then we attend to an abstraction of that object and not the object
itself. Similarly, Heidegger claims that we fail to get to grips with
experience if we see the object we experience as "formed matter" – for
that would lead us to understand the object only in terms of the
*purpose*, according to which the matter of the object has been formed
and thus, to mistake the utility or "equipmental" value of the object for
the object itself. On the contrary, Heidegger is concerned with

understanding the objects of our experience in terms of "the dynamic of care with which [*Dasein*] is concerned about its own future and its own being".[7] Thus, in his well-known meditation on Van Gogh's painting of a pair of peasant's shoes, Heidegger eulogizes that the worn insides and "rugged heaviness of the shoes" hold together, on the one hand, the dampness and richness, ripening and fallowness of the *earth*, which the peasant has trod to do her work, and, on the other hand, the careworn *world* that this work sustains.[8]

To be sure, the functional mode of Lehmen's method encourages the dancer to understand her or his body in terms of its functional ability and particular potential, and thus just the abstract structure of the sensations which it experiences. However, as my earlier examples indicate, the historical and fantastical modalities, which predominate in Lehmen's work, oblige the dancer to understand her or his body not as an utopian abstraction or idealization, but through its concerned inter-action with remembered or fantasized objects that constitute the possibilities of her or his own existence. For both Heidegger and Lehmen, understanding is not the intellectual grasp over what we do, it is the practical know-how we gain in the doing. More importantly, understanding is framed as self-understanding grasped as the "possi-bility of my own self that is played out in understanding" within the limitations of my own finitude and historical situation.[9] I would contend that, by contrast, the bodywork practices that support much post-modern dance tend to understand the body more in terms of its essential functionality and ultimately as a psychosomatic idealization, independent of historical context.[10]

Moreover, for Heidegger (in *Being and Time*) and Lehmen, human understanding of the world consists of the "fore-having" of the possibil-ities that we perceive an object possesses even *before* we interpret it.[11] For Gadamer, the realization of these possibilities constitutes the object's "effective history" or *Bildung* (the accumulation of how it has evolved into being within a tradition). "[A]ll understanding", then, "is [...] already thrown into an interpreted world".[12] Lehmen's approach to sourcing material is grounded in this notion of "thrown projection" in so far as the dancer sets out to realize the possibilities that he or she projects onto the "ready-to-hand" objects found within the actual, remembered or fantasized worlds that he or she explores through improvisation. This might assume, however, that understanding is caught in an "hermeneutic circle" in which "the possibilities of action

[...] are projected onto [an] *already experienced* [and thus self-validating] interpretation".[13] However, Gadamer in particular claims that the hermeneutic circle is never a viscous circle because the *actual* answer we receive from our interactions in the world exceeds the answer we initially *projected* onto the world, and therefore, understanding is subject to continuous revision.[14]

Now my contention is that this fruitful gap between the meaning that we intend and the meaning we gain in practice reveals a truth about the nature of truth in art and that this truth is exemplified in Lehmen's work. In the first place, the gap between what we expect and what we receive is engineered by a dynamic *strife* or *rift* between disclosure and concealment that characterizes the nature of artistic truth. In this respect, Heidegger's meditation on Van Gogh's painting is salutary, for its antithesis between earth and world is, for Heidegger, paradigmatic of this tension necessary to all works of art. On the one hand, the artwork "sets up" or un-conceals a "world". For instance, in Foster's example a synecdochic representation of a river reveals the being or "river-ness" of the river by setting up a matrix of relations between its parts that would otherwise have no world. On the other hand, the artwork "sets forth" an "earth" by first "setting back" (concealing or reabsorbing) some factor or other in the making of the work. Most obviously, the disclosure of a particular synecdochic set of relations presupposes the concealment of other possible relations.

Concealment is also necessary for the *qualification* of the materials from which the artwork is made. According to Heidegger, the purposes to which, say, an axe is put entirely predetermine (and thus "use up") the qualities of the stone and wood from which the axe is made – but a sculptor "sets back" or withholds the same materials from those purposes precisely so that the "stoniness" of the stone and the "woodiness" of the wood can be set forth in a particular way. Likewise, the polyvalency and sonority of spoken language is obscured by the prosaic purposes of daily speech, but the very difficulty and strangeness of poetic language withdraws language from those purposes so that sound and meaning can be encountered anew. The same can be said of movement in dance. Indeed, Eugenio Barba identifies a reduction or "absorption principle" in the work of "performers from many different traditions".[15] Typically, he says, "the same energy which would be used to accomplish a much larger [...] action" is compressed – Heidegger would say concealed – within a foreshortened one.[16] As with the artwork in general, the dance work absorbs the ingredients of which it is composed back into itself precisely so that it can present itself in its own being and so that, in Gadamer's words, "the beholder can tarry with it".[17]

This enables us to understand concealment as a property of artistic truth. The reduction principle is precisely what I have compared in part to phenomenological reduction and have identified in the reduction of raw movement to its synecdochic essence in Lehmen's work. The energy of the whole original movement is not simply erased but retained and concealed within its synecdochic part. Thus, for Lehmen as for Heidegger, the truth of art consists not of some sort of correspondence between what the art work does or says and a fact that exists above and beyond the work. On the contrary, truth is something that happens *in and because of* the artwork *per se* – in dance, truth is the *event* that occurs when an original movement undergoes what Gadamer calls a "transformation of structure" to establish a *rift* between unconcealment and concealment in the action which that movement has become.

In this sense, truth is "what happens in being composed" and Heidegger suggest that the rift which "self-establishes" truth can be traced in the very "figure, shape, *Gestalt*" of the specific art work or what most typifies the patterning of the artist's work in general.[18] In Lehmen's case, I suggest that there is a characteristic rift between, on the one hand, the flow and sheer speed of movement *between* actions which discloses those actions as a unified sequence and, on the other hand, the retained power and clipped rhythm with which each action strives against the unity of that whole. To grasp the self-establishing truth of this rift in this way is to grasp physical action in dance as neither a mimetic representation nor as an aestheticist displacement of a reality beyond itself, but rather as a "total mediation" in which the reality of the originating context comes to its fullest self-presentation in the kinaesthetic-visual image but only because that kinaesthetic-visual image first detaches itself from its originating context by concealing it.[19]

Moreover, if the rift between the unconcealing "world" and the concealing "earth" is deliberately agitated by the artwork, then this rift also manifests itself in the paradox of the "repose" of an image with an "inner concentration" of motion which allows that image to "stand-in-itself".[20] This is certainly consistent with Barba's comment that the reduction principle encourages us to see the energy of the kinaesthetic-visual image as "something intimate, something which pulses in immobility [...], a retained power which flows in time without dispersing in space".[21] Furthermore, this is exemplified in a deceptively simple training exercise devised by Lehmen. Each dancer takes turns to stand looking at others, looking at her or himself. But what occurs, at best, is a state in which the body is neither a subject, who looks out nor an object who is looked at but rather a being beyond both "stand-ing-in-itself" in the repose of energized receptivity: a being open to the "there" in the "there-being" of *Dasein*. In Lehmen's work, this nominally "neutral" state of repose is not only used to punctuate action sequences but typifies the sensibility of his work as a whole. Here Lehmen's attitude towards dance theatre is perfectly consistent with Gadamer's theorization of play which, for Gadamer, is paradigmatic of art works in general: "[t]he primordial sense of play is the *medial* one", says Gadamer, by which he means that play is independent of and has primacy over the consciousness of the player.[22] But to understand how the medial sense of a dance work in particular comes into its own, I must turn briefly to the second stage of Lehmen's choreographic method – which, indeed, is certainly very playful![23]

## Stage 2: "Hermeneutic" Recontextualization

In this second stage, the gap between the meaning that we intend and the meaning we gain is made explicit. If the first stage is concerned with the sourcing of movement through the exploration of modes of temporalization, the second stage is concerned with the recontextualization of that movement through the exploration of modes of interpretation. The ensembles are carefully prepared for this second stage by a series of group 'games' or training exercises. In these games, performers take turns to play the 'functions' of Dancer, Manip-ulator, Interpreter, Questioner, Describer, Observer and Presenter. Whilst one member of the ensemble takes on the function of the Dancer by performing improvised or preconceived movement, the other functions are fulfilled, in different permutations, by the rest of the ensemble. The Manipulator either obstructs or redirects, and the Interpreter attempts to make personal sense, of the Dancer's movement; the Questioner asks either mundane or highly personal questions about the Dancer's motives; the Describer summarizes the actual movement as it is happening or movement that the Describer imagines in response; and the silent Observer subtly slips between passive witnessing to active scrutiny of either the Dancer or the Observer's own physical reactions to what the Dancer does. Finally, the Presenter contextualizes the whole scene for an imagined spectator by, for instance, directing that spectator's attention to different foci or by announcing, often with a microphone, what the scene is ostensibly 'about'. In the case of any of these functions, the response can take the form of movement or speech. By the time it came to organizing created movement material into *Clever*, many of these functions were *elided* in different ways by individual performers. So, within a single section of the final show there were instances in which individuals Observe, then Present then Question whoever, at any given point, was the main focus of attention, and whoever was in that position often presented or questioned her or himself.

A case in point is the section in which I was ostensibly the main focus. I stand just off from centre stage, facing the rest of the ensemble, who sit down stage centre with their backs to the auditorium. I begin with my 'cookery' material, but not before I have put it into a completely different context by proclaiming, somewhat hubristically, "Ladies and Gentlemen! I shall now perform for you a new dance work!" Ignoring another performer, who tells me I have started at the wrong point in the show, I shift in feigned rapture to my 'Bubble Bird' sequence. However, the clicking sounds that I originally produced for each burst bubble are made instead by the rest of the ensemble into a microphone. They then irreverently misconstrue these sounds as those of breaking bones. Soon those sounds are used to accompany a full-scale mock fight!

In this manner, Lehmen montages material not according to some abstract predetermined quasi-musical design, but according to the cross-currency of obstruction and facilitation, modification and replication, interest and indifference, ironic misconstruction and faithful explication, open acceptance and critical judgement, confident falsification and tentative revelation – in short, the gamut of the possibilities of concealing and un-concealing which constitute the dynamics of understanding. What, therefore, Lehmen's work is 'about' its own hermeneutic articulation, its own possibilities for understanding itself.[24]

Lehmen's work is thus, dependent upon what Gadamer calls a 'critique' – a dialectical and dialogic rule-bound social interaction, akin to a language game, which ensures that the 'horizon of understanding' that the dancer has, of the meaning of her or his material is neither confirmed nor obscured, but is rather 'fused' or synchronized with the different horizons of understanding that the rest of the ensemble project in the process of making sense of that dancer's material. As a result, the 'truth' of the dance is not univocal, intra-psychic and transcendent (as Husserl would have it), but is poly-vocal, inter-subjective and historically situated (as Gadamer insisted) and both disclosed and concealed by the pluralizing process of the event (as Heidegger claimed for the art work in general).

## Conclusion: Meaning as Movement Event

To the extent that Lehmen's ways of making dance are akin to Heidegger and Gadamer's ways of doing philosophy, I suggest that Lehmen's work in particular, exemplifies points that can be made about recent European dance theatre and physical performance in general. Chief amongst these is the point that, in *Clever* and similar works by Lehmen and others, movement is not made to fit meaning; contrarily, meaning is an *event experienced* through the manipulation of movement. Moreover, work of this kind that juxtaposes movement and text is of importance to our general understanding of the interfusion and diffusion of forms in that it is particularly reflexive about the bond between dancing and discourse, the phenomenology of the sensation of dancing and the hermeneutics of making sense of the dance. More importantly, Lehmen's work might suggest an interdependence between the two, for the stage of sourcing movement and investigating its kinaesthetic quality is dependent upon the self-understanding of that movement's meaning. And in so far as this highly reflexive hermeneutic process of manipulating movement constitutes the performance work itself, Lehmen's work suggests that the dance's object of research is its very method of inquiry, its discourse is the dance.

Finally, although my examples have been taken from a show consisting of performers from the same cultural group, Lehmen's methods not only explore the relation of the individual to the group, but even suggest a way of relating one cultural group to another in so far as they demonstrate Gadamer's belief that very different horizons of understanding need be neither conflated according to the interests of one group nor kept apart in the interests of both, but rather held together in tension within a single performance work in which the human body is the main means and focus of enquiry.[25]

## Notes

1. An earlier version of this essay was presented at *Ethnicity and Identity*, the IFTR Jaipur conference, on 7 January, 2003. My attendance at this conference was made possible through the financial assistance of the British Academy. I would also like to thank members of the Choreography and Corporeality IFTR Working Group for their responses to my paper at Jaipur.

2. My left arm meanders to forward left high where my index finger pops my first imaginary bubble; overlapping this, my right index finger traces the path of a second bubble, which I pierce at right forward high. Flow and focus turn inward as I sink low to abruptly rotate my right leg counter clockwise to crack a third bubble nestling in my groin and as I then thrust my right leg to place high to shatter a fourth bubble before whipping my whole body around in a complete clockwise circle. My left hand scoops up the moist residue of the third bubble but there I discover a bird that I usher to left forward high.

3. Thus, in the section of *Clever* that I analyze below, the three sequences that I have so far described ("Cooking", "Bubble Bird" and "Ballet Bar") follow on from each other in that order.

4. Foster, Susan Leigh (1986) *Reading Dancing: Bodies and Subjects in Contemporary American Dance*, University of California Press, Berkeley, p. 66.

5. See Sheets-Johnstone, Maxine (1999) *The Primacy of Movement*, Amsterdam and Philadelphia: John Benjamins, pp. 188-90; and Merleau-Ponty, Maurice (1968 [1964]) *The Visible And The Invisible*, ed. C. Lefort, (trans. A. Lingis, Evanston) Northwestern University Press, Illinios, p. 111.

6. Moran, Dermot (2000) *Introduction to Phenomenology*, Routledge, London and New York p. 258, 269.

7. Gadamer, Hans-Georg (1976) *Philosophical Hermeneutics*, trans. and ed. David E. Linge, University of California Press, Berkeley, p. 215.

8. Heidegger, Martin (1971) "The Origin of the Work of Art", *Poetry, Language, Thought*, trans. Albert Hofstadter, Perennial/HarperCollins, New York, p. 33.

9. Grondin, Jean (2002) "Gadamer's Basic Understanding of Understanding", in Robert J. Dostal (ed.) *The Cambridge Companion to Gadamer*, Cambridge University Press, Cambridge, pp. 37-8.

10. For instance, in Feldenkrais' exploration of "the dynamic link between standing and rising", the subject is instructed to "avoid conscious mobilization of the leg [... and] neck muscles" until he or she is left with the essential awareness of muscles in the hip joints directing a force through the spine to facilitate a smooth transition (Feldenkrais, Moshe [1977]

*Awareness Through Movement*, Harmondsworth: Penguin, p. 80). Likewise, there is a deceptively simple Body Mind Centering exercise in which the subject in a supine position draws her or his knees up into a constructive rest position. With each repetition of the exercise, the subject reduces mobilization of the quadriceps until he or she is left with nothing but the sensation of the widening and lengthening iliopsoas muscles. Similarly, the Klein Technique offers an exercise in which the subject, also in the constructive rest position, drops both knees in an arc towards the left or right. Again, through numerous repetitions any inessential effort is reduced until the subject is actively aware of the deep lateral rotators within her or his own hips. Most bodywork practices are in this way utopian in their drive towards the full awareness of a context-less functional efficiency, which, says Feldenkrais, "heralds the emergence of the truly human man" (*ibid.*: 48). In this respect, experiential anatomy is much closer than Lehmen's *tanztheater* to the transcendental project of Husserlian phenomenology.

11. See Heidegger, Martin *Being and Time*, trans. John Macquarrie and Edward Robinson,:Blackwell, Oxford 1962 [1926], sec. 32.

12. Moran, *Introduction to Phenomenology*, p. 269.

13. *Ibid.*

14. See Grondin, "Gadamer's Basic Understanding of Understanding", p. 46-50.

15. The "reduction principle" is the fourth of the five so-called transcultural laws of Theatre Anthropology. See Barba, Eugenio, the *Paper Canoe: A Guide to Theatre Anthropology*, trans. Richard Fowler, London and New York: Routledge, pp. 25-30, and Stewart, Nigel (2002) "Actor as *Refusenik*: Theatre Anthropology, Semiotics and the Paradoxical Work of the Body", in Ian Watson (ed.) *Negotiating Cultures: Eugenio Barba and the Intercultural Debate*, Manchester University Press, Manchester, 1995, pp. 47-9.

16. Barba, Eugenio and Nicola Savarese *A Dictionary of Theatre Anthropology: The Secret Art of the Performer*, ed. Richard Gough, trans. Richard Fowler, Routledge/Centre for Performance Research, London and New York, 1991, p. 15.

17. Gadamer, Hans-Georg, *Truth and Method*, 2nd ed., trans. W. Glen-Doepel, rev. trans. Joel Weinsheimer & Donald G. Marshall, Sheed & Ward, London, 1989 [1975] p. 222.

18. Heidegger, "The Origin of the Work of Art", pp. 70, 62.

19. See Gadamer, *Truth and Method*, p. xiv. So, if a dance is in anyway a representation of something it is because the dancer first "achiev[es] her or his own self-presentation" by dancing (*ibid.*: 108). The subject of a dance work is ultimately the dance work itself.

20. Heidegger, "The Origin of the Work of Art", p. 47. See also Gadamer, *Philosophical Hermeneutics*, p. 227.

21. Barba and Savarese, *A Dictionary of Theatre Anthropology*, p. 81.

22. Gadamer, *Truth and Method*, 103, 102, 104.

23. Remarkably, "the word "*Spiel*" originally meant "dance", and is still found in many word forms (*e.g.* in *Spielmann, jongleur*)" (Gadamer, *Truth and Method*, p. 103).

24. For Gadamer the concept of play is so compelling, because what he describes as the "to-and-fro movement" in the "play of light, the play of the waves, the play of gears or parts of machinery, the interplay of limbs, the play of forces, the play of gnats, even a play on words" is precisely, what is basic to the dialectic of question and answer through which any kind of understanding is produced (Gadamer, *Truth and Method*, p. 103). And in so far as Lehmen organizes movement according to the dynamics of understanding, the actual to-and-fro of movement in his dance works exemplifies the structures of the collective experience of interpretation and understanding that Gadamer sees in the paradigm of play.

25. Taylor, Charles "Gadamer on the Human Sciences", in Robert J. Dostal (ed.) *The Cambridge Companion to Gadamer*, Cambridge University Press, Cambridge, 2002, p. 126.

# 6

# I Saw It With My Own Eyes

## The Power of Messenger Reports and Teichoscopies on Stage

### Peter G.F. Eversmann

Films, novels and theatre plays tell stories. But in theatre and film this happens in a different narratological mode than in the novel. The action and the characters are shown rather than described. The spectator perceives the events and doesn't have to conjure them up in the mind's eye from a spoken or written text. It is this principle – known as ostension – that functions as one of the major characteristics in distinguishing theatrical performance from other art forms – especially literary ones – and it is also recognised as the leading principle that underlies the specific form and structure of the drama text. That text distinguishes itself from the literary story by the relative invisibility of a narrating instance and by mainly consisting of direct speech – and in this respect it is telling that descriptions or stage directions are designated as the *secondary* text.[1]

Just to give one, rather normative example of this narratological reasoning on how stories are told in the theatre I quote from a certain Hasselbach who already in 1890 wrote in his *Overzicht der Stijlleer* (Introduction to stylistics):

> Also the drama creates an image of life – just like the epic poem and the novel do – but here the events should not be narrated, they must be *shown*. [...] A drama – the word itself meaning *action* – should

therefore consist of a sequence of important events that quickly, without unnecessary delay, develop before the eyes of the audience. [...] It follows that the main requirements for drama are action and delineation of character. But stories and lyrical utterances are not completely banned from the drama; they can even clarify or embellish the [dramatic] poem, provided that the playwright takes care that they do not take up too much room and are fittingly embedded at just the right moment in time.[2]

Yet, the emphasis on showing action that speaks from this quote is somewhat biased and is not altogether confirmed by theatrical practice. There are specific moments when, on stage, stories are told instead of shown and when, moreover, one should not designate these stories as 'clarification' or 'embellishment', but rather deem them as rather important – if not crucial – in furthering the action and developing the plot. These are the moments when characters relate in words parts of the action that remain invisible for the audience and/or the other characters. One can think for example, of prologues that are worded by a character or memories that are told – but also of so-called messenger reports and teichoscopies. The messenger report deals with events from the more or less recent past, while the teichoscopy (from the Greek, literally meaning: a view from the wall) is referring to simultaneous actions: a character describes what is going on in the world of the play at the very same instance – but not visible to the spectator since it is happening in the wings, outside the frame.[3]

The specific ontological status of messenger reports and teichoscopies in the theatre – told and not shown – merits by itself a somewhat closer look at these phenomena. But there appears to be even more: in the already mentioned novel and in the film we do not find these kinds of stories. Also, with modern playwrights and in the theatre of today, there hardly seems to be a place for the story of the messenger. And if, sporadically, one encounters a kind of messenger situation where, for example, soldiers return from war and want to relate their story – then it is not so much the content of their tales but rather the incomprehensibility, the unwillingness to listen and the mechanisms of social rejection that are emphasized.

## A Classical Messenger Report: Euripides' Medea

But let us not run ahead of things and first take a look at a classical messenger report from *Medea* by Euripides. The entry of the messenger

in the production of this play by the La Mama Repertory Company
from New York, under the direction of Andrei Serban stands out in
my memory as an especially moving and truly theatrical moment. This
production was brought to the Netherlands by the Mickery theatre in
1972. It employed two languages – ancient Greek and Latin – and there
was no translation or subtitling so a modern day audience could not
understand a word. Nonetheless, the expressive acting style combined
with the audiences knowledge of the story resulted in an exciting
production that could be understood moment by moment. One of the
high points in the *mise-en-scene* was the moment that the shackled
Medea after she has sent away her children with some gifts to Kreousa –
her rival for Jason's love – is left alone on an otherwise dark stage. Then
a desperate cry from the palace is heard, coming ever closer and
growing louder to a deafening pitch, till a messenger hurls himself, half
stumbling, onto the stage a burning crown in his hand. At this sudden
horrified outburst a shock goes through the audience and the burning
diadem symbolizes the terrible story to the spectators who have just
studied the programme and hence are familiar with its meaning. The
ensuing monologue in a strange, incomprehensible language was really
unnecessary in order to understand what had happened. However, if
one could have understood the words, the report would have given a
very vivid description of the events that had just taken place inside the
palace. These are some lines from the story that the messenger has to
tell us and Medea, but now in intelligible English:

> *Enter* a MESSENGER.
> MESSENGER: *(...after having told how her children gave Medea
> presents and she has put them on...)*
> Then suddenly we saw a frightening thing. She changed
> Colour; she staggered sideways, shook in every limb.
> She was just able to collapse on to a chair,
> Or she would have fallen flat. Then one of her attendants,
> An old woman, thinking that perhaps the anger of Pan ·
> Or some other god had struck her, chanted the cry of worship.
> But then she saw, oozing from the girl's lips, white froth;
> The pupils of her eyes were twisted out of sight;
> The blood was drained from all her skin. The old woman knew
> Her mistake, and changed her chant to a despairing howl.
> One maid ran off quickly to fetch the King, another

To look for Jason and tell him what was happening
To his young bride; the whole palace was filled with a clatter
Of people running here and there. [...];
and she lay speechless, with eyes closed.
Then she came to, poor girl, and gave a frightful scream,
As two torments made war on her together: first
The golden coronet round her head discharged a stream
Of unnatural devouring fire: while the fine dress
Your children gave her – poor miserable girl! – the stuff
Was eating her clear flesh. She leapt up from her chair,
On fire, and ran, shaking her head and her long hair
This way and that, trying to shake off the coronet.
The ring of gold was fitted close and would not move;
The more she shook her head the fiercer the flame burned.
At last, exhausted by agony, she fell to the ground;
Save to her father, she was unrecognizable.
Her eyes, her face, were one grotesque disfigurement;
Down from her head dripped blood mingled with flame; her flesh,
Attacked by the invisible fangs of poison, melted
From the bare bone, like gum-drops from a pine-tree's bark –
A ghastly sight. Not one among us dared to touch
Her body. What we'd seen was lesson enough for us.
But suddenly her father came into the room.
He did not understand, poor man, what kind of death
Had struck his child. He threw himself down at her side,
And sobbed aloud, and kissed her, and took her in his arms,
And cried, 'Poor darling child, what god destroyed your life
So cruelly? Who robs me of my only child,
Old as I am, and near my grave? Oh, let me die
With you, my daughter!' Soon he ceased his tears and cries,
And tried to lift his aged body upright; and then,
As ivy sticks to laurel-branches, so he stuck
Fast to the dress. A ghastly wrestling then began;
He struggled to raise up his knee, she tugged him down.
If he used force, he tore the old flesh off his bones.
At length the King gave up his pitiful attempts;
Weakened with pain, he yielded, and gasped out his life.

Now, joined in death, daughter and father – such a sight
As tears were made for – they lie there. (...)
*Exit* MESSENGER.[4]

This messenger report of the beginning of Medea's revenge (later more horrible things will follow when she murders her children, but that is another matter) incorporates some characteristic elements that can serve to clarify functions and effects of the eyewitness accounts that messenger stories are.

First of all, it is a monologue. Messenger reports are relatively long chunks of text that, although they are directed at one or more persons and can be interrupted by a question or an exclamation, form a closed and self contained whole. Or, to adopt Mukaeovský's terminology[5], there are virtually no semantic changes of direction or reversals. The messenger doesn't jump from one subject to another and the actions are told chronologically. In other words: messenger reports are trying to convey the events in a more or less objective manner and are principally structured as "and then.... and then...and then...."

Secondly this coherent story is told by a specific kind of character – the messenger – who in some translations is also called a servant, a slave, an attendant or a soldier. This messenger is part of the cast and is a 'real' person within the internal communication system – participating in the action; but at the same time he or she is also an impersonal figure without development or the true characterization of a psychological background. Almost always the messenger speaks on stage only once: to convey that one message, to tell that one extended story. In short, the messenger has one very dominating function within both the internal and external communication system: the referential function of giving new information on an aspect of the action that is further not shown.

By the way, in my opinion these two characteristics account for the fact that such messenger reports are so popular in acting schools: on the one hand a self contained, monological story and on the other a relatively abstract and impersonal (or even: objective) dramatic figure. As practice material for beginning actors and actresses these classical messenger reports are hardly surpassed. Even more so because the content of the stories is usually very dramatic. We deal not with just average, run-of-the-mill stories, but with accounts of eyewitnesses that have seen terrible things. For example in Euripides' *Medea*: the plastic and vivid description of the effects of the poison can easily be compared to the effects of nerve gasses or napalm that we know from modern day warfare. And this is the case with messenger reports in general: atrocities that transcend ones imagination, suffering, horror, war, inhuman torture, rape, murder, fear and violence – these are the usual elements that make up a messenger report and it goes without saying that such material is more rewarding for an actor than having to describe a leisurely, uneventful stroll through the park.

## Functions of the Messenger Report

And with the content of the messenger report we also touch upon one of its functions: the fact that by using this device theatre makers can circumvent taboos. Instead of showing live rape or murder – and in doing so crossing the boundaries of decency – these things are now told. Where good taste forbids the explicit image, words can help out. Instead of appealing to the sensational and to feelings of cheap horror the audience is being confronted with the facts of the related story through their own *imagination*. We cannot avert our eyes or turn away in shock, thinking 'Oh well, its only theatre and make-believe, because there is nothing to turn away from: there is only an evocative story. And here one should also realise that the often-minute descriptions in these messenger reports can evoke before the mind's eye the details of the related horrors to even those theatregoers that are sitting in the last row of the auditorium.

And the latter points to maybe an even more important function of messenger reports: efficiency. Not only is it within the confines of certain aesthetics inappropriate to openly show terror and violence but also it is also hard to realise these things technically. It is just much simpler and much less costly to employ a narrator than to have twenty or more actors enacting a battle scene. A realistic depiction of say a shipwreck or the beheading of a stage character is quite a task for the theatre technician and the results of his efforts are often laughable, but the playwright has no difficulties whatsoever in describing such things in an imaginative way. Special effects like burning crowns on the head of an actress and flesh melting from bones are maybe not impossible to realise in the theatre, but technically and economically this costs the messenger less effort and the producer less money. In other words: the physical restraints of real space and time that are unequivocally linked to any theatrical situation with live actors, further sometimes the economic usage of stories on stage.

Connected to all this there is a third obvious function of the messenger report that derives straight from its definition: to sketch a part of the world of the play that is not visible to the spectators and, in doing so, to extend and constitute that world. The theatrical space is formed by the scenic, physically perceivable space plus a virtual, diegetic space that the spectator deduces to be there from signals in the production. In other words: a character that enters the stage is not coming from the wings and the dressing rooms, but from a part of the fictional world that just happens to be invisible. And that world doesn't have to be restricted to spaces that are in the immediate vicinity of the scene, but can extend – in the fiction – to an entire universe.

With regard to this we sometimes find a distinction being made between adjacent virtual space – directly contagious with the scene – and virtual space that lies further away. This means that – as Scolnicov has illustrated with regard to Greek tragedy – also messengers can come from nearby or far away. She draws a clarifying parallel with painting when she points out how playwrights consciously employ different locations within the virtual world in order to give relief to the fiction and the place of the scene within it:

> As in some perspective paintings the action that unfolds in the foreground is given depth by two differently distanced planes, which form its background. The best indication of these two planes in the play is provided by the two messengers, indifferently called in some translations 'messenger' and 'attendant'. But the Greeks called the one *angelos* the other *exangelos*, or the messenger who told news from a distance as opposed to the messenger who told what was doing in the house or behind the scenes.[6]

In other word, the story of the messenger and the space where he or she is coming from help to establish the scenic space within the geography of the virtual world. And, although we will not always find two different 'background planes' (more or less are also possible) Scolnicov's analysis shows nonetheless how stage figures coming from outside give substance to the world of the play and make it believable – especially when the convention of the 'unity of place' is adhered to.

## Teichoscopies

Extending the scene and giving it a place within the fictional world is also a clear feature of teichoscopies that, contrary to messenger reports, describe contemporary events in the adjacent virtual space that can be seen by the characters on stage, but not by the spectators. A good example of such a teichoscopy can be found at the end of Rosmersholm when the housekeeper looks out of the window and describes the suicide of Rosmer and Rebecca:

> [... The room is empty for a moment. Then MRS HELSETH opens the door on the right.]
>
> MRS HELSETH: Miss, the carriage is – *[Looks round her.]* Not here? Out together at this time? Well, now – I must say that's –! Hm! *[Goes out into the hall, looks round, and comes in again.]* Not on the garden seat. Well, well. *[Goes to the window and looks out.]* Good gracious! That white thing there –! Yes, upon my soul, they're both standing on the footbridge. God forgive the sinful creatures! If they're not putting their arms round each other! *[Screaming loudly.]* Ah! Over the bridge – both of them! Out into the millrace. Help! Help! *[Her knees giving way, she holds herself up, trembling, by the back of the chair and can scarcely get the words out.]* No. No help here. The dead mistress has taken them.[7]

The fact that the events offstage coincide with what happens on it makes that the teichoscopy is often somewhat different in character than the messenger report. This is most of all apparent in the status of the stage figure. With a teichoscopy this is more often a leading part that has an active role in the plot and who we see in not just one but several scenes. This means also that the description of the events is more often coloured by the perspective of the character that speaks the teichoscopy. Contrary to the messenger report the teichoscopy is not only a dry, more or less 'objective' account of the events; it rather shows the reaction of a figure and clarifies his or her character. We are not only told what is happening but are also given an insight into the psychology of the intermediating stage character.

An obvious and well-known example is the scene from Schiller's *Mary Stuart* where count Leicester stays behind on stage while his love Mary is taken to the scaffold at his command. The soliloquy that follows is also a true *vision-du-dedans* (a view into the inner life of a character that enables one to present his or her thoughts and feelings) in which Leicester expresses his despair and describes the execution of the Scottish queen that is taking place directly outside – invisible to the audience.[8]

By the way, it should be noted here that this is a somewhat special form of a teichoscopy since Leicester also does not see the execution while he describes it; he only hears what is going on. So, may be in this case, we should talk about a *teichosaudy* instead of a teichoscopy.

## Telling the Truth: The Effectiveness of Messenger Reports

Although teichoscopies are more subjectively coloured then messenger reports both phenomena have one thing in common that was not discussed yet: their *truthfulness*. Messenger stories and teichoscopies are always telling the truth: the events that are related are – within the boundaries of the fiction – real events. Only in very rare instances a messenger lies, but if this is the case the audience knows it and can appreciate or abhor the deceptive qualities. To my knowledge there is no case where it turns out later that a messenger has told a lie to both spectators and the other stage characters. Messengers and teichoscopists are always right. The stories may be told in very subjective and coloured ways, but the audience is not supposed to think for example that Leicester is just imagining things and that Mary Stuart does not die. And no one will doubt the death of Nestor and Kreousa since the messenger has been there himself and has seen with his own eyes the terrible workings of the poison.

This absolute truthfulness is part of the powerful quality of messenger reports and ensures their effectiveness. The spectator knows that the related events are true and that – especially in the case of messenger reports – they are told by eyewitnesses that are 'ordinary' people. In this regard, the messenger report works in two ways. First of all, the phantasy of the spectator is activated and stimulated because he or she has to imaginatively conjure up the events from what is told in words. Secondly, the story that is presented does not focus only on the events but also – and specifically – on the human reaction to those events. One could even say that the narrated action is more or less subordinated to its presentation – to the impact that witnessing the events has had on the narrator. It is the reaction of the messenger that gives the story depth and relief. And seen from this angle the subject of the messenger report lies not so much in the atrocities that are related, but rather in the impact of them on innocent bystanders who just happened to be present and who have to describe the horrific events as well as they can.

One can hypothesize that the ordinariness of the messenger coupled with the stimulation of the imagination enables a great measure of involvement from the spectator. As already discussed: not showing the events denies the audience the usual escape of *"oh,..it's only theatrical play and stage blood"*. And the fact that the story is told by eyewitnesses who might have been our neighbours leaves more room for emotions than the average news report and may further the spectator's empathy with the world of the play. Of course we are on speculative ground here, but it would be interesting to use reception research to investigate whether in some cases a suggestive account by a messenger could be more haunting than a meticulous enactment of the events themselves.

In any case, the ordinary human quality of the messenger is part of the challenge for the actor or actress who faces the task of enacting such a dramatically interesting character: terrible events that are emotionally moving must be communicated in the utmost clear, coherent and correct manner without having had any journalistic training. Besides, the messenger knows that he or she is the bearer of bad news that will spell disaster for the receivers. Thus, it is no surprise that messengers are often reluctant to give their account and fearful of the reactions of their listeners.

## The Absence of Messenger Reports in Novels and Films

After these preliminary remarks regarding characteristics and effects of messenger reports I would like to consider the two connected questions that were posed in the introduction. First: why do not messenger reports occur in the neighbouring disciplines of theatre – novels and films? And second, why do not we find them in contemporary drama?

A comprehensive answer to these questions – also taking into account some of the exceptions – requires in depth research and lies outside the scope of this exploration. So I will restrict myself here to some suggestions that might serve as a basis for further discussion.

Let us start at the easiest question: why are messenger reports virtually absent in the novel? The explanation is relatively simple and stems from the structural characteristics of this art form: since there already is a narrator who describes the action there is no need for a second one who – at a certain moment – has to take over in order to communicate a part of the events that the first narrator cannot or will not tell. Of course, in a novel there can be stories within a story or events can be told from different perspectives – but having a narrator who invokes a one-time messenger who then more or less takes over the narrative task does not seem a very natural way of telling stories. Such a setup is rather artificial and forced. Even more so because the recursiveness results in distancing the reader – the narrator tells how events are being told by a messenger – while the actions could also be described more directly.

It is harder to give an answer as regards film. After all, this is a multimedial art form that – at least superficially – has a lot in common with theatre. Still we hardly find any messenger reports or teichoscopies here; not even with film adaptations of theatre plays. There are several reasons for this, but in my opinion the main ones are the flexibility and the supposed 'objective' truthfulness of the camera.

In film the camera can move around the fictive world at will: it can go anywhere, shoot from any perspective, it can zoom in and out or jump to another place or time, etc. In short: the camera as narrating instance frees film makers from the fixed perspective that is character-istic for the spectator in a theatre and it can – just like a messenger – manipulate the attention of the audience, letting them concentrate on certain details and so on. In addition to this the mechanical workings of the camera give the impression that it is an objective eye that only registers 'reality'. Of course, in the final analysis we know this is not true, but we fall into the trap time and time again: with regard to the truth we prefer images over accounts from eyewitnesses. And it is precisely the emphasis on visuality that the audience seems to demand. Perhaps, it is the influence of television, but nowadays also with fiction movies the spectators apparently are not satisfied with suggestive shooting. Rather, they demand meticulous registration of the most horrifying and bloody details – if at all possible in close up and/or slow motion. And, why would filmmakers employ characters that have to be believed on their word when they can also show the events in (filmic) 'reality' and at the same time can appeal to the appetite for sensation?

In this respect the film industry can go very far indeed. Even to the point where, as was already mentioned, in adaptations of stage plays in which there is a messenger it is not at all unusual to cut this figure and replace it with pictures of the 'real' events. But, in doing this, one has to pay a price: the audience has to forego the human reaction of the messenger and the imagination is no longer stimulated. As a result suspense structure and emotional impact of a story can change drastically. For example, part of the effect of the drama *The Good Hope* by the Dutch playwright Herman Heijermans lies in the fact that for quite a long time both spectators and stage characters are uncertain about the fate of the fishing rig and her crew. At long last the irrevocable truth is revealed through a telephone call (that takes the place of the messenger here) in the following scene:

(The telephone rings. Clementine closes her book)

THE BOOKKEEPER: Mister Bos has gone out. The phone rang also a while ago.

CLEMENTINE *(listens)*: Yes? – Father is not in. – How long will he be, Kaps?

THE BOOKKEEPER: Maybe two or three minutes...

CLEMENTINE *(startled)*: What did you say? A hatch with the number 47 – and *(trembling)* – I can't hear you – *(screams, drops the horn)*

THE BOOKKEEPER: What is it? What is it?

CLEMENTINE *(shocked to tears)*: ...I dare not listen any more... O, O!

THE BOOKKEEPER: Is it the coast guard?

CLEMENTINE *(passionate)*: ...Barend is washed ashore. O God, now it's all over!

SAART: Barend?.... Barend?...

CLEMENTINE: 'A telegram from Nieuwediep –a hatch – and a body....

BOS *(enters)*: What is happening here? – Why are you crying?

THE BOOKKEEPER: A message from the *Hope*

BOS: A message?

THE BOOKKEEPER: The coast guard is on the phone

BOS: The coast guard? – Move over. –You, go away: what are you staring at!

SAART: I - I *(exits frightened)*

BOS *(on the phone)*: Hello! Who's speaking? – The coast guard? – A telegram from Nieuwediep – north of the Haaks – I can't understand

a word! Stop that crying! –a hatch you say? – Forty seven... – Yes
that's goddamn bad – that's – the body – already in a state of decay –
it's Barend, he signed up as the oldest one in the family... – Recognized by whom? – Whom? – O – The *Expectation* has docked in
Nieuwediep with some damage and skipper Maatsuiker has recognized him? – Earrings, yes, yes, silver earrings – that doesn't matter
any more. – So it's not necessary that we send someone from here to
identify the body? – Yes, it's a bloody disaster! – Our village has not
been blessed indeed. Yes – yes – Well – we have to bow to Gods will.
– Yes, yes – Personally I had no hope left. – Thank you. – Yes. – I
would like to have the official report as soon as possible. I'll notify
the assurance company. Goodbye! *(throws the horn back on the tiller)*
I'm just devastated – twelve men.[9]

In a movie version of the play from as early as 1935 the scene is a
lot shorter. Note how not only lines and characters have been cut, but
also that even the washed up hatch that is referred to in the telephone
call is visualized (cf. Figures 1-5):

(The telephone rings. Clementine enters and answers)
CLEMENTINE *(listens)*: Yes? – Father is not in. – How long will he
be, Kaps?
THE BOOKKEEPER: Maybe two or three minutes...
CLEMENTINE *(startled)*: What did you say? A hatch with the
number 47...
[cut to a shot depicting the hatch that is washed ashore. Then cut back
to]
CLEMENTINE: I can't hear you – what?...... *(clearly shocked)*...I dare
not listen any more... *(hands over the phone to the bookkeeper)*...Barend
is washed ashore.
[cut to villagers leaving their houses and assembling to hear the news.
Cut back to Clementine and the bookkeeper who now have been
joined by Bos]
BOS *(to the other two)*: Our village has not been blessed indeed. I'm
just devastated – twelve men.

It is possible for the film to shorten the scene because the
spectators already know that the *Good Hope* with all hands has perished
at sea. And they know this since they have seen themselves how the

ship went down some time before (cf. figures 6 and 7). Or, as the text on the videocassette proudly states: "Contrary to the play this film makes use of the specifics of the medium by adding the storm at sea to the story". But this adding of the storm results in a totally different kind of reception of the scene – since the audience now knows more than the characters and most of the reactions of ship owner Bos are left out.

## The Absence of Messenger Reports in Modern Drama

Finally I would like to make a few remarks on the question why in modern drama we hardly find any messenger reports? Of course, there are exceptions such as the moving account of the fall of Pnomh Penh in Helen Cixous *L'histoire terrible mais inachevée de Norodom Sihanouk, Roi du Cambodge,* that is remarkable also because it's a war story told by a female messenger – but on the whole the playwright of today foregoes the use of messengers or teichoscopies. One of the reasons for this we have just encountered when Herman Heijermans uses a telephone instead of a human messenger. From the end of the nineteenth century onwards-new means of communication such as telegraph, telephone, radio, television and computers take care of the contact between the scene on stage with the virtual world and make messengers superfluous.

But apart from this there might well be other factors that play a role here. One could, for example, point at various epic and performance-like tendencies in modern theatre that are geared towards the denial of illusionary 'as-if'-worlds. We no longer look through the proscenium arch at virtual make-beliefs. Theatre makers no longer want to create a full-fledged illusionary world; they are rather concerned with the physical aspects of the presentation, the psychology of the characters or the thematic aspects of the theatrical situation. And with the lack of such 'realistic' illusion there is less room for messengers or teichoscopies.

Of course, there are monologues in modern drama, but these are ego documents in which one stage figure tells us extensively about his or her life. In other words: these stories don't form a part of the action, but they are the action itself. Hence they are no messenger stories in the sense that they only address the audience and are not directed to other stage characters in the fictive world as well. Besides: these stories conform to postmodern thinking as they tell us a subjective truth and not the truth. In today's theatre – as in today's society – there seems to

**Figure 1**
*"How long will he be, Kaps?"*

**Figure 2**
*The hatch is washed ashore*

**Figure 3**
*"I dare not listen any more..."*

**Figure 4**
*Villagers leaving their homes*

**Figure 5**
*"I'm just devastated – twelve men."*

**Figure 6**
*Barend is drowning*

## Figure 7
*The Good Hope perishes*

be no place for the absolute trustworthiness of the messenger report. Eyewitnesses can no longer be believed on their word because we have become used to the fact that one should take into account several perspectives on any event. Reports have to be confirmed by at least one other source and the principle of speak and counter speak must be adhered to at all times. We demand tangible facts – if at all possible visual documentation on the spot – rather than personal experiences. The soldier who comes back from the war is no longer trusted and the asylum seeker has undoubtedly a hidden agenda and will depict the situation much worse than it really is. Reports for truth committees are not really attempts to find out what actually happened but are rather treated as a means for collective therapy and reconciliation. And that one's memory cannot be trusted because it is prone to suggestive manipulation is a platitude that goes without saying. Even important sports matches that are brought to you live, have to be commented upon by at least two television reporters in order to clarify multiple viewpoints. In brief: where truth itself has become fluid and where there are just subjective outlooks on that truth, there the efforts of a single messenger are doomed to fail – no matter how rhetorically or persuasively they are expressed.

## Conclusion

Perhaps this is not regrettable and there are enough productions of
classical plays so that messenger reports on stage can still be savored.
But it might be that there is also a dark side to the above model of truth
that reduces messengers to mere subjective reporters. The consequence
of this model is namely that not only the eyes of the other cannot be
trusted any more, but also that ones own perception becomes doubtful.
"I saw it with my own eyes" is no longer a valid source of knowledge
about the world.

What this can lead to is sketched by Samuel Beckett in one of the
few, but at the same time very appealing, examples of teichoscopy from
twentieth century dramatic literature – *Endgame*.

In a daring tour-de-force Beckett psychologizes in this play the
theatrical means of the teichoscopy in such a way that one not only gets
an insight in the mind of the character that describes what happens off
stage, but that one also realizes that the act of looking itself becomes the
main subject.

The space in which Beckett situates the play is a closed off interior
with two small windows high in the back wall. According to several
well-acknowledged interpretations, this space can be seen as a metaphor
for the human mind: it is as if the spectator sees the inner side of a skull
in which the two small windows represent the eyes.[10] In the play we see
the homunculus Hamm who is paralyzed in a wheelchair. For his information on the outside world he is dependent upon Clov who
sometimes climbs a ladder in order to look out of one of the windows.
The alienation of this situation and the mistrust that goes with it
provide us with a painful picture of Hamm's isolation. So, it is no
wonder that the outside world is apparently empty, void and desolated.
And it's also no wonder that at the end of the play Hamm remains
behind alone, devoid of any human contact.

In this way Beckett succeeds in adding a new dimension to the
teichoscopy whereby this means of telling a story is used as a tool of
reflection on the human condition and on the problem of perception.
And, of course, on the whole question of (theatrical) spectatorship as
well, because in the end even the audience is unsure whether Clov is
speaking the truth or playing a game.

But here we touch upon the problem of the trustworthiness of
stage figures and that is a problem that doesn't exist with the classical
messenger reports and teichoscopies. So with *Endgame* we come to the

end of this preliminary exploration into two specific modes of story-telling in the theatre. An exploration that, I hope, has shown that further research on messenger stories is certainly in order and that especially in the fields of comparative media studies and reception research interesting results can be expected.

## Notes

1. Cf. for example Pfister, M., *Das Drama. Theorie und Analy.* (Wilhelm Fink Verlag, München 1977), ch. 1 and 2.
2. Hasselbach, P.B., Overzicht der Stijllee. (Breda: P.B. Nieuwenhuijs, 1890), pp.45-46. (translation PE)
3. Cf. also Pfister, 1977, pp. 276-280.
4. Euripides, *Medea and other plays,* transl. Philip Vellacott, 1963 (Harmondsworth: Penguin Books, 1976), pp. 52-55.
5. Mukaeovský, J., *Kapitel aus der Poetik*, übers. W. Schamschula (Frankfurt: 1967). Cf. also Pfister 1977, pp. 180-184.
6. Scolnicov, H., 'Theatre Space, Theatrical Space and the Theatrical Space Without' in: J. Redmond (ed.) *The Theatrical Space.* (Themes in Drama – 9) (Cambridge: Cambridge University Press), pp. 11-26.
7. Ibsen, H., *The master builder and other plays,* transl. Una Ellis-Fermor, 1958 (Harmondsworth: Penguin Books, 1976).
8. For this example cf. also Pfister, 1977, pp. 278-280.
9. Heijermans, H., *Op hoop van zegen.* (Amsterdam: Querido, 1965), pp. 67-68 (transl. PE).
10. Cf. for example Esslin, M., *The Theatre of the Absurd* (Harmondsworth: Penguin Books, 1980), pp. 62-78.

# 7

# Ballet Frankfurt and the Re-branding of Frankfurt's Changing Identity

## Robyn Marie Campbell

From the perspective of the political, economic and cultural institutions of dance, this study engages in an investigation of globalization and image marketing, looking specifically at Ballet Frankfurt since William Forsythe's direction of the company in 1984, and the role of Ballet Frankfurt in the re-branding of Frankfurt's changing identity. This discussion is one section of a larger work looking into dance touring practices and the role of dance companies in the image marketing of nation states and the re-branding of cities.

Globalization is a complex and multidimensional process[1] with profound implications for the ways in which we make sense of our lives and the changing world we live in.[2] In his article, "Tradition and Translation: National Culture in Its Global Context", Kevin Robins asserts the geographical transformations that emerge out of the international restructuring of capitalist economies are central to contemporary cultural change.[3] Robins believes the re-organization of the international economic order has a strong effect on the nature and role of cities, and fosters new relationships between city administration and national and trans-national investments.[4] In the process of globalization, the nature and role of cities is changing.

The city of Frankfurt is an excellent example of these changes; particularly in the past two decades, Frankfurt city has experienced major changes in its economic and cultural identity, and in its politics of image marketing. Ballet Frankfurt, as one of the city's main cultural institutions, is implicated in the changes that proceed from the process of globalization. Ballet Frankfurt is currently a professional touring modern ballet company, employing 36 dancers, 2 ballet masters, 30 administrators and technicians under Artistic and Executive Director William Forsythe. It has a long and changing history; in the recent past, under the directorship of Forsythe, Ballet Frankfurt transformed from a classical repertory city-based ballet into an international modern ballet company renowned for its distinctive, radical style. Forsythe is a key figure in the identification of the ballet; many critics discuss William Forsythe and Ballet Frankfurt with an inseparability of description. Nadine Meisner, dance critic for *The Independent*, describe a Ballet Frankfurt performance by stating how William Forsythe "takes the dancing out of its traditional alignment, with twists and unbalances, unexpected timing or placing, and a casual way of walking or standing mixed in with the formality of balletic movement".[5] Performance reviews seldom fail to mention Forsythe, occasionally to the neglect of a critique of the actual performed event.[6]

In May 2002, William Forsythe was told by Frankfurt's Lord Mayor Petra Roth that the city of Frankfurt desired to move away from Ballet Frankfurt's radical ballet towards a more classically-styled ballet company. There has clearly been a great deal of speculation in the press and in the international dance community about this proposed change, evident in the volume of letters, columns and communications in international newspapers and journals that have conferred about the possible impetus of the change. Speculative discussions have contemplated the role of Ballet Frankfurt in regional, national and international contexts and questioned the ballet's touring practices, as well as considered Forsythe's personal relationship with the city. These discussions primarily concentrated on artistic or personal circumstances of the company and its members. This paper argues there is an alternative explanation to this proposed change: in its current form, Ballet Frankfurt no longer propagates the desired contemporary image of Frankfurt city that the city leaders wish to promote nationally and internationally. The city of Frankfurt seeks to re-define Ballet

Frankfurt and other cultural institutions to support its changing identity in the face of global economic competition.

A brief overview of Frankfurt city's changing identity in the social and political challenges of post-war Germany will contextualize this assertion. This overview has been drawn from the recent work of prominent German cultural theorists and historians; while there are many possible threads of historiographic interpretation of these events, the selected perspective has a strong basis of support from active researchers including Bianchini, Blacksell, Friedrichs & Dangschat, Glees, Jeffrey and Lewis & McKenzie.[7]

Friedrichs & Dungschat claim that after World War II, Germany lost its capital city of Berlin, and with the loss of its traditional political, cultural and academic centre, the western Federal Republic of Germany's (FRG) regional states gained in political power.[8] Regional capitals under these conditions grew in population and economic strength, and consolidated strong local identities.[9] Frankfurt city, the capital of Hessen, became renowned as a financial hub for banking.[10]

Prior to German unification in 1990, the FRG saw the political momentum towards economic and political integration in Western Europe as a means of re-establishing its credentials as an independent state in an international community.[11] Frankfurt, the FRG's financial centre, played an important role in fostering economic and political integration into the developing global economy and in strongly supporting capitalist ideals.[12]

After German unification, the ordeal of bringing together the FRG and the German Democratic Republic (GDR) posed huge problems for German national identity.[13] Unification raised critical challenges to the reconciling of politics and economics of two German frameworks; Germany found itself divided by a daunting ideological economic gulf between the east and the west.[14] As Jeffrey accounts, "forty-one years of separate development in ideologically opposed states have imbued easterners and westerners with differing sets of political and social values".[15] Jeffrey believes the rapidity of the unifi-cation process arguably led to the incorporation of the old GDR into the old FRG.[16] In transforming the eastern command economy and the western capitalist-market economy into a single competitive economy, the 'new Germany' established enterprise – economic, political and cultural – as one of the landmarks towards a united, strong and compet-itive Germany.[17]

With its focus on enterprise, its regional and national capitalist success, and its growing global economic influence, the city of Frankfurt contributes to the promotion of a new German image in domestic and foreign markets. Frankfurt's identity as a financial hub consolidated after unification. The home of the Deutsche Borse (the vanguard that runs the Frankfurt Stock Exchange) and the Neuer Markt (the revolutionary European exchange for high-growth, high-risk shares), Frankfurt became a centre of financial innovation that excels at combining market risks with market security[18]. *Business Week* published an article titled "Booming Frankfurt", attributing Frankfurt's financial success to its "innovation", "daring", "new dynamism", as well as its "entrepreneurial" spirit of "high-growth, high-risk capital".[19] Frankfurt is discussed in terms of its "revolutionary" measures in shareholder protection and "investor confidence".[20]

While Frankfurt developed as an influential economic hub prior to, and after unification, its negative cultural image has been a problem for its overall image. Bianchini says that until the 1980s, Frankfurt's cultural life was "under-developed and its overall image poor".[21] Friedrichs & Dangschat claim "Frankfurt for a long time had the image of an ungovernable, criminal city with always and everywhere something under construction".[22] With nicknames such as Krankfurt (from krank = sick), G'stankfurt (from stinken = to stink) or "Bank-furt", Frankfurt has been associated with some unfortunate images.[23] In the 1980s, Frankfurt set out to change its internal and external image through a vigorous round of cultural policies.

In 1977, the new Lord Mayor of Frankfurt and the Premier of the Province of Hessen, Walter Wallmann, a member of the Christian Democratic Party, broke away from traditional policies and adopted a different lifestyle than his Social Democrat predecessor, Rudi Arndt. To contrast the poor image of the city, he produced his idea of a 'new Frankfurt'. To enhance Frankfurt's cultural status, the Lord Mayor, Walter Wallmann, and Hilmar Hoffmann, the City Council's Chief Cultural Policy Officer, increased Frankfurt's municipal expenditure on cultural policy from 6% in 1970 to 11% in 1990.[24] Friedrichs & Dangschat assert the massive investment in cultural facilities, including the reconstruction of the Old Opera House and the creation of 11 museums in a new Museum-district, was intended to act as an important catalyst in revitalizing the city's social life.[25] Through its significant cultural investment, Frankfurt began to alter its negative city image to emerge as "a trend-setter of new urban lifestyles".[26]

Contributing simultaneously to Frankfurt's urban image as a culturally competitive city, Ballet Frankfurt advantageously promotes the city of Frankfurt as a unique local place of work and a distinctive global place of performance. As a traditional classical ballet whose practices encompass innovation, risk and flexibility, Ballet Frankfurt arguably reinforces Frankfurt city's desired trendsetter status. Ballet Frankfurt is widely viewed as a revolutionary ballet company, whose innovation challenges the traditions of ballet. The company is credited with bringing new dynamism to ballet through its unconventional risk-taking, while providing audiences with the security and confidence in its guarantee of quality performances and its forward-thinking artistic vision. Alongside other cultural institutions, Ballet Frankfurt is a symbol of the city's newly acquired elegance, sophistication and cosmopolitanism. Frankfurt is anxious to consolidate its competitive advantages by filling the gap between its high economic status and its relatively low cultural standing.[27] Through its residence at the Opera House, Ballet Frankfurt is directly associated with the cultural facilities quoted as being the foremost catalyst in the revitalization of the city's social life.

With a focus on urban renewal and cultural regeneration, the city of Frankfurt, through its patronage of a 'tight-loose' ballet company, re-brands regional and national identities. Not unlike global corporations, the city of Frankfurt seeks to position itself in a tight-loose network:

> tight enough to ensure predictability and stability in dealings with external collaborators; loose enough to ensure manoeuvrability and even reversibility, to permit the redirection of activities and the redrawing of organisational boundaries when that becomes necessary.[28]

Ballet Frankfurt is traditional enough to ensure its predictable classical ballet status, while modern enough to ensure manoeuvrability, flexibility and freedom. Frankfurt and Germany desire an identity reputed for its 'tight' predictability, with appeals to historical imagination (tradition, shared values and cultural belonging), and a 'loose' manoeuvrability, with appeals to cultural imagination (vision, talent, and innovation).

Haider (1992) discusses the value of image marketing in the rebranding of identity:

> image marketing [becomes] perhaps the most frequently employed marketing approach to place development used by states, cities, and various places. Image marketing can be used to reinforce existing positive images, neutralise and change unfavourable ones, or create new images where [few] or no images exist.[29]

Imminent developments in the re-identification of Ballet Frankfurt and current re-branding of the city of Frankfurt raises new questions about the changing face of globalization. Frankfurt's current Lord Mayor Petra Roth appeals for a changed image for the city, and a different face for its ballet – both pointing towards a more conservative, traditional approach.

One timely reason for this change likely pertains to the recent changes and challenges to the German economy. The adoption of a new currency, the Euro, and the establishment of the European Central Bank, has affected all participant European countries, but none more than Germany. In November 2002 the Organization for Economic Cooperation (OECD) claimed that the German economy was struggling to pull out of the most severe downturn in decades, with shell-shocked markets and rock-bottom business confidence. In an effort to prevent Germany from sinking into a full-scale recession, the European Central Bank (ECB) cut interest rates in December 2002 for the first time in more than a year. This decision by the ECB is intended to provide a counterweight to some of the existing risks to economic growth, thereby supporting confidence, according to Wim Duisenberg, the president of the ECB.

When global German identity is primarily founded on an image of financial and economic stability, clearly economic uncertainty is highly culturally and politically destabilizing. In times of economic insecurity, strengthened interests in stability and conservatism aim for rapid economic recovery. Enterprise culture and economic diplomacy form a basis for the re-branding of the German nation-state, and permeate Ballet Frankfurt's dance cultural practices.

# Notes

1. Authors' Note: Robins says the globalisation of economic activity has profound implications for identities and ways of life, and is associated with a wave of cultural transformation. This paper presents one way of looking at how urban renewal and cultural regeneration have a distinct affect on dance policies and institutions. Dance practices are firmly located within practices of urban renewal and contribute to the re-branding of regional and national image. The proposed changes to Ballet Frankfurt support the city of Frankfurt and the German nation in reinventing a sense of place, in which positive images are reinforced and unfavourable images are altered.

2. K. Robins, 'What in the world's going on?', in K. Robins, ed., in *Production of Culture/Cultures of Production* (London: Sage, 1997), p. 33.

3. K. Robins, 'Tradition and translation: national culture in its global context', in J. Corner and S. Harvey, eds., *Enterprise and Heritage: Crosscurrents of National Culture* (London: Routledge,1991), pp. 23-4.

4. K. Robins, 'Tradition and translation: national culture in its global context', in J. Corner and S. Harvey, eds., *Enterprise and Heritage: Crosscurrents of National Culture* (London: Routledge,1991), p. 24.

5. N. Meisner, 'Forsythe's chilling apocalypse', *(The Independent,* 13 November 1998), p. 10.

6. See, N. Meisner, 'Forsythe's chilling apocalypse' *(The Independent*, 13 November 1998), p. 10.

7. See, F. Bianchini, 'Remaking European cities: the role of cultural policies', in F. Bianchini & M. Parkinson, eds., *Cultural Policy and Urban Regeneration: The West European Experience* (Manchester: Manchester University Press, 1993), pp. 1-20; M. Blacksell, 'Germany as a European power', in D. Lewis & J. McKenzie, eds., *The New Germany: social, political and cultural challenges of unification* (Exeter: University of Exeter Press,1995), pp. 77-100; J. Friedrichs and J. Dangschat, 'Hamburg: culture and urban competition', in F. Bianchini and M. Parkinson, eds., *Cultural policy and urban regeneration: the West European experience* (Manchester: Manchester University Press, 1993), pp. 114-134; A. Glees, *Reinventing Germany* (Oxford: Berg, 1996); C. Jeffrey, 'The changing framework of German politics since unification', in D. Lewis and J. McKenzie, eds., *The New Germany: Social, Political and Cultural Challenges of Unification* (Exeter: University of Exeter Press, 1995), pp. 101-126; D. Lewis and J. McKenzie, eds., *The New Germany: Social, Political and Cultural Challenges of Unification* (Exeter: University of Exeter Press, 1995).

8. J. Friedrichs and J. Dangschat, 'Hamburg: culture and urban competition', in F. Bianchini and M. Parkinson, eds., *Cultural policy and urban regeneration: the West European experience* (Manchester: Manchester University Press, 1993), p. 114.

9.  J. Friedrichs and J. Dangschat, 'Hamburg: culture and urban competition', in F. Bianchini and M. Parkinson, eds., *Cultural policy and urban regeneration: the West European experience* (Manchester: Manchester University Press, 1993), p. 114.

10. J. Friedrichs and J. Dangschat, 'Hamburg: culture and urban competition', in F. Bianchini and M. Parkinson, eds., *Cultural policy and urban regeneration: the West European experience* (Manchester: Manchester University Press, 1993), p. 114; see also Ewing, J. 'Booming Frankfurt'. *BusinessWeek online* (6 September 1999) (http://www.businessweek.com/1999/99_36/b3645013.htm retrieved 20 December 2001).

11. See, D. Lewis and J. McKenzie, eds., *The New Germany: Social, Political and Cultural Challenges of Unification* (Exeter: University of Exeter Press, 1995).

12. See, J. Friedrichs and J. Dangschat, 'Hamburg: culture and urban competition', in F. Bianchini and M. Parkinson, eds., *Cultural policy and urban regeneration: the West European experience* (Manchester: Manchester University Press, 1993), pp. 114-132; D. Lewis and J. McKenzie, eds., *The New Germany: Social, Political and Cultural Challenges of Unification* (Exeter: University of Exeter Press, 1995).

13. See, F. Bianchini, 'Remaking European cities: the role of cultural policies', in F. Bianchini & M. Parkinson, eds., *Cultural Policy and Urban Regeneration: The West European Experience* (Manchester: Manchester University Press, 1993), pp. 1-20; J. Friedrichs and J. Dangschat, 'Hamburg: culture and urban competition', in F. Bianchini and M. Parkinson, eds., *Cultural policy and urban regeneration: the West European experience* (Manchester: Manchester University Press, 1993), pp. 114-134; A. Glees, *Reinventing Germany* (Oxford: Berg, 1996); C. Jeffrey, 'The changing framework of German politics since unification', in D. Lewis and J. McKenzie, eds., *The New Germany: Social, Political and Cultural Challenges of Unification* (Exeter: University of Exeter Press, 1995), pp. 101-126; D. Lewis and J. McKenzie, eds., *The New Germany: Social, Political and Cultural Challenges of Unification* (Exeter: University of Exeter Press, 1995).

14. M. Blacksell, 'Germany as a European power', in D. Lewis & J. McKenzie, eds., *The New Germany: social, political and cultural challenges of unification* (Exeter: University of Exeter Press,1995), pp. 81-82.

15. C. Jeffrey, 'The changing framework of German politics since unification', in D. Lewis and J. McKenzie, eds., *The New Germany: Social, Political and Cultural Challenges of Unification* (Exeter: University of Exeter Press, 1995), p. 103.

16. See, C. Jeffrey, 'The changing framework of German politics since unification', in D. Lewis and J. McKenzie, eds., *The New Germany: Social, Political*

*and Cultural Challenges of Unification* (Exeter: University of Exeter Press, 1995), pp. 101-126.

17. See, A. Glees, *Reinventing Germany* (Oxford: Berg, 1996); C. Jeffrey, 'The changing framework of German politics since unification', in D. Lewis and J. McKenzie, eds., *The New Germany: Social, Political and Cultural Challenges of Unification* (Exeter: University of Exeter Press, 1995), pp. 101-126; D. Lewis and J. McKenzie, eds., *The New Germany: Social, Political and Cultural Challenges of Unification* (Exeter: University of Exeter Press, 1995).

18. See, Ewing, J. 'Booming Frankfurt'. *BusinessWeek online* (6 September 1999) (http://www.businessweek.com/1999/99_36/b3645013.htm retrieved 20 December 2001).

19. See, Ewing, J. 'Booming Frankfurt'. *BusinessWeek online* (6 September 1999) (http://www.businessweek.com/1999/99_36/b3645013.htm retrieved 20 December 2001).

20. See, Ewing, J. 'Booming Frankfurt'. *BusinessWeek online* (6 September 1999) (http://www.businessweek.com/1999/99_36/b3645013.htm retrieved 20 December 2001).

21. F. Bianchini, 'Remaking European cities: the role of cultural policies', in F. Bianchini & M. Parkinson, eds., *Cultural Policy and Urban Regeneration: The West European Experience* (Manchester: Manchester University Press, 1993), p. 16.

22. J. Friedrichs and J. Dangschat, 'Hamburg: culture and urban competition', in F. Bianchini and M. Parkinson, eds., *Cultural policy and urban regeneration: the West European experience* (Manchester: Manchester University Press, 1993), pp. 121-22.

23. F. Bianchini, 'Remaking European cities: the role of cultural policies', in F. Bianchini & M. Parkinson, eds., *Cultural Policy and Urban Regeneration: The West European Experience* (Manchester: Manchester University Press, 1993), p. 16; J. Friedrichs and J. Dangschat, 'Hamburg: culture and urban competition', in F. Bianchini and M. Parkinson, eds., *Cultural policy and urban regeneration: the West European experience* (Manchester: Manchester University Press, 1993), p. 114.

24. F. Bianchini, 'Remaking European cities: the role of cultural policies', in F. Bianchini & M. Parkinson, eds., *Cultural Policy and Urban Regeneration: The West European Experience* (Manchester: Manchester University Press, 1993), p. 16.

25. J. Friedrichs and J. Dangschat, 'Hamburg: culture and urban competition', in F. Bianchini and M. Parkinson, eds., *Cultural policy and urban regeneration: the West European experience* (Manchester: Manchester University Press, 1993), pp. 122-23.

26. J. Friedrichs and J. Dangschat, 'Hamburg: culture and urban competition', in F. Bianchini and M. Parkinson, eds., *Cultural policy and urban regeneration: the West European experience* (Manchester: Manchester University Press, 1993), p. 123.

27. F. Bianchini, 'Remaking European cities: the role of cultural policies', in F. Bianchini & M. Parkinson, eds., *Cultural Policy and Urban Regeneration: The West European Experience* (Manchester: Manchester University Press, 1993), p. 16.

28. K. Robins, 'Tradition and translation: national culture in its global context', in J. Corner and S. Harvey (Eds.) *Enterprise and Heritage: Crosscurrents of National Culture* (London: Routledge, 1991), p. 28.

29. D. Haider, 'Place wars: new realities of the 1990s', *Economic development quarterly* (1992), 6(2), p. 131.

# Part II

---

Political Polarities and Identity Formation

---

# 8

# Reclaiming Cultural Identity

## The Upsurge of 'Coloured' Theatre in South Africa Since 1990

### Bett Pacey

The Apartheid policy influenced cultural perceptions and expressions in South African theatre. White and Black theatre had a definite focus, but 'Coloured' theatre found itself fragmented. Although the majority of coloured people speak the Afrikaans language, they were politically alienated (and physically barred) from state-subsidized Afrikaans theatre. Denied the acceptance of a common language and racially oppressed, 'Coloured' theatre allied itself with Black political, protest/ and anti-Apartheid theatre. Even then, the unique coloured culture took a backseat to the common call for Black consciousness. The dismantling of the Apartheid system lead to 'Coloured' theatre finding an own cultural voice. The process started early in the 1990s, gained momentum, and resulted in an explosion of what is now often referred to as 'Cape Indigenous Theatre'.

By way of introduction, I wish to remark briefly on the term 'Coloured'. In deference to the sensitivity still surrounding the term (the issue of which falls outside the scope of this paper) I have placed it in single quotation marks when referring to theatre. The term was already used in South Africa in the 1880s, with reference to all people who were 'not White'. From the early 20th century the term was assigned to people who descended from slaves who came from, *inter alia*, Indonesia, Malaysia, Madagascar and Ceylon (Sri Lanka), the indigenous Khoi and San people, as well as descendants from interracial relationships, in other words, of so-called mixed race. Under the Apartheid system severe restrictions, as well as identities, were imposed by the state on the people of the country on the basis of race and skin colour. The Population Registration act of 1950 defined Coloureds as "people who are neither White nor Native". It was in particular this classification as 'not being white enough to be White, nor black enough to be Black', which compounded identity problems.

Zimitri Erasmus stated at a conference on coloured identity held in Cape Town in 1998:

> The coloured identity has never been seen as an identity 'in it's own right'. It has been negatively defined in terms of 'lack' or taint, or in terms of a 'remainder' or excess, which does not fit a classificatory scheme.[1]

This negative and distorted perception of identity was also apparent in the theatre. Because of the Apartheid policy and accompanying legislation, there was a distinct difference between Black and White theatres. The focus of White theatre was Euro-centric, and so-called indigenous South African drama (which was considered to be English and Afrikaans language plays about South Africans, written by white dramatists) was fostered and promoted by state-subsidized theatre structures, performed by white actors to white audiences in purposely-built theatres. This included plays written in Kaaps[2] about coloured people, by white playwrights.

Black theatre received no support from the government and had to be content with rudimentary venues and equipment. It focussed in the main, but especially from the 1960s through to the 1980s, focussed on politics and protest. 'Coloured' theatre found itself hovering ambivalently between the two. It generally followed the pattern of White theatre, especially Afrikaans language theatre. This is not surprising as the majority of coloured people has Afrikaans as home language. However these Euro-centric plays or Afrikaans plays were performed under the same shoddy conditions afforded Black theatre and in addition, according to Vernon February:

> These plays were far removed from the cultural, linguistic and socio-political realities of the 'coloured' townships"[3].

In 1958 Lewis Sowden's play *The Kimberley Train* was hailed by drama critics as 'the first indigenous' theatre. The play dealt with life determined by, and love across the colour bar, a theme which would recur in 'Coloured' theatre. In 1965 Adam Small's so-called coloured play, *Kanna Hy Kô Hystoe*,[4] was first performed by coloured actors to coloured audiences in community halls, but when hailed by critics as a great Afrikaans play, it was afforded a performance in a state-subsidized theatre in 1972. Ironically the performance was by white actors to white audiences and Small could only attend by special permit.

Denied the acceptance of a common language and physically barred from White and in particular Afrikaans theatre, coloured people aligned themselves with Black theatre, particularly after the Soweto uprising in 1976, with Adam Small himself preferring to be called a Black playwright. While subscribing to Black consciousness as self-awareness, self-esteem and the rejection of white stereotypes, the coloured identity took a back seat in the common call for freedom from oppression and was in fact often overshadowed by African consciousness.

'Coloured' theatre during the 1970s and 1980s dealt mostly with issues of race classification and other anti-Apartheid issues and the tone was angry and bitter, for example The Colour of my Skin by Paul Jacobs, In Glass Houses by Robert Pearce and Senzenina – what have we done? By the Cape Flats Players. There were also more poignant expressions such as the musical collaborations by Taliep Pietersen and David Kramer, District Six and Fairyland.

With the crumbling of Apartheid in the late 1980s, the lifting of oppressive legislation in the early 1990s and a government of Black majority rule in 1994, the face of South African theatre also changed. Initially there was a celebration of the 'rainbow nation' in interracial, cross-cultural theatre free from restriction, and while this is still the case, gradually there was also a shift to ethnic identity, with Black theatre re-introducing traditional African forms of theatre and exploring the cultures of different ethnic groups on stage and White theatre grappling with the legacy of Apartheid guilt.

The most notable change occurred in 'Coloured' theatre. While many coloured people still had problems with the term 'coloured' and argued that a common 'coloured identity did not exist (a debate which is ongoing) playwrights, actors and artists explored and celebrated aspects of coloured identity on stage. While the legacy of Apartheid on the coloured people continued to be a theme, the trend in the 1990s was more towards social plays dealing specifically with issues relevant to the coloured communities.

The issue of gangsterism was dealt with by Robert Pearce in his play *Die Highbucks bende*,[5] by Joseph Mitchell in two plays, *Is Maa Net Nogga Laaitie*[6] and *Die Gangsters* – the latter examines the issue against revelations made before the Truth and Reconciliation committee, and by Coco Merckel in *No Room for Squares*, set in the drug-infested gang-lands of Westbury and Newclare townships in Johannesburg.

The Cape Flats Players, who in earlier years almost exclusively presented protest and political theatre, moved towards plays, which dealt with a variety of social issues. *Love, Lust or Guilt*, dealt with child and alcohol abuse, *Die Goodbye People*, with people living in mental institutions and *Die Invisibles* explored the lives of people rejected from society or ignored, such as vagrants, street cleaners, AIDS sufferers and prisoners.

In 1999 the play *Suip*[7] by Oscar Petersen and Heinrich Reisenhofer premiered at the Standard Bank National Arts Festival in Grahamstown. This hard-hitting play with strong language tells the story of four Bergies[8] in the new South Africa and how they cope with the changes. They also present their version of the country's history, using alcohol as a metaphor. Subsequent performances all over South Africa drew capacity houses and the play was also performed in London, Sydney and Melbourne. Notable is that the play was published in 2000 – the first 'coloured' play available in book stores since *Kanna Hy Kô Hystoe* was published in the late 1960s.

The issue of coloured identity in post-Apartheid South Africa is dealt with in several plays. In *Daai's Nou Politiek*[9] by Peter Snyders, two characters from his 1978 play, *Political Joke*, meet up again. This time Ralph feels that "dit is nou nie meer kousjer vir 'n Kleurling om swart te wees nie"[10]. Ivan Lucas, in his one-man play *Die Strondloper*[11], deals with his concerns about his plays in the new South Africa. Lueen Conning's one-woman play, *A Coloured Place*, explores the lives of six women from different coloured backgrounds coming to terms with the new social structures. Conning has since changed her name to Malika Lueen Ndlovu to reflect her Zulu heritage.

The Khoi and San heritage has for a long time been avoided. While the reasons fall outside the scope of this paper, it can be mentioned that the old term for Khoi, namely Hottentot, was used by both Blacks and

Whites as a derogatory reference to coloured people and by coloured people themselves to denote Coloureds of a lower social standing. In 2000, Heinrich Reisenhofer used Khoi and San stories of shamans who, in a trance, could turn themselves into birds as a basis for his play *Birdbrain*. This comic fantasy deals with a boy's quest to fly in a country struggling with its ideas of freedom. *Klarabelle Gaan Kaap Toe*[12] by Zenobia Kloppers (2002) deals with a woman who, because of memory loss, embarks on a journey of self-discovery. Her memories bring out stories and characters dealing with issues of roots and rootlessness, as well as pride in her Khoi heritage.

From very early on in the twentieth century Coloured characters were introduced in White theatre as comic relief. From the 1990s Coloured writers took charge of their own unique brand of humour. Actor Soli Philander has created a number of successful stand-up comedy shows in which he not only comments on general South African issues, but also in particular on Coloured issues and idiosyncrasies. Rosie September, his female character who is a housewife from coloured suburbia, has become a s well-known as the Evita Bezuidenhout character created by Pieter-Dirk Uys. Marc Lottering has portrayed a wide range of characters in his two shows *From The Cape Flats With Love* and *Big Stakes and Slap Chips*.[13] Lottering tackles contemporary issues, both local and global, and his shows have drawn large crowds from across the social spectrum, not only in South Africa, but also in Canada, New Zealand, Australia and the United Kingdom. The Ivan Lucas/Oscar Petersen two-hander, *Meet Joe Barber*, started in a café club in the Cape in 1999 and has since been continually performed throughout South Africa. Set in a barbershop on the Cape Flats, the two characters take on various personae, commenting on daily life on the Cape Flats. Audience members are drawn on stage and involved in the stories. Reflecting on identity a promotional line for the show reads:

*Dis onse mense en hulle praat onse taal.*[14]

While the debate on coloured cultural identity continues at conferences, discussion groups and in the media, theatre practitioners use the stage for exploration and affirmation. The process is best summed up in the words of actor/director/ playwright, Oscar Petersen:

It all turns on this: Who the fuck are we really? So there's reclamation going on, taking ownership of who we are.[15]

## Notes

1. Zimitri Erasmus ed., *Coloured by History, Shaped by Place: New Perspectives on Coloured Identities in Cape Town* (Cape Town: Kwela Books), p. 17.

2. A variant of Afrikaans also often called Cape Coloured Afrikaans.

3. V.A. February, *Mind Your Colour: The 'Coloured' Stereotype in South African Literature* (London & Boston: Kegan Paul International Ltd.), p. 111.

4. Roughly translated: Kanna comes home.

5. Translated: The Highbucks gang.

6. Roughly translated: It is only (yet another) little boy.

7. Afrikaans word which means to drink excessively.

8. Term used to describe homeless people in Cape Town who generally, but not always, live in the area of Table Mountain – 'berg' being the Afrikaans word for mountain.

9. Roughly translated: Now that is politics.

10. Translated: It is not kosher anymore for a Coloured to be black.

11. A 'strandloper' is a small bird found on Cape beaches. It was also a term used by early Dutch colonists for Khoi people. By changing the 'a' to an 'o' there is also wordplay on the Afrikaans 'stront', meaning shit.

12. Translated: Klarabelle goes to the Cape.

13. 'Slap chips' is a popular snack of thick-cut fried potato slices, which are not done to a crisp.

14. Translated: It is our people and they speak our language.

15. Oscar Petersen interviewed by Guy Willoughby. 'Theatre Gets Genuine', *Mail & Guardian*, 23 March 2001.

# 9

# Faking Truth

## The 'Problem' of 'Theatricality'[1]

### Glen McGillivray

It is a phenomenon of discourse that certain terms enter the critical lexicon of particular communities of interpreters and are immediately taken up because their usefulness in forming discourse is readily apparent. An example of such a term is "performativity" which originated in the relatively esoteric realm of speech-act theory in the 1950s but now is both indispensable to and commonly used in most discussions of human performance. "Theatricality" has proven to be similarly useful and is becoming equally ubiquitous. Whereas a fundamental theory of "performativity" was established by J.L. Austin and considerably elaborated on by Judith Butler and others – and this theoretical work has informed subsequent uses of the term – in contrast "theatricality" has lacked such solid theorization. Instead the term has been invoked as a kind of transcendental "catch all", an "empty" signifier, that is used as an interpretive tool in a wide range of discourses from the semiotic to the psychoanalytic, and from sociology to cognitive science. In addition, the concept of "theatricality" is complicated by the long history of the theatrical metaphor, *theatrum mundi*, whose ontological claims have strongly influenced later critical uses of "theatricality". Indeed, to speak of "theatricality" is to speak of a cluster of interpretations which are signified by terms such as "theatrical" or "dramatic" metaphor, "role", "social drama", "theatricalism", "meta-theatrical/dramatic", "theatre". "Theatricality", thus, is useful as

an interpretive umbrella for all these applications and it is under-
standable why it has been used as a, relatively unexamined,
transcendental "catch all". The key word, however, is *interpretation:*
"theatricality" is neither an essence nor a process, but is a way of interpreting particular phenomena in the world and as such it is, of course,
socio-historically specific. My argument, therefore, will first lay-out
what is meant by "theatricality" in its most common-sense and
everyday interpretation and explore the implications of this interpretation in quotidian uses of the concept – particularly how it operates by
analogy. Furthermore, I will argue that underpinning such use is an
implied or tacit understanding of what "theatre" is that is, in turn,
predicated on a Platonic moral ontology of "reality" ("good") and
"unreality" ("bad"). Finally, I will review a theory of interpretation and
cite a case study, which illustrates how "theatricality"-as-interpretation
operates.

## "Theatricality" as a Spectatorial Process

So, what is meant by the term "theatricality?" Common-sense
meanings link it to the activity of "theatre" as an art form, which
includes not only theatrical practice but also the theatre building, and
theatre as an institution. Simply put, "theatricality" refers to an idea of
"theatre" and, without analyzing it any further, this sense of the term
remains relatively unproblematic. However, in another sense of the
term, its quotidian use, "theatricality" operates as a descriptor of
behaviour, people, events and objects in the world – descriptions,
which are inflected by the idea of "theatre" as an art form but are not of
the art form *per se*. In its most simplistic, common, taken-for-granted
meaning, "theatricality" tacitly implies particular relationships of truth
and artifice, of seriousness and play, and also conjures up, from the art
form "theatre", the formalist organization of space, spectator and
performance – that is, the idea of "theatre". "Theatricality", when used
in this other sense, is enlisted in an interpretation that is predicated on
the ontological distinction of "real" versus "not real". With this sense in
mind, however, when "theatricality" is used to describe behaviour,
people, events and objects, its meaning is frequently coloured by
"anti-theatricality", as Barbara Freedman observes: *'Theatricality is* still
used today as a perjorative term to refer to behaviour that is seen
as false or inauthentic to the extent that its concern with being seen
takes precedence over, and in fact distorts, what it shows."[2] Although

Freedman's statement suggests "theatricality" itself has some agency, I think that how she sees "theatricality" operating, rather, implies the agency of a *spectator* who judges the behaviour "false or inauthentic". In other words a person, event or object in the world becomes a performance-to-be-watched – becomes "theatricalised" – when an onlooker decides to be a spectator. At this point, too, notions of "authenticity" and "fakery" – reflecting the ancient Platonic prejudice against mimesis – come into play as the flow of being is ruptured and the spectator becomes aware of him/herself watching a performance. It is by analogy, as I will discuss below, that the spectator "theatricalises" the experience of watching.

Reality is "theatricalised" when the viewing subject, for whatever reason, finds him or herself in relationship to an object, person or event and is stimulated to analogously apply his/her awareness of "theatre" to how he/she is now spectating. An object, person or event, therefore, is not inherently "theatrical" but is endowed with "theatricality" by the spectator. In other words, there are no "theatrical" things, only "theatrical" perceptions and interpretations. This insight can be attributed to a pioneering study written by Elizabeth Burns thirty years ago, according to Burns: "Theatricality is not ... a mode of behaviour or expression, but attaches to any kind of behaviour perceived and interpreted by others and described (mentally or explicitly) in theatrical terms. ... Theatricality is determined by a particular viewpoint, a mode of perception."[3] However, it is important to remember that the process of "perceiving" and "interpreting" phenomena in "theatrical terms" is a culturally encoded process. One must first have an idea of "theatre" before one can interpret things "theatrically", or, as Burns puts it: "[the onlooker] recognizes certain patterns and sequences which are analogous *to those with which he is familiar in the theatre.*"[4] Thus "theatricality" emerges from the "theatrical" looking of an inculturated spectator who is able to distinguish "theatricality" from "strangeness" (although the two are by no means exclusive).

Assuming an onlooker who is available to view the world "theatrically", then the conditions are such that "theatricality" can be perceived in a person or a thing in such a way that makes the onlooker preternaturally aware of his or her own positioning as a "spectator". Josette Féral, who acknowledges her own debt to Burns's study, similarly describes this process as part of a "series of cleavages (inscribed by the artist and recognized by the spectator)".[5] It is, however, the spectator's awareness, which creates the conditions for a theatricalised interplay of looks, an awareness which occurs when the spectator decides to demarcate the space of the exchange as theatrical (Féral's principal "cleavage"). To borrow a phenomenological term, the beholder "brackets" reality so that the "bracketed" reality is available to him or her for "theatrical" interpretation. What Burns is pointing towards is the idea of "theatricality" being a perceptual process which requires first of all a competency on the part of the spectator to be able to identify and interpret what is being seen as theatrical and, secondly, an intention on the part of the onlooker to place him or herself in a spectatorial relationship to what is being viewed. In other words, a person must know how and be willing to view any action or object in theatrical terms – a competency which has been learned through a combination of specific socio-historical phenomena. However, Burns reminds us of an important proviso to this: "[t]he perception of expressive aspects of ordinary action as significant in themselves and interesting to observe is independent of drama as a form of art".[6] Therefore – although the act of interpretation, which transforms behaviour in the world into imitative action, which is "primarily symbolic", belongs, of course, to the domain of "theatre" – it is not exclusive to "theatre", nor does it depend upon the existence of "theatre" as an art form.

## The Moral Ontology of "Theatricality"

The ontology of "theatricality", as I suggested above, is unproblematic when it occurs in an event framed as "theatre". As Burns argues, the conventions of the event "define the situation" and provide the clues for all participants that enable them to interpret what is going on.[7] The actual dynamics of what occurs, and how, in this kind of interaction are more complex than my previous sentence would suggest but, fundamentally, the act of recognition of "theatre" as a specific kind of human activity is required before any other interpretations can occur.[8] Although many contemporary performances have blurred the boundary between "reality" and "unreality", nevertheless, the position of spectator at such events is still predicated on an ontology, which distinguishes between quotidian existence and the "fictionality" of the performance. For example, at a recent production of OBS *Macbeth* the audience were in very real danger of bodily injury from the huge scaffolds on wheels that were being whirled around the space, but dodging them became a playful part of the performance. The context for this "danger" was understood as part of the definition of the situation, which was interpreted as a "theatrical" event. Outside of events that are framed as "theatre", expressive behaviour may or may not be viewed as "theatrical" – it depends on how that expressive behaviour is interpreted. In quotidian interpretations of "theatricality", it nearly always functions as a signifier for "not real" which operates on a sliding scale from outright deceit on one end to playful exaggeration on the other. In these degrees of "unreality" a moral ontology is suggested predicated on the idea of "Truth", which ontologically defines and stabilizes interpretations of "reality". At the opposite extreme to "Truth" is instrumental deception – that is, deceiving to achieve a particular "real world" outcome – which is worse than fictionality because the latter declares its status as "play". In other words, the Platonic paradigm. For example, in the recent trial of multiple child murderer, Kathleen Folbigg, her ex-husband and father of the four murdered infants used theatrical metaphors when he testified that his then wife "'cried on cue'" which was part of her "'broken sparrow routine'".[9] Craig Folbigg's use of the words "on cue" and "routine" suggested that his wife's grief over the death of her children was not only insincere but was a performance that was "put on" for effect. Clearly, such evidence relied on the competency of Folbigg and the court in interpreting these metaphors and understanding the kind of behaviour they referred to, that is, behaviour analogous to an actor on stage. Therefore, the interpretive logic of such uses of the concept of "theatricality" can be seen to be underpinned by an ontology of "real" versus what Burns call "composed" behaviour.[10]

## "Theatricality" as a Theory of Interpretation

From Craig Folbigg's testimony we can see an unproblematic acceptance of this implicit ontology of "theatricality" and, also, reference to a "near enough" definition of "theatre". The concept, however, becomes problematic when it is used in critical discourse precisely because this quotidian understanding of the term underpins its critical use and thus allows a lack of precision and interpretive ambiguity in its use.[11] Josette Féral, in a recent essay, comments on the wide use of "theatricality" – "either metaphorically or actually resorted to as an operative concept" – in fields outside of Theatre/Performance and how, in these contexts, its use is "widely divergent and contradictory". Furthermore, she writes, "when used outside the field of theater, the notion of theatricality seems to refer to familiar characteristics, as if its meaning were somehow implicit for those who use them".[12] Other contributors to the volume characterize "theatricality" as being a" still quite vague notion"[13] or as having a "meaning [which] may seem difficult to grasp when one is to make a theoretical approach to the field".[14] Similarly, in a special edition of *Modern Drama* that reconsiders Jonas Barish's *The Anti-theatrical Prejudice* (1981), the contributors examined "anti-theatricality" as a productive force in the constitution of "theatricality". As co-editor Martin Puchner observes, both terms could be viewed as "deeply intertwined systems, enabling one another and propelling one another forward in history".[15] How this occurs, Kirk Williams in the same volume argues, is because "[w]estern theatre has been concerned with its enabling conditions from its very beginning, and, for this reason, the stage itself is often the best and most persuasive setting for an exploration of its own moral failings and ontological dangers. Anti-theatricality is, in short, the trope specific to and even parasitically dependent upon theatrical representation".[16] Féral, who has been considering the concept since 1982[17], wonders whether "theatricality" has any theoretical "traction" in relation to "performativity" and feels that the former notion is "a tricky one".[18] She invokes an equally symbiotic relationship of "theatricality" to "theatre" as Williams does for "anti-theatricality": "It is precisely because the notion of theater has changed that we must constantly redefine the notion of theatricality".[19] Both Williams and Féral's comments suggest the interpretive force that ideas of "theatre" have on the concept of "theatricality" and emphasize the need to have a clear understanding of what kind of "theatre" is being referred to.

"Theatricality", thus, is identified as a site of interpretive struggle. In his essay "Structure, Sign and Play" Jacques Derrida distinguished between two interpretations of interpretation, which Samuel Weber summarizes as "nostalgic versus affirmative interpretation".[20] "Nostalgic" interpretation "'seeks to decipher, dreams of deciphering a truth or origin that transcends play and the order of the sign ... the other, no longer oriented towards origin, affirms play and strives to pass beyond man and humanism...'"[21] Weber questions the implication in Derrida's essay which prefers affirmative interpretation and suggests that what Derrida defines as the "common ground" of both interpretations of interpretation is not an acceptance of "irreducible difference" but a "struggle" to "'divide up the field of the human sciences *amongst themselves'*".[22] This process is not "neutral" but involves "the staking of claims, the effort to appropriate".[23] Thus Weber sees that "... beyond the 'irreducible difference' of nostalgic and affirmative interpretations, there is a third version, interpreting interpretation as a struggle to overwhelm and dislodge an already existing dominant interpretation and thus to establish its own authority."[24]

The "problem" of "theatricality", viewed in light of the above, can be seen as part of an on-going struggle for interpretive dominance that has in no small way been influenced by Derrida's deconstructive binarism of "nostalgic" and "affirmative" interpretation. The performance art, "theatre", that developed in European cultures "has been concerned with its enabling conditions from its very beginning" (as Williams reminded us above) and it is these "enabling conditions" which are the source/site of interpretive struggle. For example, theatre scholars are all familiar with the text/performance struggle that has characterized both the practice and study of theatre in the twentieth century. Roland Barthes's definition of "theatricality" from his essay on "Baudelaire's Theatre" as "theater-minus-text" is paradigmatic of this debate and is often quoted in arguments against the dominance of the written text.[25] Similarly, as Elin Diamond has noted, from the text/performance struggle has emerged a related interpretive struggle in the discourse of "performance" versus "theatre" (particularly in the United States). Diamond critiques this dichotomy which "charges" "theatre" with logocentrism, with representational closure, and encouraging interpretation by an audience, which is unmistakably "nostalgic". Against this, an idea of "performance" is "honoured" because it "dismantl[es] textual authority, illusionism, and the canonical body of the actor in favour of the polymorphous body of the performer", in short, it encourages "affirmative" interpretation.[26] Therefore, we can see that "theatricality" is being enlisted in this struggle when Féral asks, in her forward to SubStance, if it is "still a pertinent concept compared to performativity, which has overshadowed it in the last 15 years".[27]

### *"Theatricality" in a Case Study of a Struggle for Interpretive Dominance*

The enlisting of "theatricality" in a different struggle for interpretive dominance can be seen in the debate provoked by Michael Fried's use of the concept in his 1967 essay "Art and Objecthood".[28] As art critic

Rosalind Krauss stated, in a forum discussion with Michael Fried on the twentieth anniversary of the publication of his essay, "theatre" is "a non-thing, an emptiness, a void. Theatre is thus an empty term whose role it is to set up a system founded upon the opposition between itself and another term."[29] Furthermore, noting the Derridean hierarchical inequality that is to be found in all binary oppositions, she argues that in "Art and Objecthood": "Theater as the empty, un-locatable, amorphous member of the pair is bad, while the non-theatrical rises within the pair to be coded as good".[30] Krauss, too, identifies the Platonism of Fried's distinction, which places the "empty term" of "theatre/theatricality" in a binary opposition to "non-theatricality" thus allowing the latter term to be "coded as good". Although Krauss refers to "theatre" it is clear that in responding to Fried's essay she is not referring to the art form but to something associated with it, that is, "theatricality". However, it is also apparent that Fried himself in "Art and Objecthood" was not referring to the art form "theatre" but was invoking "theatricality" as a trope in the anti-theatricalist tradition. Such a use Martin Puchner identifies as "paranoid", because it sees "a theatre which is at work everywhere, infiltrating and corrupting everything, and which therefore demands the greatest vigilance".[31] "Theatricality" as a concept is, thus, attached to the art form of "theatre" but also can be detached from it. It is worth briefly reviewing Fried's seminal text to see how this operates.

Fried's "Art and Objecthood" is the paradigmatic "anti-theatricalist" text of the late-twentieth century and in it he defends modernist art (which just is) against minimalist work, which he deems "theatrical". Art, as the epigraph to his essay suggests, at "every moment" "ceases [to exist] and is every moment renewed"[32]. Fried's modernism requires art to be transcendental, trans-cultural and trans-historical, to manifest its "presence" as art in such a way that *"at every moment the work itself is wholly manifest"*[33], Fried's argument rehashes the ancient Platonic prejudice against mimesis which establishes the basic binary opposition of the "authentic real" and the "false copy" with the latter term being the lesser of the two. Thus his aim, explicitly stated, is to "distinguish between the authentic art of our time and other work which ... seems to me to share certain characteristics associated here with ... theater."[34] For Fried *"Art degenerates as it approaches the condition of theater"* [35] and therefore is "corrupted", "perverted" and "infected" by "theatre"[36]. These metaphors of disease and degeneracy express a modernist horror that is like a mid-twentieth century eugenicist's horror of miscegenation; a horror reinforced by his declaration that: "*What lies* between the *arts is theater*" [37]. Such a statement reinforces Samuel Weber's claim that "one of the hallmarks of the history of theatre ... in the West [is] its problematic relation to property, to politics and to established consecrated places and institutions, both private and public, political and domestic."[38] What kind of art is it that concerns Fried? In essence he is critiquing minimalist sculpture which self-reflexively declares "I am art" thus drawing attention to itself as being in relationship with a particular spectator, at a particular moment in a specific place. For Fried, such art demands theatrical spectatorship: "[T]heatre has an audience – it exists for one – in a way that the other arts do not; in fact, this more than anything else is what modernist sensibility finds intolerable in theatre generally."[39] "Theatrical" art acknowledges itself, and by so doing it is performing presence, creating a "theatrical effect or quality – a kind of stage[d] presence."[40]

Fried's use of "theatricality", as Philip Auslander argues, allowed him to structurally define a particular debate that occurred in the visual arts world in the late sixties, but the parameters established by Fried have continued to influence debates beyond his own field.[41] Indeed Fried himself arrives at a similar conclusion: "I continue to be struck by the extent to which hostile responses to 'Art and Objecthood' tend not to be deconstructive in approach but rather to attack my 'positive' terms in the interests of my 'negative' ones, so that on the whole the disputes have continued to take place within the conceptual space the essay established twenty years ago."[42] In Auslander's reading of Fried, he sees "theatricality" as signifying not the "theatre" as such but rather a postmodernist sensibility against which Fried is attempting to construct a fortress of modernism (presumably in the International Style). Although Fried may have lost the battle, Auslander suggests, he may have won the war. Visual arts discourse, in attempting to establish the discursive (interpretive) dominance of postmodernism over Friedian and Greenbergian modernism, accepts without question the field defined by Fried: "By reifying Fried's position, along with [Clement] Greenberg's, as the late modernism against which postmodernism defines itself, [it] unintentionally recuperates postmodernist art for the very critical discourse it is said to have surpassed." Thus this discourse "repeats the modernist gesture of defining itself" against a past discourse, which it views as no longer, growing or developing.[43]

## "Theatricality" as a Site of Interpretive Struggle

Returning to the question I began this paper with: 'What do we mean when we use the "theatricality"?' we can see that the issue of interpretation is fundamental to it. Firstly, following the Burns/Féral thesis, any definition of "theatricality" is necessarily an interpretive activity engaged in by a spectator who has competency to do so. In the context of "theatrical" events, such interpretation is conventionally pre-defined: the spectator knows by how the situation is defined that it is a "theatrical" situation and not some other, non-theatrical, event (notwithstanding the example of Invisible Theatre whose conventions are such that it is not identified as a theatrical event). However, in everyday situations, the spectator can choose to interpret people, events, things "theatrically" and in so doing uses an ontology of "unreality" versus "reality" signified by interpreting behaviour as either "composed" or not. Reflecting the Platonic prejudice against mimesis, "theatricality" is often the lesser term in the binary relationship with "reality". The use of theatrical metaphors in everyday discourse suggests that the analogy of "composed" behaviour to "acting" in the "theatre" is a particular interpretation that is well established in Western societies. However, as recent discussions in the field of Theatre/Performance studies have illustrated, these quotidian interpretations of "theatricality" are frequently employed as tacit understandings when the concept of "theatricality" is used in critical discourse. As Rosalind Krauss noted in Michael Fried's use of the term, "theatricality" is a cipher employed in opposition to define something *else*. Krauss's notion of "theatricality" as a cipher is persuasive and we can see that its use as such in a range of discourses is, by and large, remarkably similar. Keeping "theatricality" as an interpretive cipher in mind we become aware of how it is used in what Samuel Weber sees as struggles for interpretive dominance between "nostalgic" and "affirmative" interpretation. A critic such as Fried employs the concept of "theatricality" as the "other" which allows him to construct a discourse of "authenticity" or what Derrida spoke of as the "dream ... of truth or origin that transcends play or the order of the sign". On the other hand, as Philip Auslander argues, the attempt to invoke "theatricality" as a signifier of "affirmative" interpretation – the postmodern discourse, in opposition to modernism – only reaffirms how deeply entrenched is Fried's interpretation.

"Theatricality", thus, appears as a useful critical signifier, which can be utilized to support either "affirmative" postmodern positions, or, through negative example, function to support the teleological certainty of "nostalgic" arguments. Both uses are problematic because the truth claims that are being made for "theatricality" are claims whose foundations can be found in an unexamined idea of "theatre". I am, however, persuaded by Weber's thesis regarding the struggle of interpretations of interpretation, which is illuminating when applied to "theatricality". Viewed in the context of Weber's work "theatricality" emerges as a site of interpretive struggle. This can be observed in some of the recent scholarship re-examining Barish's notion of the "anti-theatrical prejudice" in Modern *Drama*. The interpretive struggle of "theatricality" manifests as "anti-theatricalism" which operates both as radical self-critique and as an expression of ontological anxiety. "Theatricality", as it has demonstrated through-out the twentieth century, continues to be quiescent and accommodating as a term and, as the recent discussions in SubStance and *Modern Drama* have demonstrated, can be used as a cipher within a wide range of differing discourses.

## Notes

1. The following paper is a version of the paper presented at the Jaipur IFTR/FIRT Conference which conference convenor Dr Ravi Chaturvedi encouraged me to submit in an expanded form.

2. Barbara Freedman, *Staging the Gaze, Postmodernism, Psychoanalysis and Shakespearian Comedy* (Cornell University Press, Ithaca and London, 1991), p. 50.

3. Elizabeth Burns; *Theatricality: A Study of Convention in the Theatre and Social Life* (Longman Group Ltd, London, 1972), pp. 12-13.

4. Ibid., p. 12 – my emphasis.

5. Josette Féral "Forward" *SubStance* (#98/99, Vol. 31, nos. 2 & 3 2002), p. 10.

6. Elizabeth Burns, op. cit., p. 13.

7. "Defining the situation" refers to the process whereby an individual in a social situation attempts to define what is going on by attempting to interpret the consensus of others present and thus adapt his/her behaviour to conform to or change the definition of the situation. Ibid, pp. 15-16.

8. See Willmar Sauter's *The Theatrical Event: Dynamics of Performance and Perception* (University of Iowa Press, Iowa City, 2000) for an excellent discussion of these dynamics. The importance of recognition is borne out by the example of "Invisible Theatre" which depends on the spectator *not* defining the situation as "theatre" but as an event in the quotidian. (See Josette Féral's "Theatricality: The Specificity of Theatrical Language" in *SubStance* 2002, p. 96 for a discussion of just this kind of example).

9. Lee Glendinning, "Here no evil, see no evil", *The Sydney Morning Herald* (24-25 May 2003), p. 33.

10. Elizabeth Burns, op.cit., p. 33.

11. See Marvin Carlson "Theatre History, Methodology and Distinctive Features" in *Theatre Research International* (Vol. 20 No. 2, Summer 1995) and "The Resistance to Theatricality" in *SubStance*, op. cit., for a discussion of this.

12. Josette Féral (2002), op. cit., p. 3.

13. Malgorzata Sugiera, "Theatricality and Cognitive Science": The Audience's Perception and Reception", *SubStance* 2002, p. 225.

14. Ragnhild Tronstad, "Could the World Become a Stage? Theatricality and Metaphorical Structures", Ibid., p. 216.

15. Martin Puchner, "Modernism and Anti-theatricality: An Afterword", *Modern Drama* (Vol. 44 No. 3 Fall 2001), p. 355.

16. Kirk Williams, "Anti-theatricality and the Limits of Naturalism", Ibid., p. 284.

17. Josette Féral, "Performance and Theatricality: The Subject Demystified", *Modern Drama* (Vol. 25, March 1982).

18. Josette Féral (2002), op. cit., p. 3 & 4.

19. Ibid, p. 4.

20. Samuel Weber, *Institution and Interpretation* (University of Minnesota Press, Minneapolis, 1987), p. 4.

21. Jacques Derrida, *Writing and Difference,* (1967), p. 427 qtd in Ibid, p. 3.

22. Derrida (1967) qtd in Ibid, p. 4.

23. Ibid., p. 4.

24. Ibid, p. 5.

25. Roland Barthes, *Critical Essays* (Northwestern University Press, Evanston, 1972), p. 26.

26. Elin Diamond (ed.), *Performance and Cultural Politics* (Routledge, London and New York, 1996), p. 3.

27. Josette Féral (2002), op. cit., p. 3.

28. Michael Fried, *Art and Objecthood: Essays and Reviews* (University of Chicago Press, Chicago and London,1998), pp. 148-172.

29. Krauss, Rosalind "Theories of Art after Minimalism and Pop" in Hal Foster (ed.), *Discussions in Contemporary Culture No. 1* (Bay Press, Seattle, 1987), pp. 62-63.

30. Ibid, p. 63.

31. Martin Puchner, op. cit., p. 356.

32. Michael Fried, op. cit., p. 148.

33. Ibid, p. 155, Fried's emphasis.

34. Ibid, p. 168.

35. Ibid, p. 164.

36. Ibid, p. 161.

37. Ibid, p. 164.

38. Samuel Weber, "Scene and Screen: Electronic Media and Theatricality" (author's email of speech delivered Brisbane, 13 August 1998), p. 4.

39. Michael Fried, op. cit., p. 163.

40. Ibid, p. 167.

41. Philip Auslander, *From Acting to Performance: Essays in Modernism and Postmodernism* (Routledge, London and New York, 1997), pp. 49-57.

42. Michael Fried, "Theories of Art after Minimalism and Pop" in Hal Foster (ed.), op. cit., p. 57.

43. Philip Auslander, op. cit., p. 54.

# 10

## Materialism, Intellectualism and the Dialectics of *The Oriki of a Grasshopper*

### John Warrick

It is perhaps wishful thinking that, at the time of his death in 1956, Bertolt Brecht was conceiving a materialist's response to Samuel Beckett's *Waiting for Godot*. And it is only fitting that one of Brecht's admirers, the Nigerian playwright Femi Osofisan, took up the mantle – walked a mile in Lucky's hat, so to speak – and produced what may be considered a type of *Godot* in which the circuitous and riddling *form* of the piece served only to emphasize epistemological ramifications upon the material referential *content* – that of a very real and historically grounded cultural group. Premiering in 1981, *The Oriki of a Grasshopper*, as Sandra Richards describes it, is "a brooding examination of the intellectual's relationship to society."[1] As a matter of exploration, I shall attempt to place Osofisan's text within three different, yet fundamentally related contexts: (1) that of an intercultural aesthetic hybridity between the colonial remnant and the Nigerian present, (2) broadly, that of the play's political interrogation concerning the possibility and value of social transformation, and (3) that of the role of the intellectual (theatre) scholar within a Nigerian, and ultimately Socialist worldview.

While Osofisan's *Oriki* contemplates the precepts of Nigerian socialism, the play's dramaturgical organizing principle is clearly that of Beckett's text. The protagonist of the play, Imaro, an intellectual Marxist and scholar, hosts a rehearsal for the play *Waiting for Godot*. However, like *Godot*, nothing actually takes place but the waiting: waiting for an actor, waiting for the police, and waiting for the revolution ... none of which will appear. Instead, the central question of the play is the choice of Imaro's self-determination – whether to incorporate the metaphorical tendencies of Pozzo or of Lucky into his own quest for political and cultural identity.

However, it was not a theme of Apocalyptic angst which drew the playwright to the original French text; instead, Osofisan realized a certain correspondence between Beckett's metaphysical tramps and the historical plight of the Nigerian intelligentsia.

> The *Waiting for Godot* theme was a good coincidence... it suddenly occurred to me that in spite of all the metaphysical interpretations given to it in the West, the play is in fact very much a Third World play! It exposes splendidly the plight of our intelligentsia .... This is what marks the African petty bourgeoisie, its terrible marginalization, coupled with a hope that one day a Messiah will come. Hence Godot for me is revolutionary in demonstrating this helplessness, and the vanity of its [the academy's] expectation of a messiah when it should organize and do something.[2]

The opening of the play finds Imaro, a revolutionary scholar, quietly thrumming guitar in his nearly evacuated office and awaiting the inevitable booted thuds, which are sure to announce his impending arrest. Instead of policemen, however, his old friend Claudius appears at the door, seemingly unaware of the danger and ready to begin the morning's rehearsal for their production of *Waiting for Godot*. When encountered with Imaro's sullen attitude and wrecked office, Claudius, a millionaire and avowed capitalist, comfortingly proffers cigars and a bottle of Chivas Regal. Over drinks, Imaro cryptically refers to the past week's crisis, at which the characterizations clearly turn to another level of theatrical metaphor.

CLAUDIUS.   What crisis! What of the crises – in the plural, mind you – the numerous terrible crises that we go through outside everyday?

IMARO.   Well...

CLAUDIUS.   Life goes on, my friend. As Pozzo will say!

*IMARO.*      Yes, I suppose so. Pozzo will say that. Life goes on.
             Except that you're playing Vladimir, not Pozzo. And he
             wanted to hang.[3]

Levels of characterization are somewhat blurred at the mention of
Pozzo. Within the performance, it is clear that Imaro is to play the role
of Pozzo, both as actor and, as he soon shall come to realize, as
bourgeois intellectual faced with a self-determining choice between the
capitalist Pozzo and that of the only other role left to him – according
to the form of Beckett's text, that of the proletarian Lucky.

Habit is, of course, a major determinant in the development of
these characters, and it is fitting that both Imaro and Claudius come to
agree upon the numerous crises with which life confronts the
individual. These are the catastrophes of the moment, often alleviated
with the trifles of commodity culture, and they serve to anesthetize the
revolutionary activist and intellectual. As a matter of dramaturgical
surrogation however, Osofisan's well-educated Pozzos are more than
aware of their predicaments, and Imaro laments, "But that's it,
Claudius! That's what I'm trying to say! We've been waiting all our
lives! You said it just now. We, the so-called intellectuals, we're just
professional waiters we've just..." The point is ended upon Claudius'
well-timed interruption of "Come, let's start the rehearsals" (6). Each
begins warm-up exercises to no avail as Peter, who is to perform the
role of Estragon, has already been arrested and will not make an
appearance.

Sandra Richards suggests that, trapped in the riddles of Beckett's
original text, *Oriki*'s characterizations "reaffirm an established order"[4]
of neo-colonialism and capitalist manipulation. In the proffering of
such an "absurdist" stance, even in its fully justifiable pertinence,
Richards reduces the play's meaning to conform to a certain Western
structure. It is inconceivable that such an approach does not alter the
historically determined structure and political commentary of *The
Oriki of a Grasshopper* as, first and foremost, a materially and culturally
Nigerian text.

As a matter of dramaturgical precedence, it is important to
recognize key similarities among the approaches of Osofisan, the traditional Nigerian theatre, and the epic theatre of Bertolt Brecht. Because
all such influences exist in *Oriki*, a difficulty arises in addressing the
play as an evenly interlaced, intercultural work – particularly when
both structure and content expose and reflect the receding presences of

the English and French colonial persuasions *and* the "emerging plagues of kleptocratic governments, self-perpetuating dictatorships, unrelieved poverty, an opulent and corrupt few, and the collusion of foreign commercial interests."[5] In this, Osofisan is not so much interested in writing back to the Empire, but in creating a dialectical theatre in which the processes of historicization may be viewed, critiqued, and ultimately altered ... both by and for the peoples of the community and nation. As such, the playwright attempted to locate the affinities of habit between *Godot* and the contemporary Nigerian cultural and political landscape. Consequently, his was not an intercultural attempt at cultural pageantry, nor was his an experiment at reworking planes of imbalanced exchange into a free and equilibrated swap of cultures to effect in mutual tolerance and appreciation.

*Oriki* blatantly rests upon Beckett's structure as an example of precisely that which will forever dissuade a collective movement from social transformation and revolutionary action. Habitual behaviour only equates with the certain use of tools as props in a meta-theatrical narrative of pointlessness, akin, suggests Imaro, to "relish[ing] the leftovers. Like Estragon, nibbling bones."[6] As such, *Oriki*'s characters alleviate their catastrophes of the moment with the trifles of commodity culture; the comforting pleasures of cigars and Chivas Regal serve to anesthetize any residual revolutionary drives.

The reduction of Imaro's intellectual angst within the persona of Estragon's nibbling is indicative of Osofisan's use of the parable. This narrative technique is probably most commonly associated in the West with its Brechtian counterpart, and Modupe O. Olaogun suggests that, "through the use of parables, [Brecht, and by implication Osofisan] could illustrate the injustices of the society which he wanted corrected."[7] According to Roland Barthes, this type of Brechtian presentation is "offered to the spectator for criticism, not for adherence."[8] This premise may be seen in the title to Osofisan's play, *The Oriki of a Grasshopper*. From the root word *ori*, which translates as "the head," the oriki is a "praise song about an individual's personal and ancestral history."[9] Within the play, this song relates to the matter of "moral choice" which every character makes, "when the forest heats up, in a hot season." When the forest burns, the grasshopper must flee the flames or remain and be consumed. The grasshopper, of course, is Imaro, and he must compromise regardless of his course of action. Facing the proposition that his words will effect in nothing so transformative as his own incarceration, his revolutionary spirit falters and he begs Claudius for a "producing" job within the safe confines of a government office. In response Moni, Imaro's ex-student and current mistress, admonishes, "Yes, grasshopper! Time to fly, and learn the antics of locusts" (19).

Osofisan externalizes the great psychological angst with which his characters suffer, and a certain difficulty arises in the suggestion that any judgment of character occurs on behalf of the audience. It is important to remember that the play was initially written for an audience composed largely of Imaro-type scholars, those intellectuals who conflictingly preach Marxist ideology and revolution from pulpits, which are largely provided through means of government subsidies and private oil interests. As a result, and regardless of the influence of Beckett's forms, the play takes the presence of the *montage* structure. While audiences for *Godot* may always silently urge the characters further down the road of metaphysical discovery, Beckett has constructed a rhetorical trap by which no real advance remains possible. Beckett was a firm believer in the artistic framing of chaos, and his plays follow from the larger mandate.

> What I am saying does not mean that there will henceforth be no form in art. It only means that there will be new form, and that this form will be of such a type that it admits the chaos and does not try to say that the chaos is really something else .... To find a form that accommodates the mess, that is the task of the artist now.[10]

It might be said that if Beckett employs a language, which is recedingly removed from its historical context, that a process of entropic collapse results. Within this formula, within the demise of the grounded referent, lies the power of Beckett's tragic-comedy. However, such a form – if indeed this was even Beckett's intention at all – renders aesthetic damage to the immediately, politically activist drama. This is exactly why Osofisan's text takes the existential and sublimates it in the act of infusing a cultural ground. According to Sam Ukala, explains: Osofisan (ask the author to recheck this world, Brian suggests it to be replaced).

> These are largely political issues, which makes Osofisan a playwright in politics from the perspective of subject matter. With the alter- native dramaturgical form, which subverts established forms,

Osofisan subverts established perspectives on politics, history, myths, legends and life.[11]

Ukala refers in this instance to Osofisan's split with Soyinka and his, as Fanon would posit, second phase of cultural reclamation. In Fanon's own words, this phase ultimately transforms the artist into "an awakener of the people, hence comes a fighting literature, a revolutionary literature, and a national literature."[12] Unlike Soyinka, whose work is at least occasionally self-described as containing a threnodic essence, Osofisan's plays relegate cultural "origins" only within a contemporaneous materialist discourse which is entirely dialectical in nature.

> The dialectic between the real and the imaginary, between the forces of tradition and the modernist consciousness, is the contribution that the theatre can usefully make to the process of social transformation .... this tension between the existing and the visionary, between the past, the present and the future, not as deity now but metaphor, is the god Orunmila. For it is obvious that we shall never have the truth completely within our grasp, only as a aspiration.[13]

Perhaps it is with some consideration as to the "developing" and "reclaiming" status of the Nigerian state that one forgives Osofisan for his reckless appropriation of Beckett's texts, particularly considering that Beckett rarely, indeed if ever, approved of even the slightest alteration to his work. Still, as a matter of political investigation, it might prove beneficial to briefly explore the direct intercultural implication of such a flagrant and deliberate alteration of the French source text.

*Oriki*'s structure retains from its Beckettian source a certain ambivalent attitude towards meaningful cultural practice, and as such it remains faithful to the original text as Beckett might have intended it. However, because Osofisan manipulates the content to his own purposes, it would be fair to acknowledge his intention to thoroughly exploit *Godot* against its very creator. It might prove most beneficial to consider the practical side to such an irreverent rewriting. Sam Ukala posits that *interculturalism* as an aesthetic concept is largely outdated and suspiciously, seemingly Utopian in its practices. The writer, in the very act of borrowing – or even being influenced by – a text, cannot help but reduce, distill, and even inadvertently invalidate the original's rich cultural grounding, thereby committing an act of cultural theft.

However, if theft is somehow endemic to the process of aesthetic influence, the artist then must choose his or her affinities, be they the source material or the present audience.

In consideration of source and target cultural events, "Bharucha's position neglects the primary notion of adaptation as a reductionist process. In fact, no matter its rationalizations, an intercultural experiment that seeks the satisfaction of both source and target audiences satisfy neither. Performative meaning, social significance and the representation of socio-political identities are culturally determined, not politically negotiated.[14]

Osofisan clearly pins his political aims upon the always-present, contemporary audience, and it is somewhat noteworthy that the talkback session for the original production lasted twice the length of the play itself. Such is the nature of truly dialectical theatre. If one were to bestow any critical judgment upon the relative worth of such a practice, it seems that Oriki's *montage* appropriately proffered an open-ended, valid, and culturally engaging challenge to the intellectuals in the audience, one that elicited the response of a debate as to the directed quality of scholarship and artistic endeavor within a Nigerian social state.

While Brechtian of quality, and as he certainly generally promotes Marxist ideals grounded in materialist practices, Osofisan's play does not directly employ a *not/but* scenario, and Brecht has been criticized that his formulae too often and logically progress *only* to the Marxist solution. Osofisan, despite his Marxist tendencies, regularly depicts the most unfortunate of circumstances and the most limited of solutions, and if one were to qualify his scenarios within a simplified form, it may be said that his plays illustrate a montage whereby both *not/but* and *not/not* reactions are promoted. His revolutionary spirit lies not in the activation of the specifically Marxist activist, but simply with the dialectical critic. These two categories of discourse need not be mutually inclusive, and Imaro's dilemma – whether to continue professing the revolution or to capitulate to the capitalist structure – is ultimately not released from the grip of its powerful consternation.

Words, Osofisan suggests, contain within themselves the power of revolutionary change. Imaro's university has been shut down, and those students and teachers that have not been arrested have been sent home, excised from the source of their power – their words. On the other hand, there exists within the play a consistent commentary on the nearly ontological deferral of social transformation as espoused in academic settings. Change, it seems, crawls at a pace, which turns hypocrite the very function of social transformation.

CLAUDIUS.  Yes, tell me! What is it like, this revolution I hear so much about? This Godot that will sweep everything away and bring paradise? A scene in a play? All the words you throw about, your savage gestures, your wild-waving fists in the air, what do they all amount to? To a room in a prison cell? Boots in the crotch? Or electrodes on the nerve centers? You think those will make you more of a revolutionary and less of a fake?

MONI.  I don't have to convince you, sir. When the day comes, [the revolution] will have enough words to describe itself. (18)

Imaro cannot recognize that what "breaks" his students is exactly that which has broken him: a combination of fear and the daily, wearing struggle of the revolutionary thinker whose effects upon social transformation are always already deferred to a slow, spasmodic advance. Secondly is the almost direct acknowledgement that the university system might be too removed from the reality of daily struggle – a claim for which I am sure many scholars and intellectuals respond with dialectical acumen.

Abandoned by both Moni and Claudius, and isolated within an office bereft of those precious words – bereft, that is, except for Beckett's text – Imaro begins to cry the song "MANDELA! AMANDLA!" Osofisan makes one final ambivalent gesture in writing of his representative scholar: "[*Lights begin to fade. He walks round slowly, like one searching for something in the sand. His voice is broken when he speaks again*].... Let freedom come...Let freedom come...Let freedom..." (31-32). In one final twist of dramaturgical manipulation, Osofisan returns to a very representative cultural centre, the African song of freedom, seemingly emptying it of its political significance even as Imaro is committed to a state of inaction which steals his very voice. This final silence is identified by Joseph Roach as a "liturgical silence," one which does not necessarily equate to existential capitulation.[15] While it may be true that the play concludes in a moment of mournful loss, the unsung conclusion of the song still creates a type of "emotional space into which revelation can enter"[16] and into which the audience may initiate its critique even as it fills in the literal gaps of Osofisan's ellipsis. Far from the noble-nihilistic structure of Beckett's source text however, this amalgamated conclusion – uniformly following from Brecht, Beckett, and the Nigerian parable – only serves in the cultural, dialectical reassessment of Nigerian societal value systems.

## Notes

1. Sandra L. Richards has published one of a very few critical works on Femi Osofisan's plays. From *Ancient Songs Set Ablaze: The Theatre of Femi Osofisan* (Washington: Howard UP, 1996) p. 31.

2. Richards, p. 32.

3. All textual references to *Oriki* are from Femi Osofisan's anthology *The Oriki of a Grasshopper and Other Plays* (Washington: Howard University Press, 1995), p. 3. The text is not lineated, and citations are from page numbers only.

4. Richards, p. 40.

5. From Femi Osofisan's "Theatre and the rites of 'Post-Negritude' Remembering." In *Research in African Literature*, 30.1 (Spring 1999), p. 3. Osofisan's viewpoints on such matters are inseparable from his seeming support of the very notion of "nation-hood" itself.

6. Beckett, Samuel. *Waiting for Godot: A Tragicomedy in Two Acts*. Tr. Samuel Beckett (New York: Grove P, 1954), p. 6. All further citations from this text follow parenthetically.

7. Modupe O. Olaogun, "Parables in the Theatre: A brief Study of Femi Osofisan's Plays," *Okike: An African Journal of New Writing*, 27/28 (March 1988), p. 44.

8. From Roland Barthes' "Diderot, Brecht, Eisenstein," *Image – Music – Text*, trans. Stephen Heath (New York: Hill and Wang, 1977), p. 71.

9. Richards, p. 33.

10. From L. Graver and R. Federman, eds., *Samuel Beckett: The Critical Heritage* (London: Routledge UP, 1979) p. 219. The identification of nihilistic tendencies in Beckettian texts draws from this entropic model of signification; however, if one were to analyze Beckett's own personal life and his activist actions particularly during World War II, "entropy" is not the only model by which one may analyze his plays.

11. From Martin Banham, James Gibbs and Femi Osofisan, eds., *African Theatre: Playwrights and Politics* (Oxford: James Currey P, 1999), p. 32.

12. From Halford Fairchild's "Frantz Fanon's The Wretched of the Earth in Contemporary Perspective."

*Journal of Black Studies*. 25.2 (December 1994) pp. 191-199. The article condenses Fanon's phases.

13. The words are Femi Osofisan's: "Ritual and the Revolutionary Ethos." *Okike*, 22.3 (September 1982), p. 78.

14. Ukala, as cited in Martin, Gibbs and Osofisan, p. 48. I do not espouse the statement personally, but the sentiment is an important one if Nigerian critics follow such a model.

15. Joseph Roach, "The Great Hole of History: Liturgical Silence in Beckett, Osofisan, and Parks," *The South Atlantic Quarterly*, 100,1 (Winter 2001), p. 307.

16. Roach, p. 307.

# 11

## Post-operatic Encounters with History

### Nicholas Till

In this paper I want to outline some ideas I am working on for theorising a range of theatre works of the past 20 or so years as "post-operatic". My hypothesis is that although opera is clearly moribund as an artform, the operatic continues to haunt the imagination of a number of European theatre artists who work around and through the operatic: the work of musicians such as Heiner Goebbels, Giorgio Battistelli, Salvatore Sciarrino and Helmut Lachenmann, or theatre artists such as Christophe Marthaler and Societas Raffaello Sanzio. I want to suggest that this re-engagement with the operatic, which is primarily a phenomenon of German and Italian theatre, should be understood as a need by theatre artists from these countries to re-engage with history.

In Bertolucci's film *The Spider's Stratagem* of 1970 a young man returns to his family village thirty years after the war to recover the truth about the assassination of his father during the Fascist era. He finds that his father is honoured as an anti-Fascist hero, and manages to locate three of his father's former colleagues. "What was our anti-Fascism based on? ...we fancied conspiracies... *Ernani* (hums theme from *Ernani*) ... you know, conspirators. Or Samuel & Tom in *Un ballo in maschera*. We saw ourselves as such characters, but we understood nothing."

Bertolucci suggests here a striking instance of the way in which opera – or perhaps what I would call the "operatic" – has shaped the imagination of modern Italian politics. "Nature imitates art" says the Sicilian writer Leonardo Sciascia in his novel *The Day of the Owl*, in the way the culture of opera feeds into Italian life. "Ever since the time when, in the sudden silence of the orchestra pit, during *Cavalleria Rusticana*, the cry of "Hanno ammazzato cumpari Turiddu!" ("They've killed Turiddu") first chilled the spines of opera enthusiasts, criminal statistics and number systems of the lottery in Sicily have had closer links between cuckoldem and violent death."[1] The decisive contribution of Verdi in shaping the consciousness of the Risorgimento is well known. Less well known is that Giuseppe Mazzini, the great ideologue of the Risorgimento, had identified opera as the art form most likely to unite Italy because of its ability to transcend the divisions of language, its representation of an idealized national community beyond region or class in the chorus, and its powers of heroic arousal.[2] The recurrent themes of 19th century Italian opera – loyalty, conspiracy, revenge, and violent death – colour Italian politics to this day, the result of what the historian Paul Ginsborg describes as a social structure that continues to be based on familial loyalty and networks of clan patronage.[3] There are many similarities between modern Italian history and modern German history. Both countries underwent political unification during the 19th century, and in both cases there is an evident connection between the necessity to forge a supra-geographical and supra-historical national consciousness and the subsequent emergence of Fascism. And in Germany, as in Italy, opera developed during the 19th century as a key contributor to this process, although in different ways.

I want to explore the idea that is in those European countries where history has been mythologized through the operatic that artists have found themselves forced to confront the forms of the operatic to enable them to re-encounter history: Italy, where history is either melodrama or *opera buffa* – the later farcical, cynical, cruel ("cynical" is a term frequently used by Paul Ginsborg to describe Italian politicians); Germany, where history is mythologized as sacrificial tragedy. The Second World War brought the culmination and nemesis of these narratives, and in each case the postwar cultural scene in these countries was deeply influenced by a coming-to-terms with that narrative. A part of that process in both countries was the experience of a violently polarized repoliticisation in the early 70s, culminating in the state crises of 1977-78.

The third main school of opera in Europe is that of France, where history may be said to be enacted as the spectacle of grand opera. Let me start with France to suggest why opera has been strikingly irrelevant to modern French culture in contrast to Italy and Germany. In 17th century France opera was a crucial aspect of the spectacular display that so was so central to Louis XIV's establishment of power. During the 18th century the political status of opera meant that it became an important site of contestation for political and ideological disputes – the apparently trivial Guerre des Bouffons of 1752-54 between the partisans of French and Italian opera revealed the fault lines between the ideologues of absolutist rationalism and the proponents of Enlightenment naturalism. During the Revolution and the Napoleonic period grand opera provided a model for the secular spectacles in which both the Jacobins and Napoleon invested. By 1848 the gestures of revolutionary politics have become as empty as grand opera itself; we recall Marx's reading of Napoleon III's coup détat as the farcical re-enactment of the first Revolution which strips bare the true dynamic of the first revolution as a vicious bourgeois coup masked by fancy dress.[4] Operetta, not opera, is now the only suitable form for the new regime, and from this moment onwards opera and history part ways. The irrelevance of French opera ensured that after the war Boulez could issue his famous dictat against opera because, in effect, opera had in France already long ceased to carry any historical connotations that needed to be dealt with.

This is clearly not the case in Italy or Germany, where any confrontation with history demands some sort of engagement with opera. In these countries I think that one can see four distinct responses to the problematic of opera during the post-war period. What strikes me here is that these different stages might be said in some respects to map onto the development of the three waves of new cinema in Europe (Italian in the late 40s and 50s, French in the late 50s and 60s, German in the late 60s and 70s), reflecting the specific trajectory of the ability of country to come to terms with its recent history. In Italy the end of the war had already proved the existence of an extensive counter-fascist movement and as result postwar Italy experienced far more political continuity than the *Stunde nul* of Germany or the fundamental re-alignment of the political landscape in France, allowing filmakers like Rossellini or Rosi to engage with Italy's immediate history. Italian neo-realism is a clear antidote to the specious idealism and rhetoric of fascist films, and until the late 60s Italian film-makers refrained from dealing directly with the fascist era believing that the contemporary political situation in Italy warranted more urgent attention.

France had a more complex set of wartime issues to resolve, in particular the hastily forgotten complicity of the Vichy regime, and it took longer to do so. In contrast to Italian neo-realism the French New Wave presents itself a defiantly "modernist" – a reaction against conservative Gaullist nationalism. In Germany the acknowledgement of Nazism only really took place after 1968, and the recovery of history, memory, identity and even myth become prevalent themes in the films of Wenders, Herzog, Syberberg, Fassbinder and Reisz made in the 70s.

Some sort of related periodisation may be found in the trajectory of postwar music theatre and opera, in which I think there may be discerned four distinct tendencies:

1.  A rejection of opera as an impossibly compromised art form. This is the immediate response of postwar modernism, whose ambition is to effect a radical purging of the compromised rhetoric of western art music. "I wanted to make an experiment that set out from the "degree zero of writing" says Boulez, "For me this was an essay in Cartesian doubt: I wanted to question everything, to make a *tabula rasa* of the whole musical inheritance and begin again at degree zero..."[5] Even Schoenberg must be rejected for the lingering elements of romantic expressionism in his music: "c'est du Verdi sériale" was the response of one of Stockhausen's associates on first hearing Schoenberg's serial opera *Moses und Aron*. It is notable that, with the obvious exception of Boulez himself, the first generation of radical postwar modernists that centred on Darmstadt/Donaueschingen continued the Italo-German axis: Stockhausen, Berio, Nono, Maderna, Bussotti. In operatic production the equivalent to the puritanism of modernism is the move by Wieland Wagner to abstract Wagner, stripping his operas of historical and mythological associations. The development in the 1960s of forms of music theatre that explore the theatricality or ritual of musical performance, or the relationship between music and image or music and space, whilst sidestepping the operatic, is the modernist solution to the Drang nach Theater of almost all musicians – I'm thinking here of Cage,

Kagel as pioneers of the first kind of work, or the multi-media works of Stockhausen or Hans Dieter Schnebel.

2.   An effort by composers such as Hans Werner Henze in Germany or Luigi Dallopicola in Italy to reclaim opera for the humanist left, without any radical questioning of its basic theatrical or musical forms. In opera production this response is represented by the neo-realism of Visconti or the socialist humanism of Felsenstein in East Germany. By the 60s leftist modernists such as Luigi Nono or in Germany Berndt Aloys Zimmermann, are attempting a more radical retrieval of opera for both the left and modernism. The problem they are faced with, and cannot overcome, is that modernism – whether Serialist-Darmstadt or Stravinskian-neo-classical – is inherently anti-humanist.

3.   Diversion of the operatic into other media – most obviously film. This seems to have occurred primarily in Germany, where by the 1970s film has become the main medium for a re-engagement with Germany's suppressed history. I'm thinking of Alexander Kluge, Werner Schroeter, and Herzog, above all Syberberg. Syberberg's quasi-Wagnerian epic *Hitler a film from Germany* is described by film historian Anton Kaes as "the rebirth of film from the spirit of music and theater."[6] For Syberberg film becomes the essential medium for the remythologisation of German history against the bureaucratisation and americanisation of East and West Germany respectively. One might cite here also the controversial paintings of Anselm Kiefer, also effecting a problematised re-engagement with German history and myth.

4.   Writing about the New German cinema of the 70s, Wim Wenders says "I speak for everyone who, in recent years, after a long barren period, has started producing sounds and images again, in a country that has a profound mistrust of sounds and images about itself."[7] At some point one has to re-engage with the history and meaning of sounds as well as images. This entails a rejection of the deliberate amnesia of high modernism. Boulez had argued for modernist abstraction that "strong, expanding civilizations have no memory; they reject, they forget the past."[8] But by the mid-70s in Germany the suppression of historical memory had erupted in political violence. As Heiner Müller argued: "In order to get rid of the nightmare of history, you have first to acknowledge its existence. You have to know about history, otherwise it comes

back in the old-fashioned way, as nightmare, Hamlet's ghost. You have to analyse it first and then you can denounce it, get rid of it. Very important aspects of our history have been repressed for too long."[9] From the late 70s there is a more direct critical re-engagement with the meanings of music and the operatic in both Germany and Italy. The forms of opera itself remain problematic, but composers and theatre artists are seeking to address them.

Luciano Berio's *La vera storia* of 1982 is a direct attempt to engage critically with the forms of 19th-century Italian opera; it is, in effect, a deconstruction of Verdi's opera *Il trovatore* in which Berio acknowledges that the modernist composer "should always be aware that most of the operatic conventions, characters or ingredients on which he is so keen to turn his back are unavoidably present, in more or less explicit form, on stage... Every form of musical theatre played out within an opera house is also, inevitably, a parody."[10] In late 70s Germany Heiner Goebbels approaches the problem more obliquely. Goebbels, now 50, studied sociology in Frankfurt from 1972, where he encountered the critical theory of the Frankfurt School and became associated with the leftist grouping called the Frankfurter Spontis, whose members included Danny Cohn Bendt and Joschka Fisher. The Spontis were one of a number of post-68 movements who combined a Frankfurt School critique of the administered society of consumerist capitalism with a determination to make Germany face its Nazi past.

Werner Herzog has said that his generation "had no fathers, only grandfathers". Goebbels located just such a grandfather figure in Hanns Eisler. Eisler, renegade pupil of Schoenberg, friend and collaborator of Brecht and committed socialist, offered Goebbels a model for a politically engaged music practice, a possibility that he feels had simply not been available for musicians of the 1968 generation. Through Eisler Goebbels felt able "to connect to a German musical history of resistance".[11] Of particular importance to Goebbels was Eisler's dialectical understanding of the relationship between music and society, encapsulated in the phrase "Fortschritt und Zurucknahme" (progress and recuperation). Goebbels himself explains, "If you want to develop one element you have to accept the convention of another to be able to communicate", and Goebbels believes strongly in the necessity of engaging with existing musical forms and sounds. "I mistrust the idea that it is possible to be entirely original. We are all full of memories, full

of history, full of taste which is not ours; which comes from the past."
He also acknowledges a responsibility to his material, always considering the social and historical meanings of the musical gestures he draws
on, and recognising that certain forms or sounds may carry too much
baggage. He admits, for instance, that a part of his difficulty in setting
German words to music (he almost invariably uses spoken text in his
works) is because sung German – whether of opera or Lieder – "always
has a reference back, a connotation."

Film historian Thomas Elsaesser notes a prevalent *angst* in
German films of the 70s, suggesting that directors "situate history
between apocalypse and tabula rasa".[12] There is a similar sense of
"angst" in Goebbels's work, which often seems to convey a world
existing on the edge of disaster, most obvious in his sustained
engagement with texts by Heiner Muller, whose bleak dramatic
monologues are invariably located under the shadow of an "unknown
catastrophe", or in "a landscape beyond death".[13] Much of Goebbels'
music sounds like the soundtrack to some lost *film noir* of European
history. Goebbels himself acknowledges that his outlook is coloured by
the need to "face German history".

Goebbels found that he could deal with the, for him, still highly
problematic relationship of music and language after encountering the
strident, expressionist declamation of German new-wave bands such as
Einstûrzende Neubauten. Alongside his work with the art-rock band
Cassiber throughout the 80s Goebbels made radio dramas in which he
wove sound, documentary material, literary texts and vernacular
musics into complex montages. Eventually in the early 90s Goebbels
started to make theatre works which extended his methods to include
space and light. These are works that reflect on European culture and
history, employing an unembarrassed theatricality. Although
Goebbels professes himself uninterested in opera, and hardly ever
employs the classically trained voice, his most recent theatre piece
*Landscape with Distant Relatives* is described by him as an opera and
includes a chorus.

Similar tendencies are evident in the work of Goebbels' exact
contemporary the Italian composer Giorgio Battistelli. Battistelli
recounts how in the early 70s he was urged by his teachers to purge his
music of rhetoric and expressivity. But Battistelli's theatre works deliberately exploit both rhetoric and expression, and he contrasts two
forms of music-theatre which he describes as the "anorexic" and the

"bloated".[14] Like Goebbels he generally avoids vocal lyricism, preferring to use spoken or declaimed language for its associative qualities. His most striking theatre work *Experimentum Mundi* combines spoken texts about artisan production from the *Encyclopedie* with an orchestra consisting of actual artisans working their materials.

Paradoxically, the more direct re-engagement with lyricism has come from theatre artists such as Christophe Marthaler whose theatre piece *Murx* directly tackled the relationship between German romantic music and the holocaust. In Italy Societas Raffaello Sanzio have made works whose engagement with the disaster of 20th century history seems to demand a pushing of theatrical languages to the limits of the operatic – to those places where the relationship between opera and pathology becomes obvious. In their adaptation of Celine's *Voyage au Bout de la Nuit* the first person narration is sung throughout by the three female performers in a kind of reinvention of Monteverdian recitative.

Each of these examples deals with some aspect of the inheritance of the operatic in post-war Europe, and it does so with a sense of critical engagement with the problematics of opera itself.

## Notes

1. Leonardo Sciascia, *The Day of the Owl* (Granta, London, 2001), p. 36 (original publication: 1963).

2. Giuseppe Mazzini, "On Historical Drama" (1830); "The Philosophy of Music" (1833); "On Italian Literature Since 1830" (1837).

3. For detail, see Paul Ginsborg, *A History of Contemporary Italy: Society and Politics, 1943-1988* (Penguin, London, 1990).

4. Marx, 18th Brumaire of Louis Bonaparte, 1852/1869.

5. Quoted in Michael Kurz, *Stockhausen: A Biography* (Faber & Faber, London, 1992), p. 33.

6. Anton Kaes *From Hitler to Heimat: The Return of History as Film* (Cambridge, MA: Harvard, 1989), p. 45.

7. Wim Wenders, *On Film: Essays and Conversations* (Faber & Faber, London & Boston) p. 100.

8. Kurz, p. 33.

9. Heiner Muller, *Germania* (Semiotexte, New York, 1990), p. 24.

10. Berio, "Of Sounds and Images", *Cambridge Opera Journal*, Vol.9, No.3, 1997, pp. 295-299.

11. All quotations by Goebbels taken from interview with author, November 2002.

12. Thomas Elsaesser, *New German Cinema: A History* (BFI, London, 1989), p. 217.

13. Heiner Muller, *Theatremachine* (Faber & Faber, London & Boston, 1995), p. 55, 133.

14. Interview with author, July 2002.

# 12

## Intimate Interactions

### Spatializing a Postmodern Sociology of Theatre

**Rebecca Caines**

## Riding the Lines

It's 1997 and I am running seriously late for a train. Not long in Sydney and hearing rumours of muggers on every corner I rush into Redfern station, clutching my purse and eyeing every stranger with mistrust. I am pushed through the barriers by a huge impatient crowd waiting to catch the 4.27pm Penrith via Enfield express. I vaguely catch out of the corner of my eye, a girls' dance troupe competing with a saxophone player on another platform, but my view is partially obscured as two silent Tangara trains blur by, expressionless faces staring out at me and at each other as they pass. For the next four hours, I wander Western Sydney, on and off trains and platforms and station malls, watching infinitely slow martial arts. I hear about a Cambodian man's journey to Australia, and watch as a harried-looking man yells into a mobile phone, his words indistinguishable amongst the growls and squeaks of the loudspeakers. I look at someone's family photos as a drunken angry war veteran yells at me for not understanding what war is. A young group of Vietnamese Australians want to share an elaborately masked myth with me, but I am distracted by a near accident on the road nearby and end up buying a Thai pork bun from an impatient old woman at a newsagents' stand. At Granville, I share hot chips from a huge greasy bundle with a group of people from my carriage as a Koori Hip Hop Band gets the commuters to join in on a chant of "Pauline

Hanson Sucks" at the top of their lungs. A typical afternoon on Sydney public transport? Actually it was my experience of the 1997 Urban Theatre Projects theatre event *Trackwork*, a performance that spanned six train stations and the surrounding areas, interacting fluidly with the everyday workings of Western Sydney life, blurring the line between performance and social process. It was certainly an example of contemporary performance that played with the nature of theatre, deliberately undermining any possibility of a unified interpretation. Yet, *Trackwork* was also a vibrant metaphor for contemporary community in practice, one which questioned and disrupted the politics and spatiality of contemporary power relations.[1]

## Sociological Spaces

Sociology can be seen as "the study of the development structure and functioning of human society."[2] Community formations, like those utilized in *Trackwork*, and their utilizations inside contemporary performance are part of what I call sociological space, that territory in which we form our networks of social interactions, and in which we store our memories and histories of the networks and interactions of the past, present and future. Sociological space is a zone of control and of subversiveness, of rigidity and transience, of ownership and reinscription, of connection and rupture, but at all times one potentially open to challenge and transformation. Sociological surfaces are thus, contestable surfaces and sociological terrains, as frequently charted by theatre theorists, such as Maria Shevtsova,[3] are a particularly rich source of creativity and politics for performance artists. In my wider work, I go on to explore other contestable performative spaces, including the physical material spaces we move within, the conceived spaces we grid and locate, and use to control, represent and map, and the virtual and imagined spaces we form in our minds. In this larger project, I explore how contemporary performance, as a zone of these contestable intersecting spatialities, is open to a new sort of political challenge. This politics in performance is not made from spatial additions to linguistic challenges, but instead is a politics that is constituted out of spatiality itself, a respacialization, if you like of the performing avant-garde.

In this short work, I do not have room to go into the complex field of performance sociology or my new work on the spatialities of post-modern sociology. Instead, I will focus on some of the problems inherent within attempts to address twenty-first century politics. This work maps the interrelation that occurs in sociological space between contemporary community formations and the work of the 'guerrilla' artist. I trace how 'guerrilla' artists might be able to foreground a particularly contemporary sense of community in performance; to simultaneously engage with the strangeness and wonder of everyday living whilst encouraging contradiction, difference and social challenge in both the process, form and the content of their work.

This paper is a recontextualization of new work, recently published in *Australasian Drama Studies* journal, April 2003, under the title *Guerrillas in our Midst: Contemporary Guerrilla Performance and the Post-Structural Community*

## Shifting Notions of the Guerrilla Artist

With one foot in the art world and the other in the world of political activism and community organizing, a remarkable hybrid has emerged in the mid-1970s, expanded in the 1980s and is reaching critical mass ... in the 1990s. This new activist cultural practice is the subject of conferences and articles, museum exhibitions and museum sponsored community based projects. It provides the impetus and programme for several magazines and organizations, and it has also led to much critical and theoretical speculation, raising many unanswered questions...[4]

When I think of a 'guerrilla', I think of an activist or soldier affiliated with a radical political cause, someone who is not afraid of the sudden violent action, someone who can appear suddenly without warning and then disappear as suddenly; perhaps someone who lives as a nomad and who fights in small, zealous groups. The etymology is Spanish, a mutation from "guerra", war to "guerrilla", little war. The Oxford suggests it's an "irregular war", by "small groups (usu. political)" perhaps "acting independently"[5]. Mao Tse Tung and Che Guevara both wrote passionate manifestos and then became (in)famous heroes of this "terrifying new form of fighting on a massive scale"[6]. It is a notion that suggests camouflage, mobility and subterfuge and at times, fanaticism. In today's political climate, it has uncomfortable insinuations of terrorism, violence and retaliation.

The phrase 'guerrilla art' rose to particular prominence in the 1960s and 1970s, as a description of the student or artist-led street protest, particularly around issues such as the Vietnam War. In theatre, the term 'guerrilla' was often used by theorists, to refer to the low budget, impromptu, left-wing political performance, that would occur at public sites as a way of 'educating' the public and disseminating opinions and in some cases aiming to inspire direct political blockades or mass protests. Companies discussed in Lesnick's 1973 anthology of American guerrilla theatre included mostly street theatre and counter culture companies, whilst Filewod and Watt sum up 1960s and 70s guerrilla art as "worker student alliances...with a romantic tendency towards Marxist analysis".[7]

These guerrilla artists had clear political objectives and attempted to directly affect the votes of citizens and the policies of governments. This particular type of oppositional street performance can be traced today in the work of environmental and social justice agencies such as Greenpeace and in student protests across the world.[8] Guerrilla is, however, still a seductive term, particularly for modern avant-garde artists, who feel their mission is to disturb and disrupt through radical arts action. Perhaps due to its military and subversive connotations, it offers artists a way of naming themselves onto the cutting edge, placing themselves in the front line of artistic protest and disruption. Despite its colourful history, however, 'guerrilla art' is still a phrase that is indiscriminately used and under defined.

There have been some attempts, through what Nina Felshin calls 'activist art' to locate a changing historical notion of what we might call 'guerrilla tactics'. "Beginning in the late 1960s, however, changes began to occur in the arts world that reflected changes in the 'real world'. The hybrid cultural practices...ha[ve] evolved from these changes. Shaped as much by the 'real world' as by the art world, activist art represents a confluence of the aesthetic, socio-political, and technological impulses of the past twenty five years or more that have attempted to challenge, explore or blur the boundaries and hierarchies traditionally defining the culture as represented by those in power. This cultural form is the culmination of a democratic urge to give voice and visibility to the disenfranchised, and to connect art to a wider audience. It springs from the union of political activism with the democratising aesthetic tendencies originating in Conceptual art of the late 1960s and early 1970s."[9]

Very little work, however, has been done to synthesize or explore the specific characteristics of contemporary late twentieth and early twenty-first century guerrilla art. Those described as guerrilla artists, most recently, have ranged from activists that undertake poster and sticker campaigns, graffiti or media heists[10] to those, who construct radical internet websites or attempt invasive hacking[11] or those who have been especially confronting in their performance techniques.[12] There are also links between the 1960s notion of guerrilla art and the anti-globalization and anti-corporate techniques of the ad-busters and culture-jammers, those who use and manipulate corporate brands, marketing campaigns and design features to create art, fashion and media that exposes the dubious human rights records, employment abuses and unsavoury environmental practices of large multinationals.[13]. There is also an increasing tendency in performance theory to call any piece that is controversial or mobile in form as 'guerrilla art'. Hill and Paris, for example, in their work *Guerrilla Performance and Multimedia* group together thirty years of contemporary performance practice and live art, from Birringer's multimedia dance to Stellarc's cyborg explorations of the body, from the boundary breaking performance of Rachel Rosenthal and the artists from the Wooster group to the fragmented museum pieces of Guillermo Gomez Peòa, and title it 'guerrilla art' without any description of what guerrilla theatre is or how it interacts with the complexities of post-modern politics.[14]

If we sum up the notion of politics, not as some sort of engagement with how individuals work with governments, but instead as the manoeuvring, establishing or contesting of power relations, where contemporary power are the forces that shape and construct us and which we use to shape and construct the way we live and the way we act, then of all the guerrilla arts, theatre has particularly immanent political possibilities. It may prove a useful start in mapping the territory of the contemporary guerrilla artist to both broaden and refine the lens and define a piece 'guerrilla', if it effectively contests power relations in its specific cultural context in any form and if it directly engages with this contemporary politics in ways that are localized, intimate, unexpected and difficult to control.

General characteristics of contemporary guerrilla performance which separate it from any art with a political edge, seem to include a desire to radically confront and challenge society without necessarily replacing one major narrative with another, a particular affinity with the actual realities of peoples' existence and content that contains personal experiences and histories. Twenty first century guerrilla art is also dependent on some sort of ability to manipulate space, particularly public space in interesting and manifold ways, the ability to simultaneously produce multiple texts and performance forms and the utilization of multiple entities independently working within the larger arena of the performance event, whether these entities be individuals with distinct and separated agendas or self contained artistic or social groups, such as the community dance groups, choirs, bands, religious organizations and youth and physical theatre companies that appeared in Urban Theatre Project's *Trackwork*. Nina Felshin maps out the edges of the growing field when she states: "...these artists...are all characterized by the innovative use of public space to address issues of socio-political and cultural significance, and to encourage community or public participation as a means of effecting social change."[15]

Contemporary guerrilla performance does not seem to have to be anonymous, on the street or directly oppositional to the current state government to be guerrilla. In fact, what we could name contemporary guerrilla politics has been documented inside organizations that have state support or performed in mainstream theatre venues. The guerrilla artist's main contemporary function, instead, seems to be to probe into the sociological space, into the actual personal narratives, spatial histories, local catastrophes and everyday injustices to citizens. This guerrilla activism influences and interrupts the ways that individuals interact with each other and with the powers that shape their lives and does so in a manner that creates confrontation and challenge. Guerrilla art continually shifts its strategies in order to cope with the particular political milieu, and in this climate of post-modern dispersed and nomadic power structures, it thus becomes dispersed and nomadic in order to continue to dispute and to disrupt.

As Rebecca Schneider notes:

> Power is neither visible nor stable, thus effective resistance must make use of the invisible and unstable... direct political action today necessitates invisibility and non-locatability, but pedagogical actions can slide into the space between location and dislocation, visibility and invisibility.[16]

In Australia, I might map a particularly nomadic guerrilla art arising out of alternative lifestyle events and festivals such as, Woodford or Canberra Folk Festivals, ConFest or Stamping Ground Dance Festival and in the raves, electronic and hip hop music movements and student-led street demonstrations, particularly the activities of anti-globalization and anti-corporate collectives and organizations like Reclaim the Streets. In Australian theatre, I see an attention to sub-cultural or non-oppositional politics in the works of youth theatre companies, particularly in regional Australia,[17] urban community companies like Urban Theatre Projects, and work curated for Peter Sellars's 2002 Adelaide Festival of the Arts, all of which radically disrupt ideas of personal and social identity by replacing the single narrative with the multiple whilst engaging with the personal histories of the participants. Internationally a return to public art, to performative citizen protest and to site-specific mutations of space and identity, based in a history of activist art and rising out of the community movements of the 1980s and the hybridizing intercultural and interdisciplinary multimedia performance explosions of the 1990s, is a field rapidly receiving growing critical attention. Before we can analyse the strategies, which some of these 'guerrilla' practitioners use, it is first better to place them in context with the significant and disturbing problems that face artists attempting to engage in some sort of politics in the postmodern sphere.

## Performing 'Postmodern' Politics?

Baz Kershaw notes that "Historians and critics [and to his list, I might add theatre theorists and practitioners] have habitually fought shy of committing themselves to unambiguous claims about the possibility of a more extensive socio-political efficacy of performance", and I agree with him when he asks, "surely such efficacy is the fundamental purpose of performance?"[18] Kershaw used a model of ideological trans-action in his work to effectively map the direct political effect of certain types of 1970s, 1980s and 1990s local community theatre on the British voting citizen. In order to map the political actions of contemporary companies in countries like Australia that embrace a different set of fluid performance forms and technologies, we must, however, look at the dispersed political conditions which mark the post-modern sphere, and then look at the ways that by foregrounding intimate social arrangements, contemporary performance events like *Trackwork* have allowed individuals, inside sociological space, outside the hierarchies of local, state and federal structures, to question their identities, form unexpected and transient strategic alliances, disrupt the governing strategies that structure their lives and reclaim the differences that both separate and connect us all.

As Jessica Kulnych notes:

> To say that the world is now "post-modern" is to highlight funda-
> mental changes in both the condition of the contemporary world,
> and in our attitude towards this world. The unique political and
> economic configuration of advanced, welfare state capitalism, the
> subtlety and ubiquity of disciplinary power, the simultaneous solidi-
> fication and fracture of personal and collective identity, and the
> advance of technology and bureaucracy combine with an increasing
> philosophical skepticism toward truth and subjectivity to produce a
> world that is often incompatible with our traditional understandings
> of democracy. These fundamental changes inevitably alter the meaning
> of basic democratic concepts, such as political participation."[19]

Placing oneself inside such theoretical territory, in order to debate
contemporary politics, is an activity that produces a peculiar type of
nausea, inertia and vertigo. Governmentality theorists have shown us
the ways in which the forces that shape our lives are not sovereign or
placed easily in a hierarchical progression, but rather are made up strategies that shape the language we understand as rational, the actions we
understand as possible, the knowledge we count as expert fact and the
choices we believe are desirable. Kulynych goes on to note:

> As Foucault explains, what was formerly considered apolitical, or
> social rather than political, is revealed as the foundation of technol-
> ogies of state control. Contests over identity and everyday social life
> are not merely additions to the realm of the political, but actually
> create the very character of those things traditionally considered
> political...Thus it is contestations at the micro-level, over the intri-
> cacies of everyday life, that provide the raw material for global
> domination, and the key to disrupting global strategies of
> domination. Therefore, the location of political participation extends
> way beyond the formal apparatus of government, or the formal
> organization of the workplace, to the intimacy of daily actions and
> iterations.[20]

It is the diffuse and at times seductive nature of capital power that
has made it so difficult to contest through the deconstruction of traditional notions of 'the community'. We may, however be able to see
possibilities for a different type of localized group politics and through
understanding the intersection between contemporary ideas of

community and performance, begin to understand how contemporary guerrilla artists, particularly in Australia, engage with and bypass problems of post-modern political resistance.

## Intimate Insurrections: Performative Community Spaces

Performance and community are interwoven processes, as the creation of a piece of performance requires the formation of a complex and influential 'performance community', made up of the artists and audience and the surrounding historical and social context.[21] Performance also foregrounds multiple other community narratives inside each event, both inside the script/focus material, and through the actions and contexts of each member of the performance community, themselves members of multiple other communities. A performance event *can* aim to foreground the characteristics of a traditional community, the appeal of spontaneous unmediated communities within structures which will promote a sense of continuity, stability and cohesion, but in terms of political challenge, such an event unfortunately strives for what Anna Yeatman calls "… the kind of agency that requires to be expressed as singular, unambiguous and, preferably, reasoned purpose." The problem with this sort of community structure is, despite its appeal, 'it does not easily accommodate ambivalences, ambiguities, contradictions, incoherencies, multiplicities of intention and purpose and… For this to occur, the politics of choice and representation latent within the heterogeneity of perspectives and interests must be suppressed.'[22]

In contrast, contemporary performance companies, like UTP, can embrace the transience and partiality of a much more contemporary understanding of community, celebrating radical difference and connecting people in social formations that shift and change. This type of event embraces theatre's potential to become what Hakim Bey, problematic theorist, who has recently been embraced by Rave and Alternative living movements, famously calls a T.A.Z. or Temporary Autonomous Zone, a "… guerrilla operation which liberates an area (of land, of time, of imagination) and then dissolves itself to re-form elsewhere/else when before the State can crush it)".[23]

The spatiality of these guerrilla performers is one of sliding, relocating, sociological landscapes. Perhaps why the image of the UTP production of *Trackwork* lingers and recurs throughout my work is due to the fact that it so clearly represents for me the ways community can operate in the contemporary sphere. First, through the engagement of multiple spaces on trains, platforms and streets, multiple performance and advocacy groups and multiple stories and fragmented imagery, the performance highlighted the way that contemporary individuals are involved simultaneously in various and sometimes contradictory communities, but not limited to communities of geographical location, networks of voluntary interest and association including interests in popular culture, communities of social inter grouping, such as ethnic, sexuality, disability; urban neighbourhood networks and groups of similar socio-economic disadvantage. It showed how individuals gain different benefits from different communities, and in some cases how community formations can trap individuals, limiting their options for development. It also foregrounded the creation of the community initialized by the performance event itself, that made up of the performers, the technical and creative crew, the paying audience and the commuters and passers-by intimately interacting together, bringing isolated people corporally together, without imposing a rigid structure on their behaviour.

Second, through the presentation of fragmented and partial narratives, constantly interrupted by competing groups, the noise and activity of public spaces and the practicalities of travelling between and through performance spaces, the event re-emphasized the transience and partiality of community formations, created around a set of issues or questions, but dissolving, mutating and reforming as individuals and their desires shift and disperse. Through the mixing of fantasy and biographical stories, the piece encouraged the re-imagination of identity, particularly the re-imagination of what it means to live in Australia in the late twentieth and early twenty-first century. Through the construction of many different ideas of Western Sydney reality, it highlighted that identity and society are constructed notions, and thus are open to reconstruction.

Third, *Trackwork* brought audience into spaces that they perhaps would never have seen, the often crowded and colourful train stations and platforms, the street malls that mix multicultural food and clothing with mass produced mainstream retail outlets, the busy suburban streets, the deserted concreted parks, grafittied toilet blocks and empty parking lots of a large area of Western Sydney. The performance event not only confronted the audience with narratives from the performance groups engaged in the performance event, but also with the everyday lives and narratives of the people, who inhabit those public spaces, creating a mix of 'real' and 'performed', 'scripted' and unscripted personal stories and confronting people with lives and experiences that were radically different to their own.

Overall the facilitators aimed and succeeded in creating spaces in which the simultaneously subjugated and celebratory voices of a host of different communities could be heard, foregrounding other ways of seeing, hearing, eating, travelling, working and living. They showed up the imbalances in economic development between communities, highlighted the hypocrisies inherent in some of the fears and anxieties of Australians and disrupted a coherent notion of one Australian identity with the simultaneous foregrounding of multiple different realities.

The site-specificity of Urban Theatre Projects performances does not select a theatrically laden space and perform in it, but rather combines performance and everyday experience in ways which allow the space to perform back, forcing audience to not just watch but to take part in the workings of everyday living together. This was also evident in the Urban Theatre Projects more recent works, including the 2002 Adelaide Festival productions of *The Cement Garage* and *The Longest Night*, created with the members of the local communities, discussing issues of domestic and political disturbance, performed inside the community cultural centre at dusk whilst the users of the centre continued their daily business.

The performance forced participants to remap the city, to move through spaces and to cross multiple borders. Eugene Van Erven in his chapter on Urban Theatre Projects, in his 2001 *Community Theatre: Global Perspectives*, cites two inner city youngsters on their way to Stanmore for a barbecue, who ended up following *Trackwork* all the way to Granville. "We weren't imagining to find anything out West, but we discovered it was really good to get out here."[24] As Burvill also notes in his 2001 article on Urban Theatre Projects, some "... participants [in Urban Theatre Projects production events] have to travel from the inner city... thereby, they are also required to embark upon a class journey across social boundaries."[25] The audience for *Trackwork* stood in long queues and were jostled in hot carriages, rushed to avoid congested traffic, had conversations with the other commuters, avoided the syringe in the public toilet, laughed at the antics of excited kids and cheered the buskers. The event allowed locals and visitors together to experience the specific contrasts that mark the spaces traversed by the performance event.

Although there is certainly not room in this paper, it is possible, through the work of post-modern sociologists, feminist post-structural theorists and cultural philosophers, to further sketch the territory for this model of community not based on the traditional characteristics of unity, stability, continuity or location, but rather based on strategic alliances, arbitrary closures, the mixing of rational and irrational social formations, the promotion of radical difference and the construction of transient spaces for imagination and the reformation of personal and social identity. All of these are potentially radical guerrilla actions.

Contemporary communities and the guerrilla performances, which embrace them, highlight how inside existing sociological terrains there are a host of intimate spaces where contradiction, confrontation and disagreement are not just tolerated, they are encouraged. Perhaps, most excitingly, these developing cultural practices have the potential to form new sociological 'gaps', cracks and fissures, in which subjugated ways of speaking and knowing may be heard, and in which, eventually, new specialities of social challenge may be born.

## Notes

1.  Rebecca Caines, 'Guerrillas in our Midst: Contemporary Guerrilla Performance and the Post Structural Community', *Australasian Drama Studies*, No. 42, April 2003, p. 75.

2.  Alan Bullock and Stephen Trombley, *The New Fontana Dictionary of Modern Thought*, (UK: Harper Collins Publishers, 1999), p. 797.

3.  See Maria Shevtsova, 'The Sociology of the Theatre', Parts One, Two and Three, appearing in *New Theatre Quarterly*, Vol. 5, No. 17, 18 and 19, 1989.

4.  Nina Felshin, *But is it Art? The Spirit of Art as Activism*, Seattle: Bay Press, 1995, p. 9.

5.  R.E. Allen, *The Concise O.E.D.*, (Oxford: Oxford University Press), 1990.

6.  Captain B.H.Liddell Hart, (ed.), *Mao Tse-Tung on Guerrrilla Warfare and Che Guevara on Guerrilla Warfare*, (London: Cassell, 1962), p. 7.

7.  Alan Filewod and David Watt, *Workers' Playtime: Theatre and the Labour Movement, Since 1970*, (Sydney: Currency Press, 2001), p. 17.

8.  Baz Kershaw, 'Fighting in the Streets: Dramaturgies of Popular Protest, 1968-1989', *New Theatre Quarterly*, Vol.5, No. 14 (August 1997), pp.

255-27. In this article Kershaw traces a contemporary shift away from politics in theatre to theatricalization of politics in moments of political activism by organizations such as Greenpeace and Friends of the Earth.

9. Nina Felshin, *But is it Art? The Spirit of Art as Activism* (Seattle: Bay Press, 1995), p. 10.

10. For example, the high exposure poster, sticker and media art of the New York group Guerrilla Girls, who state in their website www.ggbb.org, that they are, "an anonymous, collaborative group of women artists of all disciplines.. [who] dubbed [themselves the "conscience of the art world". They began making posters in 1985, that "bluntly stated the facts of arts discrimination, and used humour to convey information, provoke discussion and to show that feminists can be funny". Guerrilla Girls Theatre was established in 1996 and Guerrilla Girls Broad Band in 1999.

11. For example, 'hacktivists' associated with groups, such as S11, Kulturejam and the mayday protesters, who work against organizations such as the World Bank, the International Monetary Fund and the International World Trade Conferences and associated corporations and individuals. For a history of hacktivism, see Naomi Klein, *No Logo* (Toronto: Random House, 2000).

12. For example, the work on eugenics and scientific experiments from New York company Critical Art Ensemble, see Rebecca Schneider, 'Nomadmedia', *TDR*, Winter 2000, Vol. 44, No. 4, p. 120.

13. For a history of adbusting and culture jamming see Naomi Klein, *No Logo* (Toronto: Random House, 2000).

14. Leslie Hill and Helen Paris *Guerrilla Performance and Multimedia*, (London and New York: Continuum Books, 2001).

15. Nina Felshin (ed.), *But is it Art? The Spirit of Art as Activism*, (Seattle: Bay Press, 1995), p. 9.

16. Rebecca Schneider, 'Nomadmedia', *op. cit.*, p. 120.

17. For example, in New South Wales, Shopfront, Erth, Lucky Dip, Greymantle Productions; in Western Australia, Laughing Gecko; and in Tasmania, Salamanca Youth Theatre.

18. Baz Kershaw, *The Politics of Performance*, (London: Routledge, 1992), p. 2.

19. Jessica J. Kulynych, 'Performing Politics: Foucault, Habermas, and Postmodern Participation', *Polity*, Vol.30 No.2 (Winter 1997), p. 315.

20. Ibid.

21. For an expanded view of the community of the performance event, see Richard L. Barr, *Rooms With a View, the Stages of Community in Modern Theatre*, (Michigan: University of Michigan Press, 1998) and Richard Schechner, *Between Theatre and Anthropology* (University of Pennsylvania Press, 1985)

22. Anna Yeatman, *Postmodern Revisionings of the Political* (New York: Routledge, 1994), p. 81.

23. Hakim Bey quoted in Graham St John, 'Alternative Cultural Heterotopia and the Liminoid Body: Beyond Turner at ConFest', *The Australian Journal of Anthropology*, Vol.12 No.1 (April 2001), p. 47.

24. Eugene Van Erven, *Community Theatre: Global Perspectives* (London: Routledge, 2001).

25. Tom Burvill, 'Urban Theatre Projects: Re-siting Marginal Communities in Outer Western Sydney', in Marc Maufort and Franca Bellarsi (ed.), *Siting the Other: Re-visions of Marginality in Australian and English-Canadian Drama* (Brussels and New York: PIE Lang, 2001), p. 139.

# 13

## Surviving the Monoculture

### Land, Language, Identity Corpses, Zombies or Life after McDonald's

**Tim Prentki**

The social injustice and widespread misery inflicted upon billions of people in all parts of the world as a result of the neo-colonial process which operates today under the label of globalisation is now recognised by many diverse groups who form themselves into resistance movements aimed at redressing some of the more blatant inequalities of the system. Less clearly understood are the longer-term consequences of the globalised monoculture for the survival of the human species. The argument running through this article concerns two parallel sets of processes, both of which are concerned with the functions of culture in relation to the socio-economic forces which shape the lives of all those presently living on this planet. One process centres on the transition from a colonial to a neo-colonial state that is often misleading labelled 'postcolonial'. This is a transition that takes its victims from conditions of slavery, imprisonment and other forms of physical subjugation – the colonisation of the body (corpse) – to a state in which the body's freedom is spurious because the mind which controls that body has had its deepest desires, its patterns of thought, the language of its dreams infiltrated by cultural controllers operating from some distant vantage point – the colonisation of the mind (zombie). I am describing this transition as the evolution of the victimised human being from corpse to zombie, which, while it looks like progress, may actually constitute a step backwards for the majority of the peoples of the earth. The second process is about the ways in which the response of colonised peoples has to adapt in order to survive the monoculture of neo-liberal capitalism. Colonisation was more or less successfully resisted at times and in places by the physical resistance of mass movements against the acts of the coloniser in their own lands. In the present age of globalisation such forms of resistance may be at best inappropriate and at worst futile since the strategies of the coloniser mostly have switched from military to cultural invasion.

In seeking a new kind of resistance I am suggesting that it is to the cultural rather than the military arena that we should look. Release from the dominant, neo-liberal paradigms of globalisation may emerge in future by moving from resistance to liberation, from dependence on the knowledge of the outsider to a new found confidence in indigenous knowledge systems; from the over-determinations of the trans-national corporations to the self-determination of the local community. The capacity of communities to maintain a dynamic cultural life in a constant state of dialogue or hybrid negotiation between inside and outside elements will be critical to the survival of the inhabitants of the globe. If there is to be life after McDonald's, it is to be sought among those indigenous cultures, which develop the means of survival without losing all contact with their histories, myths and former identities.

Theatre for Development can play a significant role in such a process through its capacity to combine reality with imagination, story with social analysis and equally through its formal flexibility which enables traditional, local elements of performance culture to be combined with other elements culled from colonial and globalised practices. The paradox at the heart of cultural identity is that if a particular form of identity lays itself entirely open to the socio-economic forces of the dominant model of globalisation, it will be destroyed; but if it attempts to cut itself off from outside influences, it will atrophy into slow death by heritage. Cultures survive by means of hybridisation but the process is implicated at every level in relations of power. Who determines which cultural practice is grafted onto the main stem of the dominant? Alternatively, how does the marginal culture decide which elements of external cultures can strengthen and be revived without inflicting damage upon identity? Land, language and patterns of social relationships are the sites upon which the practices of hybridity, like those of colonisation, are played out. Therefore I argue this as a significant site for cultural contestation.

First let us consider some of the factors behind today's cultural maps. The colonial project was unambiguous in its earliest intentions and its practices. The worth of the indigenous culture was weighed in the gold that could be carried back to the imperial centre; for example:

During the three or four months I was there, more than seven thousand children died of hunger, after their parents had been shipped off to the mines, and I saw many other horrors also. It was later decided to hunt down the natives who had fled into the mountains, and the subsequent hunting parties were responsible for carnage beyond belief. Thus it was that the whole of the island was devastated and depopulated, and it now affords, as we discovered on a recent visit, a moving and heart-rending spectacle, transformed, as it has been, into one vast, barren wasteland.[1]

Las Casas is here describing the genocide of the native population of Cuba by the Spanish conquistadors in 1512. At a stroke, the knowledge, culture, socio-economics and human understanding of a whole people were lost to the rest of mankind. Even in the act of stealing the mineral wealth that would underpin the domination of the European nations in the centuries to follow, the total store of what it is to be human was being reduced. Perhaps the very means of survival of the species was being wantonly cast away. The cultural memory of the Cuban so-called Indians was consigned to oblivion since corpses are only the bearers of those memories written into their flesh and bone and therefore destined to decay beyond the reclamation of culture.

The historical space that is officially designated as the colonial period is crammed with narratives which describe the various ways in which the 'great' nations of Europe set about the plundering of the earth accompanied by the enslavement, elimination or subjugation to varying degrees of non-European peoples. There are many records of European 'gains', 'achievements' and 'successes' during this period, but far fewer memorials or archives of the indigenous losses. Colonisation did not begin or end with the colonial period and all surviving records of human behaviour suggest that the inclination of one set of people to impose themselves by setting up colonies in the territories of another set constitutes part of what is involved in being human. Whether or not this was always the case, such behaviour is today what Edward Wilson has termed an epigenetic rule[2], that is a reflex response learned persistently over many ages to the point of ingrained habit indistinguishable from the rest of a human's genetic code. Even as children who are victims of parental abuse are vulnerable to becoming abusers of their own children as a result of internalising learnt behaviour, so the colonised are prone to identify even more marginalized peoples as targets of their own colonising tendencies. Just as we talk of cycles of violence or vicious circles, we can also speak of cycles of colonisation. This is the process depicted by John McGrath in his play *The Cheviot, the Stag and the Black, Black Oil*:

> ...the Red Indians were reduced to the same state as our fathers after Culloden – defeated, hunted, treated like the scum of the earth, their culture polluted and torn out with slow deliberation and their land no longer their own.... But still we came. From all over Europe. The highland exploitation chain-reacted around the world; in Australia the aborigines were hunted like animals; in Tasmania not one aborigine was left alive; all over Africa, black men were massacred and brought to heel. In America the plains were emptied of men and buffalo, and the seeds of the next century's imperialist power were firmly planted.[3]

The Highland Clearances were a concerted, deliberate assault upon a way of life which stood in the path of profit. The roots of the obstacle were land (crofting), language (Gaelic), and identity (the clan) and these were torn up and destroyed to create an un-peopled wilderness across which sheep might roam. The relationship between capitalism and colonialism is direct and clear. While capitalism did not invent colonialism, the need for cheap raw materials and labour to maximise profit gave an enormous motivating boost to conquest and slavery. The concept and practice of slavery was familiar to ancient Greek, Roman and Arabian societies amongst others, but it was only with the development of capitalism that it became a mode of production integrally linked to the economic well being of a nation. The Highlanders who were the victims of the Clearances became some of the colonial settlers of Canada, Australia and New Zealand, carrying with them the tattered remnants of language in the cultural memories of a life they had been forced to renounce. The lesson was clear. To succeed in this world it was necessary to behave like their oppressors: to seize land by force and to destroy the language and culture of any who resisted. From now on survival could only be permitted on the terms of the coloniser – assimilation or genocide; reservation or death.

In Canada the notorious Residential Schools were one of the means to achieve the subjugation and consequent eradication of a culture; to turn Native Americans, Cree and Mohawk, into Canadian citizens. Again land, language and culture were the key ingredients. Native children were forced to travel long distances from their homelands to get the scent of home out of their nostrils. They were beaten and ridiculed for speaking in their own tongue and they were required to dress as white children.

Today, Indians charge the Canadian government with destruction of their indigenous languages and cultures, and they denounce the government for failing to provide for Indian language and cultural instruction to their children as part of the school curriculum. Clearly, the Canadian government committed a great crime against Indians and their cultures when it forced Indian children at ages five to fifteen to attend residential schools where they were severely punished by their teachers if they spoke their indigenous language. The long years spent in residential schools subverted the parents' human right to teach the tribal language to their children. In consequence, the main vehicle of *Indian* cultural expression was critically impaired.[4]

In consequence the native population became alienated from the sources of their cultural identities without being allowed to participate effectively in the newly imposed one within which they were, at best, second-class citizens on the margins of society. By culture I understand the whole complex of significations through which an individual makes meaning out of the experiences of reality. Particular societies assign shared meanings to certain phenomena which then operate as a kind of shorthand enabling those who participate in that society to subscribe automatically to those meanings. Out of this process emerge a sense of belonging and a feeling of having an entitlement to a place in the world. The experience of colonised peoples all over the world has been of having that sense destroyed by an external force, which has not made good the loss. The consequence has been a slowly degenerative process of alienation and despair, which manifests itself in material and psychological deprivation. This has been the recent history of the native peoples of North America, chronicled in countless tales from the 'victim' culture of alcoholism, drug abuse and teenage suicide.

I move now to look at a particular instance with some reflection on the potential and place of cultural intervention. In the spring of 1999 one white Australian woman and one white English woman, students from the MA programme in Theatre for Development at King Alfred's College, Winchester, UK, took up the invitation from Darrel Wildcat to undertake their fieldwork project on a reserve of the Cree nation at Hobbema, on the wind-swept prairie south of Edmonton. The place took its name from a Dutch landscape painter of whose work it is reputed to be reminiscent. Thus is it mapped onto the cultural memory of the dominant, leaving the indigenous inhabitants to survive in a world they have not named? Tourists heading south on highway 2A from Wetaskiwin to Ponoka pass through Hobbema in about thirty seconds, scarcely aware that they are crossing the ancestral lands of four bands of Cree; lands floating on a sea of oil. Though the boom was past its peak, the legacy of cash in hand from the sale of leases to oil companies combined with the crisis of cultural identity was written in the high incidences of foetal alcohol syndrome, drug abuse, diabetes and teenage suicide. The recipe of consumption mixed with alienation, here as elsewhere, was producing deadly results. The colonised mind projected itself into poor self-esteem, which in turn transmitted itself into abuse of the body.

Among the specific initiatives the students engaged with during this placement was a project with some of the young people attending the Alternate School, and spending time with some of the older people who were inmates of the hospital on the reservation. The small group of young people who regularly participated in the School were among those whose self-image had been severely distorted by the ravages of drug or domestic abuse brought on by the desolation of living with cash in their pockets and without an image of who they are or whence they have come. For these young people the notion of school conjures up cultural memories of the front line in the battle to empty their souls and douse their spirits with the cold learning of the white man's world. The Alternate School was alternative in at least two important ways: it was as anti-authoritarian as was compatible with the base lines of health and safety and it sought to draw upon the students' knowledge and understanding of their own world, rather than displace these with an orthodox curriculum. The student facilitators worked on unlocking their innate creativity, which they then directed towards an identification with the School in the form of advertisements that they devised to encourage others to enrol for the coming Fall Semester. The process was, at times, painfully slow as the pupils tried to find and identify their authentic voices among the echoes, fragments and debris left to them by the invasive culture. But, in most cases, they were found and with their discovery came confidence, self-assertion and the beginnings of an identity in harmony with the tattered remnants of their cultural memories. The highlight of the process was the visit to the community radio station where the advertisements were recorded for later transmission. From being voiceless beyond the margins of their already marginal society, these young people, at least for a few moments, became, quite literally, the voice of their community.

The MA students also spent considerable time with two women in their late 50s who were suffering from terminal illnesses and who had been more or less left to their own devices for their remaining period of life. As trust developed conversations turned to stories of their traditional childhoods, brought up according to the rhythms of the hunter-gatherer way of life, following the paths of the Great Spirit. It soon became apparent that the stories and details which these women were sharing with the students, were largely unknown to the generation of their own children due to the forced intervention of the residential schools that caused a fatal break in the transmission of culture between generations. The plight of the two women seemed increasingly like a metaphor for the position of Native American culture. Although the hospital was strategically located at the heart of the reservation, its patients were forgotten people whose store of knowledge, stories, myths was destined to die with them, leaving that particular reservation, the Cree nation, and humanity in general all the poorer for having lost some of the means of creative, self-determined survival. Slowly, gradually over the weeks these women were persuaded to share the wealth of their understanding with the wider community through a performance. The combination of their infirmities and shyness ruled out conventional theatre but a story-telling form using shadow puppets and narrative was devised with the support of the students and this was augmented by musical accompaniment from a relative.

The performance took place inside the hospital one evening. The audience was composed of peers, the children's generation and the grandchildren's generation. The nature of the responses to the stories, which evoked a largely forgotten way of life, was markedly different from generation to generation. The narrators' own peers greeted the performance with a mixture of admiration for the bravery of the women mixed with delight at sharing the recollections of times when their identity and sense of self had been so much more secure. Simple incidents such as fetching fresh water from the stream and falling off a pony became imbued not only with the joyful glow of nostalgia but also with the increasing confidence and sense of solidarity emanating from shared cultural memory. By contrast, their children, the so-called 'lost' generation of residential school victims had difficulty relating to the event and appeared awkward and ill at ease with the ghostly echoes of a past that was and was not their own. The third generation, however, expressed great excitement and interest in the whole event and many in the audience used that evening as the stimulus from which to open dialogues with their grandparents. These dialogues became, in effect, not only channels of communication but also channels of resistance through which the young people could assert their right to an identity not dependent upon the dominant culture. Perhaps for the first time the notion of their place in the world, a world in which they had a right to exist, began to take shape as a creative and imagined reality, as a response to the challenge set down by Boldt:

> At present, more than half of Canada's Indian population are under eighteen years of age. Except for the 'expressive' aspect of their traditional cultures, most are receiving virtually no exposure to fundamental *Indian* philosophies and principles. Indian elders who should play an essential role of interpretation and transmission of traditional philosophies and principles have been largely relegated to symbolic functions, which they perform in a language most youths do not understand. Even the expressive culture is coming under increasing pressure, as it must compete with the values and appeal of North American pop culture for the minds of Indian young people.[5]

Citing this example is not to make an exaggerated claim for the possibilities of theatre but rather to suggest that this type of cultural intervention, arising from within the community and tapping sources of creativity, imagination and knowledge, because of its collective nature in performance, has the potential to foster the coming together and mutual confidence giving which is necessary to embark on such a formidable task as countering the forces of neo-liberal globalisation. The role of the external facilitator is critical in opening up a space of possibility, a fictive space grounded in the reality of lived experience. The very presence of the facilitator in the community can act as, what Brecht termed, a *Verfremdungseffekt* whereby a way of life which has become engrained by habit as 'normal' – alcohol, drugs, glue, arson, domestic violence – can be repositioned in the creative imagination through the evocation of alternatives. These alternatives must be proposed by the community not the facilitators but may only be articulated as a result of the counter-hegemonic intervention, which creates the space for articulation.

The facilitators were able to work in that location because they approached this community in a spirit of dialogue, curiosity and humility; the qualities identified by Paulo Freire as essential prerequisites to learning. Here was an outside intervention not aimed at selling Nike trainers or Molson beer but at releasing creativity for the benefit of the indigenous community. A counter-model of cultural intervention was used to assist in resisting the ravages of the dominant, neo-liberal model. A dialogue was made between the community which offered its context-specific knowledge and experience – in this case of traditions and cultural forms on the verge of extinction – and the facilitators who gave their skills in communicating through performance languages.

This dialogical process is the antidote to the imposition of the neo-liberal monologue, for which the case of McDonald's serves as a paradigm. The concept behind the golden arches is that the manufacturing process is so standardised that it can be exactly reproduced anywhere in the world, thereby effacing any contextual variety. One of the consequences of exposure to its culinary convenience and marketing of desire is that indigenous ways of cooking, eating and performing all the social rituals which accompany these activities can fall into disuse and then become forgotten.

The worldwide simplification of architecture, clothing, and daily objects assaults the eye; the accompanying eclipse of variegated languages, customs and gestures is already less visible; and the standardization of desires and dreams occurs deep down in the subconscious of societies. Market, state, and science have been the great universalising powers; admen, experts and educators have relentlessly expanded their reign. Of course, as in Montezuma's time, conquerors have often been warmly welcomed, only to unveil their victory. The mental space in which people dream and act is largely occupied today by Western imagery. The vast furrows of cultural monoculture left behind are, as in all monocultures, both barren and dangerous. They have eliminated the innumerable varieties of being human and have turned the world into a place deprived of adventure and surprise; the 'Other' has vanished with development. Moreover, the spreading monoculture has eroded viable alternatives to the industrial, growth-oriented society and dangerously crippled human-kind's capacity to meet an increasingly different future with creative responses. The last 40 years have considerably impoverished the potential for cultural evolution.[6]

This question of 'mental space' is crucial in relation to the effects of the globalisation of the media via satellite television and the internet. The control of the satellite networks in the hands of three or four multinational corporations means that the capacity to colonise and silence the minds of much of the world's population rests with a little club of media moguls who, from the safety and quiet of their air-conditioned offices, exercise a degree of power unprecedented in the history of civilisations, undreamt of by Alexander the Great, Ghengis Kahn or Queen Victoria. Aside from the small circle described by our own direct experience, our knowledge and understanding of the condition of the planet is largely in the hands of this tiny group who can, in effect, become the gatekeepers of our consciousness. The colonising of our minds is not a dangerous possibility but an ever-present reality of our daily lives.

Paradoxically, those who live beyond the reach of satellite broad-casting or who lack the means of consuming its offerings, by and large the poorest and most economically marginalized peoples of the earth, may be the ones best placed to maintain a living contact with their indigenous cultural forms. As with the exotic species of the natural world, those who have had the least contact with the all conquering monoculture may also be those from whom the rest of us can learn most about the elements necessary for human survival. But the precon-ditions for this learning to take place require a major change of perception on the part of both learners and teachers. Those of 'us' who have been educated within the paradigms of Western progress and civilisation have to set aside our most cherished norms and prejudices about our way of doing things in order that our minds become sufficiently open to receive a different kind of wisdom and under-standing. The closer one lives to the seats of power, both economic and political, the longer and more painful will be the journey to a new kind of knowing. Those who deal in the monologues of conventional Western wisdom – Alan Greenspan, Bill Gates, Ted Turner, Rupert Murdoch – will be the most intractable to engage in the processes of dialogue out of which a different way of organising cultures may emerge. For the teachers it is a problem of confidence, of finding a safe space from which to articulate their understanding of injustice and tyranny without fear of reprisal and intimidation. Where it happens, the process is inspiring to witness but to make it happen on a scale where fundamental changes to societies can take place is the immense challenge that faces those committed to the support of cultures of resis-tance and self-determination.

One small-scale example of such a process occurred during a training workshop I was co-facilitating for Save the Children (UK) in rural Andhra Pradesh, South India. The participants in this workshop were aged between seven and fifteen and came from two village communities. The majority of the young people were the children of Jorgins. These are women who were not allowed to get married because they had undergone, as young girls, a ceremony in which their lives were dedicated as brides to the Mother of All. In practice most girls who were dedicated to the temple in this way were either deemed unmarriageable by their parents due to mental or physical defects, or else were being kept in the parental home through this device to support parents in old age. It had been customary for higher caste men to take these women as additional sexual partners into their households until pregnancy, boredom or shame caused them to be cast out. Their children, denied the possibility of a father who would acknowledge their identity, thus find themselves as the most marginalized and vulnerable people in a patriarchal society that is already on the margins of existence. As facilitators we had been warned to be very circumspect about alluding to the children's status as the offspring of Jorgins only to find that the children themselves elected to show us their version of the ceremony of dedication, which their mothers had formerly undergone. Not only was this done as a demonstration in the workshop but also it was later built into the structure of the performance to the two villages. Whatever the outsiders' feelings about the place of these children within the local culture, the children themselves found an identity, a cultural location within their designation. The rest of their perfor-mance went on to present short scenes depicting the injustices they suffer in the areas of health, education and social security as a result of discrimination, offered as a challenge to their whole community in general and to the elders in particular.

These children, hitherto the least regarded members of their society, were for one evening the teachers of that community. They literally held centre stage and became the focus of attention. Rather than shrinking beneath the weight of that responsibility, they blossomed and grew visibly in confidence as they began to feel that their experiences were worthy of consideration by the whole community. Through art, previously unspeakable aspects of that community's life were articulated in public and, as a result, that community was furnished with the means of addressing contradictions, which were barriers to its self-actualisation. The Theatre for Devel-opment process was used as an intervention from which to begin a process of dialogue for self-determination that was not predicated on Western notions of progress that would lead the community in alien directions but rather on their own socio-cultural realities. Though this is a micro instance in an ocean of globalisation, it may be indicative of the possibilities for a type of resistance to the narratives of dominant movements.

During the historical period labelled 'colonial', the battle lines were clearly drawn, the maps shaded in, the battalions deployed, the gunboats despatched. Resistance usually resulted in death but the martyr knew what s/he was resisting. In the neo-colonial period of neo-liberalism the war is waged on all fronts and the weapons are more likely to be words than guns, though their effects (think of 'debt', 'free market', 'terrorism', 'democracy') are deadly on a much wider scale, maiming and destroying the lives of millions. As in all wars supply lines are crucial. In this war it is the flow of information through the control of satellite and computer technology, which gives the major advantage. Juggernauts marked 'Microsoft', 'CNN' and 'Coca Cola' thunder down the super-highway until they come to a halt in the minds of the silent majority for this is a battle of cultures and the prize is the minds of people defeated as citizens so they can be born again as consumers. What's different this time is that the defeated may not live to fight another day since the victory of the trans-national corporations is also the defeat of the planet, sacrificed to the ineffable logic of capitalism, sentenced to death by consumption.

The triumph of what is today commonly referred to as 'the West', absurdly sub-titled by Francis Fukuyama as 'the end of history', has been a long time in the making and owes much to accidents of geography, life-style and technology as Jared Diamond has so vividly demonstrated.[7] Perhaps the area to which Diamond gives insufficient attention is culture and the evolution of cultural forms into the dominant myths that rule the mind-sets of the powerful. For instance, his thesis clearly articulates the significance of what he calls 'farmer power', that process through which settlers were ultimately and inevitably destined to uproot, disperse or destroy hunter-gatherer civilisations but he does not follow the process through into the mythical realm by considering the role of the Creation story in legitimising farming at the expense of hunter-gathering. Adam and Eve forfeit the right to continue as hunter-gatherers in the Garden of Eden where all their needs are met by their environment and are banished to a life outside Eden where they can only subsist by tilling the soil. The consequences of imposing this myth upon peoples whose founding stories are to do with their harmonious relationship to nature rather than their alienation from it have been terrible in every part of the planet and nowhere more so than in the catalogue of genocide which was perpetrated under the banner of 'manifest destiny' by the European settlers in North America. The angry god of the Judeo-Christian tradition was more than a match for the gentle ways of Wakan Tanka (the Great Spirit of the Lakota nations) when it came to a straight fight:

> Forests were mowed down, the buffalo exterminated, the beaver driven to extinction and his wonderfully constructed dams dynamited, allowing flood waters to wreak further havoc, and the very birds of the air silenced. Great grassy plains that sweetened the air have been upturned; springs, streams, and lakes that lived no longer ago than my boyhood have dried, and a whole people harassed to degradation and death. The white man has come to be the symbol of extinction for all things natural to this continent. Between him and the animal there is no rapport and they have learned to flee from his approach, for they cannot live on the same ground.[8]

Today organisations such as Greenpeace and Friends of the Earth run sophisticated campaigns to alert us to the speed at which rain forests are being destroyed and animal and bird species driven to extinction. But even now the significance of the loss of different ways of being human has barely dawned on the descendants of those most responsible for inflicting the monoculture on the planet. Writing in *The Guardian* newspaper of Saturday, 25 May 2002, David Ward informs us that researchers from the University of Manchester predict that 90% of the world's languages will disappear by 2050. Nigel Vincent, Professor of Linguistics draws out the significance of this trend:

> If the youngest speakers of a language are in their forties, then the language will have gone when they die. When we lose a language, we lose something of the world's diversity. Every language is the repository of the culture of the people who speak it. When you lose the last speaker, you lose the people's cultural memory.[9]

Hugh Brody who spent years among different hunter-gatherer societies of North America, is unambiguous about the extent of the loss suffered by colonialism and its legacies:

> The world is also shaped by stories. What people feel, know and need to pass on from generation to generation has existed in words: words that speak of how the world began, of how humans emerged in it and found both places to live and ways to deal with one another.

> Words are entitlement to these places. The stories of farmers, including the Creation as described in Genesis, give meaning to their ways of life. The stories of hunter-gatherers give meaning to theirs. These are different meanings, different kinds of stories. The history of the one has dominated and, to a large extent, silenced the other.

> Many hunter-gatherer ways of knowing the world have disappeared, along with hunter-gatherer languages. These are rich and unique parts of human history that cannot be recovered. If the words are gone, so are the stories. A particular shape is lost forever. There are fears that hundreds more languages – many of them those of hunter-gatherers – will have disappeared within another generation. Each such case represents a harm that is inestimable: the cumulative loss of language constitutes a diminution in the range of what it means to be human.[10]

Language is the means by which thought is articulated; some would claim there is no thought without it. As languages are lost, the level in the potential reservoir from which the creative imagination may draw is lowered until it plunges to the crisis point of global mono-language: a language pool like a gene pool that has only one combination or set of structures on which to draw. When that moment is reached it is time to send in the clones who will be content to live in one system; neo-liberal capitalism, to speak one language; English, wear one make of trainers; Nike, and eat one kind of food; McDonald's. Given the resources stacked on the side of the globalisers conventional forms of resistance may be useless. However, this does not preclude the resort to the guerrilla warfare of popular culture, which appropriates elements from the culture of the dominant and repositions them in subversive contexts. There is a continuous process of reciprocal dialectic between the dominant and the popular. But the seesaw is tipping irrevocably towards the pole of the dominant as the cultural resources of the popular suffer terminal erosion.

As the earlier example of the Cree bands in Alberta demonstrates, many indigenous peoples have been cut off from their own traditions by the interventions of colonialism and left to live off the second-hand scraps from an alien culture while their own is buried under the dust of disuse and museum archives. Recently a research student, Rev. Dr. Elias Asiama, developed a fieldwork project among his own people, the Buem of north-eastern Ghana, as part of his doctoral thesis under the title *The Reinvention of Tradition*. The aim of the fieldwork was to use his 'outsider-insider' status with the community to stimulate a range of activities, some performative, some not, in order to investigate which of their almost vanished traditions were capable of resuscitation and worth resuscitating in terms of their potential value in restoring notions of identity, self-worth and the capacity for self-determination.

One of the strongest features to emerge from this process was the way in which one element of the reinvention process sparked off another, creating a chain reaction of interlinked activities, which encompassed almost every aspect of the cultural life of that community. For example, the Ohinto creation myth of the nation, being intimately linked to a formerly sacred site of the people now devalued by commercial land transactions, has been revived as a metaphor for the degradation of the environment stemming from the loss of the ancient bond between the people and their homelands. Other initiatives have witnessed the resurgence of traditional medical practices, indigenous crafts, dances, performances and erstwhile significant rites of passage of the community. But it should be made clear that this is not a heritage and tourism project. The importance of rediscovering these cultural expressions is for the people engaged in their processes; through their active interventions enabling them to judge for themselves whether or not there is life left in them. Culture never stands still and there can never be a going back to some supposedly virginal pre-colonial state. Yet these reinventions carry with them the possibility of evolving new hybrid forms from the dialogue between Western and indigenous, global and local. Part of the process is to enable a community to judge for itself which of the elements of the monoculture it wishes to exploit on its own terms, adapted to the needs of the local context. As long as the terms are dictated by the World Bank, the International Monetary Fund and the World Trade Organisation without regard for cultural diversity and local experience, they will always be an ugly, scarring imposition of the kind perpetrated by Structural Adjustment Policies.

So much of the cultural damage of colonialism has been exacerbated not ameliorated by the politics of post-independence in Africa, Asia and South America. That very nationalism which served as the rallying cry for the forces dedicated to resisting and removing the colonial presence has also been responsible for perpetrating those hierarchies and injustices which characterised colonial regimes. Perhaps this is not really surprising, given that it was the model of the nation-state, which the colonising powers of Europe exported across the globe. All too often independence has brought little more than a distorted mirror image of the governance of the former period with liberation reduced from a process to an event; a fixed and definitive historical moment: the Russian Revolution or the falling of the Berlin Wall. The repeated tying of our sense of identity to events leaves us cultural cripples, ill equipped to understand and move with the dynamic forces constantly shaping and reshaping our realities. One of the assets of Theatre for Development as a form is that it is essentially concerned with processes. For even where it makes use of performances, their value lies in their contribution to a process of social analysis owned by the community. Rather than create an event like a mark on a calendar, the TFD intervention should be aimed at articulating major contradictions in ways, which enable them to be addressed by the community as a spring-board to social transformation. Many of these contradictions are likely to arise from the effects of neo-colonialism as experienced in the realms of culture, economics and politics.

In the later chapters of his intellectually immense and compelling work, *Culture & Imperialism*, Edward Said turns his attention to the search for new paradigms which can take colonised nations beyond the neo-colonial impasse which is their common, current fate. In so doing his intuitions lead him into the territory of process and culture as a fluid form in a constant state of becoming:

> One has the impression in reading the final pages of *The Wretched of the Earth* that having committed himself to combat both imperialism and orthodox nationalism by a counter-narrative of great deconstructive power, Fanon could not make the complexity and anti-identitarian force of that counter-narrative explicit. But in the obscurity and difficulty of Fanon's prose, there are enough poetic and visionary suggestions to make the case for liberation as a *process* and not as a goal contained automatically by the newly independent nations. Throughout *The Wretched of the Earth* (written in French), Fanon wants somehow to bind the European as well as the native together in a new non-adversarial community of awareness and anti-imperialism.
>
> In Fanon's imprecations against and solicitations of European attention, we find much the same cultural energy that we see in the fiction of Ngugi, Achebe, and Salih. Its messages are we must strive to liberate all mankind from imperialism; we must all write our histories and cultures re-scriptively in a new way; we share the same history, even though for some of us that history enslaved. This, in short, is writing from the colonies co-terminous with the real potential of post-colonial liberation.... Once again it is culture and cultural effort that presage the course of things to come – well in advance of the cultural politics of the post-colonial period dominated by the United States, the surviving superpower.[11]

These 'poetic and visionary suggestions' are at risk of mental erosion by the monoculture that reduces our capacity to think outside the parameters of its own discourses. Imagination and creativity do not survive in a vacuum but depend upon the nourishment of cultural diversity that throws up many different, perhaps contradictory, ways of being human. Colonisation, as history repeatedly shows us, is resistible. Whether colonisation of the mind is also amenable to resistance and liberation is less certain. On a daily basis those minds that are inclined to dissent from the mainstream are given fewer and fewer resources from which to construct their opposition. As the force of the mainstream increases there are progressively fewer rocks and branches to support us as we attempt to swim against the current.

Those who work inside and on behalf of communities that attempt to resist the neo-liberal tide know well how painful is the struggle to move from resistance to liberation. In the resistance phase the contours of the enemy are clearly delineated and the community unites around the shared objects of hatred, scorn and 'otherness'. The danger is that resistance can become a fixed state of mind and being, so that the community allows itself to be defined by its opposition to neo-liberal imperialism. Rather than rediscovering and expressing its identity, it is the shadow or grotesque of that which it strives against. The liminal state of transition between resistance and liberation is depicted vividly in the cultural work of Derry Frontline as chronicled by Dan Baron Cohen through a collection of some of their plays, *Theatre of Self-Determination*. In his introduction he quotes from the programme note of their final production, elucidating the vital role of contradiction in an attempt to produce change, to develop out of a static state into a state of becoming:

> Because our cultural work has been so intimately linked to the everyday needs and development of the community, our plays and murals have themselves contributed to exposing the contradictions which might have served as useful barricades, but obstruct genuine freedom. In mapping out the often painful thresholds of change, our workshops have revealed how difficult it is to become democratic and how much personal courage is needed to 'decolonise the mind'. We have made mistakes in finding our way through this unchartered [*sic*] territory: but each mistake has yielded new knowledges, and confirmed that we are our own most precious resource for change.[12]

Self-determination is the key concept of the work and the plays depict a community which is struggling to find a way forward which answers their needs rather than those of all the external agencies – political, religious and military – which intervene constantly to manipulate the lives of those whom history has exposed to their control. At the climax of *Inside Out* the young man, Sean Doherty, makes the connection between personal and national self-determination with the clear implication that each individual is responsible for undertaking their own liberation:

> Abortion's as hard as armed struggle. But you know who calls it murder? Those who drain our life's blood slowly and deliberately over sixty years! Those who pay others to lie! And we don't see it. We don't talk about it. We keep it inside behind locked doors and sealed lips. It's the same everywhere! But we all pretend the world stops at the front door. It's not just when we're raided that the world breaks in! They're inside our heads! And until we change that they'll own us for life![13]

The situations explored in the plays of this collection repeatedly show that we cannot turn our backs on the monoculture and live undisturbed in our own little worlds. There are no hiding places; no places apart even inside our heads. This is the reality of globalisation. Liberation can only emerge out of resistance, not flight.

This analysis began in Cuba at the moment when the indigenous people and their culture was wiped out. It is fitting that it ends back in Cuba where the hybrid combination of exploiters and slaves who inherited the desolate island has now become one of the world's last bastions of resistance to neo-liberal imperialism. But Fidel Castro's reading of globalisation makes it clear that the nation's destiny cannot reside in resistance, important though that phase was. The neo-liberals have been quick enough to intervene to shore up their interests all over the world. Those who can imagine a different version of our future must emerge from behind the barricades and add their voices to the dialogue as Castro urged in a speech at the opening session of the South Summit, convened by the Group of 77 in Havana on April 12, 2000:

> Globalisation (sic) is an objective reality underlining the fact that we are all passengers on the same vessel – this planet where we all live. But passengers on this vessel are traveling (*sic*) in very different conditions.
>
> A trifling minority is travelling (*sic*) in luxurious cabins furnished with the internet, cell phones and access to global communication networks. They enjoy a nutritional, abundant and balanced diet as well as clean water supplies. They have access to sophisticated medical care and culture.

The overwhelming and suffering majority is travelling (*sic*) in conditions that resemble the terrible slave trade from Africa to America in our colonial past. That is, 85 percent of the passengers on this ship are crowded together in its dirty hold, suffering hunger, disease and helplessness.

Obviously, this vessel is carrying too much injustice to remain afloat; pursuing such an irrational and senseless route that it cannot call on a safe port. This vessel seems destined to crash into an iceberg. If that happened, we would all sink with it.

Two days later in the closing address, Castro finished off his trope by alluding to the dialectical relationship between First and Third Worlds instead of the conventional binary opposition, which has taken the planet close to extinction. Globalisation is a fact of life. But must globalisation lead to the irreversible triumph of the monoculture?

We are fighting for the most sacred rights of the poor countries; but we are also fighting for the salvation of a First World incapable of preserving the existence of the human species, of governing itself in the midst of contradictions and self-serving interests and much less of governing the world whose leadership must be democratically shared.

This is the only way that we can prevent the ship...from colliding with the iceberg that could sink us all. This is the only way that we can look forward to life not death.[14]

The monoculture may be survived but if it is not we will not be here to lament it. Large-scale social transformation tends only to occur at moments in history when the contradictions in the way we organise our lives become intolerable. The contradiction between the unequal consumption of finite global resources and the continuing quest for profit by trans-national corporations unchecked by increasingly feeble national governments that act as their agents is becoming daily more acute. It will arrive at the crisis point of transformation sooner rather than later. As that crisis approaches, it is vital that humankind maintains, within its collective cultural memories, sufficient store of alternative ways of existing in order to develop, creatively and imaginatively, a more just, democratic and also sustainable means of ordering life within spaceship earth. Colonialism paved the way for globalisation. Those whose history and cultural memory is of resistance to colonisation may be best placed to offer their experience in the service of survival. Robert Chambers sub-titled his book, *Rural Development*, 'Putting the Last First' [Longman, 1983]. If the human race is not to be lost, its victory may, paradoxically, have to be entrusted to those who have traditionally been last in the greedy scramble labelled 'progress'. If there is to be life after McDonald's, it will only be worth living for those who have decolonised their minds in order to pursue their own, not their oppressors', dreams.

## Notes

1. Bartolome de Las Casas, *A Short Account of the Destruction of the Indies*, Penguin, Harmondsworth, 1992, p. 30.
2. Edward O. Wilson, *Consilience*, Abacus, 1999.
3. Mcgrath, J., *The Cheviot, the Stag and the Black, Black Oil*, West Highland Publishing Company, Isle of Skyem, 1977, p. 17.
4. Boldt, M., *Surviving as Indians*, University of Toronto Press, Toronto 1993, pp. 187-88.
5. *Ibid.*, p. 218.
6. Sachs, W. (ed.), *The Development Dictionary*, Zed Books, London, 1995, p. 4.
7. Diamond, J., *Guns, Germs and Steel*, Vintage, London, 1998.
8. Standing Bear, Oglala in Miller, L. (ed.), *From the Heart*, Pimlico, London, 1995, p. 225.
9. Vincent, N. in *The Guardian*, May 25, 2002.
10. Brody, H., *The Other Side of Eden*, Faber and Faber, London, 2001, p. 314.
11. Said, E., *Culture & Imperialism*, Chatto & Windus, London, 1993, p. 331.
12. Baron Cohen, D., *Theatre of Self-Determination*, Guildhall Press, Derry, 2001, pp. 16-17.
13. *Ibid.*, p. 77.
14. Castro, F., Speech to the opening session of the South Summit, convened by the group of 77 in Havana, April 12, 2000 in DEUTSCHMANN, D. (ed.) Capitalism in Crisis, Ocean Press, Melbourne, pp. 279-80 and 291-92.

# 14

# Ethnic Symbolism in the Plays of Wole Soyinka

**Vibha Sharma**

Culture has always been producing constructs and lending them to literature. Every nation and every civilization because of its inevitable novelty possesses a distinct culture and subsequently the culture gives birth to various institutions. When a particular nation or its civilization interacts with an already existing construct then also it creates a novel system of culturally empowered landmarks in that construct. In a paper read at a literary conference in Sweden in 1967 Wole Soyinka declared that the "artist has always been functional in African Society as the record of the masses and experience of his society and voices and vision in his time".[1] Such is also true of the literary endeavour of African civilizations in the English language. Like every nation, the African tradition too has provided a distinct ethos to world literature in English. This posits the notion that the identity of a nation or a culture in literature is too strong to be crushed under the canons in literature.

Wole Soyinka's plays stand as testimonials to the aforesaid argument. Soyinka's plays are essentially African in their ethos and their appeal is worldwide. One need not search for a definition of African identity in his plays, as the ethos is too full of African themes. One is often led to believe in the phraseology of African writers, American writers, Canadian writers, Indian writers etc. To use such terms for a chronological study of literature is reasonable but the use of these phrasal distinctions beyond this creates an over-emphasis on the distinction of writers based on their origins. This is often taken for granted as a need for identity whereas a writer's texts, if they are true to their culture, are sufficient in themselves to create an identity of their canon.

Joseph Okapaku quotes the statement of Soyinka, "Soyinka says we do not want to be African writers but writers."[2] This hinges on the fact that the identity of a culture comes into question when the realization of it being crushed arises. This realization leads to the endorsement of the presence of the suppressors. Soyinka's plays in a very subtle manner create ethnic paraphernalia. Soyinka does not make any point; he just presents a display of West African cultural traditions and imagery, which speak for themselves. The present study attempts at extracting the aforesaid notion from the famous place of Soyinka like *A Dance of the Forests*, *The Road*, *The Lion and the Jewel* and *The Swamp Dwellers*.

In *A Dance of the Forests*, a Nigerian Independence play, Soyinka borrows from basic Yoruba beliefs to produce an atmosphere in which at one and the same time we are in contact with the living and the dead, the unearthly and earthly, with the present, the past and the future. According to beliefs in Africa the continuity of life from before to after death is common. Soyinka's own culture (Yoruba) also strongly holds firm to the belief. Soyinka extends through the play this idea and gives it physical reality. The play opens with a couple coming straight out of the earth to walk among the living. "An empty clearing in the forest. Suddenly the soil appears to be breaking and the head of the Dead Woman pushes its way up. Some distance from her, another head begins to appear, that of a man. They both come up slowly. The man is fat and bloated, wears a dated warrior's outfits, now mouldy. The woman is pregnant. They come up, appear to listen."[3]

Soyinka ushers the audience into a fantastic folk-tale world where the dead mingle with the living and gods with men. With the proceedings of play we are taken further and further into significant fantasy. The Dead Woman is pregnant for eight centuries at the beginning of the play and gives birth at the end. The woman is a symbol of ambivalent fusion of the dead and the living. The Dead Woman carries life in her, the past carries the unfulfilled vision of future and the present becomes a venue for the fusion and the developments thereafter. The ethnic mould in which the action is crafted is simply mesmerizing. The child born is only a symbolic half-child and appears in the final showdown. The build-up to the last pageant comprises of mingling of numerous ethnic themes. The totem of Demoke and the rivalry caused due to it brings an added interest in the final showdown. By using this world of extended fantasy Soyinka liberates himself from a particular area of space and a special liberating quality of the folk tradition. All human characters have double histories whom Soyinka releases from the prison of particularity and makes them symbols of general humanity. Thus ethnicity transcends time and setting. The last section is full of complex symbolism engaged in the choric invocation of future. The general assembly comprises of all the various kinds of characters in the play: humans who by this time have been shown in the present as well as the past, the 'guests of honour' who have come from the world of the dead, and the gods and spirits. Besides these there are purely symbolic figures – the spirits of the Palm, Darkness, Precious Stones, Pachyderms, etc. At this juncture the present and the past become a contrasting backdrop against which the dramatist looks at the future of mankind. All the characters play out a scene to enact this equation. Soyinka skillfully contrives the use of his human characters. The human characters spell the dreadful words predicting the future as each of the symbolic spirits makes his appearance. The form adopted here is that of the *egungun*[4] masque tradition. The humans are in a state of possession: "The Interpreter moves and masks the three protagonists. The mask motif is as their state of mind – resigned passivity. Once masked, each begins to move in a slowly widening circle, but they stop to speak, and resume their sedate pace as they chorus the last world."[5]

Soyinka creates a double image through the use of *egungun* tradition. The human characters who were creating pranks in their folly are now full of earthly wisdom. Their forms are human but their voices are not their own. The ethnic masque convention enables them to predict for themselves a doomed future, which comes from a more than human vision and has a more than human authority:

> *White skeins wove me, I, spirit of the Palm*
> *Now course I red.*
> *I who suckle blackened hearts, know*
> *Heads will fall down,*
> *Crimson in their bed!*

Similarly, the spirit of the Rivers:

*From Limopo to the Nile coils but one snake*
*On mud banks, and sandy bed*
*I who mock the deserts, shed a tear*
*Of pity to form palm-ringed oases*
*Stain my bowels red!*[6]

This speech full of pithy and sententious imports of *egungun* form repeats the plainer words of the disgraced warrior to the court physician in Mata Kharibu's court. "Unborn generations will be cannibals most worshipful physicians. Unborn generations will, as we have done, eat up one another",[7] says the author in a despairing prognosis.

Soyinka's technique is balanced in that it comprises of traditional rooting and modern influence at the same time. At one time we find the *egungun* pattern and at the same time we find the flash back technique as in *The Lion and the Jewel*. Similarly, there is a play in the play in *The Dance of the Forests*. The play shows this soldier standing within by watching the future being conjured up a hundred generations later, and it becomes symbolically clear that in fact nothing has changed and that his earlier prediction is still valid.

The Dead Man and the Deat Woman are the bearer of the truth of the past. The Dead man was "one of those who journeyed in the market ships of blood". They are the witness of an inglorious history and were treated abominably in the past. In the present too they are abominably treated. The Old Man says: "We were sent the wrong people. We asked for statesman and we were sent the executioners."[8]

This ill-treatment is in fact a witness of the "willful blindness to the truth about the past and an arrogant rejection of that past as it is enshrined in these two representative figures".[9] Soyinka has written that the past should not be "a flash point for escapist indulgence" rather it should be accepted, because it exists "now, this moment; it is co-existent in present awareness" and "it clarifies the present and explains the future". The experience of the Dead Man and his wife conveys the fact that men's appalling behaviour has been persistent from past to present and will remain so in the future too. The exploitation of the subalterns has been a persistent phenomenon cutting across ages.

Finally the dialogue between the Ant leader and the Forest Head that followed the roll-call of the spirits sums up memorably the essential ethnic needs of African civilization, i.e. remembering the truths about mankind in general and about Africans and their history in particular but more important than this is Soyinka's interminable concern for an introspection on the part of a newly-freed Nigerian ethnicity and thus a self-criticism which Chinua Achebe sought for in *Presence Africaine.*

| Forest Head: | Have you a grievance |
|---|---|
| Ant Leader: | None, Father, except great clods of earth |
| | Pressed on our feet. The world is old. |
| | But the rust of a million years |
| | Has left the chains unloosened. |
| | ... |
| Forest Head: | Have you a cause, or shall I |
| | Preserve you like a riddle? |
| Ant Leader: | We are ones remembered |
| | When nations build... |
| Another: | ...with tombs tones |
| Another: | We are the headless bodies when |
| | The spade of progress delves. |
| Another: | Down the axis of the world, from |
| | The Whirlwind to the frozen driffs, |
| | We are the ever legion of the world |
| | Smitten, for – 'good to come'.[10] |

This moment in the play is the culmination of the invocation of history and the future to present a pessimistic view of the human race. Thus in an ethnic mould the thematic concerns of modern civilization is cast, thereby creating a compatible approach to past, present and future vis-à-vis the development of the human race. All characters testify to the fact that a spiritual stagnation has crept into the human beings. The fate of the half child, symbolizing the future of mankind, is entrusted to Demoke, the artist, whose work has been earlier described by no less than Forest Head in the guise of Obaneji as the kind of action that redeems mankind? Hope is there for essential human progress in souls like these. They should never stop trying.

In *The Road*, the title itself is a realization of the fertile central motif. The scenes of the play are enacted beside a Nigerian road. But at a profound level the symbolic relevance of the road lies in its being a road of life inevitable for all men to travel along. Along the road they must travel either individually or collectively as nations. It is the road between life and death, which connects this world and the other world running through a hazy landscape.

This road is watched over by Ogun, the greedy god who lives on the butchery that the roads daily provide him with. Ogun is a symbol of duality, his life feeds on the dead regularly. The drivers who drive along the road uphold their devotion to Ogun. The most common sacrifice offered to Ogun are the dogs that stray onto the road. But Ogun does not care for this forever and therefore so many of the road's 'heroes' in the play – Zorro, Akanini the lizard, Sigdi Ope, Sapele Joe, Saidu-Say, Indian Charlie, Humphrey Progart, Cimarron Kid, Muftau, and Sergeant Burma – are dead.

In fact, all the central figures of the play are under the spell of death: they are either probing towards death or are actually dead and undergoing decomposition, their voices are echoing from this hazy zone in a moving manner.

The road is a middle ground, a sort of land completely uninhabited by the flesh as well as the spirit. Professor is the illustration of several ethnic concerns of Soyinka. He has a Victorian costume, an academic title earned through expertise in forgery; he has a past connection with the Christian Church but has leanings towards *Ifa*.[11] Professor is a symbol of confusion and bafflement of the African psyche influenced by modernization. He is neither a complete African nor a complete European, neither wholly spiritual nor wholly material-istic. Soyinka in a way scoffs at the blind way the Africans would follow the fashions of Europe and could never catch up. They remain suspended in between. Thus Professor is a manifestation of a state in between. He seeks after the Word, i.e. the knowledge of the essence of death but he is himself a genuine criminal, selfish and rapacious. He has a proximity to the devotees of Ogun and has a past connection with Christianity. He himself chooses to sleep in two camps, in the cemetery where he can best keep his ear to the ground for the Word. There is a paradox in his mission, he wants complete knowledge of death without actually dying as he says: "I cannot yet believe that death's revelation must be total, or not at all." He engineers accidents by removing road signs from dangerous points on the highway and sells spare parts, old shoes, and clothes in his shop. Professor, the drivers and thugs all symbolize an unpleasant mingling of Africa and Europe. Their names are inspired by American crime and western films yet they sing traditional Yoruba praise songs and worship Ogun, e.g., Say Tokyo Kid. "Say Tokyo is an ugly fusion of the traditionally African and hard-headed materialism of an alien culture."[12] Murano is a very important character in the play, who is neither dead nor living; neither speaks nor hears. As professor says: "He has no mind. He neither speaks nor hears." It is he in whom the Professor is interested and finally he puts on the *egungun* mask at the end and he is closest to the spirit world, which the *egungun* professionally deals with.

*The Road* is the writing on the wall for Africa. The society and hence ethnic populace is on the road to death and dissolution, a society for which there seems no hope, Professor symbolizes those who will have to die before learning the truth of death. He speaks of death as "the moment of our rehabilitation". Rebirth is only possible after death. The movement itself overpowered by the mask at the end of the play, which drowns gradually until "it appears to be nothing beyond a heap of cloth and raffia". Thus, Soyinka presents the case of ethnicity as the problem of races and tribes.

Similarly in the plays like *The Lion and the Jewel* and *The Swamp Dwellers*, Soyinka upholds the powers of ethnicity and stresses the revived faith in one's culture and tradition with a rational acceptance of modernity. *The Lion and the Jewel* focuses the attack on Lakunle a westernized schoolteacher who is shown to be ridiculous with his blind faith in book learning, his self-obsession imbibed with preposterous arrogance. Lakunle's lack of taste is heralded by his clothes while Sidi's single cloth proclaimed her essential integrity. He calls his people 'a race of savages' and feels himself as the harbinger of the new order. His contempt for ancestral ways makes him drag his community into the modern world. He finds his vehement attempts to be in vain when his beloved denounces him for a traditional marriage with Sidi, (the head of the tribe). Thus, Teacher and Professor both suggestively stand as the teachers of new order who work for a futile end and this carries a reinforced faith in one's traditions. 'Teacher', though, symbolizes through contrast the hunger for literacy in Africa but at the same time this symbol culminates in only a superficial notion of progress. To quote Eldred Jones: "In *Lion and the Jewel* Soyinka satirizes the dangerously superficial concept of progress in the school teacher Lakunle."[13]

In *The Swamp Dwellers*, a similar theme is inherent. The twin sons of Alu are separated in their life's battle as one decides to live in the city neglecting the cause of his people. The other son is shattered as he is unable to decide either to live a village life or seek a job in the city. He is thus a sufferer in general and a victim of his own environment in particular, which is torn with reshuffling airs of the new order and lasting influence of tradition. This family is the prey of the new order and in the backdrop is the village, facing drought. Even in this drought the village priest Kadiye exploits the piety of those whom he represents before the local god. The swamp is a witness to the struggle of the civilization bearing the brunt of the waves of change and disorder.

Thus, Soyinka takes up through his plays not only the themes and concerns of his ethnicity but he sets them in an aura essentially African. But despite this fact the concerns in the play transcend all geographical boundaries and explain the chaos and crises of the psyche of all nations who passed through a similar juncture in their development. When Soyinka visited the University of California in 1998 he said in an interview, "I was thoroughly surrounded and immersed in aspects of the Yoruba culture".[14] To conclude one must say that Soyinka's symbolism is enshrined in ethnic paraphernalia subscribing to West Africa but his plays belie a need to stress the search for identity for what his plays show is that identity is part of one's ethnicity. By just reviving a faith in one's culture and traditions and respecting others' at the same time makes the human being complete. The Yoruba culture in his play is always an amiable face of the civilization which is welcoming a balanced control of the new order but denouncing the hostile attempts misleading people to lose faith in their ethnicity and hence their identity. I conclude by quoting Soyinka's lines:

> "*I borrow seasons from an alien land*
> *In brotherhood of ill, pride of race around me*
> *Strewn in Sunlit shards. I borrow alien lands*
> *To stay the season of a mind.*"[15]

## Notes

1. *Journal of Commonwealth Literature*, Vol. XVIII, No. 1, 1982, p. 107. "Soyinka and the Voice of Vision", Brian Crow with Abah and Saddik Tafawa Balewa.

2. Wright, Edgen. *The Critical Evaluation of African Literature*, Heinmann, London, 1973.

3. Soyinka, Wole. *Collected Plays*. Oxford University Press, Oxford, 1971, Vol. 1, p. 3.

4. *Egungun* is a very different kind of mask, which is made out of layers of colourful strips of cloth. It belongs to Yoruba of Nigeria. The egungun danced whirls the costume so that the bits of cloth decorated with ribbons, mirrors and metal fly through air.

5. Ibid., p. 73.

6. Ibid., pp. 73-75.

7. Ibid., p. 75.

8. Ibid., p. 4.

9. Rosocoe, A., *Mother is Gold: A Study in West African Literature*, Cambridge University Press, Cambridge, 1971, p. 224.

10. Ibid., p. 226.

11. *Ifa* is an African religion.

12. Ibid., p. 230.

13. Heywood, Christopher ed., Eldred Jones in *Perspectives on African Literature*, Heinemann, London 1971, p. 130.

14. Online interview on the site to University of California.

15. Soyinka, Wole, *'Massacre, October '66'*, Idanre Methuen, London, 1967, p. 52.

# Part III

## Ethnic Issues and Challenges

# 15

# Ethnicity and Style in Productions at the Royal Court Theatre, London, 1956-1966

**Amelia Howekritzer**

The year 1956 has been designated, by virtually unanimous agreement, as the year in which British drama turned decisively and took off in a new direction. Critic Kenneth Tynan called 1956 the year in which "the English theatre" was "dragged... kicking and screaming, into the twentieth century."[1] The new drama declared Tynan, was "serious in intent, contemporary in theme."[2] The ten years following 1956 came to be known as the "angry decade," with plays by John Osborne, Arnold Wesker, John Arden, and Edward Bond achieving international recognition not only as individual works, but also as part of a discernible movement in British theatre. Although a considerable number of the era's hallmark plays originated in other theatres, such as Joan Littlewood's Theatre Workshop, it was the English Stage Company at the Royal Court that came to be considered the centre of Britain's "theatrical revolution"[3] – the venue in which work by young writers of working-class origins was channeled into the mainstream of British culture. Thus, among Britain's cultural institutions, the Royal Court became the "symbolic centre of rebellion [and] dissent."[4]

The question with which I approached the "angry decade" is this: what was the relationship of the Royal Court's work to British social formations of the postwar period? Clearly, the "angry decade" played a part in defining working class mobility within postwar English society, underscoring changes that had begun during the industrial revolution. This same decade, however, witnessed a truly revolutionary change in British society – the entry into the English working class of considerable numbers of people from Commonwealth nations in the West Indies, Asia, and Africa. A recent account describes the initiating event. "The arrival of the troopship Empire Windrush at Tilbury Docks on 21 June 1948 was a landmark. It is now recognized and celebrated as the official commencement of the large-scale post-war migration of Commonwealth citizens from the Caribbean to Britain."[5] In the decade following Windrush, about 125,000 Caribbean migrants arrived in Britain; this group was soon joined by newcomers from Africa, the Indian subcontinent, and East Asia.[6] The migrants joined Britain's urban working class, as the recovery and industrial growth within postwar England demanded increasing numbers of labourers. In London's East End, they joined immigrants who had been living in England for a generation or so – primarily Jewish Eastern Europeans who had fled pogroms and Nazism. This major relocation marked the beginning of the multicultural Britain that exists today.

In examining how the Royal Court Theatre responded to changes in the British working class during the ten years following the watershed year 1956, it is necessary to look both at new plays and at production choices. During this time, the Royal Court was headed by George Devine, who gathered around him a small team of directors including Tony Richardson, Lindsay Anderson, Anthony Page, William Gaskill, and John Dexter; and designers including Stephen Doncaster, Clare Jeffery, Alan Tagg, Jocelyn Herbert, Margaret Harris, and Sophie Devine. Many members of this group were people new to theatre, recruited and trained by Devine. Thus, it is not surprising that the productions over the ten-year period of 1956-66 show a remarkable consistency of vision that came to exemplify, along with its encouragement of new writers, the Royal Court's uniqueness. Lindsay Anderson, in the Royal Court retrospective published in 1981, has addressed himself to what became known as "The Court Style". "The Royal Court impulse," writes Anderson, "was a 'realist' impulse.... [and] style, it was understood, was just as important a part of the theatrical experiences as theme or content."[7] The Court style, Anderson continues, was "above all, serious....The playing was natural, civilized, unforced. And the presentation was similarly lucid and economic. The settings were realistic, but not fussily or extravagantly naturalistic: they stood out with elegant clarity against a pure, white surround. There was no bowing and scraping to us, the audience; and there was no bullying either. In English culture, where 'serious' is most often used as a mocking epithet, this made the experience a refreshing and even a touching one."[8] Anderson sums up the Royal Court aesthetic by identifying it with the Periclean ideal, which he first quotes in Greek and then translates as: "We pursue beauty without extravagance and knowledge without effeminacy."[9] Lindsay Anderson's citing of Pericles suggests that the aesthetic ideal pursued by the Royal Court Theatre during the "angry decade," rather than offering a radical break with the past, shows a significant and largely deliberate renewal of connection with social and theatrical forces that predate the twentieth century. Anderson's quotations suggest a strong predisposition toward a classical vision.

The classical drama constructs a conceptual order with timeless, essential mankind at its centre. It serves to universalize the particular. The classical vision is centred in an assumption of unified subjectivity. The unity of the classical subject may be broken apart in tragedy or incompletely realized in comedy, but remains the ideal, evoking pity and fear in tragedy or humour in comedy. Despite influence and selective borrowing from Bertolt Brecht, who attempted to articulate and practise an anti-classical theatre, the Royal Court productions seldom deviated from classical principles. In Brecht's insistence on stage props that would authentically evoke a particular historical and social situation, Devine found simply a focus on theatre materials and craftsmanship. "When there has to be a door... it's a real door and beautifully made," he replied to William Gaskill's question "What's the Berliner Ensemble like?[10]

The Royal Court's realignment of Brechtian elements to support a vision of unity is seen in its typical production arrangements during the decade following 1956. The refurbishment of the Royal Court under Devine's direction originally included a permanent stage surround of white cloth covered in net. This surround was Devine's solution to the problem of "how to create, in [a] limited and encumbered area, a feeling of space and air... a solution [that] must appear to be essential, as opposed to ideological, functional as opposed to decorative, natural as opposed to theoretical."[11] Although the surround was discarded at the end of the first season, because large scene pieces often caught on the net when they were flown in or out), the Court style evolved with this surround as its unified and universalized conceptual frame. Interestingly, the exposed lighting instruments that were a hallmark of Brechtian theatre, were used in a way that, rather than disrupting a unified concept of the production, instead helped to construct a visual unity that, even more than in a traditionally illusionistic scene design, limited the conceptual perspective of the production. Thus, in Jocelyn Herbert's influential design for Arnold Wesker's *The Kitchen*, the shape of the lighting grid followed the outline of the set. The visual metaphor is one of wholeness, balance, and above all, internal unity.

While it used Brechtian elements to subvert Brecht's epic-theatre ideas, production at the Royal Court also rebelled against pictorial realism. The Royal Court's stylized realism aimed at conceptual unity rather than visual verisimilitude. Jocelyn Herbert, in her contribution to the Royal Court retrospective, emphasizes the actor-centred nature of the Court style:

> George Devine wanted to get away from swamping the stage with decorative and naturalistic scenery; to let in light and air; to take the stage away from the director and designer and restore it to the actor and text. This meant leaving space around the actors, and that meant the minimum of scenery and props, i.e., only those that served the actors and play: nothing that was for decorative purposes only, unless the text, or the style of the play, demanded it....Perhaps it was the beginning of what I call 'considering the actors as part of the design': considering where the actors will be on the stage and what they will need as the basis of the design; not creating an elaborate picture and then sticking actors in it.[12]

Pictorial realism – an outgrowth of the early twentieth-century social dramas of Pinero, Galsworthy, Shaw and Maugham – grew out of and tended to foster an assumption that the human is a product of her or his environment. Rejection of pictorial realism rejuvenated the assumption that man is the apex and centre of creation, environments merely the projection of human will. In centring the conceptual unity of the production in the intersection between the actor's body and the playwright's words, the Court style relegated social setting to a 'background' that helped bind together text and performance. The Court style thus used the elements of production to establish an apparently natural coherence, rather than to explore areas of disunity or disjunction.

The Royal Court productions aimed to represent in both common senses of the word. The Court style during this decade was a straightforwardly mimetic style; it did not question the idea that art holds a mirror up to nature, or inquire into the construction of this familiar dichotomy, as the modernists had done. Representativeness, in the sense of a single individual standing for a larger group of people, was established by means of props, costumes, and dialects. John Arden's iconoclastic antiwar play, *Sergeant Musgrave's Dance* (1959), which the author subtitled "An Unhistorical Parable," was given the costume, decor, and dialect of a mining town in Northern England during the late 1800s. Ann Jellicoe's experimental piece, *The Sport of My Mad Mother* (1958), was given contemporary specificity by portraying the young male characters with the inflections, gestures, and clothing of the London gang members known as Teddy Boys. The careful use of such everyday details as working-class dialect and the combination living-sleeping room that became almost obligatory for the angry plays, had the overall effect of universalizing the particular lives of working-class people in mid-twentieth-century England. In striving to establish a working-class identity that could be taken seriously in mainstream culture, the Royal Court at the same time reified this identity in such a way that excluded questioning of the way it was constructed.

The tendency to promote a classical concept of unified subjectivity at the expense of political and social concerns manifested itself in textual as well as production choices. For example, in the Royal Court's production of Miller's *The Crucible*, as reported by William Gaskill, the part of "Giles Corey, the one character who gives the play its economic and political perspective" was cut.[13] Similarly, Kenneth Tynan criticized George Devine's production of *The Good Woman of Setzuan* for its cutting of the final scene, an epilogue which addresses the audience directly and challenges them to provide a happy ending to the play.[14]

The production style and new plays associated with the "angry decade," focused on the work of white men of working-class origin who had received enough education to achieve social mobility. Despite their association with a presumed working-class viewpoint, these stagings universalized concerns regarding identity and status rather than exploring their particular sociopolitical aspects. The prototype of the decade, Jimmy Porter, in *Look Back in Anger,* expresses anger and despair so specific and at the same so universalized as to confound audience identification. He positively refuses to connect his anger with social or political issues, famously declaring that "there aren't any good, brave causes left."[15] In his classical quest for status and power in a world that constantly threatens to disrupt his unified subjectivity, Jimmy Porter is comparable to the more frankly universalized characters of Pinter's *The Dumb Waiter* or Beckett's *Endgame.* Even more than in its characters, these plays revealed a framework of classical unity in the viewpoint, which was invariably white, male, and European, without any acknowledgement of these biases.

The intensity of the Royal Court's focus, during the angry decade, on a universalized concept of man permitted little space for differences of viewpoint. The English Stage Company's financial backers felt strongly that it should concentrate on English plays.[16] Although the plays produced during the decade addressed a variety of experiences, these experiences were usually encompassed within an assumption of unified subjectivity. Notable exceptions to this assumption were the two playwrights whose first plays brought the subject of ethnic minorities in Britain to Royal Court audiences. These playwrights were Arnold Wesker, the son of Eastern European Jewish immigrants to England, and Barry Reckord, a West Indian whose family had been among the first wave of migrants. The first plays and subsequent work of these two dramatists provide instructive examples of the way in which the Royal Court's production style interacted with ethnicity.

Wesker structured his first play, *Chicken Soup with Barley* (produced in 1958) around the sociopolitical commitments and interpersonal dynamics of a Jewish family in prewar England. The play covers a period of twenty years in the life of this family in London's East End – famous for its association with new arrivals, ethnicity, and poverty. The drama centres around the energetic and strong-willed mother of the family, Sarah Kahn. She, unlike the prototypic "angry" character, is not concerned primarily for herself. Her dominant concern is for her children – especially Ronnie, the son with whom she is closest. Her primary desire is that Ronnie remain close to the family and continue the belief system and political activism she has embraced as a lifetime Socialist. Her ideals focus on caring for others inside and outside of the family. In her climactic speech, she argues, "You've got to care. You've got to care, or you'll die."[17] The divided consciousness exemplified by Sarah is typical of the ethnic subject within a dominant majority; divided between two cultures. In this play, Wesker gives the division a political cast, but it plays out as a contest between maintaining difference versus assimilating to the majority, as Ronnie's siblings both leave their East London family environment and pursue individualistic goals, leaving Ronnie as the emblematic figure who must make a choice.

The divided consciousness evident in *Chicken Soup with Barley* created problems from the beginning. George Devine did not really want to produce the play. With director Lindsay Anderson advocating strongly for its production, Devine compromised by setting up a tryout production at the Belgrade Coventry; only after passing this test was the play performed at the Royal Court.[18] This production met with an initially weak response at the Royal Court, and its team of artistic directors continued to treat Wesker's work with what he termed "mistrust" and "resistance."[19] Wesker, in turn, responded by moving away from the representation of ethnicity. His subsequent plays, *Roots*, *I'm Talking about Jerusalem*, *Chips with Everything*, and *The Kitchen* (produced 1959-1960) downplayed or avoided the issue through a focus on mainstream groups, institutions, and experiences. The success of the later plays influenced the response to *Chips with Everything*, and it was revived successfully in 1960 as part of the Wesker trilogy. Reviewing the trilogy, critic Kenneth Tynan emphasized that Wesker's viewpoint was that of a "Jewish writer"; he identified the theme of the play as "the erosion of political certainties, and their replacement by apathy," but complains that the cast lacked "Jewish dynamism" and "Jewish wit." At the same time, Tynan acknowledges the play's aims, ending the review with the observation that the Kahns "are not arguing about a way of earning, or a way of spending, or a way of making love. They are arguing about a way of life."[20]

Barry Reckord, the first West Indian dramatist to have a play professionally produced in England, made his Royal Court debut with *Flesh to a Tiger* in 1958. It focuses on a Jamaican woman living in poverty whose child is critically ill. In seeking treatment for her child, she is forced to choose between the traditional methods of a local shepherd and the alien medicine of an English doctor. This conflict between superstition and cultural defensiveness on the one hand and exploitation and attitudes of cultural superiority on the other destroys both the child and the mother. Again, a divided consciousness is evident, and interestingly again exemplified by a female character. Although the Royal Court attempted to meet the challenge of performing Reckord's first play, by removing the white surround to make way for more realistic scenery and by bringing in black actors, the play did not appeal to Royal Court audiences. Its box office for a twenty-nine-performance run was only fifteen percent.[21]

Record joined the Royal Court writers' group, and he, like Wesker, modified the content of his plays. His next play, *You in Your Small Corner* ((1960) focused on a black family in Brixton attempting to establish themselves in the middle class. This family does not exemplify divided consciousness, since they display loyalty only to their adopted culture, seeking to assert social superiority within it. This play was produced by the Cheltenham Theatre and received only one performance at the Royal Court, in its Sunday night, without-décor series. Reckord finally achieved Royal Court success in 1963, with *Skyvers*, a play about a group of lower-class white youths attending an urban comprehensive secondary school and, essentially, learning how to fail. Critic John Russell Taylor sums up Record's three Royal Court plays in this way:

> Among...Royal Court discoveries, mention must be made of Barry Reckord, a young Jamaican dramatist...whose first play, *Flesh to a Tiger*, was staged at the Royal Court in May 1958. This was a disappointing shanty-town melodrama with too much extraneous local colour and too little working out of loaded situations.... But with his second play, *You in Your Small Corner*, which played one night at the Royal Court and was later revived at the Arts, he showed a considerable advance in dramatic technique...though there were still certain awkwardnesses in the narration, the story... had a number of salutary surprises in store for the conventionally minded.... [H]is latest play, *Skyvers*, first produced at the Royal Court in 1963... offers a sympathetic and impeccably accurate account of life in a London secondary modern school. Young people and teachers alike are observed with rare fairness and precision, and for once, this is not at all a 'Negro play', but just a play, and there is not even a single coloured character or reference to the colour problem. In *Skyvers* Reckord justifies up to the hilt his right to be considered a British dramatist just like any other, though much more accomplished than most.[22]

Reckord went on to work with other theatres, returning, once he had ceased to associate with the Royal Court, addressing racial conflict explicitly in the 1969 stage play *Don't Gas the Blacks*, the 1973 radio play *Malcolm X*, and the 1975 television play, *In the Beautiful Caribbean*. The plays of Barry Reckord, unlike those of Arnold Wesker, have fallen into obscurity, but they merit study in the context of 1960s and 1970s Britain.

The Court style, which combined a commitment to stylized realism with the classical vision of wholeness, could not offer a theatrical language in which to comprehend divided subjectivity. With its univocal tone, its sequential unitary sets, and its spare and consistent detail, the style confined imaginative time within the single, linear narrative. This containment of imagination contributed to closure of the theatrical artifact and protected it from disruption. It thus reinforced acceptance of the assumptions that make possible the existing social and theatrical status quo and discouraged questioning and change of those configurations. By paring down the amount of visual detail in productions, the Court style subordinated theatre's communicative density – its theatricality – to a thematic and stylistic unity of production determined by the playwright's point of view. The reining in of complexity that characterized the Royal Court's return to the classical standards of simplicity and restraint, offered the audience, in Catherine Belsey's terms, "a position of knowingness which is also a position of identification with the narrative voice."[23] The author's narrative voice, occupying the apex in the "hierarchy of discourses"[24] within a theatre, which identified itself as a writers' theatre, both demanded and received legitimation from a Court production. The stylized realism and especially the emphasis on conceptual unity in the Royal Court style served to reduce the range of meanings of a dramatic work within the boundaries of a single voice. The selectivity and consistency of the Court style – what Lindsay Anderson referred to as its "elegance 'without extravagance'"[25] – drew attention to the message of that voice and away from the means by which the voice was produced. The play was performed from the standpoint of what its author had to say, without any attempt to examine how either the voice or the statement had been constructed.

The "angry decade" at the Royal Court has been celebrated for putting social alienation on the stage. However, its production style lent itself to an Aristotelian catharsis rather than analysis. Viewing the emotional pain of individual characters isolated within a theatrical artifact that universalizes their suffering leads, as Brecht has made us aware, to resignation and apathy rather than to awareness of social problems that should be corrected. In many ways, the Royal Court, in its angry decade was looking back, rather than to the future. Before it could represent the changes taking place in Britain in the postwar period, it had to abandon the Court style and discover new theatrical languages.

## Notes

1. Kenneth Tynan, *A View of the English Stage* (St. Albans: Paladin, 1976), p. 251.
2. *Ibid.*, pp. 272-3.
3. Craig, Sandy, "Eflexes of the Future: The Beginnings of the Fringe," *Dreams and Deconstructios: Alternative Theatre in Britain* (Ambergate: Amber Lane Press, 1980), p. 11.
4. Findlater, Richard, ed., *At the Royal Court: 25 Years of the English Stage Company* (New York: Grove Press, 1981), p. 29.
5. Bourne, Stephen and Sav Kyriacou, *A Ship and a Prayer: The Black Presence in Hammersmith and Fulham* (London: Borough of Hammersmith and Fulham, 1999), p. 26.
6. Kershen, Anne J., *London: The Promised Land? The Migrant Experience in a Capital City* (Avebury: Ashgate Publishing, 1997), p. 113.
7. Findlater, p. 143.
8. *Ibid.*, p. 144.
9. *Ibid.*, p. 148.
10. William Gaskill, *A Sense of Direction* (London: Faber and Faber, 1988), p. 11.
11. Philip Roberts, *The Royal Court Theatre and the Modern Stage.* (Cambridge: Cambridge University Press, 1999), p. 34.
12. Findlater, p. 84.
13. Gaskill, pp. 12-13.
14. Kenneth Tynan, *A View of the English Stage* (Frogmore: Paladin, 1976), p. 183.
15. John Osborne, *Look Back in Anger* (New York: Bantam, 1965), p. 104.
16. Roberts, p. 36.

17. Arnold Wesker, "Chicken Soup with Barley", in *The Wesker Trilogy* (New York: Random House, 1960), p. 77.

18. Findlater, pp. 78-79.

19. *Ibid.*, p. 81.

20. Kenneth Tynan, *A View of the English Stage* (London: Paladin, 1976), pp. 290-91.

21. Roberts, p. 64.

22. John Russell Taylor, *Anger and After: A Guide to the New British Drama* (Harmondsworth: Penguin Books, 1963), pp. 94-95.

23. Catherine Belsey, "Constructing the Subject: Deconstructing the Text," in *Feminist Criticism and Social Change*, ed. by Judith Newton and Deborah Rosenfelt (New York: Methuen, 1985), p. 53.

24. Belsey, quoting Roland Barthes, p. 53.

25. Findlater, p. 148.

# 16

## Cultural Memory and Ethnic Surrogation in Sleep Deprivation Chamber

### Elizabeth Bonjean

I am thy father's spirit
Doomed for a certain time to walk the night
And for the day confined to fast in fires
Till the foul crimes done in my days of nature
Are burnt and purged away...

*Hamlet*, I,v: 10-14 qtd. in *Sleep Deprivation Chamber*

Caught between two worlds, the Ghost of Hamlet's Father wanders the earth when there is no light, receding with the break of dawn. His restricted movement between the land of the living and that of the afterworld defines his place in Purgatory – that space where tortured souls endure suffering. The innocent spirit whose crime was to live when another deemed him unworthy of existence, is not only a subject of Shakespeare's *Hamlet*, but the focus of mother and son writing team, Adrienne Kennedy and Adam P. Kennedy in their play, *Sleep Deprivation Chamber*.

Written in 1996, *Sleep Deprivation Chamber* is the re-telling of Adam Kennedy's personal experience as a young African-American man who encountered violent racism at the hands of white policemen in 1994. While visiting his father in Arlington, Virginia, Adam was stopped late one night for having a non-functioning taillight on his car.

He was beaten without provocation, and then arrested on false charges that he had acted as a "hostile citizen" and had struck a police officer. The police brutality continued at the station, in the hopes of "convincing" Adam to sign a confession. Adam's ethnic identity was a signifier to the law enforcement that he was unmistakably in the wrong neighborhood – which was ironically just several feet away from his father's house in a predominantly white, upper-middle class suburb. This story ultimately concerns a family whose ethnic and cultural identities are shaken from their foundations in response to this episode and Adam's subsequent trial.

The 2001 production of *Sleep Deprivation Chamber* at the University of Washington School of Drama is the focus of this paper, which explores how the physical theatrical space is used as a tool of transformation for the characters – space mapped as part of the reclamation process of African-American cultural memory. Secondly, it looks at the role of the Other in this production, which has been refigured through a deliberate use of the *surrogation* process as defined by Joseph Roach. A significant aspect of the intercultural nature of this production stems from a particular directorial choice: the casting of a multi-ethnic actor in the pivotal role of a white police officer. Here, the notion of *substitution* brings up ethical issues of cultural exchange, and the possible aims and complications of production choices that elicit new conceptions of Othering. The "Ghost" of *this* play is the ghost of African enslavement in the United States and the racism that persists in contemporary American culture.

*Sleep Deprivation Chamber* is a memory play – one filled with so many painful memories of racial injustice that they seem to fill the margins of the play text, and have a similar effect in production, where they lurk above, below, to the side – even in the corners of the theatrical space. Director Valerie Curtis-Newton emphasizes this aspect by delegating specific places on an intimate thrust stage for different characters and incidents, and by making racism ever-present in the set design. A black metal-framed bed hovers persistently over the stage. And at times, the stark white sheets serve as a canopy of illumination. The large contrasting squares of a black and white checkerboard floor are the surface upon which acts of racial hatred and issues of justice are played out. Racism resides in a large pit that opens in the middle of the stage, and it is housed in small boxes that open here and there throughout the course of the play. Racism hides behind a stone wall which acts as the backdrop of the setting. Later a section will open to reveal a black wall littered with white paper – the countless unanswered letters a mother has written to officials in support of her son. The letters hang affixed there appearing like a collection of moths persistently drawn to the illumination of a light. The wall also serves as a seat of justice, whereupon the judge presiding over Teddy's case looms high above the rest of the action of the play.

Teddy's mother, Suzanne, exists within the space of the stage and never leaves it. Yet she lives in two worlds – that of fitful dreams juxtaposed alongside her anxious waking hours. Her single-minded purpose in aiding her son manifests itself into a ceaseless, formal letter-writing campaign to every government official and human rights organization she can locate. Suzanne is sleep-deprived and that canopy of illumination serves to define her own prison-like purgatory where she subsists looking for a shaft of light that will free her son and release her, too, along the way. Like the Ghost in *Hamlet* who must retreat to his prison house with the daylight, Suzanne is trapped in space. If she sleeps, she loses precious moments when her focus should be on obtaining her son's release. And when she does sleep, the past and the present collide as she relives childhood memories of her father, who as a member of the NAACP had fought for racial equality, alongside a plague of terrifying dreams that reenact the violent crimes just committed against her son. Suzanne is haunted by the recognition that the colour of Teddy's skin is a determinant in whether or not his story will be believed, and that despite her prominent position as an American artist and citizen her appeals are not just being denied but ignored.

> Dear Governor Wilder:
>
> My name is Suzanne Alexander. I am a black writer. I am writing to you again about the Arlington, Virginia Police Department ... We are an outstanding black American family. My former husband, David, is head of Africa/USA. My plays and stories are published and taught widely. We are now a grieved family. Our son is being persecuted by the Arlington Police Department just as surely as happened in the Deep South in the 1930s or during Emmett Till's time.
>
> *Sleep Deprivation Chamber*, i: p. 9

The line between the past and the present, between what real movement has been made in the way of racial equality in the generations that have passed between her father and her son, has been effectively blurred.

Teddy is the only other character to remain stuck within the structure of the stage area. Yet he is allowed one alternate form of movement – he may step below into the rectangular grave-like pit. The space he moves in mirrors the limited scope of opportunities available to him – those that hinge on the power of a judicial system to either liberate him or relegate him to a spiritual if not physical death. The areas that Suzanne and Teddy occupy are designed in combination with the space inhabited by another character – old Uncle March, a retired university professor, who remains on the periphery of the theatrical space. When Uncle March appears, costumed in colourful African dress, he moves to the beat of drums. He walks, as his name implies, with a deliberate, unhurried gait. To his family, he has strayed away again – but March is "walking" in the de Certeauian sense. His seemingly aimless wandering is an act of mapping the landscape of the white dominant culture. "His depression about the conditions of African-Americans has worsened," Suzanne explains.[1] She reminds us that March was "one of the first blacks to go to Africa to live," and as such, a clear conduit between African cultural memory and contemporary African American culture.[2] March moves around and through the audience, and to the edges of the stage space, and he stands along the perimeter of the epicentre of the dominant culture in which Suzanne and Teddy had ostensibly integrated themselves. The discovery or rediscovery is that their ethnic identity marks them in the fixed role of the Other. March's function in the play is to bear witness to the long-standing great divide between whites and blacks – the "difference" that his family has begun to forget. His walking is a carefully worn path ingraining the memory of African roots in America.

For Joseph Roach, memory requires such "public enactments of forgetting either to blur the obvious discontinuities, misalliances, and ruptures, or more desperately, to exaggerate them..."[3] Director Curtis-Newton further complicates the notion of "public enactment" with a carefully chosen racial *substitution* in the character of the white police officer. The "whiteness" of Officer Holzer is central to the story and script, as it reflects the authenticity of the real life incident. Thus Curtis-Newton's deliberate choice of casting a non-white actor to play the role seeks to disrupt accepted racial tensions embedded in American culture. The surreptitious manner in which she presents this actor to us, further intensifies this disruption.

The initial introduction of Officer Holzer to the audience is solely auditory. We hear his authoritative voice yelling, "Get back in your car," but are blinded by the same high-beamed light as Teddy, who in that moment has been detained by the officer. The first glimpse of Holzer finds the ethnicity of the actor veiled behind dark glasses and police gear, remaining barely distinguishable in the bright light. It is not until late in the play, during Teddy's trial, that we are actually met with the ethnic identity of the police officer – or are we? This question is posed in response to what was a surprisingly insignificant amount of reaction on the part of the audience to this conceptual casting choice – with a good portion of the audience successfully blurring the "obvious [ethnic] discontinuities," having determined that perhaps because the actor was "light-skinned enough" and his ethnicity indeterminate, that he could be interchangeable with a white man. Such a reception admits the multiplicity of meanings at the crux of this casting choice. Was this merely a case of colour-blind casting, or was a representative from another marginalized race used to deepen the exploration into racial identity and intercultural relations?

The action of *Sleep Deprivation Chamber* demonstrates the process whereby a culture reproduces and recreates itself, or what Joseph Roach terms *surrogation*. Comprised of substitution, memory, and performance, surrogation is a continuum as "actual or perceived vacancies occur in the network of relations that constitute the social fabric. Into the cavities created by loss through death or other forms of departure," Roach says, "survivors attempt to fit satisfactory alternates."[4] For Curtis-Newton, herself an African-American, the satisfactory alternate disrupts our preconceived notions of both who the Other *is* and who *does* the Othering.

In my interview with the director about this production Curtis-Newton made note of a strong cultural association between whites and Asians in the United States – a view that she stated is commonly held by African-Americans. Such a connection is in direct contrast to Rustom Bharucha's discussion of the "intracultural" or "the interaction of local cultures within the boundaries of a particular state."[5] While Curtis-Newton points to the "intracultural" as a factor of acceptable ethnic interchangeability due to an understood acculturation of Asian-Americans into the dominant white culture, Bharucha sees a pressing need to explore social difference "at a time when globalizing forces are in the process of homogenizing 'indigenous' cultures everywhere."[6] With the emphasis on discovering and respecting unique cultural traits, intracultural interaction could, according to Bharucha, be the sole instance in which local cultures can be rightfully acknowledged from both inside and outside of their social sphere.

Curtis-Newton described the rehearsal process as a difficult one for the entire cast, who with the exception of this single role of the police officer, were cast racially-appropriate. Dealing with contemporary instances of racial prejudice and violence created a hesitancy between some of the actors offstage who found themselves confronted by cultural stereotypes and realities which they found painful to engage in even at the level of performance. The actor who played the role of Officer Holzer is of Filipino descent, and Curtis-Newton described him as identifying ethnically as "Asian". What is more, that he went through the same agonizing process in approaching the racial prejudice in the play as the white actors because his lived experience had so closely mirrored their own. Thus, we are presented with a specific example of what Curtis-Newton has argued is culturally understood in the African-American community – an acceptable blurring of racial lines between white and Asian Americans. In this instance, then, the Other remains the same but through surrogation the perpetrators of Othering extend beyond the conventional structure of what the dominant culture might consider ethnically "white." This conflation of cultural ethnicity additionally proposes a configuration, which can be read as a form of Othering of the Asian American by the African-American.

In production, director Curtis-Newton strategizes ways to engage disparate cultural communities into a rare dialogue. The act of presenting this production, too, is in-and-of-itself an aspect of the surrogatory process. Director Curtis-Newton advanced this practice through what she terms "community events" which were incorporated into the production schedule. Here, specific performances were targeted with the goal to allow openness for public discussion. In addition to the predominantly white subscription and student audience, invitations were extended to groups from the African-American community, such as the ACLU, the Human Rights Council on Racial Profiling, and African-American churches, as well as government officials and the police department. Curtis-Newton looked for a critical balance of race representation in order to simply facilitate dialogue in a room where issues of racial prejudice are acted out. It is a step, she believes, on the path toward communication between racial communities and *breaking* rather than continually spinning the cycle of prejudice. As the facilitator of these post-show discussions, she sees intrinsic value in validating the feelings expressed by audience members who were able to articulate their outrage or even uncomfortability with the events they had just witnessed in a racially-mixed environment. But then she pushed for a response that went one step further. "It is great that you *see* the racism, that you acknowledge the problem exists. Now, what is the *action*?," she asks. It is a question for which at the moment there are no simple curative responses, only attempts at translating, understanding, and upholding a wealth of varying cultural communities. Curtis-Newton's "response" was an effort to disrupt the staid expectations of her actors and the audience alike. In doing so, she forged a deliberate path that encouraged the acceptance of distinctive cultures, somewhat akin to the very process of intracultural examination where Rustom Bharucha sees hope and affirmation. Part of Curtis-Newton's work seemed to contradict such goals of intracultural awareness through the complicated notions of race and culture in America that she obscures through her surrogatory casting choice. Yet, with the combination of both the production and an open forum, it is hoped that the seeds of exchange between the white and black communities in America's long-standing battle for racial quality, might ignite the possibility of *continued* communication and perhaps someday solutions within a newly-formed, albeit tenuous, collective community. A system in which the ghosts of the past roam freely as reminders of that which needs to be remembered and shared in order to reach deeper understandings within the structure of intracultural reciprocity.

## Notes

1. Adam P. Kennedy and Adrienne Kennedy, *Sleep Deprivation Chamber* (New York: Dramatists Play Service, 1996), p. 30.
2. Ibid.

3. Joseph Roach, *Cities of the Dead: Circum Atlantic Performance* (New York: Columbia University Press, 1996), p. 2.

4. Ibid.

5. Rustom Bharucha, "Somebody's Other: Disorientations in the Cultural Politics of our Times" in *The Intercultural Performance Reader* ed. by Patrice Pavis (London: Routledge, 1996), p. 200.

6. Ibid.

# 17

## Un-Presented Reality

### On Self-identification of the Polish Society in Drama After 1989

**Ewa Wachocka**

The transformations that took place in the social and political life of Poland after 1989, the year of the downfall of the communist regime and of the beginning of democratic government, triggered a profound, albeit rapid, cultural change. Clearly, the twilight of the communist model of economy and politics coincided with the exhaustion of a certain version of culture. The culture before 1989, sub-divided into various spheres depending on the impact its products were expected to have upon reality, developed in a context in which various artists and artistic institutions, whose orientation with respect to the authorities was meticulously observed by the regime, were either granted favour and influence, or were banished backstage – if not literally exiled. For Polish theatre and dramatic arts, the collapse of the exhausted model of culture boded well in all respects: it could have brought healing changes in the forms of communication and, more importantly, it could have marked the beginning of a new quality in dramatic art. In the eyes of optimists, the end of the old system opened up brand new, unexplored perspectives – especially in the context of the newly restored freedom of speech. Such optimistic visions do not come as a surprise; after all, analogous cultural developments took place at similar moments in the 20th century history of Poland: in 1918, 1945, and, to a certain extent, also in 1956. Indeed, Polish theatre took its chance, although its trans-formation did not come about without the pain of lifesaving surgery and necessary revaluations. In the writing of drama, however, the consequences of changes proved to be of insignificant import. Against all expectations, the breakthrough associated with the year 1989 did not particularly reverberate in drama, passing largely unnoticed. The abolition of censorship undoubtedly opened up artistic space for themes up to then disapproved of or forbidden outright, but did this fact inspire contemporary drama to make any serious efforts towards reorienting itself in the new reality? Was drama powerful enough to make a diagnosis that would permit true self-knowledge on the part of society? Did it manage to offer a valid description of the state of social consciousness, or an analysis of the painstaking process of self-identification and recognition?

It is worth remembering that post-war Polish theatre was wholly political. For obvious reasons, to outsmart censorship, it strove to speak of the times by resorting either to canonical classics of drama (predominantly of Romantic provenance), or to parables like Slawomir Mrozek. Such an escape into historical costume and Aesopic language is one explanation of the monothematic character of drama and the narrow spectrum of genres within dramatic arts of the period. In the beginning of the 1990s, however, this mode of communication with the audience lost its currency and soon its lack of value became obvious. This resulted in an alarming recognition of the grave instability of values. A common understanding of what is worth what in art vanished. Moreover, social expectations with respect to theatre (and culture in general) became blurred as well. It was therefore inevitable that questions about the place of art and the position of art's audience within the new reality would sooner or later have to emerge.

Rather abruptly, other preferences of the audience came to the fore – or perhaps, quite simply, new circumstances created a favourable climate for the audiences to manifest their long-held tastes. Indeed, the language of political allusion lost its position, yet this did not mean that political themes vanished from the artistic arena altogether. However, what these tendencies disclosed most evidently was the painful lack of new, modern techniques of communication with the audience. Especially in drama, the lack of a language in which addressing issues of a political nature (or generally, issues of significance) would be possible without resorting to allusion or parable was experienced as a major obstacle.

Thus, in broad terms, the restoration of state sovereignty in Poland not only brought an end to the career of the easy "theatre of allusion", but also marked the moment when the Romantic tradition[1] – the basic paradigm of Polish literature – lost its cultural productivity and had to be removed from its central position. Moreover, the twilight of the Romantic paradigm was preceded by the exhaustion of the theatre of the absurd,[2] described by Martin Esslin. Bearing in mind that no other paradigm as distinct, as productive, or as expansive as those has emerged to replace them, it comes as no surprise that today, in a situation dominated by the urgent need to devise new ways of addressing reality, drama is starting over, beginning with the penetration of what at first sight appears to be exclusively the zone of privacy. It begins anew with modest, individual stories, focusing around family matters (not infrequently grotesque), or portraying the fates of outsiders at odds with life, sometimes presented in various shades from the Romantic palette, or – more frequently – in naturalist tones. In this context, the relatively small number of plays attempting to settle accounts with the past and to reassess the ideological and moral problems of recent history appears to be symptomatic of the broader tendency in drama.

The first literary echoes of the martial law conspiracy sounded in Pawel Mossakowski's *Identification* (*Identyfikacja*) of 1986, where – among folk-heroic, flawless heroes of the patriotic underground and mean confidantes of the totalitarian regime – honest, weak people, overwhelmed in the face of the oppressiveness of communist militia, are portrayed as well. A still broader spectrum of phenomena characteristic of Polish reality after the political breakthrough of August 1980 informs the plays by Eustachy Rylski. Three of his plays, *A Chilly Autumn*, *The Scent of Wisteria*, and *The Wolf of Kazan* (*Chlodna jesien*, *Zapach wistarii* and *Wilk kazanski*) form a bitter contemporary trilogy offering both a vision, and an accounting of the gains and losses of the Polish struggle for freedom. In each of the three plays, Rylski attempts to portray a "hero of our time", who would exemplify the central ethical questions of the present-day reality. In the first play of the trilogy, the "hero" is an artist in the service of the regime, a writer who grows towards rebellion against oppressive powers. The hero of the second play is an intellectual, a politician siding with the Church. The last play of the trilogy, *The Wolf of Kazan*, features the character of a young businessman, a lonely workaholic, who – having become entangled in shady business with the mafia – eventually becomes a gangster. Rylski's original set of plays comprises a drama of the break-through, which offers a portrayal of the subsequent formative stages of the new consciousness of the Poles. By and large, however, his plays represent the only attempts at a painterly reassessment of history and at uncovering its truth in drama.

It would be hard to criticise contemporary playwrights for their incapacity to observe the world. More frequently, critique targets a contrary tendency: drama duplicates bits and pieces of life and carries them off the street and out of the household directly onto the stage. Critics, striving to diagnose the essence of drama's difficulties with the veritable depiction of reality, have long cited the ideological blurredness, or perhaps ideological uprootedness of art – symptomatic of the post-modern climate of our time – as the major pathogenic factor at work. Drama, so to say, wanders in the margins, describes periph-eries, but fails to reach its destination, ignorant of the way to the centre. It suffers from lack of synthesis, and is wanting in sources of deeper reflection on the period it reflects and, in some way, co-creates.

Even if the drama of today is indeed incapable of attaining greater universality, or unable to formulate a more profound diagnosis of the present, playwrights can by no means be criticised for lack of courage and inventiveness in addressing current issues. Undoubtedly, the trans-formations and conflicts of the transitional period in the history of Poland, resulting in the collapse of former organising structures and an acute crisis of values, proved to be one of the most seminal sources of dramatic inspiration. On the one hand, the major themes derived from this source include the maladies and flaws of the new system, the moral degeneration of the former patriotic conspirators, and the selling-out of the best "Solidarity" ideals in the merciless reality of the free-market tug-of-war. On the other hand, themes inspired by recent history oscillate between visions of predatory capitalism, dangerous, yet alluring, built upon the ruin of the old titles and proprietorships of the past, as in the vision Pawel Huelle created in his *The Ostrov Spa* (*Kapielisko Ostrów*); and the drama of the loss of ethnic identity and economic independence, as in the plays by Stanislaw Bieniasz. It should be noted, however, that in drama addressing such issues, historical processes are usually shown in the light of interpersonal relations, rather than through the broad perspective of the general transfor-mation of the system. And still, apart from themes informed with a clear political undertone, the subjects of family crisis, the generation gap, and the histories of outsiders, losers, and people unable to adapt to the new reality loom large in drama. These, in other words, are the "dramas of life", developed and artistically transformed in a variety of ways.

It is not accidental that family-oriented subjects, and, more precisely, analyses of the degeneration of human relations, should find an important place among themes in contemporary drama. As if to confirm the alarming reports of sociologists, playwrights seem to warn that the collapse of family relations is the primary source of most of the problems haunting contemporary man. Hence, the degeneration or atrophy of elementary human ties has become a significant point of reference in the fate of a dramatic persona, even though the symptoms of the malady identified in Polish drama are still far in their intensity from the tragic events of Marius von Mayenburg's famous *Fireface* (Ger. *Feuergesicht*). Depicted with clinical precision in such plays as *Spam* (*Mielonka*) by Dagna Slepowronska, *Abortus* (*Wyskrobek*) by Damian Dewitz, or *Let's Talk about Life and Death* (*Porozmawiajmy o zyciu i smierci*) by Krzysztof Bizio, the images of emotional numbness, growing indifference, mental battles fought incessantly within one's self – are all more reminiscent of the gloomy portrait of family relations painted in *Jamaica* (Ger. *Bis Denver!*) by another German playwright, Oliver Bukowski, than they are of Mayenburg's tragic vision. Polish playwrights seem predominantly concerned with the individual dimension of the process of alienation, and with its particular psychological consequences; the sociological dimension of the problem interests them only inasmuch as it provides the context in which the experience of loneliness may gain a tangible texture, and thus also become legible. This is probably the reason why dramatic attempts to relate individual alienation to more general, large-scale transformations, or to seek ways to express the peculiarity of the situation of an individual clashing with the culture of post modernity, are rare. In this regard, a play by Lidia Ameyko titled *When Reason Sleeps, the Answering Machine Turns On* (*Gdy rozum spi – wlacza sie automatyczna sekretarka*) deserves special attention, as it portrays the impossibility of communicating in a world increasingly subordinated to technological transformation. Similarly, Ewa Lachnitt's *The Man of Trash* (*Czlowiek ze smieci*), a play offering a picture of the disintegration of forms of life in huge urban agglomerations, cut off from their roots, is an important attempt to address the relationship between the individual and the culture within which he or she functions.

The determination to face everyday reality manifests itself also in the appearance of particularly troubling themes which until recently were basically alien to the Polish stage. Such a tendency is readily observed in new plays striving to underpin the most burning issues of the present reality and to diagnose the incurable diseases afflicting the "here and now," such as social pathologies (e.g. drug addiction), and the overall increase in aggression and various forms of violence. Illustrative examples of this trend are the depictions of the environment of juvenile delinquents in the shocking *Youthful Death* (*Mloda smieræ*), a series of para-documentary études by Grzegorz Nawrocki, and in Marek Bukowski's more "literary" but likewise disconcerting *Deadman* (*Truposz*). This innovative trend in the Polish drama – which, it should be noted, has never had any long-lasting realist traditions – could be described as "drastic realism," a local, Polish analogue to the European "new brutalism."

The ability of such tendencies to lower the stylistic register is much greater than usually realised. The drama of most recent years, read as a mirror of reality, sparks protest and frequently fills the audiences with repulsion. The latter results from the transgression of all possible taboos both in the sphere of language and in the space of stage imagery. And yet it is not only plays investigating the problems of the social margins that shock the audiences with the violence of the events they depict and the vulgarity of their idiom. Cruelty and coarseness, a complex *signum temporis*, are among the most characteristic traits of the new Polish drama. And even though the brutality of these Polish plays is still far from the intensity of rape, violence, and deviations of all sorts that pervade the oeuvre of British "brutalists" such as Sarah Kane and Mark Ravenhill, and even though their vulgarity does not go as far in transgressing cultural norms as does the abhorrent verbal provocations of Werner Schwab's "Fäkaliendramen" – its function, still, seems to be similar. Language anchored in a degenerate everyday reality expresses every hideous thought, as if the character wished to break free from it by making it materialise in words. It is only infrequently, however, that the most recent Polish drama – treated as metaphor – meets Richard Rorty's criterion. Rorty, putting literature at the top of his hierarchy of discourses, argues that literature has taken over the function of philosophy and helps us to build our own

autonomy, determine our identity and, effectively, become less cruel –
or, in other words, to realise the consequences our private idiosyncrasies have for others[3]. In fact, the new Polish drama hardly ever
facilitates self-identification, recognition, or reflection.

All of the above inevitably makes one wonder whether the reason
for the present state of affairs does not lie in the fact that the dramatic
persona of today is no longer capable of carrying the burden of representation, and – at the same time – of filling the role, which by
definition mediates between the stage and the audience. In such a stage
personality, the whole theatrical and paratheatrical reality ought to
find its reflection: the artists' self-consciousness along with the needs of
the audience. The contemporary protagonist, however, is immobilised
by apathy, immersed in profound depression, stuck in idleness, permanently alienated and, in a sense, thoughtless. Indeed, the observation
that the dramatic persona has undergone a far-reaching disintegration is
anything but revolutionary. Yet what appears striking in the development of the dramatic arts of today is that the defining characteristic
of new drama (in Western Europe as much as in Russia or Poland) is the
persona's *depressive* condition, and – consequently – a depressed,
morbid vision of reality matched by depressed, morbid reactions to it.
Authors of different social and economic backgrounds, representing
experiences of living within frames of dissimilar political systems,
essentially confirm the same diagnosis of the present-day reality.
Irrespective of the sociopolitical conditioning of the playwright, the
existential situation of man in the contemporary world is presented in
the same fashion throughout Europe; hopelessness, or more precisely,
depression, becomes its central metaphor. Today, the helpless, passive,
lost protagonist is almost a norm: both in new plays and in contemporary reinterpretations of the drama of the past. The protagonist of
today's drama is a hero incapable of recognising the rules of the
surrounding world and unable to properly acknowledge his or her own
participation in it, who vacillates irresolutely and willessly in the
incomprehensible chaos of incoherent events, a hero doomed to live
life in a fragmented space, devoid of coordinates, disordered.

Forty years ago, Tadeusz Rózewicz's *The Files* – with its hero
idling his time away in bed, with its grotesque chorus of senile men
prompting him towards action with the now famous "Say something,
do something, in theatre one has to *play*, something *must* be happening
here..."[4] – came as a shock to the Polish audience. Today, Marek

Koterski deliberately alludes to this artistic gesture of contestation, showing the same character, that of an intellectual suffering from chronic impotence, in each of his subsequent plays. His character is a man haunted by bad luck: born too late to live in the "good old pre-war" Poland, and too soon to be able to accept "new" Poland as his true homeland. The difference between the characters created by Rózewicz and Koterski lies exclusively in the *motivation* of the respective hero's incapacity: if the passivity of the Rózewicz hero results from the overburden of his experience of tragic history, the passivity of Koterski's *everyman* is an expression of his indifference, a position assumed *a priori*. All his plays are characteristic for their consistency in laying bare the misery of everyday life. Beginning with *The Community* (*Spoleczns'c'*), through *The Inner Life* (*Zycie wewnetrzne*) and *The Day of a Loony* (*Dzien swira*) – each of his plays offers a description of a life-consuming struggle with the inertia of life itself. The reality Koterski portrays is that of life confined in a district of high-rise apartment blocks, a life before the television set, life disturbed by the noise of the elevator right behind the wall – and yet life lived in the rhythm of obsessive monologues, through which the artist narrates the boundlessness of his unfulfilment, complexes, fears and frustration, in which he tells the story of the huge reserve of ill-invested, wasted energy.

All of the above brings one to the conclusion that the basic problem of drama, which is its inability to reach into the centre of reality instead of wandering at its periphery, does not in fact lie in the insufficiency of contemporary themes, but in the serious lack of artistic will to enter into contact with the spectator. Drama has ceased to be the space of conflict; in a gesture of escapism, it has come to avoid presenting events and characters in a fashion that would make confrontation possible. Escaping into the realm of nebulous generalities, withdrawing into illustration of assumptions adopted *a priori*, retreating into dispassionate objectivism – Polish drama unwittingly signs its act of capitulation, the tangible expression of which is its retreat from reality. Predominantly, this tendency towards resignation manifests itself in the practice of mean, paltry, flat realism.

Unsurprisingly then, the most interesting works addressing the problems of contemporary Poland are those that steer clear of realist conventions (*The Scattered Files* [*Kartoteka rozrzucona*] by Tadeusz Rózewicz and Wieslaw Mysliwski's *Requiem to a Housekeeper* [*Requiem dla gospodyni*]), while the playwrights who could be said to have truly succeeded in communicating with the audience are those who managed to create their own, unique language – a language of myth and psychology – and, *through* this language, to call a whole unique world into existence. Tadeusz Slobodzianek, for instance, alludes to, recovers, and reconstructs the past – both the past told by histories, and that of the realm of the legend – and in so doing, he composes what one could term "alternative history." Drawing on myths, stories, and truths of the oral tradition, the artist calls into being a polyphonic and polysemic, de-mythologized version of fossilised events – a version which is neither the only nor the last alternative to the History accepted by tradition. Ingmar Villqist (pseudonym of a Polish playwright), in turn, invents a mysterious town named Ellmit (located somewhere in Scandinavia), inhabited by strange, traumatised and emotionally bruised characters. Ellmit becomes the artist's "laboratory", a secluded space of experimentation upon the living "human tissue," where he can scrutinise emotions, close human relationships, and the mechanisms of concealed tensions.

Both Rózewicz and Mysliwski show a multidimensional, if at times grotesque, image of the condition of the society in the face of essential transformations and the consequences of the new, mentally "undomesticated" reality. *The Scattered Files* is a unique sequel to the play Rózewicz wrote thirty years earlier. *The Files*, "the original" as well as the "the scattered," are heavily burdened with history. On the one hand, it is a history less remote: that of World War II, of the experiences of Stalinism, of the thaw of September 1956, and – especially in *The Scattered Files* – of the subsequent stages of the Polish struggle for sovereignty; shown, however, without pathos, portrayed as if they took place somewhere between the parliamentary space of the Polish Sejm and a bazaar. On the other hand, the recent history informing both plays is immediately contextualised by what has always already loomed large in their very essence: the other, remote history – familiar, yet not a part of the playwright's curriculum vitae – interiorised from countless pages of literature as the memory of the nation. Above all, this history is embodied in the Salon of Warsaw from Adam Mickiewicz's *Forefathers' Eve*, in the dilemmas of Konrad and Kordian, the heroes of the masterpieces of Polish Romanticism, in the reminiscences of *The Wedding* by Stanislaw Wyspianski, and in the patriotic sermons of Piotr Skarga. Interestingly, unlike in the allusions Rózewicz makes to the remote past, his dramatic narrative of recent history is notable for its shortage of facts of grand scale, facts of the kind of significant dates in a history coursebook. Instead, it is informed with the shallow, trifling, everyday quality of passing time; no occurrences of great significance leave their mark upon it, and it is only a close scrutiny that allows one to discover subtle waves on its surface and, at its bottom, the delicate debris of the momentous events taking place in the background. And yet, even in Rózewicz's presentation of history as tradition, the remote past reverberates with the distant echoes of the pathos of the stereotype, with the obsolete sublimity of gesture and pose, and sometimes carries with it an only too obvious, and at times ridiculously pathetic, political allusion. Nothing is to be taken for granted; everything is twisted in a distorted gesture, distorted grimace; fossilised, and therefore dead; artificial, and therefore inauthentic.

Unlike that of Rózewicz, Mysliwski's drama shows the friction between the old and the new, between the traditional rural culture (which somehow has not yet lost its subtle poetic aura), and the expansive, loud culture of the urban agglomeration. It mellifluously combines the present with the past, the real with the imagined, thus emphasising the sense of misdirection, the inability to find one's own place in a world which abides by the rules of commonsense pragmatism. The past inscribes itself into the timeless order of nature and religion, providing a solid foundation upon which human consciousness can rest; the present, conversely, is nothing but chaotic contingency, devoid of stable points of reference.

The holistic, distanced perspective of history pervading the drama of Rózewicz gives rise to parodic, grotesquely disfigured images. In turn, the self-presencing of the space of myth in Mysliwski's plays awakens nostalgia for tradition, which is irrevocably fading away. Rózewicz seems to be pointing to what the stereotypes of our contemporary concept of history indeed rigidly fix in our vision. This is possibly the reason why in his *Scattered Files*, at the end of the scene in the Salon of Warsaw, the whole stage is covered with a black shroud. With such a theatrical gesture, as if in accord with Francis Fukuyama, Rózewicz seems to declare the "end of history." He cancels history – and yet he does so only to return to history, but this time choosing a different approach. Returning, Rózewicz reassesses history from the perspective of the mediocre, poor, and unrepeatable reality, found exclusively in the concreteness of ordinary human existence. In this respect Rózewicz shares a vision with Mysliwski, who likewise shows the cultural and historical breakthrough of the year 1989 from within the space of a village cabin.

Thus, next to grand images (always shown in their stereotyped versions), the drama of Mysliwski and Rózewicz employs minor histories of modest, humble, and sometimes plainly stupid, ordinary people. Rózewicz speaks of the end of history understood as metanarration, and, at the same time, of the beginning of philosophy of history conceived in terms of the description of the mechanism of the multiplicity and divergence of individual fates. Great History does not exist; what *does* exist, however, is the limitless multiplicity of the dimensions of human fate, which cannot be reduced to anything but an individual truth, to the sensations and experiences of a unique human being. Exemplary in this respect is the character of Hela, the girl who "knew nothing of Caesar and died [...] If Hela did not know that Caesar had crossed the Rubicon – then Caesar *never* crossed the Rubicon [...] [Thus,] Hela rendered history null and void."[5]

The characters peopling Rózewicz's plays are neither distinguished nor pre-eminently gifted. Rank and file, they do not aspire to realise the fates of their generation; all they wish for is to be able to represent themselves, to follow their own fate.

The texts of Rózewicz and Mysliwski stand out from the otherwise uniform practice of contemporary Polish drama, haunted by the spectre of the un-presented reality. Meanwhile, however, it is the young theatre that is replacing drama in what used to be drama's sovereign domain: the difficult art of careful, tender analysis. Evidently, the lively interest in the new epoch, the need to understand its uniqueness, both are bringing about its serious criticism. In the Poland of today, experiencing milestone transformations in politics, the economy, customs, manners, social structures and interpersonal relations, this young theatre is driven by a will to be in touch with the fast-flowing current of everyday events. The common impression, or, better still, a frequent observation made by those "younger and more gifted ones", as they are frequently called, is the Artaudian thought that "all our ideas about life must be revised in a period when nothing any longer adheres to life"[6]. Artists such as Grzegorz Jarzyna, Anna Augustynowicz, Piotr Cieplak and Zbigniew Brzoza are creating their theatre in the cracks and fissures between everyday life and its representations; they strive to stick back onto life what has peeled off of it, but without which it is not possible to live a normal life. And hence, quite unsurprisingly, the focal points of their interest – and those that determine their artistic strategy – are building the ethics of the new reality, creating new models of morality, and developing social awareness of the importance of ethical norms.

## Notes

1. Cf. M. Piwinska, *Legenda romantyczna i szydercy* [The Romantic Legend and its Scoffers] (Warszawa: PIW, 1973).

2. Z. Majchrowski, "Ucieczki od dramatu." ["Escapes from Drama"] in: "Dialog" 1997, No 4.

3. R. Rorty, *Contingency, Irony and Solidarity* (Cambridge: Cambridge University Press, 1989).

4. T. Rózewicz, *Teatr* (Kraków: Wydawnictwo Literackie, 1988), Vol. 1, p. 90.

5. T. Rózewicz, "Kartoteka rozrzucona" ["The Scattered Files"] in: "Dialog" 1994, No 10, p. 27.

6. A. Artaud, *Teatr i jego sobowtór* (Warszawa: WAiF, 1978), p. 34.

# 18

# An Echo of Phenomenological Reflection in the Analysis of the Butoh Bodily States

## Jelena Rajak

### "To become a puppet": An emblematical exercise

One of the distinctive features of the Butoh method is the practice of *visualization*, even though the term "visualization" is not to be taken literally. In fact, rather than to perceive the world by means of sight, the point is to see with an "inner" eye, for example, the one that is mentioned in the yoga meditation techniques. To be more precise, the starting point of the *visualization* is a sequence of mental images that one concentrates on. In the next phase, the physical attitude is transformed under the influence of the initial image. In this way, the reverberations of the images of the mind, which belong generally to the sphere of the spirit, are felt in the body.

However, one should not think that the body subordinates itself to the instructions of the spirit because the Butoh method incorporates at the same time a very keen perception of physical action, an analysis of bodily sensations (proprioceptive sensitivity). That is to say, the two poles, the pole of the concrete, the way of the body, and the pole of the abstract, the way of imagination, are joined and confirm that elements of flesh and elements of spirit complement each other.

The puppet movement is probably one of the most representative exercises of the Butoh training, which is also often developed in-performance. It resumes metaphorically the mere essence of this dance technique. As in other cases of transformation in Butoh, the dancer should not seek to resemble a puppet but to create his own puppet, according to the "essential nature", the internal principles of a puppet. Two characteristics define the essence of a puppet: firstly, to be hanging on (invisible) strings which control the movement of the limbs and, secondly, to move as a result of another person's will. The imaginary action consists of several phases. In the first place, somebody (or something) gives the order to move, by pulling the strings, which bring into movement the dancer's body.

The nature of the movement that is originated by this process is unique. Since the imaginary strings move before the body does, there appears a delay, a slowdown. Moreover, the body seems not to be reacting according to its own will. It becomes an inanimate, lifeless object. It looks as if the movement were controlled from an imaginary point exterior to the subject of the movement but which is, at the same time, created by the subject himself. Instead of thinking of making a movement, the dancer rather thinks of someone (or something) inflicting the movement on him. The movement is driven by impulses created by the mental image, that of a puppet, not by the dancer's conscious choices. One aims to have the most intense sensation possible of what one imagines, in order to avoid the idea of having an intention to act. In other words, if the imagination of the situation is strong enough, the body will move because it feels the need to respond to the situation that, although imagined, becomes *real* for the body.

This exercise might remind of an approach that is often considered dangerous, where "a man reinforces the separation between the mind, which directs, and the body, which becomes manipulated as a puppet."[1] In order to elucidate this point, we can refer to what the cognitive psychology says about the conceptions related to action. In the most complex sensorimotor activities, especially in dance, the locomotion requires the integration of intentional and anticipative cognitive aspects. However, Pailhous and Bonnard observe, "a locomotion that obeys a subject's intentions and anticipations is not a voluntary movement in its entirety, [...] but a *voluntarily modified automatic movement,*[2]" therefore often unconscious.

It appears to us that the Jerzy Grotowski's writings from the final phase of his work, at the Workcenter of Jerzy Grotowski, in Pontedera, Italy, provide us with the elements for interpretation of the training based on *visualization*, a source of the "transformations" representative of Butoh. This is how Grotowski speaks of the performer's dual nature:

> One can read in ancient manuscripts: "We are two. A bird that pecks and a bird that observes. One will die, one will live." Enraptured by existing inside of time, anxious to peck, we forget to keep the observing part of ourselves alive. Consequently there is a danger of existing only inside of time and never out of time. Feeling as if being watched by the other part of oneself, the part that seems out of time, reveals the other dimension. There is an I-I. The second I is almost virtual; it is not the look of the others in us, nor their judgement, it's like an immobile gaze: a silent presence, like a sun that illuminates things, and that is all. Every person's process can be accomplished solely in the context of that immobile presence. I-I: in the experience, the couple doesn't appear to be separated, but whole, undivided.[3]

Grotowski observes the presence of two layers in every original being: the one that is real, the other that is virtual. Could that correspond, applied to Butoh, to the layer that acts, which is immersed into action, and to the layer that imagines? Although it seems that the act of imagination is the one that gives birth to movement, is it possible to know at which point the action begins? And if the fluidity of images does not fade as long as the dance lasts, the question is how that potential existence is actualized? What makes the presence "keep the silence", and prevents it from turning into a representation? How can one establish a correlation between the concept of *intentionality*, in its phenomenological sense, according to which the consciousness is defined by its directedness towards an object, and the fact that the voluntary act is banned, as it were, from performing arts?

## "To become an object" of the Butoh body

In phenomenology, the crucial paradigm of "being-in-the-world" designates the primordial experience constituted as a subject's encounter with the world, which overcomes the opposition between the subject (ego) and the object (world). In fact, the "subject" and the "object" are nothing but "two abstract aspects of that unique structure called *presence*."[4] We can consider them as conceptual elements that compose a phase that western thinking has to go through to think the unity. In numerous theorizations of the performer's work, we can recognize a similar situation, that is, the thought that one has to "start from the experience of separation in order to reach for the organic unity."[5] Butoh in particular asks for that way of thinking, not only because it is an example of "acculturation" techniques, characterized by body states that differ from those which are used in everyday life, but also because it is based on the singular technique of "becoming an object".

The notion of "becoming an object" can be traced back to the imaginary world of one of the founders of Butoh dance, Tatsumi Hijikata. He states in one of his interviews: "I want to become a body which has but eyes wide open, a body tensed to the point of cracking in response to the majestic landscape that surrounds it."[6] It is important to know that this key notion does not come from a dualistic point of understanding because, on the contrary, "to become an object", as Hijikata's words show, signifies "to become a recipient", to become nature, to open oneself to the environment, and to erase the boundary between ego and the world. This conception is reminiscent of the theories that look at man as a microcosm that contains all the elements of the macrocosm, of the matter that the world is made of. It is in light of these theories that one can also interpret the notion of *"natural rhythm"*, recurrent in the Butoh dancers' vocabulary. In this case, *natural* exactly means in harmony with the world, inert as the matter, non-intentional. That is why in the visualization exercises, based on the process of successive transformations, the point is not in imitating a precise external form, but in letting the form be born, emerge to the surface.

Another important characteristic of the concept "to become an object" is related to the fact that Hijikata felt particularly attracted to the body states close to human motor disabilities and the early stages of a child's psychomotor development. In those states, the individual fails to adapt himself to the world, which is manifested mostly by him being incapable of manipulating objects or his own body. Accordingly, Hijikata refers indirectly to a case of apraxy, when a person cannot perform voluntary goal-oriented movements: "When I tried to take hold of something, another hand grasped my hand. A hand chasing another hand ends up being a senile hand, unable to reach anything."[7] He states also that the origins of the Butoh dance are hidden in the "physical sensation that our arm does not really belong to us,"[8] that of a baby who does not recognize its limbs yet, or that of patient suffering from asomatognosia, who does not recognize one part of his body image. In addition, Hijikata enjoys switching places of the *animate* and the *inanimate*. For instance, he is fascinated by a handicap, he likes it when "a part of the body is transformed into a thing, an artificial leg, for example,"[9] or the opposite, he acknowledges that he was very much inspired by the behaviour of the children who fuse with objects by giving them a life of their own.[10]

All these cases of "becoming an object" seem to demonstrate that the reification occurs in the course of the process of voluntary manipulation of different body images. While preparing itself to receive the image of an object, or of a more abstract idea, the body alternates the phases of emerging and disappearing of body parts within the whole of the body scheme. Moreover, it is always necessary to think the body in its existential bond with the world because it presents itself as an "object, which uses its own parts as a general symbolic system of the world", in order that we may "frequent" this world, "comprehend" it, and attribute a meaning to it."[11]

## Consciousness of the body-object: An idea of incarnation

After giving a possible interpretation of the constitution of the body-object in Butoh, let us think now of the way in which the body-object enters in relation with the body-subject. According to Merleau-Ponty, "the objectifying consciousness presupposes the consciousness of the self,"[12] that is to say in this case that to be able to voluntarily manipulate the body image, we must have a point of reference, the sense of *our* body, and, moreover, we must make it conscious. The consciousness of the self will be born from the successive relating of the body at work and the body image that is being constantly altered.[13]

We would like to underline that the concept of "consciousness of the self" does not suggest a claim to subjectivity, because it is "the work [which] replaces the interiority."[14] Thus, as it seems impossible to exclude the concept of the volition of the process of acquisition of the Butoh body states, I would like to make clear that volition concerns the question of "intending to do" and not "intending to express."[15] Indeed, when the performer constantly directs his attention to the sensorimotor changes that occur in his body following the assimilation of the images (rather than produces a series of formalized steps and attitudes), he is in fact looking at what he is *doing*. Therefore, he is not divided because he does not think the object, which is the movement of his body; he is *within it,* while making the act of perception coincides with the action.[16] On the other hand, by aspiring to the "intention to express", he would be driven to think his movement as a product ready "to be consumed" by the audience and whose meaning is ossified, being disconnected from him.

However, since the body-object is conditioned by the existence of the body-subject, a Butoh dancer is aware that he is observed by the audience, thanks to the multiplicity-of-consciousness phenomenon. More precisely, he becomes the body-object because he is conscious of his reification, because he is a privileged witness of the work of imagination and of the movement that he is performing. Thus, by the very nature of the training, the performer is ready to face the audience because he is already his own audience.

So although the Toshiharu Kasai's theory of the Butoh body, for example, is founded on the concept of "non-objectification", conceived as a radical refusal of any presence of volition within the method, it does not exclude the possibility of "self-dissociation". This "self-dissociation" implies a reciprocal relation between the body-subject and the body-object. Kasai quotes the example of the Sankai Juku dancer who said that "there are at least three selves when he is performing: The dancing self who is watching and "objectifying" the body, a second self who is seen by the audience, and a third self who is watching from above both the dancing self and the stage."[17]

Perhaps that means that the Japanese refuse to theorize Butoh in terms of the division between the subject and the object, dualistic thought being perfectly alien to them, but that at the same time, the dancers' language does not avoid it completely. Indeed, it appears that for dancers, this seemingly dualistic discourse represents nothing but just one of many "hypotheses of the imagination" and as it does not refer to "any real thing", it is free to change.[18] On the other hand, this fact shows that the criterion of "referential exactness of the image"[19] does not apply to the work of imagination in Butoh, which marks the decisive difference between the utilitarian mental practices that aim at motor learning, and Butoh, as a primarily creative aesthetic practice.

Let us look once again upon the emblematic exercise of "becoming a puppet", in order to see how it solves the problem of the manipulating and the manipulated. It seems that by creating an intermediate instance, which transfers the intention of movement "elsewhere", in a kind of imaginary double, it becomes possible to circumvent the mind-body problem, and "to un-eat" the fruit of Tree of Knowledge.[20] Let us remind ourselves that it is this false stage of division of the dancer's ego, this stage of mediation, which results in the deceleration of the movement. At the more technical level of the dance, "slowness and precision are here actions which optimize the relation between the body and the consciousness, and create a state suitable for a finer perception of its modifications,"[21] as Ushio Amagatsu observes. A slow and continuous movement will make possible for the dancer to control it "during its execution, primarily starting from the sensory messages which result from it."[22]

Even if Heinrich von Kleist in its intriguing essay on the puppet theatre admires the puppet above all because its mental activity is absent, he acknowledges that "thus returns the grace, when the consciousness has gone through infinity; so that it appears in its purest form in this human anatomy which either has no awareness, or whose awareness is infinite, in a puppet, or a god."[23] The Butoh dancer also seeks, in a certain way, to avoid the idea of intention, that which would consist in wanting to signify and to represent something for the audience, by going through "infinity", by raising the level of consciousness to the maximum, by distributing the consciousness throughout the whole body.

One can consider that the mental images used in visualization exercises are incarnated in the body of the dancer, if one takes the verb "to incarnate" literally, meaning "to put in a body of flesh what exists in spirit."[24] The dancer's body is inhabited by images, it realizes them, by making them evolve from an abstraction to the concrete material existence. But one can also say that the incarnation of the dancer takes place, as it were, when the puppet integrates with its puppeteer, that is when the dancer acquires the capacity "to be flesh", "the body which is aware of itself at the same time as it is aware of what is around it,"[25] or according to Grotowski, "to be double,"[26] to, at the same time, be a consciousness which supervises the dance, and to dive into the world of matter. At this point we get close to Yvonne Ténenbaum's analysis of the art of presence of Carlotta Ikeda: it is because of the "withdrawal of the subject" of the dancer, who is reduced to the physical act of dance that his/her body is transformed into "impersonal flesh", placing itself amongst the objects of the world.[27]

## Metamorphoses of the body-object: Potentialization and actualization

One might say that the potentiality of the Butoh dance is the richer as the dancer aspires to the status of the matter that has an "infinite fruitfulness, undulating in its entirety with infinite possibilities which fill it with vague shivers"[28]. The dancer mobilizes his potential nature in order to respond to an imaginary situation, which has no solution, being virtual in the least. His body in itself has capacity to change. Even though this capacity has always been present within it, it is by the process of "becoming" that it must reactualize each new form or image. These forms and images are hidden in the memory of the body, and if one wants to make this life of the body palpable, one must let the bodywork "as if it was a memory,"[29] one must let it remember.

However, the memory in question corresponds only partly to "automatic recognition", which consists "of an action, and not of a representation" and must be supplemented by the "attentive recognition" which is characterized by the intervention of the "memoriesimages."[30] According to Grotowski, it would be the "phenomenon of reminiscence" which pushes the performer "to discover in himself an ancient corporeality."[31] If we put aside a certain universalizing and mystifying effect of the following metaphor, one can also speak of "the immemorial memory of the world" which is the "free awakening to the thought of possibilities that were dormant."[32]

From the moment one becomes aware of this interior source, it remains necessary to initiate the communicating principle so that a constant circulation of the images and forms is established. What rises directly from the source and indicates the mobilization of the matter that exists in possibility Grotowski names "impulses". The impulse represents the life of physical action preceding its actualization.[33] It seems that the process, which is present in Butoh resembles the organic process, which unfolds like a continual flow of the impulses[34] and which reaches nothing but a form in constant evolution. In my opinion, this is the reason for which the forms of Butoh cannot ossify nor for Butoh to be enclosed solely in its context of origin.

Moreover, "the impulses are related to the right tension"[35] and it is not accidental that the concept of "tension" is also significant in Butoh. Often, thanks to the technical and mental maturity of certain dancers, the effort of the body-mind work is not perceived as "expressionist residue", but as an integral part of the singular aesthetics of Butoh. However, the only thing those dancers are actually better at is handling this "right tension". The control of the tension might be regarded as the control of "indocility" of the body, indocility which is manifested in tremors, quivers – as many signs of effort, of the resistance of deep muscles, caused by the imaginary presence of obstacles in the body, by the postures whose balance is unstable. Indeed, "the indocility of the body" reminds us of its "mediating function."[36] The Butoh dancer fights without respite this indocility, while calling into question the mere possibility of "body control". He seems to constantly defy the existential union between the body-subject and the body-object in order to exceed it.

The dancer thus permeated by a network of "tensions" is the living symbol of the "tensional" nature of the technique that underlies his dance. Insofar as the deployment of the natural force of the body in action is repeatedly blocked, an imaginary intention becomes simultaneously a motor intention and one can finally speak of "violence"[37] in the Butoh method. The tremor would thus represent "the consciousness which refuses the intention and the structure to penetrate the forms."[38] The forms will remain open, capable of inexorable though unstable transformations.

In the process that is present in Butoh, it is possible to distinguish two decisive moments. On the one hand, there is visualization, a passive moment, as it were, of "letting be", during which the dancer is following the stream of images mentally. On the other hand, there is action, an active moment of mobilization of energies whose aim is to respond to the imaginary stimuli, a moment which often comprises, as I have underlined, a physical effort, characterized by muscular inertia, and a mental one, characterized by the consciousness refusing a static structure. According to Paul Ricœur, "one can assimilate this relationship between effort and letting be to the relation between actualization and potentialization."[39] I will thus conclude that, in Butoh, the genesis of forms occur through the successive stages of actualization and of repotentialization. The dance is nothing but a series of passages from the existence in possibility to the existence in actuality.

## Notes

1. Grotowski, Jerzy, "De la compagnie théâtrale à l'art comme véhicule (1993)", in Richards, Thomas, *Travailler avec Grotowski sur les actions physiques (At Work With Grotowski On Physical Actions)*, Arles: Actes Sud/Paris: Académie expérimentale des théâtres, 1995, p. 193.

2. Pailhous, Jean, Bonnard, Mireille, "L'Espace locomoteur: intégration sensorimotrice et cognitive", in *Le Corps en jeu*, ed. by Odette Aslan, Paris: CNRS Editions, 1993, p. 37.

3. Grotowski, Jerzy, "Le Performer", in *Centro di Lavoro di Jerzy Grotowski*, Potedera (Italie): Centro per la Sperimentazione e la Ricerca Teatrale, 1988, p. 55.

4. Merleau-Ponty, Maurice, *Phénoménologie de la perception*, Paris: Gallimard, 1945, p. 492.

5. Barba, Eugenio, "Le Corps crédible", in *Le Corps en jeu, op. cit.*, p. 252.

6. Hijikata, Tatsumi to Shibusawa, Tatsuhiko, "Plucking off the Drakness of the Flesh", in *The Drama Review*, Vol. 44, No 1 (T 165), spring 2000, p. 53.

7. Hijikata, Tatsumi, "Wind Daruma", in *The Drama Review*, Vol. 44, No 1 (T 165), *op. cit.*, p. 77.

8. Idem, "Plucking off the Darkness of the Flesh", *loc. cit.* p. 53.

9. Idem, "Plucking off the Darkness of the Flesh", *loc. cit.* p. 53.

10. "Once I took a dipper secretly and left it in the middle of a field. I did it because I felt sorry for it, laying in the darkness of the kitchen, and because I wanted to show it the world outside." IDEM, "Wind Daruma", *loc. cit.*, p. 75.

11. Merleau-Ponty, M., *op. cit.*, p. 274.

12. Idem, *ibidem*, p. 274.

13. Cf. Rosenfield, Israel, *Une anatomie de la conscience. L'étrange, le familier, l'oublié (The Strange, Familiar, and Forgotten. An Anatomy of Consciousness, 1992)*, Paris: Flammarion, 1996, pp. 18-19.

14. Barthes, Roland, *L'Empire des signes* (1970), Paris: Skira, 1993, p. 81.

15. Cf. Barba, Eugenio, Savarese, Nicola, "Pré/expressivité", in *Anatomie de l'acteur. Un dictionnaire d'anthropologie théâtrale*, Cazilhac: Bouffonneries-Contrastes/Rome: Zeami Libri/Holstebro: ISTA, 1986, p. 22.

16. Cf. Merleau-Ponty, M., *op. cit.*, pp. 275-76.

17. Kasai, Toshiharu, "A Note on Butoh Body", in *Memoir of Hokkaido Institute of Technology*, Vol. 28, 2000.
    (http:/www.ne.jp/asahi/butoh/itto)

18. Amagatsu, Ushio, "Corps et virtualité", in *Dialogue avec la gravité*, Arles: Actes Sud, 2000, p. 35.

19. "If it is indispensable that the images which are developed during the mental practice of a physical activity have a maximum degree of activation, and that the subject keeps controlling them cognitively, the *figurative content of the images needs also to accurately reflect the situation that the images refer to.*" Denis, Michel, *Image et cognition*, Paris: PUF, 1989, p. 243.

20. Kleist, Heinrich von, "*Sur le théâtre de marionnette*" (1810), Paris: Milles et une nuits, 1993, p. 14.

21. Amagatsu, Ushio, "Douceur et précision", in *Dialogue avec la gravité, op. cit.*, p. 25.

22. Pailhous, Jean, Bonnard, Mireille, "Programmation et contrôle du mouvement", in *Traité de psychologie cognitive 1, Perception, action, langage*, ed. by Claude Bonnet, Rodolphe Ghiglione, Jean-François Richard, Paris: Bordas (Dunod), 1989, p. 147.

23. Kleist, H. v., *op. cit.*, p. 20.

24. Souriau, Étienne, *Vocabulaire d'esthétique*, ed. by Anne Souriau, Paris: Quadrige/PUF, 1990, p. 875.

25. Henry, Michel, *Incarnation. Une philosophie de la chair*, Paris: Seuil, 2000, p. 8.

26. Grotowski, J., "Le Performer", *loc. cit.*, p. 55.

27. Ténenbaum, Yvonne, "Ikeda Carlotta, un art de la présence", in *Butô(s)*, ed. by Odette Aslan and Béatrice Picon-Vallin, Paris: CNRS Éditions, 2002, p. 216.

28. Schulz, Bruno, "Traité des mannequins ou la seconde Genèse", *Les Boutiques de cannelle* (1974), Paris: Gallimard, 1992, p. 77.

29. Grotowski, Jerzy, *Lignée organique au théâtre et dans le rituel. Session du 23 juin 1997 au théâtre Odéon*, audio recording, Loubejac: Le Livre qui parle, 1998.

30. Cf. Bergson, Henri, *Matière et mémoire. Essai sur la relation du corps à l'esprit* (1939), Paris: Quadrige/PUF, 1999, pp. 100-107.

31. Grotowski, J., "Le Performer", *loc. cit.*, p. 56.

32. Henry, M., *op. cit.*, p. 206 and 208.

33. Grotowski, Jerzy, "Liège Conference", Cirque Divers, 2nd January 1986, unpublished, quoted by Thomas Richard in *At Work With Grotowski On Physical Actions, op. cit.*, pp. 154-55.

34. Grotowski, Jerzy, *Lignée organique au théâtre et dans le rituel. Leçon inaugurale au Théâtre des Bouffes du Nord*, 24th March 1997, audio recording, Villefranche-du-Périgord: Le Livre qui parle, No 24550, 1997.

35. Richard, Thomas, *Travailler avec Grotowski sur les actions physiques, op. cit.*, p. 157.

36. Ricœur, Paul, *Philosophie de la volonté. Le volontaire et l'involontaire,* (1950), Paris: Aubier, 1988, p. 200.

37. "[...] by definition, an act is a violent passage from what I have got to what I aim at, from what I am to what I have the intention to be." Merleau-Ponty, M., *op. cit.,* p. 438.

38. Sakurai, Keisuke, "The Body as Dance. An Introduction to the Study of Butoh-logy", in *Butoh kaden,* CD-ROM, ed. by Yukio Waguri, Tokyo: JustSystem, 1998.

39. Ricœur, P., *op. cit.,* p. 312.

# 19

## The Fadime Sahindal Story

### Honour Killings as "Death by Culture" in Sweden 2002

**Tiina Rosenberg**

> For a while, Fadime Sahindal seemed an ideal symbol of second-generation immigrant success in a country that prides itself on its openness and tolerance./.../But it was this very desire for independence that provoked her father into a rage so great that he killed her in January turning her into the tragic emblem of a European society's failure to bridge the gap in attitudes between its own culture and those of its newer arrivals.
>
> *New York Times*, 23 July 2002[1]

Do I detect a certain malicious pleasure in this commentary from the *New York Times*, as though it were time to point a finger at the failure of the European integration of non-western immigrants, after years of European criticism of the Americans for their racist politics? At a time of rising anti-immigrant, and clearly islamophobic, sentiments across the continent of Europe (not to mention the US), even many Swedes' attitudes have hardened toward non-Nordic immigrants. Sweden has, of course, never been free from racism, but lately the things have changed considerably. It is as though the feeling of solidarity has vanished and attitudes that would have been politically unthinkable, say, say ten years ago, are now openly acknowledged. On top of the growing pan-European xenophobia, Sweden had a spectacular case of "honour killing" in January 2002, when the Swedish-Kurdish woman

Fadime Sahindal was brutally murdered by her father. The Fadime story was given extraordinary media coverage. It introduced the expression honour killing to the Swedish media vocabulary and placed the phenomena itself on the very top of the Swedish media agenda.

Honour killings had been discussed in the Swedish media occasionally even before Fadime Sahindal. Between 1984 and 2001 there have been around 30 honour killings in Sweden, but it was not until after the murder of Fadime that they were intensely discussed and analysed. However, the term itself is not clearly defined. In the mainstream media the term honour killing is used as follows: (1) one or more men (2) murder (3) a woman they know well (4) who has offended their honour. The use of the term honour killing places this kind of violence in foreign cultures (cultural otherness) and neglects the fact that violence against women is also a part of Swedish everyday life.

The tragic story of Fadime Sahindal, which shocked and provoked the Swedish public and media, was – perhaps predictably – received slightly differently in different parts of the Swedish media landscape. This paper focuses on the four main discourses of honour killing in the Swedish media: (1) the death by culture discourse; (2) the feminist discourse; (3) the individualizing discourse; (4) the hybrid discourse; and relates them to three theatre productions on the topic honour killings: *Electra, Heder (Honour)* and *Vem ska trösta Mona eller Sveriges förlorade heder (Who Will Comfort Mona or The Lost Honour of Sweden)*.

## The Fadime Story in Short

Fadime Sahindal, 26, was killed by her father in January 2002 as she sat in her sister's flat in Uppsala. The doorbell rang. Her father burst in and shot Fadime in the head. For four years Fadime's father had been threatening to kill her. But in her last week she took the risk of going to bid farewell to her mother and sisters before leaving to study in Africa. She died in her mother's arms.

The family moved to Sweden from Turkey in 1980, and Fadime had grown up in the university town of Uppsala. At a computer course in 1996, Fadime met and fell in love with a young Swedish man, Patrik Lindesjö. The couple kept their relationship secret for a year, and when her father finally found out, Fadime moved to another town to escape her father and brothers. The police merely advised her to stop talking to her family. Instead, Fadime turned to the press, giving interviews about the conditions of Kurdish girls and women in Sweden.

Single-handedly she started a debate about integration and double standards.

The police's passivity in the face of her father's threats infuriated the Swedish public. Fadime was given a state funeral in the Protestant Cathedral, attended by the Swedish Crown Princess Victoria and members of the Swedish political elite. Symbolically, another important funeral took place in Sweden around the same week, namely that of Astrid Lindgren, the Swedish author who created Pippi Långstrump (Pippi Longstocking), the archetypal subversive and anarchic girl rebel of Swedish post-war literature.

The Fadime story has stirred deep emotions in Sweden and generated a heated debate on honour killings that was very much used in the latest elections in September 2002. In order to investigate xenophobic attitudes among Swedish politicians, two Swedish journalists from a television documentary series called *Kalla fakta (Cold Facts)* used a hidden camera and microphone while interviewing politicians on and off the record. Their political statements were very different depending on if they thought they were being taped or not. The documentary was broadcast a few days prior to the Swedish elections and caused great political turbulence. The two journalists were accused of using unethical methods, but were also awarded the Swedish Journalist of the Year Award.

At the same time, Swedish theatre has turned sharply towards more political themes. In 2001, racism, post-colonialism, integration and social justice were already on the theatre agenda, and in 2002 the move to political questions has been even more pronounced. In that part of the repertoire we find the performances mentioned earlier: *Electra, Honour* and *Who Will Comfort Mona?*

## The Death by Culture Discourse

The death by culture discourse emphasizes cultural specificity and how this is manifested in people's actions. Those who argued for this discourse sought the reason for the extreme action of Fadime's father in the Kurdish culture. According to this perspective, the norms of the Kurdish culture justify honour killings. In order to prevent further honour killings in Sweden we must acknowledge cultural specificity and promote intercultural exchange (meaning: "they" have to learn from "us").

The most active spokesman for the death-by-culture discourse has been the anthropologist Mikael Kurkiala. In his first article in the leading Swedish newspaper *Dagens Nyheter*, entitled "The great fear of differences", he challenged those who individualized the Fadime case, inferring that it was simply the desperate action of a madman who could just as well have been a Swede. The main representatives of this standpoint are two influential journalists, Jan Guillou and the Swedish-Kurdish Kurdo Baksi. Furthermore, Kurkiala criticised feminists for defining Fadime as the victim of patriarchal values and practices. The feminists he was pointing at were Left Party leader Gudrun Schyman and the feminist writer Moa Matthis. Kurkiala also underlined that his views were strongly supported by Kurdish women. He also wrote that nobody dared put the blame on Kurdish culture for fear of being labelled as racists, and thereby contributing to the growing xenophobia in Sweden and the western world.

My first theatre example, *Electra,* relates to this discourse. *Electra* (opened in March 2001) was an adaptation of Sophocles' *Electra* but transplanted to Uppsala, the very town where Fadime lived. It was directed by Birgitta Englin, who has won several awards for her contemporary adaptations of classics. At the time of the production of *Electra* at Uppsala City Theatre Fadime was already known as a spokeswoman for threatened immigrant girls and women. Birgitta Englin gathered a reference group of these women while working on her *Electra*. The production process of *Electra* surrounded Fadime's life and death while the play was running.

*Electra* opens with a dark stage and a DJ in full action. The set consisted of video screenings on TV monitors, a big closet for Clytemnestra, a sofa and sort of phone box with a computer. On the screen the text "Orestes come here!" blinked insistently as people ran back and forth, joking, arguing.

The tragedy of Agamemnon, who sacrifices his daughter Iphigenia for good wind and success in war and is killed by his wife Clytemnestra, is one of the master narratives of the Western literary canon, with the message: blood craves more blood. Englin's production focuses on the abused daughter, Electra: a modern, angry young woman dressed in a short skirt, Doctor Marten's shoes and a Palestine shawl wrapped around her neck. She is full of hatred: "Fuck you, fuck you, fuck you!" she screams, while her best friends Linda and Cissi – the chorus of the Mycenaean women in Sophocles' play – do their very best to calm her down. Electra is sexually harassed by Aigisthos, and when her brother Orestes finally arrives and kills their mother, he is angered by what he finds. Electra is too outward-going, modern and provocative for his taste, and she is killed too.

*Electra* was an extremely intense and energetic production, well suited for younger audiences. Swedish theatre critics voted it performance of the year in 2001 and it was performed to full houses for two years. But at the same time there was something problematic in this production, as Yael Feiler pointed out. The emphasis on Electra's anger and disappointment is very promising up to the point when Orestes enters the stage, introducing the "death by culture" discourse. By representing Moslem men as illiterate desert brothers, the whole discussion was placed too firmly in a foreign and very unpleasant context where the two cultures, Electra's Swedish modernity based on equality between the sexes, and her culture of origin – represented by her brother Orestes – with its traditional reactionary values, rather overshadowed the feminist ambitions of the performance by bringing in racist bias.

## The Feminist Discourse

The feminist debate on honour killings in *Dagens Nyheter* emphasised patriarchal structures in all cultures. This, however, did not mean that the feminist debate perceived "patriarchy" as a universal, unchanging, deterministic social structure based on denying *agency* to women. The term patriarchy was used in a narrower sense, referring to a form of male dominance whereby fathers control families and families are the unit of social and economic power.[2]

The first article, entitled "Fadime – a victim of male oppression", within this discourse was written by Gudrun Schyman, a feminist and leader of the Left Party in Sweden. According to Schyman, Fadime's death was not a "death by culture". She was sacrificed because of the patriarchal culture that oppresses women everywhere in the world. There are, of course, different degrees of oppression, but basically she did not see that there was much difference between Afghanistan led by the talibans and Sweden with its highly-praised equality policies, where women still get beaten up by their husbands, boyfriends or unknown men. She later gave a political talk on this theme, dubbed by the Swedish media as "Schyman's taliban speech".

Gudrun Schyman received a furious retort from the feminist historian Yvonne Hirdman who differentiated between patriarchies, meaning that it is impossible to compare Sweden with the taliban regime in Afghanistan. Hirdman's article clearly inferred that the white Swedish patriarchy is better than any patriarchy of colour. This is not stated explicitly but is obvious in her article. According to Hirdman, a gender system is culturally and historically specific and the Swedish gender system is founded on a policy of equality. It is therefore dangerous to universalise patriarchy in the way that Schyman did.

This in turn infuriated the postcolonial feminists. Paulina de los Reyes, Irene Molina and Diana Mulinari wrote an answer to Hirdman's article in *Aftonbladet*, accusing Hirdman and the Swedish feminist project of racism. Hirdman has later modified her argument. Her main point was: (1) it didn't make any sense to claim that honour killings were unrelated to culture, (2) it is absurd to separate power from culture, (3) "why can't we say that something is good in this country without being accused of racism?"

Moa Mathis, a feminist writer, in turn, wrote that Fadime's father, Rahmi Sahindal, is a part of Swedish contemporary society, and consequently Swedes have to get to grips with the violence against women. It is far too simplistic to single out the Kurdish people and hold the Kurdish culture responsible for what has happened. There was also one male voice supporting the feminist discourse, namely Kurdo Baksi, a frequent debater on immigrant topics. He pointed out that all human actions are in one way or another culturally specific. But if honour killing is regarded merely as a Kurdish or Middle Eastern problem, one easily turns a blind eye to its gender specificity, to social injustice and to poverty. He warns against the "death by culture" discourse, which unavoidably sets two cultures against each other. This kind of comparison leads easily to a description of the "other" culture as reactionary and something that must be fought and changed for the "better", according to our own standards. This leads to xenophobia and enhances patriarchal structures.

## The Individualizing Discourse

The individualizing discourse puts the blame on Fadime's father, Rahmi Sahindal. He is described as a sick and confused man with deeply rooted values from his former homeland. Central to this perspective is that it does not single out an ethnic group or a specific culture, but an individual.

## The Hybrid Discourse

The hybrid discourse focuses on the complexity of the Fadime case. Here we can find parts of the "death by culture" discourse, but the hybrid discourse is quick to emphasise that the Kurdish culture is not homogeneous. There are also feminist voices in support of the hybrid discourse, underlining the patriarchal dimension of the Fadime case. Nevertheless, there is a focus on the fact that Rahmi Sahindal – regardless of his Kurdish origins – is a part of the Swedish society that has to face up to the violence against women. At the same the hybrid discourse insists that Kurdish organizations now have to take their responsibility and work more efficiently for equality.

One of the articles within the hybrid discourse, entitled "Don't force us to choose between anthropology and feminism", was written by the Swedish-Jewish journalist and theatre critic Leif Zern. According to Zern, the different perspectives are not necessarily exclusive of one another. The murder of Fadime and honour killings must be explained from both cultural and feminist perspectives. It is important to analyse the phenomenon both from a larger perspective (patriarchal structures) and on a more detailed level (cultural specificity) if we want to prevent honour killings in the future.

I am placing the productions *Honour* and *Who Is Going to Comfort Mona?* in this category.

Ironically, the play *Honour (Heder)*, written by the Swedish-Jewish playwright Marianne Goldman, was in production at the time of Fadime's murder. Marianne Goldman had written this play in response to another honour killing of a woman called Sara in 1996, but no theatre was interested in producing it at the time. Goldman finally found Teatro Sandino, a free theatre group led by the Swedish-Chilean director Igor Cantillana. And suddenly the play gained an extreme actuality in the shooting of Fadime.

In *Honour* everything seems to be hopeless. The play is set in Rinkeby, a Stockholm suburb dominated by immigrants. The youngest daughter Leila is brought up in Sweden and wants to have a Swedish lifestyle, which to her is synonymous with freedom and modernity. The play's sub-title *Fast Forward* refers to Leila's wish to get on fast, while the father would choose rewind if he had the opportunity to make such a choice. Leila wants to be Swedish, while the father, not unlike Fadime's father, refuses to learn Swedish and has a nostalgic longing for his home village. Leila challenges her father, and her mother leaves the family when her husband beats her up. Leila, however, turns up at her sister's wedding, looking for reconciliation, but gets killed.

Marianne Goldman's play clearly condemns honour killings, but on her way to this final condemnation she puts up a few stations. She describes the Swedish ambition "att försörja sig själv" (to support oneself) as a kind of religion and underlines that far too many Swedes today live alone, with an alienated life style no values other than work and career status. Goldman describes loneliness as a disease of civilization. Against this she contrasts the immigrant family with intimacy and kinship as its framework. While the Swedes glorify the individual, immigrants celebrate the collective, Goldman seems to say. One of the characters comments the cultural difference between the Western and Muslim worlds by saying that it is only a difference of degree, not a difference in species. This was emphasized by the stage sets that turned the theatre space into a nomad tent framing both the actors and the audience, to bridge the gap between "us" and "them". A series of video images with motifs from refugee camps and life from Rinkeby were projected on the tent canvas.

*Vem ska trösta Mona eller Sveriges förlorade heder* (a play on words paraphrasing titles of works by Tove Jansson and Rainer Werner Fassbinder) opened in May 2002. It was a theatrical installation by Richard Turpin, and Frida Röhl at Teater Tribunalen, a political theatre space in Stockholm. The project was initiated by a young woman, "Leyla", in a situation similar to that of Fadime. The play was built around letters from young women with an immigrant background, but it also commented on developments in Sweden after the murder of Fadime. The result was an ironic sampling of voices, attitudes, opinions and ideologies where the voices of the women were mixed with comments on how the establishment profits from tragedies such as that of Fadime. The text did not offer any obvious answers or "truths" about immigration, refugees, honour killings or Swedish law practices. Instead it was a chorus of very disparate voices and options that wrestled with one another.

With irony as its weapon, Teater Tribunalen was literally attacking the Swedish media discussion, but the real core of the performance remained the collection of letters and interviews with young women with an immigrant background. On stage, several young women related their own experiences. Meanwhile, a panel of Swedish experts were trying to solve the problems and negotiate all the contradictions. "Well, who's fault was it?" asked one voice and there are many answers available: the father is to be blamed, the cultural difference, it could be everybody's fault. A feminist, a liberal democrat, an islamophobic couple, an empathetic female citizen – everybody seemed to have something to say.

The performance space was decorated with yellow and blue balloons (the Swedish national colours). A chorus of young women sang summer songs. A young man played the violin in national costume. Swedishness lay like a thick blanket over the prologue and continued to do so throughout the performance. While the young women told their stories, *Big Brother* and other docusoaps were shown on video. The stories of these young women were commented by the docusoaps, where young Swedish women and men were drinking heavily and having sex in the front of the television cameras. This theatre installation was choreographed in a very rapid pace and the multiple chorus of voices formed a collective scream on the failure of social integration.

If these three productions had anything in common – apart from the thematic focus on honour killings – it was their strong emphasis on contemporaneity and political authenticity. Various kinds of videos were as visual links with the outside reality used in all the three productions, thereby contextualising the theme with the world outside.

## The Fadime Story: Death by Culture?

The complex discussions around the topic of honour killings are far from finished. I would like to see more of a feminist discussion that acknowledges the connections between the gender-specific everyday domestic violence in Sweden without trying to place the so-called honour killings outside our own cultural context. The Indian scholar Uma Narayan actually does this when she juxtaposes domestic violence in western contexts and dowry-murders in India and discovers how provocative this connection is to westerners:

> The juxtaposition of domestic violence in Western contexts and dowry-murders in India will likely seem odd to some readers, or at

least a juxtaposition that is not self-evident. It is precisely the fact that significance of this juxtaposition will not be self-evident to many that prompts me to start with this "joining together" of two phenomena that are taken by many Westerners to be "unconnected". I know they are often taken to be unconnected because I have had several conversations in which Americans seemed to have been startled by my matter-of-fact claim that dowry-murders are not only often preceded by domestic violence but that they also constitute one extreme form of domestic violence. I no longer make this claim, since I have become aware of its oddly polemical weight. I have, in turn, been startled by the fact that the proposition that dowry-murders were a form of domestic violence was "news" to my audience here. What follows is an attempt to make sense of why the connection between dowry-murders and domestic violence is not "visible" to many Americans, as well as an attempt to make this connection.[3]

What Uma Narayan points out is that in the explanations that generate the "death by culture", "religious views" or "traditional views" often become virtually synonymous with "culture" at large. When honour killing, as in the case of Fadime, becomes associated with Middle Eastern culture in the Swedish debate, the debate easily ignores the violence and, in fact, similar honour killings in Swedish culture. Let me give you one final example:

In 2001, .the Stockholm Municipal Council organized a huge campaign against domestic violence, with huge pictures all over the city showing ordinary Swedish men with the numbers of women who had been killed by husbands, boyfriends or other men. A large number of men were enraged and bombarded the Swedish media with wild protests. They were not upset because so many Swedish women are abused in different ways. No, they found it outrageous that "normal", well-behaved Swedish men were humiliated in this way. What happened? In some parts of the city the pictures were taken down, but not everywhere. This form of violence is clearly gender-specific and must be approached accordingly. In practice, in a country that prides itself on being the most egalitarian country in the world – women are still demanding, and not automatically getting, equality.

But when Fadime was killed there was a sudden chorus of male voices condemning the deed and speaking up loudly against domestic violence. It was as if one of the favourite Western racist tales, as the

Indian feminist scholar Gayatri Spivak calls it, had come alive: the story of how the white man rescues the woman of colour from the man of colour. There are obviously patriarchies. "Our" men are good while the others are bad, seems to be the result of the moral panic after the killing of Fadime. I do not deny that there have been sincere voices demanding justice for Fadime, but I cannot turn a blind eye to the fact that Fadime has been used as a symbolic weapon against the patriarchy of colour that is oppressive while the white patriarchy is not. Seen in this light, other cultures always will be a threat to us, a political attitude that is today very clearly manifested not only in Western European politics, but above all by the US hysteria about terrorism.

When the Swedish author Liza Marklund (who spent her late teens in the Middle East, where she met her first husband) wrote in *Expressen* in April 2002 that the murder of Fadime was governed by the same patriarchal structure as the murders of other women, it earned her a great deal of criticism. "OK," Marklund replied, "there are of course varying degrees of hell, but what difference does that make to the murdered women?"

## Notes

1. Sarah Lyall, "Lost in Sweden: A Kurdish Daughter is Sacrificed", *New York Times*, 23 July 2002.

2. Linda Gordon, *Heroes of Their Own Lifes: The Politics and History of Family Violence – Boston 1880-1960* (New York: Viking), 1988, p. vi.

3. Uma Narayan, "Cross-Cultural Connections, Border-Crossings and 'Death by Culture'. Thinking About Dowry-Murders in India and Domestic-Violence in the United States", in *Dislocating Cultures. Identities, Traditions, and Third World Feminisms* (London & New York: Routledge, 1997), pp. 88-89.

# 20

# A Bizarre Entrance of the *Ethnic Other*

## Yael Feiler

Over the past two years it has been possible to observe the entrance of the *ethnic other* upon the Swedish stage. The change is quite visible. New themes are appearing in original Swedish plays and major theatres have begun to introduce actors with diverse ethnic backgrounds.

This paper will concentrate on an early, somewhat shy, secret and bizarre entrance of the *ethnic other*. It was actually so veiled that, other than myself, hardly anyone seems to have noticed it...

The play in which this hidden entrance takes place is called *Hannas midsommar*, written by the established Swedish woman playwright, Margareta Garpe, and performed at the Swedish National Theatre, Dramaten 1997.[1] The action of the play takes place in present day Sweden, on a very Swedish holiday, Midsummer (the same holiday during which Miss Julie freaks out). The protagonist, Hanna, a middle-aged woman lawyer, has recently moved (with her husband Gerhard and her daughter Billie) back to her old home on the Swedish island of Gotland. She is now preparing the Midsummer party while waiting for her best friend, Helen who's expected after two years abroad. The atmosphere is idyllic, but some dark clouds are appearing on the horizon: (1) The daughter Billie is leaving the family nest. She is to be engaged to the island's only black man, Jack, and will follow him on a trip to Africa. (2) Helen, Hanna's best friend, recently back from two years abroad as a medical worker in Africa, turns out to be newly divorced and out of balance, which, we learn, causes her to seek comfort in Gerhard. This act of "mutual comfort" takes place during the midsummer celebration on the seashore. Hanna, thus betrayed, proceeds to get very drunk and than drives home and falls asleep. The following morning she realises that she has run over her daughter's boyfriend and killed him. The questions that she confronts – after all she is a lawyer – concern guilt, responsibility and the importance of truth.

What's the problem than? Well, one major problem that I, as an audience, confronted when first watching the performance was the missing Jack. The black adoptive son, Jack who is engaged to the protagonist's daughter, and who gets killed and causes the play's (official) moral dilemma is actually missing on stage. Reading the play I realised that he is also missing as a written character. Black Jack serves an important purpose in the play. His existence makes the island go round, so to speak. But still, he doesn't really exist. I resolved to discover the meaning of this absence.

The part of me that is theatre scholar could not find any good dramaturgical reason for Jack's absence. To draw a comparison, one might choose a very well known absence in drama, Lorca's Pepe Romano in *The House of Bernarda Alba*.[2] In his case, though, the absence is well motivated. His very absence is the root of the dramatic development, or as Ponica puts it: "...they're women without men, that's all" (Lorca [1936] tr.1987). Jack on the contrary, I would argue, is absent because his function in the play is neither a conscious, nor a carefully prepared one. He "happens" to be in the background, he "happens" to be black and he "happens" to get killed. At the same time, this unconscious existence becomes a channel through which fears, anxieties and prejudices become visible. Therefore, I read this play as a story about Sweden and *the others*. Jack is a symbol for and a fantasy about *the others,* while the island Gotland is a symbol for Sweden.

This might be the right place to mention my own position in relation to this matter. Besides being a theatre scholar, (for whom it's only natural to be alert and critical) I also have a personal motive for my interest and engagement. Being regarded as an *ethnic other* in the Swedish context, I felt that this twisted representation includes me. And since I realised that I was more or less alone making this observation (since the absent Jack was hardly mentioned in any review, or any coverage of the event), I understood that the production was not aimed to be seen through my, and my fellow *others'* eyes. I realised, though, that since my observations are unique I might perceive something that the target audience, including critics, would miss. In other words, I had "a mission".

**Plate 1**
*Cover*

According to the official presentation of the play, in the programme for example, and according to the reviews, the questions, which this play deals with, are universal and moral ones, hence, it deals with life and death, truth and lies, friendship and treachery, guilt and mercy. The audiences are expected to relate to a play about Hanna in her late 40's.

Encouraged by Jonathan Culler's statement on the importance of asking "...questions the text does not encourage one to ask..." I chose however to read what I was not expected to, aiming to find out "...not what the work has in mind but what it forgets, not what it says but what it takes for granted."[3] Consequently, my so-called mission was to unveil the story of Jack, to compensate him, by making him visible. Rather than merely emphasising Jack's absence, I am going thus to tell you his story and in a way to rewrite the play. A play about Sweden and *the others*.

The picture on the programme cover speaks for itself: it exemplifies the fantasy about summer in the Swedish countryside (in reality it always rains you know): the green meadows, the stonewalls, the cloudless sky in the twilight of the summer night, the blue sea and the red Volvo PV. I mention particularly the Volvo PV because it is a symbol for the now dying Swedish Welfare State.

You can see for yourself that "Volvo" is presented as a symbol of the safe, secure and just Sweden. A Sweden one wishes to be back in....

Together with Hanna's yellow dress the colour composition signals an idyll. At the same time one could interpret the blue horizon as a barrier (it's not so simple to escape from an island), and the darkening sky as an approaching threat, en ending, death. Gotland, the Swedish island that we encounter through the play, is indeed both

**Plate 2**
*Volvo*

idyllic and threatened. It is isolated, which means both protected and desolate. The empty car and the empty dress make it feel even more deserted. This proves to be true.

The very existence of each family introduced in the play is threatened by degeneration. As is their cultural existence. Let me show you a simple scheme:

SWEDEN/ISLAND OF GOTLAND
SVEN + SOLVEIG = CHILDLESS
Solveig is also dying of Cancer
HELEN + MARCUS = CHILDLESS
HANNA + GERHARD = BILLIE

As you can see for yourself: two of the three couples introduced are childless while the third faces separation from a child. At the same time all three couples relate their problems to Africa:

| SWEDEN | AFRICA |
|---|---|
| Sven + Solveig = childless | Jack = Adopted |
| Helen + Marcus = childless | Markus + Fatma = Expecting |
| Hanna + Gerhard = Billie | Billie + Jack = ? |

Sven and Solveig adopt a child from Africa – Jack. Helen and Marcus are also childless. Both go to Africa to work as doctors, where, we learn, Helen hopes to get pregnant probably inspired by the fertile atmosphere, working as midwife, helping "thousands of children" to be born.[4] This plan doesn't succeed. Instead her husband "succeeds" in making an African woman, Fatma, pregnant, which results in his leaving Helen. Hanna and Gerhard, however, have a child, Billie.

Instead, it is their chicken farm, which is incapable of producing eggs... Billie, the young one sums up the island's fertility related problems in a statement about her mother's farm: "Something's wrong with Hanna's chicken-farm, no one knows why..."[5]

It's quite obvious that "Africa" in this context is constructed in a good Orientalistic tradition, as an opposite to the island or to Sweden if you wish. It's both promising and fertile, full of life but at the same time seductive and dangerous: Africa "steals" Helen's husband and causes her to "steal" Gerhard, which in turn causes Hanna to drive drunk and kill Jack. Also, Africa is aiming to steal Billie.

Jack, who is African by origin, is in the same way both promising and dangerous and I would argue that he is unconsciously constructed exactly that way. Let me give you an example.

In one of the early dialogues in the play we learn that Hjalmar, the village's fiddler and a representative of the Old Swedish music tradition, is about to retire.[6] Later he declares, though, that "the fiddle must go on playing,"[7] and he is going to pass it on to Jack, because "Jack is the only one who shows interest and talent."[8] The "native" young generation is presumably not interested in passing the Swedish culture forward, which means that the Swedish culture is in the process of dying. The only one with capacity to save it is Jack. Coming from Africa, which here is constructed as a source of health, energy and the well-known "rhythm in the blood", he seems to be the right one. The reaction of the rest of the population is ambivalent, though. His adoptive father Sven calls it "a sensitive matter", while Hjalmar counters that "that's the way *they* look like nowadays,"[9] which means that Jack's "look alike(s)" already have taken over the Swedish Culture... In other words: Jack is badly needed, but he is also being blamed for the help he is ready to offer since he, and *the others,* are not aware that they "go too far" in their role as "cultural saviours".

Jack's health and fertility is also badly needed for reasons already mentioned. The Island's population seems to be sterile, and moreover, his adoptive mother is dying of cancer. As representative of reproductive couples of the island, Billie's choice of Jack from Africa is a promising one in terms of fertility. She also mentions that he is "warm, sexy and has a good heart."[10] Her parents object to her plans. They don't support the idea of her becoming engaged to Jack, and Hanna declares that she "will never let her go to Africa."[11]

Jack is hence both needed and rejected, but in the end of the day the rejection takes over. Jack is killed. The fiddle will be buried with him, Hjalmar declares, (better dead culture than culture carried by the wrong representatives), and Billie is safe, she can stay with her mother for a while...

The play about "Sweden and *the others*" which is hidden between the written lines of *Hannas midsommar* includes many other interesting revelations which I don't have the time to share with you. Finally, though, I would like to make a point concerning the choice of making Jack black. In the play it is mentioned that Jack is a Tuareg. The Tuareg people are known to be nomads, originally living in the Sahara desert. Within the African context they are also called "whites".

**Plate 3**
*Tuareg*

Choosing a Tuareg identity for Jack, and at the same time emphasising his blackness, describing him in the text as "coal-black"[12], indicates not only a generalisation of *otherness* and a proof of ignorance, it also confirms my reading of his blackness as a sign. A sign for the alien. For that which is not "white", for that which is not Swedish. A sign representing the *ethnic other*.

In conclusion, *Hannas midsommar* appears on stage when Sweden is actually confronted with visible *ethnic otherness*. The dominant discourse on issues of *ethnicity* begins to be challenged. Crimes defined as racist are being committed and at the same time the well-meant exotism of *the other* is questioned in a number of debates. With reference to the examples mentioned above, the dramatic text, which I regard as a discursive act, cannot avoid these questions. That is why *Hannas Midsommar* includes traces of the different tendencies in the discussion of ethnicity and integration in modern-day Sweden.

Consequently, Jack personifies a visible *ethnic other*. That's why he's black. He is innocent and exotic, he is a source of energy and health but he is also a danger, victimised and finally eliminated.

## Notes

1. Garpe, Margareta, *Hannas midsommar,* unpublished manuscript, Stockholm, 1997.
2. Lorca, Federico Garcia, *The House of Bernarda Alba* (1936), trans. Dewell, 1987.
3. Culler, Jonathan, in Eco ed., *Interpretation and overinterpretation,* Cambridge, 1992, p. 114.
4. Ibid., Garpe, Margareta, *Hannas midsommar,* p. 28.
5. Ibid., p. 18.
6. Ibid., p. 3.
7. Ibid., p. 56.
8. Ibid., p. 57.
9. Ibid., p. 56.
10. Ibid., p. 104.
11. Ibid., p. 82.
12. Ibid., p. 53.

# Part IV

Ethnic Roots and Cultural Confrontation

# 21

# Performance, Context, Power and Transformation

## A Study Based on Two Performances in Kerala

### B. Ananthakrishnan

There are two incidents, which lead me to this paper. Both of them happened a couple of years ago in the countryside of Kerala – a state located in the southern part of India. I saw an incident before a house in a remote village. Along with two policemen a group of people gathered, two *chenda* players were playing *chenda* vigorously and spectators eagerly looking on. I got down near to the place and enquired about it. The reply was very interesting. It was a revenue recovery by a bank with support of the government machinery. I could not understand the meaning of using chenda for recovering a debt from an ordinary citizen who had taken out a loan for his agricultural purposes and could not pay it back within the stipulated and extended period of time by the bank. Of course, it is the bank's discretion and their authority that they have to recover the money from the defaulter who had mortgaged his immovable property for the availability of loan. As a citizen living in the same political environment, I also became involved in a humanitarian concern over the helpless condition of the farmer or the ordinary citizen who is trying to make ends meet, but failed. But the major question came to my mind was that, why the *chenda* was used for this exercise. I have seen the performance of chenda only in specified contexts such as wherever chenda is a prerogative to the context.

The other one happened near my house. There was a public function in which one minister had to inaugurate a government scheme for drinking water. Amidst the announcements and the high alert for the minister, a group of chenda players were preparing for a performance to welcome the minister. There was another group of young women who were preparing for a *thalappoli* to welcome the minister. Here I must give brief mention to the form *thalappoli*, a ritual oriented performance of Kerala. *Thalappoli* is a performance of women, normally performed during different auspicious occasions like marriages and similar domestic contexts. But originally it had a ritual context in which it is directly related to a myth and was performed as a realization of the myth in a temple. The original myth goes back to the *Kali Darika* conflict, the popular myth behind all the major ritual performance genres of Kerala. In the myth, *Bhadrakali* the incarnation of Siva, kills the demon *Darika*, who was creating a lot of trouble for the gods and human beings using the boon secured from lord Indra after a long period of penance that he should not be killed by anybody else other than a woman. So, the normal strong human beings in the ordinary world and celestial world couldn't kill him and get rid of the turmoil of *Darika*. Lord Siva created the strong celestial woman Bhadrakali to kill the troubling *Darika*, who was strong to have a long combat with *Kali*. For this, *Kali* reaches her maximum peak of wrath and kills *Darika*. Even after killing *Darika* she was still angry. The human beings and the celestial beings were struck by fear because of the uncontrollable anger of the goddess *Kali* and they were in search of some alternative measures to pacify *Kali*.[1] Thalappoli was one of the measures they could perform before Kali through which they could control her wrath. The word *thalappoli* is a combination of two Malayalam words *thalam* and *poli*. *Thalam* means a sacred metal tray or plate and the latter means flourishing or offering, literally an offering in a sacred tray. The tray consists of a sacred lamp lit in a half coconut piece, a piece of white cloth, a bunch of coconut flowers, and some other flowers. Normally *thalappoli* is performed during the temple festivals to please the Goddess Devi or Kali. In many of the devi temples thalappoli is mandatory for the festival. It asserts the belief on Kali and the objective of devotees is that since Kali is the goddess of smallpox and other disastrous epidemics, the performance to please Kali will ward off such epidemics.

The first performance of chenda also has a sacred ambience in its origin according to the bearers of tradition. There are many myths behind the origin of *chenda*. The presence of chenda is a mandatory component for almost all the auspicious occasions of everyday life performances and ritually designated performances. Generally, it is the creation of an extension of a sound pattern to relate with the super natural world. Precisely, both the performances have natural contexts associated with a myth and subsequently a function in the society concerned.

It is a fundamental feature of all Indian traditional performances that it always functions around a belief system of the concerned community. The belief system creates the performance according to the conventions of the group. So, whatever may be the studies on Indian traditional performance or similar performances of other regions keeping up an active bearing of belief-based performances, it has to be started with the basic concept of context. The functions of all such performances are always inherent in the context. "Any artistic performance should be seen from the point of view of its context in a given society. It certainly forms an important part of a particular discourse; cultural discourse for instance...Performing arts and its actual performances in the Indian context are, and should be, the most powerful expressive system of Indian world view, Indian social structure, Indian aesthetics, and ideology and India's social and cultural metaphor."[2] As the new studies on performance concentrates on the concepts of context, especially in the area of folklore, which always underlines the history and function of a performance within the community, where a performance is primarily exists among the community with its natural function. This was a continuation of the rise of a new orientation by Richard M. Dorson, which he called the 'contextual approach'[3] to folklore research. "The emphasis of such an approach shifts from the text to its function as a performative and communicative act in a particular cultural situation."[4] As most of the Indian traditional performing arts genres are functioning around the belief system/custom of the concerned community and community finds a meaning in it through which they are ascertaining different kinds of social relationships within the society, it seems that the theory of context is pertinent. "These heightened and focused forms are performed in different socio-cultural situations. Their dimensions also vary according to time, space, caste, religion and culture of a given society."[5] Here, the interwoven relationship within the performance structure and performance to the society in its different layered structure are relevant.

Before going to the basic argument of the paper let me see some of the important theoretical explorations happening in the area of performance and its context. Most of the studies on and concepts of context in relation to performance emerged in the areas of socio-linguistics, sociology, anthropology, folklore, and later only in the area of theatre studies or performance studies. Here, it has to be underlined that the term performance studies mentioned here is only that which directly addresses the components of theatre. The developments in linguistics were centred on the concept of 'speech act theory' by J.L. Austin.[6] Major sociological explorations in performance start with the work of Nicholas Evreinoff in his book *The Theatre in Life*, published in 1927. His prominent argument is more related to theatre expression in which he asserts that "the art of theatre is pre-aesthetic, and not aesthetic, for the simple reason that *transformation,* which is after all the essence of all theatrical art, is more primitive and more easily attainable than *formation,* which is the essence of aesthetic arts."[7] Here, the formation and transformation argument is interesting in terms of its seminal quality and it could be related with the concepts of Eugenio Barba and others. Later I will be coming back to this idea at the concluding part of the paper. Afterwards Kenneth Burke and Erving Goffman enunciated the cardinal characteristics of performance. Whereas Kenneth Burke focused on the communication process of performance rather than the theatrical aspects, Erving Goffman was particular on the everyday life in performance coining the term 'frame' as an organizing principle for setting apart social events, especially those events that, like play or performance, to normal life and normal responsibilities than the same or similar events would have as "untransformed reality" outside the confines of the frame.[8] Even though their specific targets and orientations were different, certain general or casual observations on the contextual ambience of a performance could be seen in their works. The situation of human action within a *staged* context by Burke and all the activity of an individual which occurs during a period marked by his continuous presence before a particular set of observers and which has some influence on the observers by Goffman shows their awareness about the cultural context of the performer and participant/audience.[9]

Victor Turner, Eugenio Barba and Richard Schechner are the three prominent scholars in performance studies who elucidated new theoretical axioms on theatre and it process in interaction with anthropology. Keeping a strong conceptual lenience to the Van Gennep's theories on *Rites of Passage*,[10] Victor Turner probed into the seminal process of performance generation in society. Turner's view on performance as an "anti-structural initiative," opposing the "structure" of normal cultural operations reaffirms his attitude of enquiring in to the process of performance in the society.[11] But all of his works are loaded with high theoretical abstractions rather than going into the different kinds of relationships in society which create the performance and find an appropriate context for it in their culture. This may be because of his otherness in the cultures where he had worked. The same kind of otherness may be one of the reasons for Eugenio Barba seeing the performer as an isolated phenomenon in different traditional performance cultures. Sometimes it may be because of his migrant nature as elucidated by Rustom Barucha.[12] "Barba places the foundations of performance not in the situation of its enactment (its cultural 'frame' or making), but in a basic level of organization in the performer's body, the "pre expressive level", the operations of which cause the spectator to recognize behavior as performance."[13] One of the major problems in the observations of Barba is that his theory of pre expressive behaviour and his division of performer's process into three categories, i.e., daily technique, transformation and extra daily technique[14], arbitrarily reaching to a universal conclusion about performers process. In a way the Schechnerian approach also reinforces the attitude of Barba, seeing the performer as an isolated entity during his work in the area of traditional performances. "Performing artists – and, I would say mediators, shamans and trancer-dancers too – work on themselves, trying to induce deep psychophysical transformations either of a temporary or of a permanent kind. The external art work – the performance the spectators see – is the visible trialogue among: (1) the conventions or givens of a genre, (2) the stretching, distorting, or invention of new conventions and, (3) brain-centred psychophysical transformation of the self."[15] Of course, this statement is a continuity of his earlier axiom on performance treating it as a "restored behavior"[16], "emphasizing the process of repetition or continued awareness of some 'original behavior', however distant or corrupted by myth or memory, which serves a kind of grounding for the restoration.[17] Schechner also limits the performers process, which is deeply related with its complex and eclectic social and cultural context to "physical action". To Richard Schechner performer and performance, which are inseparable in many cultures, are isolated phenomena from their cultural context, from where the performance emerged. "Schechner frequently neutralizes the context of a particular ritual (or 'meaning' as he prefers to call it) by concentrating on its *physical action*."[18]

But the case in folklorise is drastically different from the narrated theoretical situations. Even though it is mainly located in the area of oral tradition the works and innovations happening there are concentrated on the different aspects of context and its interminable role in creating the dynamics of cultural expression within the community. Keeping context as the fundamental principle for analyzing folklore expression created several concepts and it brought many disciplines together under the same umbrella of performance studies relevant to the folkloristic, especially in the area of oral tradition of folklore. "In recent years, the concept of performance has begun to assume central importance in the orientation of increasing numbers of folklorists and others interested in verbal art. ...*Performance* has been used to convey a dual sense of artistic action – the doing of folklore – and artistic event – the performance situation, involving performer, art form, and setting – both of which are developing the performance approach."[19] The mutual relationship between text and context has been very much explored in this area. "No text can exist without its context. Meaning and form is created in accordance with the nature of context."[20] We can see the beginning of this approach from the work of Malinovsky and later developed through the works of Del Hymes. "That developed from Malinovsky's functionalism to Hymes 'ethnography of speaking', which enables us not only to study but also to define folklore in its context."[21] Context is the fundamental principle, which differentiates traditional performances from other performances. Always the context determines the meaning and form of the performance, which encompasses a variety of elements rooted in the psyche of the community. A performance would appear in many different contexts according to its functions with different kinds of meanings. So, a general attribution of a single meaning to a performance is not a reality in terms of its entity in society.

The contribution of Kenneth Goldstein is immensely rich in this area. In his book *'A guide to Field Workers in Folklore'* he gives various constituents of context to the field workers to observe during the performance. To get a comprehensive awareness of the performance context the researcher has to concentrate on (a) the material or physical structure of the society/community; (b) social structure; (c) enactment or interaction between the performers; (d) activities involved in the performance or the total enactment; (e) time and time duration of the performance; (f) emotional expression; (g) observers or participants or audience and; (h) other observations.[22] Later Dan Ben-Amos also joined with him for further endeavours in the area of contextual studies. They could see that a "text require proxemics, kinetic, paralinguistic, interactional, discriptional all of which might provides clues to the principle underlying the communicative process of folklore and its performative attributes."[23] To understand precisely an action of a performer or performance whether it is a ritual or ordinary observation, a researcher or practitioner has to see the original context of the performance. Considerable number of works has been happening in the direction of folklore studies, especially in the area of oral traditions. But unfortunately it is not the case of studies in Indian traditional theatre or performance tradition. To carry out a study in any on the traditional performing art genres of India whether it is theoretical or with a practice outlook, it has to contain its immediate and elaborate context. Many of the intercultural studies on Indian traditional performing arts are also lacking this. "If we in India need to pursue a study of interculturalism in the theatre, we need to contextualize our research within the inner necessities of our history."[24] Even though Rustom Barucha's statement is on interculturalism it is applicable to our theatre directors too, who all are creating avant-garde theatre in interaction with our traditional performing arts genres.

Let me come back to the two performance incidents I have narrated in the beginning of the paper. The *chenda* performance and *thalappoli* performance are having different natural contexts in Kerala's cultural context. Each varies from the tribal community to the elite classical community. Myth, structure of the performance, cast relationships within the performance matrix, self and the internal process in the performer, physicalisation, relationships to the participants, and performance authorizations are different in each context. For instance, the *chenda* performance at the time of an evening ritual in a temple holding a higher myth is different from the performance of the same in a tribal temple. Again the performance of *chenda* before the event of

Kathakali is totally different from all others. In each context, the psycho-physical realm of the performer is different and it creates the real performance ambience. It is applicable to the participants or audience too. There is neither a neutral performer nor a neutral performance process. But, the context that has been mentioned in the beginning of this paper shows a kind of neutrality for whole the performance as it appears in a context of power exercise.

The same neutrality could be seen in the second performance, *thalappoli* also in the context, which I have mentioned. The myth behind *thalappoli* is highly significant. Different communities strongly believe in the power of Kali so that they are maintaining the performance of *thalappoli* during their festival in all Kali temples. In many contexts, the participant of *thalappoli* has to undergo, at least for one week, a maintenance of purity and other observations. The participant has to maintain a particular mental state during this period. Moreover, generally it does not have an independent entity in the whole performance matrix happening during the festival, in many cases. It comes as an inevitable part in the performance web, which is constituted by a series of different performances, observations and cast authorizations, represented through different manifestations. In a sense, a ritual performance "is a token of well-established ideology, realized in a certain form and according to the rules of a communicative rhetorical praxis."[25]

While going to the original contexts of the two performances mentioned here, it is clearly evident that both of the forms are having a certain kind of relationship with the power of the supernatural. The performance's internally inter-woven linkages may be according to the power relationship of the society where the community is living or the performance is normally happening. But abstractly it is directly related to the power, located in the frame of the belief system. Annual, periodical or regular observation is an affirmation of it. It is a part of communicative rhetorical praxis varied according to the contexts. In the myth behind *thalappoli* Bhadrakali is a saviour with all the vigour of celestial power to society.

It is paradoxical when we see these two performances in two different contexts, closely associated with power structures. The first one was implementing the power of government machinery in respect of a revenue recovery from a farmer who failed to pay off the loan. The second one was on the occasion of a minister's visit to inaugurate a public scheme. The question pertinent here is that why are these performances placed in such contexts? Of course these are not the natural contexts of the forms. There are many theoretical observations about folklore out of its context under the rubric of folklorism. "The folklorism debate would seem to be an excellent point of departure for integrating academic and public realms through ideological awareness. Applied folklore and its effect, be it caused by the state, industry, the mass media, or folklorists themselves, cannot remain outside our concept of folklore."[26] According to the transition of society, folklore and folk related performances will be acquiring new contexts with different magnitudes. Probably it may be within the cultural frame of the same community or allied community spheres. This is apart from the industrial use of cultural performance and other traditions. Many times it would be an attempt by the same society to place their expressions in a different space. Sometimes, it would be used for aesthetic purposes as in India the theatre movement started to synthesize Indian traditional forms for the construction of a new theatre sensibility. All these kinds of tendencies cannot be scaled with same tool. Because the dynamics of traditional performance culture in India is unique by its entity. It has a more vibrant and vigorous existence with an organic function than modern performance tradition. Along with all the advanced technological means of artistic expressions, traditional performing arts also survive without any deliberate cultural subsidy from any other expressions. So it is not an old archival piece but it is contemporary. I am looking at these two performances from this angle.

Here, both the performances are fused with concentrated power of the supernatural. As the performances have a vibrant existence in society it is evident that the power of the supernatural operates among the community to its full extent. But the performances and their contexts narrated in the paper are not functioning in this manner. It is impossible to equate them with their original contexts. Here, it is happening exactly in the context of power relations. Systems of power have a tendency of appropriating different cultural performances for the exercise of power. In history many kings used *chenda* for governmental statements and information announcements. The king was considered as the representative of the supernatural power. So, the percussion of chenda was rationalized in that sense. But, even though, the power relation structure transformed into new mechanisms, still the same pattern was followed. The reason for this continuity may be

the power structures equation to the particular form, which traditionally occupies the meaning of a power, which is still relevant among
the people. The performance of thalappoli in the context of welcoming
the minister denotes the same kind of exercise. Here the equation is to
the powerful Bhadrakali, through which the power representation is
realized. Irrespective of times, the power structures are capable of
relocating the cultural performances from their natural context to
another context of the exercise of power.

## Notes

1. Raghavan Payyanad, *Kerala Folklore*, Folklore Fellows Malabar, Payyannur, 1997, p. 165.
2. Jawaharlal Handoo, *Performance in the Indian Context*, an unpublished paper, Mysore, 1996, p. 5.
3. Richard M. Dorson (ed.), *Folklore and Folk Life: An Introduction*, Chicago, University of Chicago Press, 1972, p. 45
4. Marvin Carlson, *Performance: A Critical Introduction*, London, Routledge, 1996, p. 16.
5. S.D. Lourdu, *Ritual Performance*, An unpublished paper presented in a National Seminar on Performance Studies, Trichur, University of Calicut 1992, p. 1.
6. J.L. Austin, *How to Do Things with Words*, Cambridge, Harvard University Press, 1975.
7. Nicholas Evreinoff, The Theatre in Life (tr. Alexander Nazaroff), New York, Brentano's, 1927, p. 24.
8. Erving Goffman, *Frame Analysis*, Garden City, N.Y., Doubleday, 1974, p. 157.
9. Marvin Carlson, *Performance: A Critical Introduction*, Routledge, London, 1996, pp. 37-38.
10. See Van Gennep, *The Rites of Passage* (tr. M.B. Vizedon and G.L. Caffee), Chicago University Press, Chicago, 1960, for general description.
11. Victor Turner, *The Ritual Process: Structure and Anti-Structure*, Aldine Publishing Co., Chicago 1969, p. 22.
12. Rustom Barucha, *Theatre and the World*, Manohar Publishers and Distributors, New Delhi, 1992, p. 83.
13. Marvin Carlson, *Performance: A Critical Introduction*, Routledge, London, 1996, p. 19.

14. See Eugino Barba, *The Secret Art of Performer* (tr. Richard Fowler), Routledge, London, 1991 for detail description.

15. Richard Schechner, *Performance Theory*, Routledge, New York, 1988, p. 279.

16. Richard Schechner, *Between Theatre and Anthropology*, University of Pennsylvania Press, Philadelphia, 1985, p. 35.

17. Marvin Carlson, *Performance: A Critical Introduction*, Routledge, London, 1996, p. 51.

18. Rustom Barucha, *Theatre and the World*, Manohar Publishers and Distributors, New Delhi, 1992, p. 39.

19. Richard Bauman, *Verbal Art as Performance*, Waveland Press Inc., Illinois, p. 4.

20. Peter J. Clous and Fank J. Korom, *Folkloristic and Indian Folklore*, Regional Resource Centre, Udupi, 1991, p. 13.

21. Dan Ben-Amos, *Folklore in Context*, South Asian Publishers, New Delhi, 1982, p. 10.

22. Kenneth Gold Stein, *A Guide to Fieldwork In Folklore*, Folklore Associates, Pennsylvania, 1964, p. 59.

23. Dan Ben-Amos and Kenneth Gold Stein, *Folklore, Performance and Communication*, The Haugue, Mouton, 1975, p. 6.

24. Rustom Barucha, *Theatre and the World*, Manohar Publishers and Distributors, New Delhi, 1992, p. 49.

25. Johannes Fabian, *Power and Performance*, The University of Wisconsin Press, Wisconsin, 1990, p. 29.

26. Regina Bendix, *Folklorism: A Challenge of Concept*, International Folklore Review, 1988, p. 13.

# 22

# Writing Back From the Empire

## Indian Images on the English Stage

### Christopher Innes

This IFTR conference in Jaipur focuses, rightly, on Asian perceptions of the contemporary post-colonial experience. But, it is also valuable to put this in a perspective from the other side: writing-back from the Empire, to twist a phrase.

For over two centuries, the cultures of India and England were increasingly intertwined – with English becoming the language of official India and Shakespeare an adopted theatrical icon, while Indian expressions flooded into English vocabulary and India was reflected as the epitome of Empire in military melodramas, the novels and poetry of Rudyard Kipling or E.M. Forster. Even half a century after liberation, India still remains a central subliminal factor in the British psyche – as the immense popularity of a TV serial like "The Jewel in the Crown" indicates. And, India has also made its mark on the English stage. Still more to the point: there are increasing signs of cross-fertilization – cultural interpenetration, or one might even say, productive artistic miscegenation.

As is only to be expected, during the Victorian heyday of imperialism, standard melodramas – for instance dealing with the Siege of Lucknow, or heavily romanticized stories of mystery and magic revolving round immense diamonds like the fabled Koor-I-Nohr – portrayed Indians as savages, sinister villains, exploiting the clichéd association between dark skin and evil, or (occasionally) as happily subservient servants. So, it would be fair to say that during the 19th Century popular English theatre crudely and unapologetically confirmed the colonial system, projecting the image of the subjugated 'Other' and the cultural/religious imperative of what Kipling notoriously called 'the white man's burden'.[1]

But already by 1896, this imperialist picture was being challenged in a play by Bernard Shaw's friend Gilbert Murray titled *Carlyon Sahib*. Though now long forgotten, it was performed by Granville-Barker and Mrs. Pat Campbell (as a rather unlikely Indian princess) and highly critical of British colonial attitudes. And it is notable that here drama led the way, prefiguring the critique in E.M. Forster's *Passage to India*.

From then on, whenever English plays include Indian figures, they are a corrective to imperialist attitudes, challenge restrictive notions of cultural identity, or are presented as embodiments of positive political or cultural values. Significantly too, although through the 1920s, exoticized treatments of the orientalized 'other' (usually in idealizations of their pre-colonized state) were common, these were limited to Arabic or Chinese figures, as in Flecker's highly poetic Persian fantasy, *Hassan*, or Oscar Asche's musical spectacular, *Chu Chin Chow*. By contrast, India was not romanticized on the stage, with the one exception of William Archer's *The Green Goddess*, which was first produced in 1920.

Like Gilbert Murray's *Carlyon Sahib*, Archer satirizes the attitudes of the British in India through reversing the standard biases of racism and colonialism. When a plane-crash lands three representatives of imperialism (an army major, his wife, and a doctor) in an isolated Hindu kingdom in the Himalayas, they are greeted by "a wild procession... headed by a gigantic Negro flourishing two naked sabers, and gyrating in a barbaric war-dance".[2] This, of course, epitomizes western views of the East as an exoticized other: ('barbaric' is a frequently used word in the play). But it is immediately undercut by the Raja, who dresses in exquisitely cut European clothes, even quotes Bernard Shaw – commenting that 'his impudence entertains me' – and reminds them that while the Negro's sword "is a barbarous weapon compared with [the Major's] revolver...it was worn by my ancestors when yours were daubing themselves blue" (in other words naked ancient Britons).[3] And the Raja, who reads Nietzsche and has a degree in "Moral and Political Science" from the University of Cambridge, as well as being identified with the Shavian "Superman", is revealed to be an articulate spokesman against imperialism – declaring "Asia has a long score against you swaggering, blustering, whey-faced lords of creation" (which is an all-too accurate description of the Major) and demanding "vengeance for centuries of subjection and insult".[4] But sadly, Archer was finally unable to free his play from the stereotypes he was trying to attack; and *The Green Goddess* succumbs to romanticism. An early indication of this is when the Raja "plagiarizes" a surprise effect "from the excellent Walter Scott"; and indeed the plot descends into standard military melodrama. The Raja turns out to be barbaric after all. He shoots the major, then attempts to seduce the Major's wife, imprisons her and the doctor in chains, and is on the point of sacrificing them to the title-figure – the statue of "a six-armed Goddess of forbidding aspect, coloured dark green" – when the British air-force arrives just in the nick of time, bomb him into submission and save the Empire by rescuing its representatives.[5]

Although Archer's colleague and one-time collaborator Bernard Shaw never set a play in India, preferring Ireland or the Egypt of *Caesar & Cleopatra* to anatomize colonialism, in his 1930s play, *On the Rocks*, he introduces an Indian who has risen to the top of British society, but rejects everything it stands for when underlying racist attitudes emerge and he is contemptuously called "a silly nigger pretending to be an English gentleman". Justifiably outraged, he makes the same point as Archer's Raja: that when the British "were naked savages worshipping acorns and mistletoe in the woods", *his* ancestors were founding an enlightened "civilization, compared to which your little kingdom is no more than a concentration camp". (Already the historical superiority of Indian civilization over Britain has become a standard trope – so 40 years later in Stoppard's *Indian Ink* one of the Indian characters declares "*We* were the Romans! We were up to date when you were a backward nation. The foreigners who invaded you found a third world country!")[6] He then storms out, announcing "I return to India to detach it wholly from England, and leave you to perish in your ignorance, your vain conceit and your abominable manners" – and the Prime Minister comments, "That one word nigger will cost us India".[7] Even though written in 1933, Shaw's argument for Indian freedom is prescient; and just over 40 years later, David Edgar's play *Destiny*, which looks back in its opening scene to the British withdrawal at Independence, shows the pattern reversing itself.

Almost all the main characters in *Destiny* have served in India; and the play documents what happens to them on their return to Britain, after 1947. A Colonel finds himself an out-of-place anachronism – his Major and a Sergeant, disillusioned by the impoverishment and corruption of post-war England, take over a neo-fascist political party – and two Indian factory workers in Birmingham (one-time soldiers in the British Indian Army), represent the mass migration of people from the Commonwealth, who were all (at least initially) granted British citizenship. As one of them introduces himself:

> Gurjeet Singh Khera,
> Once a slave,
> Returns to haunt the Empire's grave.[8]

Their coming exposes racism in Britain. They provide a target for the extreme right and the play holds the Indians up as the only people, acting on true socialist principles and capable of fighting the fascist threat.

All this is a fairly obvious – even superficial – response to the developing colonial relationship with India and its aftermath. While the Indian characters may be spokesmen for independence (well in advance of British public and political opinion) or victims demonstrating the continuing racism in English society, all are depicted from an external perspective. They remain "the other". But just as the British population has become more multi-ethnic – and it is very much a sign of this that David Edgar's play, staged just 25 years ago in 1976, was the first to have Indian characters played by actors of Indian origin. (By contrast, Archer's *Green Goddess* was standard in having the Raja and his tribesmen all played by white actors in black-face.) So, in some recent works the treatment has been far more interesting, because authors have pursed an integrated viewpoint, creating examples of successful cross-fertilization.

The first of these, which Jan-Claude Carrière and Peter Brook started working on in the same year as Edgar's play, although it only reached the stage in 1985, was *The Mahabharata*. A well-known theatrical landmark, this epic production celebrated Indian culture through adapting the ancient Sanskrit epic, at the same time as staging it with a magnificently choreographed bravura display of symbolic acting that was deliberately intended to be universal. This was pure physical theatre, ranging from hieratic pose· ·o breath-taking acrobatics. And,

although it included some vestigial elements of Kathakali theatre, the
style seemed to me to be an amalgam of techniques derived from
Brook's search for theatrical "roots" in Iran and Africa, as well as from
the Polish and French avant-garde. Similarly, while the costumes were
based on heavily simplified Indian dress, the actors were a truly international, but largely European mix. A cynic might well call it cultural
neo-colonialism – an expropriation of mythology – yet the effect was
ascetic as well as exotic. So, *The Mahabharata* should be seen as one
model for interpenetration.

Perhaps, it's not coincidental that one of the key texts for artistic
cross-fertilization is *A Passage to India* – and indeed the earliest sign of
this comes, when Forster's novel was adapted for the stage in 1960,
with the author of the play-version being a well known Indian writer,
Santha Rama Rau.

And when Tom Stoppard (who was incidentally born in India)
turns to Indian themes in *Indian Ink*, the play is a positive re-writing of
*A Passage to India*. It also depicts a history of cultural interpenetration.
Staged in 1995, *Indian Ink* explores the reciprocal merging of artistic
cultures through a double time-frame of the 1930s (the start of Gandhi's
campaign of civil disobedience) and the present. As in Forster, a visiting
English woman is attracted to an Indian, who admires and emulates
British culture. But here, Flora, who has made her reputation on erotic
poetry and suffers from tuberculosis, finds authentic emotion in the
last days before her early death. She develops a romantic relationship
with a young Indian artist, who does two paintings of her.

The first, abandoned unfinished, which shows her in a blue dress
sitting under a tree with a monkey (representing the god Hanuman) in
its branches, is Nirad Dass' attempt to depict Flora from a borrowed
English perspective. As she comments: "you're trying to paint me from
my point of view instead of yours – what you *think* is my point of
view." The result is technicolour realism, described as "fairly ghastly,
like an Indian cinema poster" – and to Flora this lack of an independent
and authentically Indian mode of expression in Dass' art means that:
"You *deserve* the bloody empire".[9]

However, his second painting of Flora is a nude, which is
compared (and indeed confused) with a classical Rajasthani miniature
depicting the love between the God Krishna and "Radha the most
beautiful of the herdswomen" in Hindu mythology. And it stands for a
fruitful merging of western realism (in the way Flora's European body

is depicted) and eastern tradition, with "everything on different scales" so "you can't tell if the painter is in the house or outside looking in, and with "birds singing in the border – and the tree in bloom" all represented as flat and brilliant like enamel, following the key principle of Hindu art that "everything is to be interpreted in the language of symbols".[10]

On a wider level this erotic painting – and indeed Flora's romance with the painter – is a metaphor for the English love-affair with 'the Raj' and India's fascination with England. The colonized 'Other', Nirad Dass, whose art at first is overwhelmed by English models (specifically Holman Hunt and the Pre-Raphaelites or Alma-Tadema's soft-porn Orientalism), learns to value his native heritage through his love for an English woman. And it is as a result of his relationship with Flora that he not only recuperates Rajasthani aesthetics (in what – particularly appropriate for where we are now, in the centre of Rajasthan – the play clearly presents as a viable modern form), but also becomes a Nationalist and takes a leading part in protests against the British rule. At the same time, Stoppard makes Flora the epitome of European culture: having appeared as an actress in Shaw's *Pygmalion*, and being one of H.G. Wells' former mistresses, whom Modigliani had also, earlier painted in the nude. And Flora's poetry changes too, through being made aware of *Rasa* – the "essence" of Hindu art, referring to "the emotion which the artist must arouse" in the reader or spectator.[11]

Beyond that *Indian Ink* (which is also the title for the collection of poems Flora writes while in India) combines her 1930s story with that of her younger sister (now an elderly widow) and Nirad Dass' on in the present. Her sister – who in turn also made a pilgrimage to India to see Flora's grave and, marrying an English officer, stayed on until 1947 and independence – still refers to India as "home". While the young Dass (a painter like his father) now lives in London, and has abandoned Hindu art for contemporary English "deconstructionist" painting. But, the play as a whole sets up the interchange between the 1930s painter and poet, and the intercultural integration it produced, as a superior vision to the alienating absorption in the other's culture of the present-day characters. Firstly, by demonstrating that indeed Flora's "soul" does "stay behind as a smudge of paint on paper, as if I'd always been here, like Radha, who was the most beautiful of the herdswomen, undressed for love in an empty house".[12] And secondly, in the way the two different time-frames are integrated, making the play itself a study in perception.

Much the same sort of intercultural merger, but coming from the other direction, can be seen in a recent film by the Canadian director, Deepa Mehta, called *Bollywood/Hollywood*. The leading man (acted by a Bollywood star) is a wealthy young Indian, whose family own jewelery stores in Toronto, but who is rebelling against his Indian heritage, and refusing to marry any Indian girl. However, his sister will not be allowed to marry before he gets engaged – and she tells him that she is pregnant. So, when a university student, moonlighting as an escort, picks him up in a bar and presents herself as Spanish, he pays her to pretend she is his fiancée, dresses her up in a sari, provides her with Indian jewelery, and introduces her to his family as his future wife. Inevitably, following standard movie conventions, they fall in love – and naturally his family culture and the Hindu status quo is preserved, since she turns out to be Indian, after all. But if the story is pure Hollywood (and very obviously copies the Julia Roberts/Richard Gere vehicle, *Pretty Woman*) the form is typically Bollywood, with the characters breaking into set-piece songs or energetically choreographed dances, complete with Hindi subtitles, at each and every emotional point.

Cinema may not seem directly relevant, in a conference devoted to drama and the stage. Still, there's a striking theatrical equivalent to this movie in the contemporary London musical, *Bombay Dreams*. For a start, some simple counting shows a lot. While the music is authentically Indian – or at least authentically Bollywood, being by A.R. Rahman, who has won numerous prizes for his music and (as the program boasts) composed highly popular soundtracks for over fifty films made in India – the lyrics are all by a Brit, who has collaborated with Andrew Lloyd-Webber on three previous shows, and written the songs for several James Bond films. Similarly, although one of the two choreographers comes from India and has worked on a variety of Bollywood films, as well as *Monsoon Wedding*, the other choreographer is English, as are the rest of the production team (all of whom have worked on Lloyd-Webber shows before); and 25 out of the 34-strong Ensemble are also English. However, the "book" was written by an Indian born and raised in England; and exactly the same background is shared by seven of the eight lead actors, all of whom were trained in British theatre schools, with only one coming from India and being an authentic Bollywood actor (Dalip Tahil, who plays the villain of the piece, JK).

On the surface, the plot is straight Bollywood melodrama – a violent dispossession and illegal eviction of Mumbai slum dwellers, and a mafia take-over of the film industry – complete with the meteoric rise of a slum boy to film star, a crooked lawyer (engaged to the heroine), the shooting of her film-director father, the strangling of a eunuch entertainer, and an obligatory "wet-sari" scene – and the action climaxes with "hero number one" freeing himself from the corruption of success to lead the slum-dwellers in an assault on the mafia boss's penthouse, where the heroine's marriage is taking place. Single-handedly, he takes on the mafia boss, his goons and the lawyer in a bravura display of kick-boxing and wrestling; and – joined by the heroine, who repudiates her new husband once she learns of his guilt – defeats all the forces of evil. The mafia boss makes a last minute escape by helicopter (shades of *Miss Saigon*); and the hero is just in time to stop the slum demolition, standing in the path of a monstrous digger (a mechanized Godzilla).

But as those visual images suggest, there are distinct parallels between Bollywood and the contemporary London Musical. The defining quality of both is that they inject songs and dances into acted scenes, as well as sharing slick production values. But *Bombay Dreams* clearly aspires to going beyond either form, using the vitality of Bollywood conventions to extend the standard Musical, and the direct communication of live performance to enhance the emotional appeal of Bollywood. In effect, however, this also implies a critique of both – as in the ending, where the Hero declares, "All Bollywood films must have a happy ending..." (he could just as well have said "All Musicals..."), only to have the heroine move away from his embrace, with the reply: "We aren't ready, we have to find ourselves, first..." – and this leads to parody, for example in lyrics of appalling banality, such as, "Shakalaka baby, Shakalaka baby, won't you Shakalaka with me..." or in the way the characters are designated, JK "The Big Boss", Madan "The Movie Mogul", Rani "The Temptress", Sweetie (the eunuch) as "The Dreamer" and so on.[13]

And beyond that, *Bombay Dreams* is self-referential on multiple levels. The Bollywood plot (with the slum even being razed for a multiplex cinema) revolves around the making of Bollywood movies – one a historical spectacular by the independent film-director, who is gunned down at its gala opening; the other being made by the heroine (the dead director's daughter who takes over his studio, unwittingly giving it over to mafia control). Derisively described as "a documentary with songs" by the hero, this film deals with a mafia-financed eviction of slum-dwellers, exactly echoing the situation in the Musical – but in romanticized, sanitized terms (implying that the Musical is far more realistic).

But *Bombay Dreams* is also self-referential for its target audience. With all the ensemble songs by the slum dwellers, plus isolated lines in several of the other lyrics being in Hindi, the Musical is specifically designed for a British/Indian audience. And on the night I saw the show, over 60 per cent of the spectators were Indians, now living in Britain. So the slum boy's abandonment of his home, his rise to riches, followed by his saving recognition of his true roots, is clearly intended to reflect the movement of immigrants from their native land to England, their achievement of wealth – as signaled by being able to afford the expensive West End ticket prices! – and the retrospective yearning for their own culture, as represented by the popularity of Bollywood movies in Britain.

With these stage works, the Empire has been decisively transcended. In a very real sense, the 0 different approaches *Indian Ink* and *Bombay Dreams*, each represent a positive solution, moving beyond colonial or even post-colonial attitudes, to show how inter-cultural cross-fertilization can produce vital and viable theatrical works. Both are intentionally programmatic, merging the two artistic traditions while respecting ethnic identity. And together they mark a paradigm shift, in my view signalling a new beginning – or at the least opening the way for further intriguing developments.

## Notes

1. It should be noted that the poem, in which this line occurs, was specifically intended by Kipling as helpful advice to the Americans, following their takeover of the Philippines.

2. William Archer, *The Green Goddess*, New York. Alfred A. Knopf, 1921, p. 15.

3. Ibid., pp. 45 and 18.

4. Ibid., pp. 58, 52, 75 and 112.

5. Ibid., pp. 1 and 24.

6. Bernard Shaw, "On the Rocks", in *Three Plays By Bernard Shaw*, London. Constable & Co., 1934, pp. 255; Tom Stoppard, *Indian Ink*, London. Faber & Faber, 1995, p. 17.

7. Bernard Shaw, *On the Rocks*, pp. 255-56.

8. David Edgar, *Destiny*, London. Methuen, 1978, p. 38.

9. Tom Stoppard, *Indian Ink*, pp. 43 and 10.

10. Ibid., pp. 28 and 68.

11. Ibid., pp. 18 and 83.

12. Ibid., p. 29.

13. The text of *Bombay Dreams* was still unpublished at the time of writing this essay, and the quoted dialogue is from notes made during a performance of the opening run in London. The character descriptions are taken from an illustrated leaflet, advertising the show.

# 23

## Fritz Benewitz in India

### A Co-operative Research Project

### David G. John

The following is a summary of the contribution I read at the Jaipur conference, reactions to it, and their consequences for my research. When the call for papers came in early 2002, I had been working on Fritz Benewitz (1926-95) for about four years. Most of this research had taken place in the Benewitz archive in Leipzig, and was concentrated primarily on his seven productions of Goethe's *Faust*, three of them both parts of the tragedy, the other four part one alone.[1] I approached Benewitz and his *Faust* productions as a Germanist whose specializations are eighteenth-century and classical German drama, Goethe, and *Faust*, but over the past decade I have shifted my methodological approach from seeing dramatic works primarily as examples of a literary genre, to their performance. In other words, I have come to straddle the fields of German and Theatre Studies, and as an extension of this methodological shift, my interest has come to centre on performance analysis in intercultural contexts. The challenge of tackling an unusual variety of *Faust* productions is what attracted me first to Benewitz, for his long career and seven *Fausts* are a rare collection of intercultural experimentation and expression.

Benewitz directed plays in the German Democratic Republic for three decades from the nineteen-sixties until the late eighties, more than a hundred works by many authors, and more than twenty for East German television. Three of his seven *Fausts*, those including both parts, were produced and performed for the *Nationaltheater* stage in Weimar, the classical centre of the GDR, and before the creation of that state in 1948 the heart of classicism for all of Germany. These *Fausts* were spaced from 1965 to 1975 to 1981, the last running until the reunification in 1989 in almost a hundred performances, and since they were created for what his state continued to call its *Nationaltheater*, their different interpretations of the same work can be read as a reflection of social, political, artistic and cultural trends in that country, a continuum that differed considerably from its parallel in the Federal Republic of Germany to the west. These productions already offered a worthwhile focus for me as an investigator of intercultural theatre, for there is no question that East and West Germany then, and even to a great extent still today, represented two very different socio-political and cultural entities.

Benewitz's four other *Fausts*, albeit in each case part one alone, are stunning in their intercultural range. In 1978, upon the invitation of Ellen Stewart, founder of the La MaMa Experimental Theatre Club in New York, he directed the work on that stage in English translation, as well as at Princeton University in excerpted form, using a multiracial group of actors and casting Gretchen for the first time in theatre history as a black person. In 1994, upon the invitation of Vijaya Mehta, director of the National Centre for the Performing Arts in Bombay, he directed the work on the NCPA's Tata theatre stage, using Indian actors, among them the Bollywood stars Pankaj Kapur (Faust) and Naseeruddin Shah (Mephistopheles), in Hindi. In the same year, upon the invitation of Rody Vera, who also served as translator of the play into the local Tagalog language, he directed it in the Philippine capital of Manila. Benewitz prepared his final *Faust* for production in 1995 (his death prevented him from experiencing the première) in yet another country and cultural setting. This was in the small city of Meiningen, formerly in East Germany, but now part of his new united homeland. Each of these *Fausts* was of interest for my research and became part of a major project: "Fritz Benewitz and *Faust*." Benewitz has received scant attention in the critical literature of theatre studies, even in West German publications, though he was frequently an object of discussion in the GDR. Because of his unusual contribution to the history of *Faust* stagings, I was convinced of the merit of this project, and still am as I work to its conclusion. Some of the results have already appeared in academic publications or are scheduled to soon,[2] and I hope to complete a book on all of his *Fausts* in 2004.

Although Benewitz remained intensively involved in the theatre of his own country, by the seventies his primary interest moved abroad. In the last two decades of his career he brought to international audiences dozens of German plays, mostly in the native host language, in eighteen different countries around the world, including Bangladesh, Belgium, Bulgaria, Czechoslovakia, the Federal Republic of Germany, Holland, India, Italy, Luxembourg, the Philippines, Romania, Russia, Sri Lanka, Switzerland, Syria, the United States, Venezuela and Yugoslavia. He specialized in Brecht and Shakespeare. The list of countries in which he worked includes an extremely wide range in geographical, economic, political, and racial terms, which speaks to his personal and artistic philosophies. He also repeated visits, and when judged by their number and length it is clear that India was by far his favourite destination. From the sparse secondary literature about him, supplemented by my own research in the Benewitz archive, I learned that he had travelled to India twenty-six times to direct plays by Brecht and Shakespeare in addition to his *Faust*, in many cities, and almost always in the local language.[3] His conviction that the local language must be used as the play's vehicle of communication was essential to his commitment to cultural understanding. Hence, he used Indian actors and their languages, engaging in an extensive learning process to familiarize himself sufficiently with these languages and their cultural associations to correct and direct the actors. He also tried to integrate himself into Indian daily life, and faced hardships with this adjustment. He usually chose simple quarters to live in, like those of most of his actors. The venues in which Benewitz directed plays included Bangalore, Bhopal, Bombay, Calcutta, Chandigarh, Heggodu, Karnataka, Lucknow, Mysore, New Delhi, Poona and Vishakapatnam; and the plays Brecht's *Arturo Ui, Caucasian Chalk Circle, Galileo Galilei, Good Woman of Sezuan, Man is Man, Mother Courage, Puntila and his Man Matti,* and *The Threepenny Opera;* and Shakespeare's *Hamlet, King Lear, Midsummer Night's Dream, Othello, Taming of the Shrew,* and *Twelfth Night.* Benewitz's first Indian Brecht production, *The Threepenny Opera* in 1970, was sponsored by the International Theatre Institute (ITI) as well as the GDR and Indian ministries of culture, and marked the beginning of decades of artistic co-operation and friendship between himself and Vijaya Mehta at the National

School for Drama in New Delhi and thereafter the National Centre for Performing Arts in Bombay. With justification, Benewitz claimed that their co-directed *Chalk Circle* of 1973 introduced a new stage in Indian Brecht reception.[4] It later led the way for his entry to New York and Manila, was the first Indian play to be invited to the Berliner Festtage, and engendered further Brecht productions by Indian directors such as M.K. Rainas, (*The Caucasian Chalk Circle*, *The Mother*) and Habib Tanvirs (*The Good Woman of Sezuan*). Benewitz genuinely wished to encourage intercultural exchange and believed that fundamental commonalities among peoples could be demonstrated through the works of these playwrights. His personal and artistic friendships resulted in Indian colleagues and actors visiting the GDR and mounting Indian productions of Sanskrit plays there on several occasions: Vijaya Mehta (Weimar, *Mudrarakshasa* 1976), Kalidasa (Leipzig, *Shakuntala* 1980), and Girish Karnad (Weimar, *Hayavadana* 1984). After the reunification in 1989, such activity was intensified when September 1991 to April 1992 was designated in Germany for the theatre "Festival of India" with guest performances by Indian troupes during the Berliner Festtage. The President of India awarded Benewitz the Sangeet Natak Akademi Award in early 1992 for his lifetime contribution to theatre in India and his homeland.

Roland Beer's official *GDR-India. Cultural Relations* summarizes Benewitz's activities from 1970-84, including the official state exchange agreements and connected reciprocal visits.[5] Benewitz's own reports, "India overview" and "Internationale Co-operation auf dem Theater" enrich this account through their description of the essential elements of traditional Indian folk theatre which he kept in mind when adapting his productions.[6] This type of theatre received an enormous boost when India achieved its independence in 1947 and the new government strove to support traditional art forms after two centuries of British colonial rule. Ironically, the beginning of India's post-colonial period coincided almost exactly with the creation of the GDR in 1948, so that one might venture to say that the creative liberty Benewitz enjoyed in India compensated for artistic restrictions at home. In his "India overview," with reference to the *Natyashastra* (*A Treatise on Theatre*), a poetics comparable to Aristotle's and attributed to *Bharatamuni* (*Bharata the Sage*), he summarized what he understood to be the essential characteristics of traditional Indian theatre:

- The significance of music and dance. Traditional Indian theatre is more danced and sung than spoken, with choreographic interludes both independent and integrated into plays.
- Rules for the stylisation of language, the alternation of verse and prose which from Sanskrit drama is part of the characterization of the play's personae.
- The role of the chorus.
- The absence of stage sets and decoration and the role of the actors to describe it in an imaginary fashion.
- The use of masks and the ritualistic art of make-up.
- The significance of costumes and colours.
- The meaning of gestures and mimic expressions.
- The relationship between actors and audience.
- The position of the audience and movements of actors with respect to it.
- The various functions of dialogue, to narrate, to describe, and to comment.
- Reliance on the great Indian epics, *Mahabharata* and *Ramayana*, the *Puranas*, medieval legends and folk tales as almost exclusive, and seemingly inexhaustible sources of plots.
- The tendency of folk theatre to integrate local gossip, current politics and social criticism into their action; and to use alienating techniques.

His objective as a director in India was to integrate these characteristics into his productions, and a primary goal of my future research will be to assess the extent to which he was successful.

Renate Frank has organized the holdings of the Benewitz archive into chronologically arranged volumes of his large personal and professional correspondence, his theoretical writings, his phases of activity at the Weimar *Nationaltheater*, and his major productions. Many documents, such as director's books, scene and costume sketches, playbills, programs, recordings, production notes and letters are there in original or photocopied form. The correspondence itself is a massive repository bearing testimony to his wide range of friendships and associations in the theatre world, and especially in India. I have read enough of it to know that he felt a remarkably close relationship with India and its theatre folk, and that many Indians felt similarly about him.

Three major problems faced me if I was to undertake more intensive research on Benewitz and India. First, since much of his work there was done in the local languages, my ignorance of those languages is a severe, even prohibitive, handicap. Second, until the Jaipur conference, I had only slight professional contacts in Canada and India to whom I could turn for advice. Third, I had no experience living in India and was daunted by the cultural difference itself. Much of my work to date on German theatre outside German-speaking countries has relied on the scholarly foundation and methodological approaches of Germanists, blended in the last few years with aspects of performance theory, primarily that of Richard Schechner.[7] I had been using the term "intercultural" freely, as I have until now in this account, and felt myself in good company. The Jaipur conference triggered in me a complete re-orientation of this perspective and its terminology. I was grateful that a goodly number of Indian colleagues attended my paper, and was delighted with their responses in the discussion immediately following and at informal sessions in the next few days. The strongest response, and the one that affected my thinking profoundly, was Rustom Bharucha's. His intellectual intensity and passion, his personal commitment to Indian theatre and to the inherent dignity, value and significance of every cultural expression moved me. In the open discussion following my paper Bharucha spoke of his personal friendship with Benewitz and admiration for him, and although he encouraged me to pursue my project he challenged my approach severely on several fronts, causing me to re-think my future course. A number of other colleagues voiced support, encouragement, guidance and also warnings about the complications of investigating this cultural relationship. My blithe use of the term "interculturalism" had collided with Bharucha's insistence on the primacy of "intraculturalism," as presented in his *Theatre and the World: Performance and the Politics of Culture* and developed by himself and others since.[8] His critique of intercultural theatre from an Asian perspective, questioning of the assumptions of western critics with regard to India and its many cultures, and his rejection of the almost universally acclaimed work of renowned theorists and practitioners such as Artaud, Brook, Grotowski, Pavis and Schechner was widely known and regarded in the field of theatre and cultural studies, but had not yet penetrated my thinking sufficiently. His fearless rejection of iconical positions and careful crafting of counter arguments in *Theatre and the World*, his brutal honesty toward himself and his cultural sphere, and his fairness in debate despite his severity and polemics impressed me enormously.

Since his response to my paper, and that of several other colleagues along the same lines, I have been re-examining my position in relation to Benewitz and the cultural groups of India to develop a firmer theoretical position and methodology for my investigation.

Following the conference I spent three weeks travelling through India, along the way stopping in numerous places to learn more about the culture and theatre of the region and meet with individuals who might advise me further. In Mumbai I was able to discuss my project with Vijaya Mehta at the National Centre for Performing Arts, where she had collaborated with Benewitz on *Faust I* in 1994, and review their archival holdings on Benewitz with the assistance of librarian Shrimathi Madiman; and with the Bollywood stars Naseeruddin Shah and Pankaj Kapur, Benewitz's Mephisto and Faust, both of whom expressed their willingness to help me in my investigation. Further south I visited the Kathakali Academy in Kalamandalam for two days to observe the techniques and training of that dance form, and Professor Aymanam Krishna Kaimal of the Vrindavan Academy in Kottayam who in 1978 translated *Faust* into Malayam and used that published text as a foundation for a unique Kathakali production of *Faust* which toured several Indian cities until 1981.[9] Then in New Delhi I met artists, writers, educators and cultural administrators at the Sangeet Natak Akademi and National School of Drama, many of whom knew and worked with Benewitz, allowed recorded interviews, and offered their assistance in the future. My four weeks in India, from the Jaipur conference to my departure for Germany, left me culturally and intellectually enriched, more aware of the complications of my project, and grateful for the generosity of Indian colleagues to help me along the way.

In Germany, I resumed my work in connection with the Benewitz archive in Leipzig and those associated with it, and shall continue to do so in Canada when I return there at the conclusion of my six-month research sabbatical. I have been invited by a colleague in the University of Leipzig's department of Indology and Asian Studies to co-supervise a doctoral candidate writing on Benewitz and India, and I continue to correspond with colleagues at Indian universities in an attempt to formulate together an approach to investigating Benewitz's activities and impact there. I hope that within a few months decisions can be made about approaching Canadian, Indian and German granting agencies for support, and joining together in a research project, which could involve an international partnership of professors and graduate students from all three countries.

[Note: I wish to thank the Social Sciences and Humanities Federation of Canada (SSHRC) for funding that enabled me to attend this conference.]

## Notes

1. The Fritz Bennewitz Archive is maintained by the "Arbeits-und Freundeskreis Fritz Bennewitz E.V.," c/o Prof. Dr. Rolf Rohmer, e-mail: rohmer@rz.uni-leipzig.de.

2. David G. John, "The First Black Gretchen: Fritz Bennewitz's *Faust I* in New York," *Monatshefte für den deutschen Unterricht*, 94/4 (2002), pp.441-57; and "Fritz Bennewitz in India and the 'First' Indian *Faust*," Collected contributions to the Fourth International Thalia Germanica conference, Lund (Sweden), 2001, in press.

3. Jochanan Ch. Trilse-Finkelstein and Klaus Hammer, eds., *Lexikon Theater International* (Henschel, Berlin, 1995). pp. 86-7.

4. Fritz Bennewitz, "Theatererfahrungen in der Dritten Welt. Gespräch mit Fritz Bennewitz," Ingeborg Pietzsch, interviewer, *Theater der Zeit* 1983/5, p. 43.

5. Roland Beer, *GDR-India. Cultural Relations. A Survey in Review*, Edited by the Ministry of Culture – German Democratic Republic, n.p., n.d. [ca. 1984]: pp. 5-6; pp. 43-47.

6. Fritz Bennewitz, [India overview. An account of theatre co-operation between the GDR and India.] 6 typescript pp., n.d.; and "Internationale Co-operation auf dem Theater. Bericht über Arbeitserfahrungen im Kulturaustausch DDR-INDIEN," 3 typescript pp., n.d., pencil notation at top: "UNESCO EFFEKTIVITÄT." Fritz Bennewitz Archive, Leipzig.

7. Richard Schechner, *Between Theater and Anthropology* (U. Pennsylvania Press, Philadephia, 1985); *Performance Theory*, revised and expanded edition (Routledge, New York, London, 1988); *Essays on Performance Theory*, revised and expanded edition (Routledge, New York, London, 1994).

8. Rustom Bharucha, *Theatre and the World: Performance and the Politics of Culture* (India: Manohar, 1990; rev. Routledge, London, New York, 1993), p. 48.

9. Aymanam Krishna Kaimal, *Doctor Faust Kathakali* [In Malayalam] (M.S. Printers, Aymanam, 1979).

# 24

## Bombay Dreams

### Commodity Production

**David Whitton**

No one living in Britain or visiting it at the present time could fail to be aware that the country is experiencing one of its periodic infatuations with all things Indian. The scale and nature of the love affair can be judged from the following events, all of them programmed in the summer of 2002:

- at the British Film Institute and other venues throughout the country: 'Imagine Asia', an eight-month festival of South Asian films;[1]
- at the Victoria and Albert Museum: 'The Art of Bollywood', an exhibition of Indian cinema posters and hoardings, together with work of contemporary artists who have been influenced by Bollywood images;[2]
- on Channel Four television: a season entitled 'Indian Summer' with events and films scheduled around coverage of the cricket season;[3]
- also on Channel Four: a ten-part series entitled 'Bollywood Women';
- in London's Hyde Park: a musical and dance extravaganza performed by top Bollywood stars;[4]
- at Selfridges: a themed make-over of the Oxford Street departmental store for a festival of Indian food and fashion; and
- at cinemas everywhere, *Lagaan, Devdas, Monsoon Wedding. Bend it like Beckham, The Guru...*

The 'Bollywood effect' currently affecting western popular entertainment, visual culture, performance and decorative arts is by no means restricted to Britain. Nor is it unprecedented, of course. Where it differs from previous orientalist vogues is its origination in popular performance culture. A perhaps surprising phenomenon of recent years has been the way that elements of British Asian popular culture – notably music, film and comedy – which previously occupied a minority cultural space have been adopted by mainstream audiences to an extent that would have been difficult to predict as recently as ten years ago, when Indian film music was an alien sound to the average European ear. Indian films, which once played predominantly to migrants from the sub-continent, have been taken up enthusiastically by second-generation Asians and are now also playing with subtitles to white audiences. Together with the increasing familiarity of *filmi*, Bhangra too found a new audience in the 1990s through bands such as The Sahotas and record labels like IRS devoted to generating mainstream Bhangra/Western fusion music. At roughly the same time, mainstream television audiences discovered a new genre in 'Asian comedy' (of which more later).

One consequence of the mainstreaming of what might be considered 'authentic' Asian culture is the spawning of hybrid cultural commodities designed to target the crossover market that has opened up. *Bombay Dreams* (Apollo Theatre, 19 June 2002) constitutes such a product. It is not the first production to bring a Bollywood theme to the London stage. In 1998 the Tamasha Group staged an award-winning *Fourteen Songs, Two Weddings and a Funeral*, a musical play adapted from the Hindi film *Hum Aapke Hain Koun*.[5] But *Bombay Dreams*, produced by Andrew Lloyd Webber and the Really Useful Theatre Company, is the most high profile and heavily promoted event of its type, receiving almost obsessive coverage in the British media. It has also become the object of intense media interest in India. These facts, and the production's obvious potential for global consumption, identify *Bombay Dreams* as an inescapable subject for the present conference devoted to ethnicity and identity in the age of global performance.

From one perspective *Bombay Dreams* may be considered as a formulaic musical that takes currently fashionable tropes and re-packages them in a familiar envelope for the West End stage. In this perspective, Bollywood serves as a trope those functions in a similar way to silent-era Hollywood in *Sunset Boulevard*, 1950s Argentina in *Evita* or Disney-Africa in *The Lion King*. More contestably, however, the musical has also been represented as an important breakthrough for British Asian performers, giving them, and Asian audiences, a major stake in the West End theatre for the first time. Commercially, this claim is justified. With all except one of the original cast of forty-two being British, it is one of the largest employers and the most prominent showcase for Asian artists ever seen in Britain. Audiences too appear to include an unprecedentedly high proportion of non-white spectators. From a cultural perspective, the notion of 'breakthrough' seems more ambiguous. If there is a breakthrough, what does it consist of, and what does it signify? In an attempt to start to address these questions, this paper considers *Bombay Dreams* from the angle of commodity production. I will argue that it is a deracinated cultural hybrid designed to occupy a position in a global market where multi-culturalism constitutes a brand.

The pre-production publicity materials, as well as indicating what the production is about, clearly define the target audience as cine-literate. The promotional video, packaged to look like a Bollywood film, is designed as a movie trailer. The video consists of a compilation of scenes filmed in rehearsal, with clips to evoke a rags-to-riches story of true love, gang warfare and *dharma*, set against the backdrop of Bombay shanty towns and the Bombay film industry. Using a convention borrowed from movie trailers, the scenes are commentated by a male voice-over portentously enunciating sensational prose. Nothing in the video suggests that the production is a stage musical rather than a movie, a strategy repeated in the highly coloured posters. Evidently, the publicity is pitched at an audience that is presumed to be either familiar with, or disposed to be attracted to, the style of Bollywood films.

The concept for the musical came from Andrew Lloyd Webber who encountered Indian film and the music of A.R. Rahman around 1998 when Channel Four started screening Bollywood movies. Lloyd Webber speaks of it as a revelation. Previously, he said, he had expected the main regenerative influence on Western music to come from Eastern Europe after the collapse of the Soviet Union. Instead, he now realized that it was Asian popular music with its vast worldwide audiences that was transforming the local musical scene.[6] Shortly afterwards, he met the director Shekhar Kapur who invited him to Bombay where the two sketched out the basic storyline for a stage musical. To assemble *Bombay Dreams* he brought together a team of high-profile artists from India and Britain. Along with the Muslim Indian composer A.R. Rahman, the main credits are the British Indian writer and actor Meerya Syal who developed the book; the Bombay film choreographer Farrah Kahn working with British co-choreographer Anthony van Laast; lyricist Don Black (the lyricist of *Aspects of Love* and *Sunset Boulevard*, and a regular collaborator with Lloyd Webber) and Stephen Pimlott, company director of the Royal Shakespeare Company. As a creative team, it provides a model illustration of best practice in crossover product design.

Rahman, whose previous credits include the soundtrack for some fifty films in Tamil or Hindi, was until recently relatively unknown to non-Asians in the UK outside specialist music circles. In the Asian diaspora he has a massive following and is reported to have sold over two hundred million albums world-wide, famously exceeding the combined sales of Madonna and Britney Spears. The music for *Bombay Dreams* is a fusion of European and (mainly) Indian. The show includes four re-cycled hits from the composer's back-catalogue, including 'Shakalaka Baby' from the film *Nayak* and 'Chiayya Chiayya' from the iconic dance sequence on the roof of a traveling train in *Dil Se*, also choreographed by Farrah Kahn. The storyline accommodates these by staging them as big numbers, which spectators see being filmed on a Bombay movie set. The inclusion of earlier hits is neither lazy nor accidental but part of a consistent inter-textual strategy, which exploits the audience's familiarity with the musical's source materials.

Meera Syal was engaged to develop the storyline sketched out by Lloyd Webber and Shekhar Kapur. In the context of a show that sets out to capture a West End crossover market, the choice of Syal as writer is revealing. A recipient of the 'Asian Woman of the Year' award in 2002, she occupies a particular position that straddles the British Asian community and the Establishment. Despite having no previous experience of scripting musicals, she brought impeccable credentials as a writer with a high profile among crossover audiences and who understands their tastes. As script-writer and performer, author of *Bhaji on the Beach* and *Anita and Me*, and more especially as one of the team that took so-called Asian comedy mainstream in the 1990s with the satirical fast-show *Goodness Gracious Me!*, she has played a key role in helping to create the cultural space that made it possible to conceive of a project like *Bombay Dreams*.

*Goodness Gracious Me!* originated in the 1990s as a radio show, developed a cult following, and was commissioned for television in 1996 with three series transmitted between 1996 and 1998. The writers' strategy was to combine sketches that played to both white and Asian experience, satirizing stereotypes and prejudices at the same time as making fun of authentic Indian traditions. One of its specialties was an inversion sketch, which transposed behavioral patterns from one culture to another. In one such sketch a group of Bombay youths having a night on the town go for an 'English' at the Mountbatten Restaurant where they are seen harassing the waiters and daring each other to try the blandest items on the menu. In another, Indian students visiting England on holiday complain about the beggars in London and insist that in order to see the real England one has to go out to the villages.

Meera Syal and her co-writer Anil Gupta have claimed not to have had a crossover agenda but to have aspired only to create 'general comedy'. However, it seems clear from the examples mentioned above that the writers were intent on developing material from their own culture that would transfer successfully to the mainstream audience. In a country where, according to the 2000 population census, 7.1 per cent identified themselves as belonging to an ethnic minority, this means a predominantly white audience. In fact, 80 per cent of the audience of 3.8 million for the third series were reported to be white, and similar levels of crossover have been reported in other counties where it was exported. In numerical terms the programme's achievement is indisputable. Its success, however, was not unproblematic. In the UK the show won awards from the Commission for Racial Equality but it also brought complaints from viewers who felt that it made fun of Hindu religion. Reportedly, it is perceived by many second-generation Asian spectators to validate their perspectives, a view not shared by distinguished Asian cultural commentators such as Suman Bhuchar, an artistic co-director of Tamasha Theatre and consultant for Asian Art (London), who says "it gives the English the opportunity to laugh at us without thinking about it".[7] Browsing through British Asian websites in July-August 2002 one could encounter similarly mixed reactions to *Bombay Dreams*. Satisfaction at the prominence being given to an aspect of Asian culture was accompanied by negative feelings about the stereotypical portrayal of Asians and the reductive impression of Indian cinema conveyed by clichés drawn solely from masala movies.

These ambivalent reactions point to what is potentially at stake when minority culture goes mainstream. I began by positing a distinction between what might be thought of as 'authentic' forms of minority culture circulating within an enlarged space, on the one hand, and on the other hand hybridized cultural entities designed to exploit opportunities created by the popularity of the former. In reality, though, this is an impossible distinction. What we are looking at, rather, is a cultural and economic space that accommodates a spectrum of cultural products with diverse and overlapping constituencies but no clear demarcation lines. What does seem clear, however, is that in order for mainstream crossover to occur, evolution of majority tastes is not sufficient on its own but must be accompanied by some adaptation on the part of minority cultural forms. Audience surveys for British TV repeatedly confirm that white viewers generally abstain from watching shows, which they perceive to be directed at an ethnic minority.[8] The demographic penetration of *Goodness Gracious Me!* may be remarkable but it still has be understood in the context of a situation where minority culture apparently becomes palatable to the majority only when it ceases to be identified as the property of its source culture. It therefore becomes necessary, in talking about audience crossover, to consider what concessions are made by a minority culture, and what subsists of it, when it addresses itself to the majority.

Applying these considerations to *Bombay Dreams*, a salient property of the production is its cultural hybridity. That is to be expected in any West End stage musical based on Bollywood movies (which themselves constitute a culturally hybrid genre). A more disturbing feature, but one that has also come to be associated with mass-market musicals, is its deracination. Despite the insistent foregrounding of culturally-referenced iconography, sounds, dance movements, etc., the production seems meticulously devoid of any precise local context. Or rather, there is a hyper-abundance of apparently localized reference – to the Bombay film industry and to Bombay itself, rendered in sanitized and easily assimilated clichés, to the narrative tropes of Bollywood movies, to familiar personalities, images and recycled jokes of screen media, to the specific forms of the West End musical, and so on. But, being grounded everywhere and nowhere, it seems incapable of communicating anything significant about the experience of the Indian diaspora in Britain, nor about its relationship to India. It is precisely this deracinated aspect that makes it a suitable commodity, if not for global consumption, then at least for consumption across a very wide market. It therefore comes as no surprise that plans have been drawn up for the concept to transfer to other venues. Casting took place in 2002 for a production in Toronto due to open in 2003, there are plans for an opening on Broadway early in 2004, and a delegation from the Really Useful Group was scheduled to visit Delhi and Bombay in February 2003 to set up bases for an Indian production.

Who, finally, constitutes the target audience for this show, and how does it address them? At a primary level, and disregarding any culturally specific iconography, the answer lies in the economic imperatives of stage musicals. Whilst all markets are intent on selling products to identifiable consumers, the musical stage targets a mass market. This is an economic necessity for a genre of which glamorous extravagance is perceived to be a necessary ingredient. In the case of *Bombay Dreams* the up-front production costs amounted to slightly less than $7 million. Caroline Sims, the marketing manager of the Really Useful Group, confirmed that the company's objective was "to exploit the production in every language, in every place where there is a theatre, every place where we can make money for the company and for the people who have invested in it".[9]

In reality, however, no truly mass market is a homogeneous entity but comprises innumerable sub-groups, which may be more or less readily identifiable. In these circumstances, the mass-market commodity needs to capture the widest possible spread of sub-groups. This is why it is both true and misleading to claim, as many have done, that *Bombay Dreams* is significant as the first West End musical addressed to British Asian tastes. It *does* address Asian audiences, specifically those British Asians with sufficient purchasing power (a minority within a minority) to be constituted as target consumers of West End theatre. But the economics of the musical and the demographics of the UK are such that commercial success must depend primarily on its appeal to the other local audiences and tourists who constitute the core market for stage musicals. *Bombay Dreams* presumably conforms to orthodox marketing strategy in having been put together with an awareness of the different groups that comprise its potential market. What is unusual is that rather than seeking to establish a common denominator, it appears to exploit multiple audience denominators. By this I mean that instead of submerging the identities of its diverse constituencies in a homogenous mass, it maintains their visibility, addressing them with differentiated and targeted devices. Examples here are the alternation between English and Hindi, jokes of the "Home is where the *shanti* is" variety, and the intertextual references to other cultural forms. For the production to offer different levels of accessibility is not in itself remarkable, since that is an inherent property of all culture. What is worth remarking upon, in a commercial enterprise, is the foregrounding of varying levels of accessibility as an integral part of the spectator's experience. In other circumstances, this accentuation of insider-outsider status might be considered a risky commercial strategy. In the context of the crossover market I have been describing, it might be considered astute. It has certainly proved a successful strategy since, despite real doubts at the start of the run about its viability; the production went on to recover its costs in a record-breaking five months.[10]

What I conclude from this is that *Bombay Dreams* offers something significantly different from previous Western infatuations with India. Rather than an orientalism that plays to a naïve fascination with the exotic, it proposes a knowingly post-modern cultural *masala*. Opening at a time of heightened global tension over border disputes and international terrorism, the show adopts multi-culturalism as brand. Its appeal depends less on the seductive and/or disturbing power of an exotic Other than on the satisfying affirmation, in defiance of external evidence, of feel-good cultural hybridity. It is this unproblematized version of the multi-cultural global village, one might feel, that constitutes the real 'Bombay Dream'.

## Notes

1. For details see
   http://www.visitingarts.org.uk/features/02imagineasia.html.
2. Exhibition website at
   http://www.vam.ac.uk/vastatic/microsites/1153_cinema_india/
3. An accompanying book was published: Archie Baron, *An Indian Affair: From Riches to Raj* (Sidgwick & Jackson/Pan Macmillan: 2001).
4. Security concerns led to this event being cancelled.
5. Lyric Theatre Hammersmith, November 1998. Co-production with Birmingham Repertory Theatre.

6. 'I thought when the Berlin Wall falls, the country that produced Shostakovich, Tchaikovsky, Rachmaninof, has by definition to produce something that is going to completely revolutionize western musical thinking. I was so wrong! What we've got is the Eurovision Song Contest. So when I heard Rahman I thought: I was right about one thing – it was going to come from somewhere else. But I never thought it would be India' (Omnibus: 'Making Bombay Dreams', BBC2 12 June 2002.

7. *Guardian,* 20 February 1999. Similar reservations were voiced by the author Yasmin Alibhai-Brown: "I hope people aren't laughing at us rather than with us. If you are Asian, you take a completely different set of messages from it" (*Observer,* 16 June 2002).

8. For example, a poll conducted by the award-winning television series 'Black Britain' found that 25 per cent of whites would not tune in simply because it contained the word black in the title.

9. In conversation with the author, 13 December 2002.

10. 'Bombay Dreams' press release (Really Useful Group), December 2002. According to the press release, the box office had taken £10 million in the first five months.

# 25

## Indra

### "The Drinker of Soma" and His Role in Indian Theatre

#### Elzabieta Koldrzak

As Bharata-Muni teaches, the idea of the theatre was born in Indra – the King of Vedic Gods, when demons spread their power all over the Earth. Indra came to Brahma – the Creator of the World – and asked him to create theatre itself. This mythological description that comes from the first lesson of the *Natyasastra*[1] named *Natyotpatti adhyaya*, gives the very first information. Indra – since the idea of the theatre was born in his mind – has given to the theatre his presence, which is permanently manifested through his patronage for each of the essential theatre factors.

### Who is Indra?

According to McDonnell[2] Indra is the favourite national god of the Vedic Indians. His importance is indicated by the fact that about 250 hymns of *Rgveda* (which is nearly one-fourth of the total number of hymns) celebrate his greatness. Indra is primarily the god of thunder. He is the dominant deity of middle region of the cosmos.

Generally, Indra is the god, who is the conqueror of the demons of darkness and the winner of the light[3]; He is the god of battle.[4] Even all the assembled gods cannot conquer him in war[5]. The thunderbolt is the weapon exclusively associated to Indra.[6] His well-known epithets are "Lord Bountiful"[7], "Sovran Lord"[8], "The Mighty"[9], "Having a hundred powers"[10], "Vrytra slayer"[11].

In between Indra's greatest cosmogonies deeds there are some creative in nature:

In the cosmic action he rends asunder – heaven and earth as two wheels that are kept apart by the axe that unites them.[12] With his might he didst grasp the holder-up of heaven also in the seats of earth,[13] Indra with his might, upon the framework of the heaven, he didst fix, across, air's region firmly, unremoved.[14] He measured out mid-air when the mighty Heaven and Earth, those bright expanses, that have no wheels, joyed.[15] He gave life to Sun and Dawn and Heaven.[16]

Other descriptions show Indra's power of purification, ea. When Indra drove the great dragon from the air, bright were the flaming fires, the Sun gave forth his shine, and Soma, Indra's juice, shone forth.[17] Some other descriptions indicate Indra's power of concentrating energy in the form of light – He hath found light even in the blinding darkness.[18] He is said to sweep away Assures with his wheel[19] and to consume the Raksasas with his bolt, as fire might a dry forest.[20]

Indra has also his particular personal features: He is strong, nimble, victorious, heroic, of unbounded force, of irresistible might.[21] As he was born of truth he does not pauses to think.[22] He is mighty through wisdom[23] and able to surprise the gods.[24] Indra has performed his grandest cosmic feats under the influence of *Soma*[25] – the essence of being, the essence of immorality. He, whose name is "Soma-drinker",[26] shares the divine nectar with other gods and even with men.

If those limited examples given above may do clear Indra's role in the Vedic idea of reality and do show his primary role in the Vedic concept of cosmic action, let them be also the background for explanation of Indra's major role in the concept of Indian theatre.

In fact, it is not possible to find any aspect of theatrical action, which does not manifest connection with Indra. Let me describe only few crucial examples, which are the most expressive elements of the theatrical vision. Those that affirm Indra's kingly power as well as his cosmic might of lighting up the truth and the wisdom.

### Indra as Sorvan Lord – Performance as the Glory of Indra Praising

In *Natyotpatti adhyaya* (mentioned above lesson of *Natyasastra*) Bharata gives a general description of the first theatrical performance.[27] This happened at the time of the Festival named *Indramaha*, which was a celebration of Indra's honoured victory under Assures that were killed by him. Here Bharata suggests the union between idea of the theatre and Indra's victory celebration. Theatrical event appears as essentially united with the act of praising Indra's – King's of Gods – Glorious activity.

## The Mighty Indra – Performance as a Battle

In the next passage of same lesson[28] Bharata gives the view of first performance. Here Bharata introduces and explains another aspect of the theatrical event. He focuses his description on the action (the conflict of Gods and Daityas – *Daivasuram*). Bharata mentions two following parts of the performance. The first one – benediction containing blessing with words – where he develops main idea of the performance's attitude, shoving performance as an act of prayer as well as an act of God's activity praising. The second one – the situation in which the Daityas were defeated by Gods representing an altercation and tumult as well as mutual cutting off of limbs and piercing of bodies – where Bharata defines the performance's matter, which in the sense is introduced not only as representation and reflection of the victorious cosmic battle, but as this battle undertaking. The interpretation of the performance as the battle with demons supports latter part of this lesson.[29] There Bharata mentions about the attack of demons, who stopped the performance with aggressive behaviour against the actors, whose speech and memory were paralysed. He shows that the demons did not like to watch any such action which presenting them as defeated. They could not attack the gods, but they could harm the actors. For this occasion Bharata describes Indra's intervening with his power – demons – who destroyed the performance – had been slain. Indra beat them to death with his *Jarjara*, the cosmic *Vajra* – thunderbolt. Finally Indra offered his weapon, which represents his might, to protect the actors on the stage. This incident – attack of demons and Indra's victorious fight, supports suggestion that presenting on the stage God's exploits can't be understand completely through category that of mimicry, but should be conceived as a kind of battle, which at any time may provoke demons to unexpected attack. Thus, the *Jarjara* has to be kept on the stage for the performance's duration. Only Indra's protection to the actors and keeping demons away from the stage do open a way for acting and celebrating of the cosmic battle, in which demons are defeated. Describing the performance as a battle, Bharata employs mythological vision of the reality known as conflict *Daiwasuram* and shows its manifestation on a humane level. Indra's role expressed here indirectly and than directly is a clear example of his kingship in the world of Gods as well as his might in the mid-air region. Thus Indra protects the performance – a battle in the name of him.

## Indra, the Creator – Performance (Purvaranga) and Mid-air Region Creation

Other passages indicating Indra's essential role in the theatre Bharata put into fifth lesson of the *Natyasastra*. These descriptions deal with *Purvaranga*, which is the very first, ritualised preliminary part of performance. In the time of *Purvaranga* the director of a theatrical troupe – *sutradhar* – enters to the stage with *Jarjara*. In examined aspect that is Indra's cosmic creative activity, the symbolism of *Jarjara* may be interpreted on a part of mythological figure of the cosmic axe, held by Indra between heaven and earth. When *sutradhar* moves through the stage, he does do very peculiar steps, which he puts in very particular points of the stage space. *Sutradhar's* movements are a part of the ritual named *ranga-puja* – the Sanctifying of the stage space. This action suggests clearly that *sutradhar* directs his steps according to the graphic imagination of the cosmos called *vastupurusha-mandala*. What special for this design is that represents the cosmic order only in the flat ground level. Thus it becomes possible to interpretate of *sutradhar's* movements as the creation of the mid-air region that takes place in the time of *Purvaranga*. Using *Jarjara* he raises the space between earth – symbolised by the diagram *vastupurusha-mandala* and heaven – symbolised by the roof covering the stage space. The basic connection between the *Purvaranga* ritual and Indra's cosmic action in the middle region may also indicate the manner of using of the curtain in the time of *Purvaranga*. Bharata mentions 18 parts of *Purvaranga*. Among them 9, which should be performed behind a curtain and another 9, acted without a curtain.[30] The 14th element of *Purvaranga* called *sushkavakryshta dhruva* includes verses for *Jarjara*, which are sung in the open stage.[31] The practice of the curtain using seems to be related to the act of middle region creation, what supports following *Rgveda's* description: *when Indra parted the air between heaven and earth both of them became visible to each other.*[32] The parts of *Purvaranga* played behind curtain may represent here the heavenly region and other, played without the curtain, may do heavenly action to be visible to the earthly region. Thus comes the interpretation that the middle region created by Indra (including the symbolism of the stage space and curtain) plays the role of a mirror, which focuses the heavenly and earthly actions in united perspective.

## Indra the Soma-Drinker – Drama's Hero and the Actor

Indra who is praised for his heroic acts, who with his might protects theatrical performance, and who creates the space to perform the victorious deeds, at the same time is a prototype of the main drama hero and the main actor. Those features of Indra such as heroism, wisdom, truth are reflected equally in the hero's actions and in the actor's play. Bharata teaches that:

> The drama and the theatre is mimicry of the exploits of gods, Asuras, kings, as well as house-holders.[33]

> It depicted humane nature with its joys and sorrow, by means of representation through gestures, words, costume and temperament.[34]

Bharata shows that Indra's personal features and his heroic acts may be transformed and reflected in a humane level. He also defines it as the level of the experiences of joy and sorrow. Does Bharata suggest that Indra participate in human joy and sorrow? Or rather, does he mean that those human emotions, when purified by specific Indra's features – heroism and wisdom – employed to the drama hero's thoughts and to the actor's art, may become the weapons against demons, against ignorance and personal restrictions? Bharata, when he explains the value of the theatre, says:

> The man who properly attends the performance of music and dramas will attain
> the happy and meritorious path in the company of Brahman sages.[35]

Does the idea of Indra, the King of Gods, apply to the theatre lead to the feast of *Soma* similarly to the Vedic ritual?[36] Theatre – if take it as the ritual of purification of the emotions, which gives to human company of Indra sharing his divine nectar with victorious beings – seems does do.

What mystery covers the words *Soma* – the favourite drink of Indra? Taking its meaning in the context of purification, *Soma* signifies more the process of extracting of juice, than some particular object. It is supposed to be the final substance, the essence that appears in the time of transformation or after destruction of the temporal forms of being. The suggested meaning of this name indicates also that not all forms of being may be transformed into *Soma*. The positive examples are the Gods, who drink *Soma* – which is also the Self (*The Soma is within him, in his frame vast strength*[37]). Negative examples are demons, which may not drink *Soma* – which means don't include it in the self. In the process of purification demons are killed.

In the context of theatrical action the process of purification and extracting of *Soma* may be related to the eight emotional permanent states, mentioned by Bharata.[38] Those are supposed to be the forms of experience that may be transformed into *Soma*. The process of extracting of *Soma* starts in the theatre from heroic mood (*vira rasa*) and ends with the mood of wonder (*adbhuta rasa*). Both of them are closely connected with Indra – as a hero and as a victor. Beside two mentioned moods there is one more, which may be recognised as typical for Vedic Hero. This is well known from mythology that Indra in his Heaven – when his fight is over, when he tastes his victory – he watches the performance given by Gandharvas and Apsaras. Indra's heavenly mood is than nothing more than *sryngara* (love). Thus we can see a dual significance of Indra's representation or presence both in drama's hero and in actor's acting. One kind of representation is related to the battle – when Indra gives heroism, leading to the victory. Second kind is related to the situation when battle is over, to the state of love. The crucial aspect of both emotional levels is that they exist simultaneously. Indra's might comes from his knowledge of love, which he got before he had done his fights (*Desiring food he came unto his Mother, and on her breast beheld the pungent Soma*[39]). The coming conclusion is that – to the victory leads the heroism that groves from the love. Such a combined emotions – in the combination love may be unmanifested or manifested, but heroism is always manifested) – create personality of drama's hero and determinate actor's play.

What are the idea that lays in a background of supposed identity of Soma – love – and the light of victory? This question seems to illuminate the main sense of *Indramaha* Festival as well as the main sense of the theatrical performance. Similarly to Indra's cosmic action, the theatrical action leads human thoughts and emotions to the testing victory of light. Thus similarly to Indra the spectator and the actor tests *Soma* in the time of battle for light. The meaning of *Soma* is the state of harmony of all beings after excluding evil. This is the state of primal unity. On the level of the thought light and unity symbolises the consciousness. On the level of the emotions these qualities may be understood as the state of love (*Thus in the Soma, in wild joy the Brahman hath exalted thee.*)[40] In the time of performance, being the manifestation of the *Daivasuram* conflict, unity (love) has to be differentiated into other emotional states. However, they should be still able to keep the test of the primary state, they should be linked with it. In such a sense, love as *Soma* is tested in the time of performance through gradually extracted and finally distracted emotions. Finally, as the result of performance, at the conclusion of the theatrical action, the test of love – *Kama* is supposed to appear in its pure and real form that of *Soma*.[41]

Indra, the Guardian and the Patron of the theatre, is also the Guarantee of the unity, existing in the theatre within many representations.

## Notes

1. *The Natyasastra* (1950), I.1-7.
2. McDonnell (1995), pp. 54-66.
3. Ea. "When thou with might, upon the framework of the heaven, didn't fix, across, air's region firmly, unremoved, In the light-winning war, Indra, in rapturous joy, thou smotest Vrytra dead and broughtest floods of rain.", *The Hymns of the Rgveda* (1995), I.LVI.5; or: "I glorify that Ram who finds the light of heaven, whose hundred nobly-natured ones go forth with him.", I.LII.1.
4. Ea. "Yet verily the Warrior in his vigorous strength stirreth up with his might great battles for mankind. And men have faith in Indra, the resplendent One, what time he hurleth down his bolt, his dart of death.", *The Hymns of the Rgveda*, I.LV.5.
5. Ea. "Not even all the gathered Gods conquered thee, Indra, in the war, When thou didst lengthen days by night.", *The Hymns of the Rgveda*, IV.XXX.3.
6. Ea. "Even the Heaven and Earth bow down before him, before his very breath the mountains tremble. Known as the Soma-drinker, armed with thunder, who wields the bolt, He, yea men, is Indra.", *The Hymns of the Rgveda*, II.XII.13.
7. Ea. "Impetuous as a bull, he chose the Soma, and in three sacred beakers drank the juices. Maghavan grasped the thunder for his weapon, and smote

to death this firstborn of the dragons.", *The Hymns of the Rgveda*, I.XXXII.3; Maghavan: the wealthy and liberal, see: p. 20.

8. Ea. "He who is Sovran Lord of great and perfect strength, Exeter of heroic might, Who bears the fearless thunder as a father bears his darling son.", *The Hymns of the Rgveda*, X.XXII.3.

9. Ea. "Him, him we seek for friendship, him for riches and heroic might. For Indra, he is Œakra, he shall aid us while he gives us wealth.", *The Hymns of the Rgveda*, I.X.6; Œakra: mighty, the powerful, able to, see: p. 6.

10. Ea. "Thou, Œatakratu, drankest this and wast the Vrytras' slayer; thou Helpest the warrior in the fray.", *The Hymns of the Rgveda*, I.IV.8; Œatakratu: he who is connected with a hundred acts, religious rites, either as their performer or their object; or: endowed with great wisdom, see: p. 3.

11. Ea. "The men have lifted Indra up, the Vrytra-slayer, to joy and strength: Him, verily, we invocate in battles whether great or small: be he our aid in deeds of might.", *The Hymns of the Rgveda*, I.LXXXI.1.

12. *The Hymns of the Rgveda*, I.CIII.1

13. *Ibid.*, I.LVI.6.

14. *Ibid.*, I.LVI.5.

15. *Ibid.*, I.CXXI.11.

16. *Ibid.*, I.XXXII.4.

17. *Ibid.*, VIII.III.20.

18. *Ibid.*, I.C.8.

19. *Ibid.*, VIII.LXXXV.9.

20. *Ibid.*, VI.XVIII.10.

21. Ea. "His arms win kine, his power is boundless, in each act best, with a hundred helps, waker of battle's din Is Indra: none may rival him in mighty strength. Hence, eager for the spoil, the people call on him.", *The Hymns of the Rgveda*, I.CII.6.

22. Ea. "So even, Lord of Power and Might, the people call thee Maghavan, Giver, who pauses not to think.", *The Hymns of the Rgveda*, IV.XXXI.7.

23. Ea. "Mighty through wisdom, as he lists, terrible, he hath waxed in strength.", *The Hymns of the Rgveda*, I.LXXXI.4.

24. Ea. "He hath surpassed all measure in his brightness, yea, and the Gods, for none may be his equal.", *The Hymns of the Rgveda*, III.XLVI.3.

25. Ea. "In the wild joy of Soma I demolished Œaramba's forts, ninety-nine, together.", *The Hymns of the Rgveda*, IV.XXVI.3.

26. Ea. "Come thou to our libations, drink Soma, Soma-drinker thou!", *The Hymns of the Rgveda*, I.IV.1.

27. *The Natyasastra* (1950), op. cit., I.53-55.

28. *Ibid.*, I.55-58.

29. *Ibid.*, I.66-73.

30. *Ibid.*, V.8-11; V.1-15.

31. *Ibid.*, V.5-6.

32. *The Hymns of the Rgveda*, op. cit., II.XIII.5.

33. *The Natyasastra* (1950), op. cit., I.120.

34. *Ibid.*, I.121.

35. *The Natyasastra* (1961), XXXVI.8.

36. Many other than Bharata's *Natyasastra* sources give a lot of evidence that prove close relations between the concept of Indian theatre and the Vedic sacrificial rituals; see: Boner B., Sarma A., S.R. Baumer S.R. (1996); Byrski M.K. (1974); Gonda J. (1980); Lidova N. (1994); Staal F. (1983), (1996); Uni N.P. (1990); Varadpande M.L. (1987).

37. *The Hymns of the Rgveda*, op. cit., II.XVI.2.

38. Originally Bharata describes four main sentiments that are erotic, furious, heroic and odious. Than he adds another four, which are coming as follow: comic from erotic, pathetic from furious, marvellous from heroic and terrible from odious. It is clear from Bharata's description of the style of communication (vrrti; XXII.2-5) and his description of furious sentiment (VI. 64) that it is closely connected to Raksassas and Danavas action, as they are naturally furious, they are violent even making love. The furious sentiment is a very good example of the idea relating the sentiments with the dominant states. It describes connection between *rasas* and *bhavas*. Furious sentiment through which Raksassa and Danavas are pictured gives rise to anger, which is the dominant state of this emotion. Other dominant states are as follows: erotic – love, comic – laughter, pathetic – sorrow, heroic – energy, terrible – fear, odious – disgust, marvellous – astonishment.

39. *The Hymns of the Rgveda*, op. cit., III.XLVIII.3.

40. *Ibid.*, I.LXXX.1.

41. Such a statement gives a brief summary of the discussion about the meaning of *œanta rasa* sentiment. As the subject has numerous interpretations it is not possible to give here its full explanation; see: Gnoli R. (1956); Masson J.L., Patwardhan M.V. (1969); Uni N.P. (1998); see also: Raghavan V. (1978) and Byrski M.K. (2001), pp. 12-21.

# 26

## Image of the String Puppet

### Female Sacrifice and the Case of
### Queen Padmini of Chittor

**Poh Sim Plowright**

The image of the string puppet in its literal and metaphorical sense bespeaks the highest and most effective form of control: hence in India, the Creator, Brahma, is perceived as the Supreme *String Puppeteer* (*Sutradhara* or 'String-Holder'), controlling human beings as puppets with three strings. Nowhere in Asia is the eloquence of the String Puppet more striking than in Rajasthan where string puppetry, many scholars claim, began. Here evolved a theatrical genre which, merging with, and reinforced by, the religious and philosophical concept of Brahma as supreme String Puppeteer, became the most effective form of puppetry in the world: a form which implies an extraordinary *Control* system that can be explored from the literal, political, social and psychical perspective.

But why have I bracketed the 'string puppet' with 'female sacrifice' in the title of this paper and how does Queen Padmini of Chittor fit into the equation? If Brahma is the Divine String Puppeteer, the God Shiva is even more closely associated with puppets.[1] Shiva is regarded as the God of Dance or Movement *and* of Puppets, enabling us to identify *primal* movement with Puppet movement. So the iconography of the *Dancing* Shiva constitutes an important part of Indian philosophy, imparting order and purpose to the universe and, by implication, giving the same power to puppet movement. Even more significant, for the argument of this paper, is the role of Shiva's wife, Parvati, in the story of the *origin* of string puppetry. According to legend, it was Parvati who was seen as the *motivator* of this art form: impressed by the great beauty of a doll, lovingly crafted by the carpenter, Sevakram, she prompted her husband, Shiva, to bring it to life. The carpenter's pleasure knew no bounds and when the dancing doll came to a halt, so the story goes, it was Parvati who again persuaded her husband to instruct Sevakram to insert *strings* into its limbs and so manipulate it into action. Thus, it is said, string puppetry began.[2]

But Parvati is not only concerned with string puppetry; she is also credited, if we dig into mythology, with the origin of *satism* or 'female immolation': to avenge an insult to her husband, Shiva – he had been omitted from her father's invitation to an entertainment – she immolated herself in the presence of the assembled gods.[3] With this act of *absolute* fealty to her husband, Parvati sets a *divine* example, fusing in her person the image of string puppetry (which she instigated) with that of female sacrifice.

I want to set against this the sacrificial death by fire (*jauhar*) of the 14th century Queen Padmini of Chittor on receipt of the news of her husband's defeat in battle.[4] Within the system of control then prevalent in Rajasthan, where the wife's destiny was tied to that of her husband – 'Destiny' also being seen as a String Puppeteer – it is difficult not to recognise the interwoven threads of string puppetry and female sacrifice.

I will return to this story with more specific reference to String Images so as to fortify my comparison of Queen Padmini to a string puppet, but, for the moment, I would like to examine, briefly, various other implications of control encoded in the string puppet image across Asia.

My research over the past seven years has taken me to China, Japan, Singapore and Thailand, considering and connecting this image in various forms of human and puppet theatre, from the puppet theatre of Southern China and its 'Pear Garden' human theatre via Noh and Bunraku in Japan to the 'Manora' plays of Thailand. In all these forms, the influential and controlling power of the 'string puppet' icon is immediately apparent, not least in the puppet-like movements of Asian actors – consider, to take an example much closer to home, the

Kathakali actors of South Kerala: their resemblance to marionettes in appearance and movement is indisputable.

Like the Indians, the Chinese subscribed to the belief that deities control human beings in the manner of string puppets.[5] In the Chinese theatrical hierarchy, puppets are placed first, boy actors second and adult actors last.[6] The most powerful and exorcistic theatrical figure in Chinese belief is the string puppet, Marshal Tian, often shown dancing on the T'ai Chi symbol surrounded by 8 trigrams. This dance was considered such a potent rite of exorcism and cleansing that an audience is not required to witness it. In modern times this rite has been branded superstitious and anti-progressive and has therefore been banned in China. It is, however, still permitted in Singapore where there is a large Chinese population as well as freedom of worship.[7]

Marshal Tian or *Xianggong* was the boy protégé of the 8th-century Emperor Tang Ming Huang, who, as leader of the Emperor's actors in his 'Pear Garden' Academy and his puppeteers in his Inner Chamber, fostered the link between human and puppet movement in China. In a poem the Emperor compared *himself* to a string puppet,[8] which certainly enhanced its status. Even a mistake on the human stage is referred to as *fan hsien*, a term borrowed from string puppetry, meaning 'the strings have twisted'. But unfortunately there is no treatise in Chinese theatre spelling out the strong connection between these two different theatrical genres. For that we have to turn to a seminal 15th century treatise on Noh acting – *Kakyo* – ('The Mirror of the Flower') written by Zeami Motokiyo – one of the two founders of Noh – the oldest unchanged theatre in the world. In this treatise Zeami instructs the Noh actor to move his body as if it were a 'string' puppet controlled metaphorically by his 'heart', which assumes the role of 'puppeteer'. In Chinese and Japanese thought the ideograph for 'heart' combines the multiple meanings of heart, soul and mind – in other words the control of the 'heart' requires 100% inner concentration. There is the implication that it is an activity, which goes beyond consciousness, tapping into the Unconscious – the alpha of life itself. As the golden rule of restraint for movement in the Noh states: "Move the heart 10; move the body 7." What is perceived in outer movement is but the tip of an iceberg powered by a centrally – orchestrated inner control. Let me quote from the treatise: "The Noh actor must seek an equivalent to the puppet's strings in his heart....The heart is the centre for all connecting strings enabling the player to orchestrate his movement and synthesize his artistry." The string puppet connection, emphasising human and puppet affinity, is so dominant that Zeami called the Noh "an art tied to the heart by strings".[9] So when one watches a Noh actor move on the stage, it is difficult not to be struck by the strong resemblance of his movements to those of a string puppet. This similarity is deliberately intended, as Zeami had in no uncertain terms admonished his actors to move as though controlled by invisible strings manipulated by the 'heart' acting as the 'Unseen Puppeteer'.

In addition to the total inner control, which I have just described, defining the power of restrained outward movement (as refracted through string puppet imagery), there is another strand of control which irrevocably ties a player to his troupe. Such is the nature of psychical or superstitious control best exemplified in the obligation of a member of the *Manora* theatrical troupe in Nakhon Sri Thammarat in South Thailand to his/her leader. Once recruited, no actor dares to leave on pain of being cursed or punished by severe illness or even, it is said, death.[10] Similarly, in the world of *Khon* masked drama (the jewel of Thai theatrical art forms), where the training is so rigorous and severe that it has been referred to as 'inhuman', psychical control, alongside the severe daily discipline, produces actors who not only resemble puppets in movement but also in behaviour, becoming totally ego-less, controllable and submissive. No one dares shirk the gruelling daily training and leaving the troupe is out of the question: such is the power of superstitious control.[11]

Sometimes strict laws in training which turn trainees into puppets as well as wider implacable and constricting societal laws can, as in the case of the 17th century *Bunraku* puppet theatre, produce an art form of unimaginable beauty. The earlier name for this puppet genre was *ningyo joruri*: *ningyo* meaning 'doll' and *joruri* being the name of a 12th century heroine – Lady *Joruri* – who sacrificed her life for the love of her famous military lover – the *Genji* general, Yoshitsune. The fierce system of control and manipulation exercised by the military powers in Japan from the 12th to the 19th centuries reduced those in its grip to little more than puppets and Lady Joruri's life exemplified in a human story the mechanics of puppet control. In the puppet theatre called after her, each puppet is controlled by three puppeteers breathing in unison: the training required for the one moving the legs and the one moving the left arm takes eight years, while that for the one moving the head and right arm takes forever! Such discipline reflected the larger societal control where even the size of a peasant's hut was prescribed and every marriage contract of a samurai warrior had to be sanctioned by higher authority.[12] In contradistinction to the control in Noh, which is invisible, the control in this puppet genre is visibly, and unashamedly, demonstrated by the three black-robed puppeteers manipulating the puppet. The interaction of society and a theatrical form is manifest and the life and sacrificial death of a heroic woman, crucial.

And here I come back to the importance of Queen Padmini of Chittor. Chittor or Chittaugarh was the capital of the Mewar rulers who established one of the world's most celebrated dynasties, spanning 76 generations and 1,500 years. It also had the reputation of being the most magnificent medieval fort and, even today, it is still a site of poetic and national pilgrimage. Why does Queen Padmini occupy such a significant position in the Rajput psyche, irrespective of whether she was real or fictitious? It would seem that in the world of the psyche and symbolism, poetic truth surpasses historical accuracy in importance.

In a society where the warrior unquestionably sacrifices his life in battle – death in battle being equated with salvation – it stands to reason that the role of the *pattivrata* (that is, the wife who has vowed to protect her husband) is of vital importance. Queen Padmini, by her sacrifice, exemplifies the ultimate PATTIVRATA and her public submission to destiny, underlines and reaffirms the entire sacrificial basis of Rajput society and the distinctive role of the warrior with which she is intrinsically connected. Just as Parvati on a supernatural level glorifies absolute fealty to her lord and husband, Shiva, so Padmini's act, on a terrestrial level, identifies her with her husband's cause and the fundamental essence of Rajput chivalry and warriorship. If string puppetry and female immolation began with Parvati, these concepts were powerfully endorsed by Queen Padmini. In old Rajasthan, which was bound into a religious framework that perceived the Creator as the Supreme *String Holder* and, at a secular level, abounding in images of string control, real life was sometimes perceived as puppet drama and vice-versa. For example, it was said of the great Kautilya who laid the foundations of the Maurya empire (4th-3rd centuries BC) and wrote his political treatise, *Arthashastra*, that "he moved kings like puppets by the strings attached to his fingers in the real drama of life".[13] The *rawala* or 'court' of an eastern prince was sometimes referred to as "a labyrinth containing the strings that move the puppets." This was a society of labyrinthine control: the sacred thread put on a child at birth to the accompaniment of songs;[14] the collection of such threads from the bodies of the slain after a battle, in order to determine the number killed by the Mughal invaders;[15] the string necklaces which Rajput wives wore to preserve their husbands' health as part of a vow, the string of the necklace being renewed yearly;[16] and the use of a communication string linking mother and astrologer at a royal birth so that the latter could accurately chart the child's horoscope.[17] In such a milieu, though not directly connected with puppetry, as was the case of Lady Joruri in Japan, Queen Padmini was, in the strongest metaphorical sense, a puppet, caught and held in a political and social framework, which demanded total submission.[18] She certainly exemplified the properties and symbolic connotations of a puppet in a context in which puppets have long been connected with sacrifice, exorcism, and death rituals. Queen Padmini's own death – far more spectacular than Lady Joruri's – qualified her for entry into the sacrificial world of scapegoats and exorcists. In certain parts of the Fujian province in China, female mediums, scapegoats and puppets are denoted by the same vernacular term *ang*.[19] This provides etymological support for the indivisibility of these seemingly different functions. By her self-immolation, Queen Padmini did not only defy the invader – Sultan Alaudeen Khilji – from Delhi but Death itself. In a society strangulated by so many strings of control – feudal, social, and religious (time does not permit me to discuss the caste system) – Death by fire loosened the knot as it were, and provided a dignified release and protest.

I've introduced the element of protest deliberately for there is a Japanese story about a female puppet which when burnt as firewood, spat flames at her master/puppeteer and even managed to kill him. In the strictly controlled Japanese society where female dissension was out of the question, the gesture of protest was left to a female puppet.[20] But in whatever way one chooses to interpret Padmini's story, though not officially associated with string puppetry in Rajasthan where this art originated, it would be difficult not to perceive her as the Queen of Puppets and Sacrifice through her spectacular death which ironically turned someone so controlled into the Supreme Controller of life and death.

Before concluding, I would like to refer to two philosophical theories underpinning Asian theatrical disciplinary training. The first theory centres on the conversation between the Pandawa warrior Arjuna and the God Krishna, as the former is riding into battle against his evil cousins in the Hindu epic the *Mahabharata*. Arjuna is overcome by the futility of war, particularly against his own kinsmen, but Krishna's respónse enjoins him to perform his role as a warrior and consider it in the light of a most sacred duty. The responsibility of the outcome rests with God rather than with man. So from this exemplar, every human being is similarly exhorted to perform the role accorded to him in life, however insignificant, without demurring.[21] The 12th-century Chinese Confucian scholar, Chu Hsi, reiterates the same idea in a philosophical theory, which he calls *Ming-Fen* ('Names and Parts'). For society to function in an orderly way, and the vastness of China made order and CONTROL an imperative for survival, it was deemed necessary for every human being, like cogs in a machine, to perform the role, however humble, which had been assigned to him.[22] So within the framework of Asian theatrical training, which is permeated by these two controlling doctrines at the conscious and/or unconscious level, it is not surprising that Asian actors submit unquestioningly to the strict discipline demanded of them by their prescribed roles.

In conclusion, I will use two quotations from East and West, one by the 19th century German writer Heinrich von Kleist and the second by the 17th century Japanese swordsman, Yagyu Tajima no Kami, the first extolling the pure grace of puppet movement, and the second its effective strategy for a swordsman:

> Grace appears most purely in that human form which either has no consciousness or an infinite consciousness: that is, in a Puppet or a God.[23]

> Turn yourself into a doll (puppet) made of wood: it has no ego, it thinks nothing; and let the body and limbs work themselves out in accordance with the discipline they have undergone. This is the way to win.[24]

These two quotations, the one highly theoretical and the other essentially practical, underline for me the singular power of the puppet, as SYMBOL and as EXEMPLAR, which has run through this study of Puppets and Control and one has to conclude that the fruit of such a complex system of manipulation is not only unadulterated GRACE but a manifestation of HOW TO WIN IN ART.

## Notes

1. Further evidence connecting Shiva with string puppetry is provided by the 108 stone tablets incorporated in one of the entrance towers of the Temple of Chidabaram midway between Madras and Tanjore. The entire temple is a hymn of praise to Shiva. Each tablet bears a dancer in a puppet-like pose as described in Bharata's *Natyasastra*. 108 is a magically charged number as it reflects a belief (originally Chinese) that there are altogether 108 evil influences (72 earthly, and 36 heavenly,) in heaven and earth. In any collection of puppets in China, there are in principle, 36 heads and 72 body parts, the total adding up to 108 in order for the assembled animated puppets to counteract these malign forces in various theatrical performances. The ancient Chinese art of callisthenics *T'ai Chi Ch'uan* (*Yang* style) contains 108 forms and its practitioner is instructed to move like a string puppet while performing these movements. See Poh Sim Plowright, *Mediums, Puppets, and the Human Actor in the Theatres of the East*, Edwin Mellen Press, New York 2002, p. 194.

2. M.L. Varadpande, *Invitation to Indian Theatre*, Arnold Heinemann Publishers India Ltd., 1987, New Delhi, p. 63.

3. R. Willis (ed.), *World Mythology*, Simon and Schuster, London, 1993, p. 82.

4. There are many accounts of this event. See for example, James Todd, *Annals and Antiquities of Rajasthan*, (W.C. Samanta, Calcutta, 1895).

5. W. Dolby, *A History of Chinese Drama*, Paul Elek, London, 1976, p. 82.

6. P. Van der Loon, *The Classical Theatre and Art Song of South Fukien*, SMC Publishing, Taipei, 1972, p. 35.

7. Plowright, *op. cit.*, p. 47.

8. Dolby, *op. cit.*, p. 10.

9. Nose Asaji, *Zeami jurokubu-shu hyoshaku* (Zeami's sixteen treatises), vol.2, Tokyo, 1940, pp. 379-80. The English translation of this section of the treatise is by Naohiko Umewaka.

10. See the case of Manee Burinkoat – the leader of a *Manora* troupe – and her inability to leave her vocation. Plowright, *op. cit.*, pp. 25-26.

11. For more detailed information of *Khon* dance drama and its severe training, see Mattani, Mojdara and Rudnin, *Dance, Drama and Theatre in Thailand: The Process of Development and Modernisation*, (Yuki Graphics, Tokyo, 1993).

12. Plowright, *op. cit.*, p. 133.

13. M. L. Varadpande, *Traditional Indian Theatre*, Abhinav Publications, New Delhi, 1979, p. 31.

14. M. Prabhaskar, *Cultural Heritage of Rajasthan*, Panchsheel Prakashan, Jaipur, 1972, p. 66.

15. A. Eraly, *Emperors of Peacock Thrones: The Saga of the Great Mughals*, Penguin Books, New Delhi, 2000, p. 143.

16. L. Harlan, *Religion and Rajput Women: The Ethic of Protection in Contemporary Narratives*, University of California Press, Berkeley, 1992, p. 205.

17. R. Khullar and K. Singh, *Golden Rajasthan*, Prakash Books, New Delhi, 1990, p. 42.

18. R.S. Sharma, *Early Medieval Indian Society: A Study in Fuedalisation*, Sangam Book Ltd., London, 2000, p. 41. The 'perfect wife' in feudal times identified herself wholly with her husband's interests. This custom of a wife surrendering all her rights and devoting herself completely to serving her husband is bound up with the prevalent concept of *bhakti* (a special kind of piety). See also Harlan, *op. cit.*, p. 202.

19. Female mediums are also called *ang I* or 'puppet aunts', *ang* being the vernacular of the ideograph *wang* and this is also the same character for denoting diseased or deformed human persons. See J.J.M. de Groot, *The Religious System of China*, E.J. Brill, Leyden, 1910, p. 1194.

20. The story about this female puppet is recounted by Shinoda Jun'ichi in *Chikamatsu no Sekai*, (Heibonsha, Tokyo, 1991).

21. The famous dialogue between Arjuna and the God Krishna forms the core of the splendid philosophical poem the *Bhagavad Gita*. Of particular relevance is the line in which Krishna exhorts Arjuna to perform the duty assigned to him. See *The Bhagavad Gita* in R.C. Zaehner (tr.) *Hindu Scriptures*, J.M. Dent & Sons Ltd, London, 1966, p. 292. 'Do thou the work that is prescribed for thee.'

22. D.T. Suzuki, *Zen and Japanese Culture*, Princeton University Press, New York, 1970, p. 53.

23. I. Parry (ed.), *Hand to Mouth and Other Essays*, Carcanet Press, Manchester, 1981, p. 18.

24. D.T. Suzuki, *op. cit.*, p. 165.

# 27

## Re-dressing Shakespeare

### Ethnic Identity and Costume in Indian Performances of Shakespeare

**Poonam Trivedi**

Dress, particularly women's attire, it is a truism to say, is a key signifier of class, cultural and ethnic identity. In the post-colonial world of India today it has become a contested and contaminated terrain. During the colonial period, indigenous dress was zealously adhered to and preserved as a marker of 'authentic' Indian identity, but post-independence, the semiotics of Indian dress has been muddied by the tensions between tradition and modernity. The increasing hybridization of cultural mores, and not just through the influence of western globalization, but equally, through growing intra-regional mobility at home, has made it difficult to adjudicate what is "authentically Indian". Take the contemporary all-India popularity, even in the more conservative south, of the *'salwar-kameez'* – a costume identified before partition as belonging to the Punjab – over the *sari*. This was currently seen to be challenged by the more hip MTV blue jeans clad generation leading to a policing by certain political groups, through a proclamation, demanding that schools enforce the *salwar-kameez* (as opposed to the skirt-blouse) as the only appropriate "Indian" dress for girls. Curious cultural myopia operated here, for only a generation ago, as when I was in school, the *salwar-kameez* was commonly perceived, and often proscribed, as an "Islamic" dress! In the light of such critically sliding significations of dress, what then can we assume to be the consensual visual markers of an Indian-ness? And when we attempt to stage and perform the self through the localizations of western canonical texts like Shakespeare, such questions become especially acute. Identity issues are highlighted, because how we image ourselves is central to the scenography of localization: how we re-dress Shakespeare is conditioned/dictated by how/what we dress ourselves in.

The performance of Shakespeare in India, from the earliest period has developed along two parallel streams: one was an 'Othering,' the second an appropriation, i.e., a presentation of Shakespeare as western and foreign with a concurrent indigenisation in traditional theatre forms. This dual reaction was symptomatic of the initial appeal of Shakespeare in which a fascination with the foreign was twinned with a simultaneous need to deal with it on one's own terms.[1] It is the latter stream of indigenised Shakespeare that I wish to focus on, through some contemporary productions, to analyse the process of domesticating Shakespeare and in which image and garb it is chosen to do so and why. I will further narrow down my selection to the deployment of the 'Rajasthani' dress and its attendant codes to examine how performance negotiates identity and ethnicity.

Costume in the mainstream tradition of Shakespeare performance has always been conditioned by a tension between historical authenticity and imaginative re-creation and subjected to individual and economic constraints. In the performance of Shakespeare in non-anglophone countries, political and cultural determinants, too, affected the choice of dress and design. Initially, Shakespeare was seen as the exemplar of the west and was always performed in western, quasi-period costume. In India Shakespeare first began being performed by Indians, in English, in schools and colleges in the 1830s – the earliest visual record shows a performance of *Romeo and Juliet* by the New Bombay High School with the actors resplendent in Elizabethan and Italianate robes in front of a painted backdrop of a Renaissance street. We were then happy to become the 'Other' in doublet and hose, yet stopped short of the mimicry/emulation of the Japanese Shingeki Shakespeare, which had extended to the use of blond wigs and false noses.

It was the translating and appropriating stream of performance, which dared to radically re-dress Shakespeare and present him transformed and transmuted in variegated costumes. While some like the

**Plate 1**

**Plate 2**

Parsi theatre favoured a hybridized dramaturgy and scenography, other regional theatres, more strongly rooted in their linguistic and cultural traditions, chose to localize Shakespeare in an altogether more thorough fashion. Marathi theatre, for example, which sought to distance and differentiate itself from the populist amalgams of the Parsi theatre, wore its local characteristics as a badge of regional pride. We have stills to show well known actress Durga Khote as Lady Macbeth, in 1954, attired in a Maharastrian style sari (Plate 1) and distinctive *tika* on the forehead holding aloft a lamp of a recognizable indigenous cast. And other stills of the very popular Nana Jog's *teen anki*, three act *Hamlet* 1963-65 (incidentally, very few *Hamlets* have been indigenised until recently) reveal it as going a step further in creating a more site-specific regionalism through dress (Plate 2). Here dress, along with language, linguistic and performative, became an interventionist means of 'translation' 'carrying forward' and across to integrate Shakespeare into the very *mise en scéne* of the people/audience. If, now in the post-colonial period, this unambiguous equation between the regional dress and identity, as noted at the start of the paper, has been unfixed by a more widespread circulation and adoption of regional markers beyond given boundaries, then Plate 1 how do directors and designers image and root local specificities or ethnicities? Earlier, the adaptation of Shakespeare was an exploration of the self; the Marathi translation and adaptation would be played in Marathi dress, but today, since the semiotics of dress and identity have become scrambled and realigned, any director/designer anywhere in the country can chose to locate his/her adaptation of Shakespeare in any region of the country. And the one location that is most often resorted to is that of Rajasthan. I shall use as examples two Hindi productions, *Raja Lear* (1989) directed by Amal Allana and the National School of Drama's *Bagro Basant Hai* (1997) directed by Mohan Maharishi which both chose to root their scenography in their own versions of the Rajasthani.

The 'Rajasthani' is one of the most easily recognizable and popularised identities and ethnicities in India today. It is also a Plate 2 good example of the re-forming and newly emergent groupings of culture; therefore an investigation into its dynamics reveals the pressures and pulls which go into the construction of the new and the re-inscription of the traditional. To enumerate some of its images: geographically, it is a product of the area designated as 'Rajasthan,' the second largest state in the country. Historically, its identity is a construct, a product of multiple forces, which have grouped the many tribes, dialects, and cultures of this region. Till the twelfth century, several competing Rajput kingdoms commandeered the area in the northwest of India from the Arabian Sea to the central Gangetic plain, and it was only in 1594 that some were grouped into a province or *subah*, of Ajmer, by the Moghul emperor, Akbar. This formal delineation of Rajasthan as a composite political entity was reaffirmed by the British creation of the administrative unit of the Rajputana Agency (later renamed Rajputana province) in 1818. In 1949, twenty-two princely states of the area integrated with the Union of India, but the present configuration of the state of Rajasthan came into being in 1956.[2] In the popular imaginary Rajasthan is the land of indigenous heroes, '*raja – sthan*,' who offered armed resistance to invaders in the medieval period, as exemplified by Prithviraj Chauhan (1192, Tarain) and Rana Pratap (1576, Haldighati). And, as also, those who later resisted co-option and wrested a limited independence/autonomy during the British Raj.[3] In recent times, the state has become identified as the home and source of a vast variety of art and craft. In what began as an attempt to resurrect the indigenous cottage craft and industries around the country, Rajasthani crafts – fabrics, jewellery, stone and leather work etc., have registered a singular marketing success which has given its quintessential designs, colours, shapes and textures unprecedented exposure and acceptance all over the country. The post colonial efforts to revive the handloom sector, particularly, was dealing with a textile industry which had been the mainstay of the mercantile trade with the west from the sixteenth century onwards, but which had steadfastly been destroyed by imperial economics which exported the homegrown cotton, denying it to local handloom weavers, to Lancashire in return for mill made cloth. Theatres, too, figure in this attempt to revitalize the old. The 'back to the roots' movement of the 1960s and 70s which was a concerted attempt to bridge the urban-rural divide in Indian theatre lead to a considerable exposure and reification of the traditional folk forms of Rajasthan with their characteristic dance, music and costumes. More recently tourism has been transforming the identity of Rajasthan: its desert which was traditionally called *maru-sthal*, land of the dead, is now advertised as 'golden sands' – the gold has to be the cash collected in tourism. "Rajasthan, the Land of the Kings, is India at its exotic and colourful best with its battle scarred forts, its palaces of breathtaking grandeur and whimsical charm, its riotous colours and even its romantic sense of pride and honour," heralds the *Lonely Planet*, the Bible of tourism today, section on Rajasthan.[4]

But all development has an unpalatable underside. The story of Rajput heroism is also fraught with an equal number of treacheries, compradors, sell-outs and even inter-communal marriages as convenient alliances. The cornucopia of Rajasthani crafts, an undoubted commercial success, has nevertheless dislocated local signification leaving the ritualistic and traditional as merely the trendy 'chic.' The very 'living' dress of one area is seen as ethnic and exotic in another. Tourism, perhaps the most pernicious form of development, has put indigenous on exhibition: reality is modeled for show, villages, living beings, their lifestyles, dress, food, habits etc. become museum pieces to be ogled at, and the once fiercely proud region is now peddling itself. One does not intend to undermine these new avenues for economic growth, which do provide means of survival for thousands, but the profit needs to weighed against the cost, the expansion of the boundaries of identity versus the inevitable 'othering' of ourselves.

The use of the Rajasthani location, identity or ethnicity today is thus not transparent; it is instead fraught with overlays of both time and space, commerce and populism. Though there is frequent recourse (in advertising for instance) to its dance, music and dress, particularly, to harness the beauty of its vivid colours, patterns and sounds, a serious deployment of it in high art needs to go beyond the obvious beauty.

The two productions of Shakespeare that I wish to discuss as illustrations/paradigms, Amal Allana's *King Lear* (1989) and Mohan Maharishi's A *Midsummer Night's Dream, Bagro Basant Hai* (1997) both located the *mise en scéne* in Rajasthan, even though they were neither staging it any city nor in any of the local dialects of Rajasthan. Nor do the directors have deep personal affiliations with Rajasthan: Amal was brought up in Bombay and has spent her working life in Delhi, and though Maharishi was born in Ajmer, his adult working life, too, has been spent outside the state, mostly in Chandigarh. Their choice of location, already a stage removed, was determined more by critical and interpretative factors, than the emotive or the subjective.

For Amal Allana, it was, primarily, the 'idea' of Rajasthan more than its specificities that she used to root her view of *King Lear*. Staged in the Crafts Village of Pragati Maidan in Delhi, she re-created the characteristic 'bleak environment' of sand, stone and mud of Rajasthan in the vast open space of the Village with its monumental structures (reassembled heritage buildings) to impart a mythic and material dimension to the elemental trials and struggles of Lear. Costumes – chosen for their iconic significance – periodised the play into a remote past: "From famous tragedy to moving medieval epic" ... "set in medieval Rajasthan" heralded a review in the *Indian Post* (Bombay, 1 March 1989). The King, imaged as a feudal absolutist overlord, of medieval folklore, was clad in a loose long dark cloak elaborately

**Plate 3**

embroidered and bejeweled. The women's dress, recognizably localized, more acutely evoked a historical/ mythic Rajasthan (Plate 3). The courtiers wore short white *angarkhas*, the familiar dress of the lower class, while the fool wore a gaudy- multi- colored *angarkha* and cap, like the *vidushka* of folk theatres. A canopy painted in blue and the flaming colours of the desert sunset was strung up over part of the open-air stage and represented both the sky and the tents of the nomadic desert tribes. Played in the backdrop of a reconstructed ornately craved *haveli*, a mansion, it seemed not just to Plate 3 recreate, but to bring to life the legendary mythic world of Rajasthan. "The play ceases to be foreign and is transformed convincingly into an Indian story," commented the *Indian Post* reviewer. Its very success, in some quarters, was construed to be its undoing; it seemed too good to be true. It was critiqued by some, including Rustom Bharucha,[5] as overdone and exoticised.

The scenography of this production of King *Lear* is better under-stood if judged in the light of what Mary Louise Pratt has defined as "auto-ethnographic expression," an expression of the self as more than another's other.[6] Here the mythic identity of Rajasthan was being used to deconstruct another myth of Shakespeare's *King Lear*. There was a studied 'staginess' to the production, which functioned as the device of Brechtian 'quotation,' of representation as self-referentiality and a strategy for interruption and interrogation. The performance style was fast paced and consciously alienating, with a constant movement between the several acting locales and stages, with actors moving in and out of the audience, forcing shifts from the 'local,' to the 'real' to the 'theatrical.' By placing Lear in an obviously constructed space of a Rajasthan of the popular imaginary, the production not only extended the critical penumbra of the play, but also drew in for searching analysis some key Indian concepts.

According to Amal, the play was a story about the trauma of "divestment" – *tyaga* – of power, and the difficulties that "attachment" – *mohah* – (both well-known concepts of Indian philosophy) results in. This attachment to power was symbolically localized not in the turban or the crown, but the sword – the Rajput emblem of authority, which Lear clutched on to, even in the storm scene, a sign of the power he was so reluctant to give away. Goneril and Reagan's costumes, traditional dark ornate skirts, heavy with embroidered mirror work which glittered and rustled ostentatiously, their overload of jewelry, the large *bore* – head ornament, the bulky necklaces and bangles – all these were projected as the signs and symbols of their condition, both markers of a culture known for its fratricidal warfare and of the grossness of their own desires. Their heavy head scarves, *chunnis*, seemed to encase them

like straight jackets, signaling the continuing oppression of both a patriarchy which prescribed such dress codes, and of the tenacity of their
own appetites. They were not given a change of dress, in contrast to
Cordelia and Lear, who, as the play progressed, learnt to shed their egos
like outer skins and shed their heavy oppressive garments too; in the
reunion scene Cordelia and Lear were seen in simple, skin-coloured,
natural-looking shifts. In this *mise en scéne* of the Rajput aristocracy,
legendary for its warrior values, and female virility too – it is the
progenitor of *sati* and *jauhar*, rituals of the self-immolation of the
widow on the death of the husband – Goneril and Regan became less
monstrous, their power lust more believable. The observations of
Henry T. Prinsep (1792-1878), Assistant Secretary to Hastings, on the
Rajputs, seem to eerily underscore the world of Shakespeare's *King
Lear* as well:

> The hereditary chiefs of Rajasthan are the slaves of forms and
> ceremonious etiquette whose lives are passed within palace walls, in
> search of selfish, sensual enjoyment, diversified with occasions of osten-
> tatious display to gratify a pompous ignorant pride.[7]

Mohan Maharishi's *Bagro Basant- Hai* (*A Midsummer Night's
Dream*) performed by the students of the National School of Drama,
Delhi, (1997) also clearly situated itself in Rajasthan. "Shakespeare goes
Rajasthani," announced *The Statesman*'s drama critic's by-line (8
December 1997). But since this was a comedy it took the liberty of an
ironic, playful perspective on the whole. The entire play was
overlooked by an ass's head framed and mirrored at a window in the
rear. The opening scene swiftly keyed the Rajasthani ambience.
Theseus was renamed Sanbal Singh, Demetrius and Lysander, Joravar
Singh and Kamal, typical north Indian *Kshatriya* (warrior caste) names.
But it was their attire which most clearly underscored their identity:
Rajasthani *kurta* or long overshirt with tight pajamas, waist sash, cloth
turban with distinctive patterns, light leather *mojaris* or moccasins,
with swords dangling on the side, these were Rajput elite unmistakably.
The women, Hermia and Helena, or Champa and Chameli were
similarly dressed in the instantly recognizable *ghagra choli* and *dupatta*
(skirt, top and head scarf). Staged in the small studio theatre of the
National School of Drama, with virtually no stage props, the opening
scene established the *mise en scéne* through costume and then through
action. A very vehement and physical friction between Demetrius and
Lysander evoked the populist image of Rajasthan as a land of fractious

and indulgent feudal lords; they were full of a touchy honour, eager to come to blows. Rajasthani patriarchy, valorized for its total control over the women, again dovetailed with the patriarchal fury of Egeus who would have his daughter killed for refusing to accept the parental choice for marriage. Other deft touches added to this evocation of a specific time and space: the mechanicals in their enthusiasm to perform combined themselves into the "Dilshad Nautanki Company" the *nautanki* being a Rajasthani popular folk theatre of itinerant players which traditionally has many tales of Rajput valour in its repertoire, (the name "Dilshad" being part of the director's childhood memory, we are told), while the Pyrmus and Thisbe story was easily paralleled by the Dhola Maru folk tale of tragic love.

It was the materials used for the costumes of the lovers, however, which raised some discordant countercurrents. Traditional Sanganeri block printed cotton with the characteristic *'cheent'* or chintz print – of a small motif in contrasting colour symmetrically replicated on a bright background – was used, a pattern which is so traditional and so overused through the handloom revolution that it has now ceased to signal a regional signification, but has instead become a cliché. This made the warring lovers look more like chic and privileged young brats straight out of a boutique than the troubled young generation of Shakespeare, making one wonder if the very costume was not meant to be ironic, reducing Shakespeare's comic types into local stereotypes. Still, not much re-interpretative energy was being generated in this intercultural encounter, until one turned to Hippolyta, or when she caught one's attention. Not much significance is usually attached to Hippolyta's status as an Amazon in Indian productions, but here she was dressed as a dark skinned Bhil tribal, a virile but subordinated community, in a *ghagara choli* of a particular style and laden with heavy chunky necklets and earrings and large white bangles worn on the upper arm – all which are the known symbols of this tribe. She was also decidedly sullen in mood and her mannerisms clearly revealed that she had been brought to Theseus' court under duress. This Theseus, however, was besotted with her, his prize catch, and was bending over backwards to please her. An interesting interventionist moment was created when Thesues was trying to adjudicate between the lovers and the father, this tribal Hippolyta suddenly moved from Thesues' side, stomped down and stood beside Hermia causing Theseus much nervousness and forcing him to immediately overrule Egeus. This

Plate 4

interpolated gesture of solidarity by Hippolyta, the defeated queen of
another community, between subordinated groups – women and
tribals – resonated with the history of power struggles in Rajasthan
where conquering groups coming from the west had successively
defeated and pushed out the indigenous tribal peoples (Plate 4). That
the production could use the Shakespearean text to comment on the
racial politics (tribals are held to be of the 'original' dark-skinned
Dravidian race, while the ruling Rajputs are seen as belonging to the
fairer Aryan stock) of Indian society was a sign of its successful
post-colonial interculturalism. It was helped in this by the distancing
and self-reflexive devices it adopted: the ass's head, framed and
mirrored which overlooked most of the play, the whole text thus being
subjected to a comic double turn. The production dared to critique the
very scene of royal Rajasthan it set up, playfully nudging attention
towards the cracks and gaps in the construction of identity and
ethnicity.

Both productions made considered use of the Rajasthani location.
Not for mere colourful decoration, as for example the *Ankia Nat Lear*
(also of NSD, 2001) where beautifully crafted dress and accessories
from the north east failed to integrate into the preoccupations of the
play. Both these productions through their relocations of Shakespeare
via the paradigms of Rajasthani identity and ethnicity could produce
shifts in meaning. The re-dressing of Shakespeare then becomes not a
'dressing down,' some kind of chastising of the text into
esoteria/exotica or even a dumbing down into obscurity, but a

're-dressing' which is a correcting, putting right, and putting forward of fresh perspectives and insights of meaning, not just through the dense thickets of Shakespearean interpretations, but also, and more vitally, for our own very local configuration of identity. 'Ethnicity' as a construct was used "auto-ethnographically" with the full sense of its objectified 'otherness' to negotiate regional and gender identities of the here and now.

## Notes

1. For more details about the performance of Shakespeare in India see my article "Interculturalism or Indigenisation: Modes of Exchange, Shakespeare East and West," in *Shakespeare and His Contemporaries in Performance*, (ed. Edward J. Esche, London: Ashgate, 2000), and "Introduction" to *India's Shakespeare: Translation, Interpretation and Performance*, (University of Delaware Press, forthcoming 2004).

2. See Deryck O. Lodrick; "Rajasthan as a Region: Myth or Reality?", in *The Idea of Rajasthan: Explorations in Regional Identity*, (eds. Katherine Schomer, Joan L Erdman, Deryck O. Lodrick, Lloyd L. Rudolph, Manohar, AIIS, 1994, Delhi), Vols I and II: and Rudolph, Susanne Hoeber and Lloyd I., Essays *on Rajputana: reflections on History, Culture and Administration*, (New Delhi: Concept, 1984).

3. See James Tod, *Annals and Antiquities of Rajasthan*, 2 Vols (1829) rptd. New Delhi: M.N. Publishers, 1995, for a history of the Rajputs based on indigenous sources from whence much of the 'populist' view of them derives.

4. *India*, 8th edition (Victoria, Aust: The Lonely Planet Publications, 1999), p. 642.

5. Rustom Bharucha dismissed the scenography of this production as an instance of "how we exoticise our selves" during the discussion of a paper by me, "Fusion, Diffusion and Confusion: The Dynamics of Intercultural Performance of Shakespeare in India" at the seminar on *Shakespeare Performance in the New Asias*, National University of Singapore, 28 June 2002.

6. Mary Louise Pratt; "Transculturation and Autoethnography: Peru, 1615/1980" (eds. Francis Barker, Peter Hulme and Margaret Iversen, Manchester: Manchester University Press, 1994) in *Colonial Discourse/ Postcolonial Theory*, p. 44.

7. Quoted by Shyam Singh Ratnawal, *Rajput Nobility*, (Jaipur: Panchsheel Prakashan), 1989, p. 267.

# 28

## Towards a Multicultural Theatre

### The Changing Audience for Contemporary Indian Drama in English

**Radha Ramaswamy**

*The basic concern of the Indian theatre in the post-independence period has been to try to define its "Indianness."*

*Girish Karnad*

At a seminar in Mysore in 1994, the playwright Mahesh Dattani was asked, "Why don't you write in your own language?" He answered, "I do". The questioner continued his attack, "You write about things that are not Indian. Do you know what is happening out there on the streets?" Dattani had read out extracts from his play *Bravely fought the Queen* (1991), and the speaker was objecting to the depiction of homosexuality in the play, a phenomenon that he perceived as "not Indian." The complaint that Dattani did not 'know what is happening ... on the streets' is not an unfamiliar charge. Most of the people present at the seminar seemed unaware of the fact that Dattani's latest play *Final Solutions* (1993) had been banned from the Deccan Herald Theatre festival in 1992, precisely because it showed 'what is happening out there on the streets'. Starting with the story of two Muslim boys, who are chased by a bloodthirsty mob and seek shelter in a Hindu household, *Final Solutions* explores the themes of secularism and communal understanding, showing how personal and family history often shape the contours of communal conflict. In the wake of the communal riots following the demolition of the Babri Masjid in Ayodhya, which had taken place earlier that year, the *Deccan Herald* considered it risky to permit staging of the play.

The Indian playwright in English seems trapped between conflicting perceptions of being 'unaware of reality' and being 'too real'. These conflicts are related to issues of identity in a multicultural society. How does he, and other practitioners of this theatre, engage with the seeming contradiction between these two perceptions? The Indian playwright in English addresses an audience that is English speaking, urban and middle class. This audience has, in the last few decades, been caught up in debates about its identity, sometimes overtly, at other times more subtly. Any attempt to study contemporary Indian drama in English has to take cognizance of these debates.

Let me, at the outset offer some definitions and some clarifications about my approach to my subject.

By 'Indian Drama in English', I mean the theatre that has grown around the dramatic literature written by Indians in English. Usually theatres in India are identified by language – we speak of Bengali theatre, Marathi theatre or Kannada theatre. Language is also the commonest means of distinguishing audiences in spite of the overlap, in some cases, between audiences of different language theatres. IDE, unlike other language theatres, has no regional base.

I would distinguish this also from the English language theatre, which is theatre in English, but works in a completely different performance context from IDE. I do not have space in this presentation to elaborate on this, but would like to point out that though they share the language and to some extent the audience, their politics is different.

IDE in my title refers to plays written by Indians originally in English, and by 'contemporary' I mean IDE of the 80s and after. The reason for that date will become clear in the course of this paper.

IDE uses English as its medium of expression, a language that in India can never be free of connotations of power and privilege, and provokes deeply ambivalent responses. IDE is thus, placed at the cutting edge of contemporary debates about identity. In our everyday life, in our artistic endeavours, in every creative act of communication with our fellow human beings, ideally we attempt to deal with the multicultural reality of the world we live in. Any form of cultural expression that contributes to and sharpens our awareness of this process is valuable. It is as such a form of cultural expression that I am looking at IDE.

IDE texts are not canonical texts. I examine them as cultural texts rather than as literary texts. ("The act of *creating theatre*", says John McGrath, founder of the British popular theatre company 7:84, "has nothing to do with the making of dramatic literature: dramatic literature is what is sometimes left behind when theatre has been and gone" emphasis in original)[1]. I also believe that culture does not transcend the material forces and elements of production and consumption. In addition to these ideas of multiculturalism, and cultural texts, I draw on recent studies of the institution of English studies in India (Joshi, 1994; Tharu, 1991; Sunder Rajan, 1992; Ahmad, 1994), which have uncovered the multi-layered links between the teaching/learning of English and race, class and gender.

Some of the issues frequently raised in critical discourse about post-Independence IDE are (pre-independence IDE was mostly closet drama, plays that were written for reading rather than for staging, and I do not think much can be gained by discussing them here): that IDE is not "Indian", because it uses English, the language of the colonizer; that it is "elitist", because it caters to an audience that enjoys the power and privilege that England gives to those who have access to it in India today; and lastly, because IDE is seen as having no roots in any region, and so is "cut off" from all "Indian" (again that word!) literary, theatrical or other cultural traditions, it must be shallow and superficial in its concerns. Thus, the identity of IDE, its reason to exist, its purpose and function, have been contested from the very beginning. How has IDE reacted to such perceptions and debates about its identity?

Playwrights in the decades immediately after Independence tended to write plays that consciously attempted "Indian" themes, e.g. plots and themes drawn from history and mythology. Some experimented with Indian English. The response from audiences and critics was both confused and confusing. Playwrights were advised to look back for inspiration, and also to look ahead, to urban, contemporary Indian themes and contexts. Actually IDE found itself in a double bind – it was not Indian enough; and it was not western enough – either way, it could not please. Critical approaches to IDE in the 1960s and 1970s were preoccupied with the post-Independent national agenda of fashioning a 'national' theatre culture, which seemed to have guided audiences of the time. Much emphasis was laid on a search for "Indian" features in this drama. "No art can naturally grow unless it is rooted in the soil," declares Bhatta, and goes on to suggest that the IDE playwright "should find his roots in the rich tradition of Classical Sanskrit Drama and folk-stage as well as in the culture of the country" (1987:202). What might this "culture of the country" be? We get some idea of what Bhatta might have in mind, in his remarks on Partap Sharma's *The Professor Has A War Cry*: "Obviously bent upon shocking the public by his uninhibited treatment of sex, Sharma resorts to gross exaggeration and melodrama. For example, we hear that Virendra's mother, who has the professor as her lover, is raped by Saleem, a Muslim, and then by an English officer, so that Virendra is flabbergasted by the discovery that he is not a child of marriage or love but of rape." (152). In these comments, one is not sure what is being labelled as "melodrama" and "gross exaggeration", the double rape, "by Saleem, a Muslim, and then by an English officer", or that Virendra is a child "not ... of marriage or love but of rape". One wonders: would one rape have been more acceptable than two, and a "child born out of wedlock" preferable to a "child of rape"? Many such critical comments on IDE of this period are based on assumptions about simplistically drawn connections between culture, morality and a national literary tradition.

The audience for IDE in the 1960s and 1970s appears to have been a fairly small and culturally homogeneous section of society. Its responses to IDE suggest that this audience approached IDE from a perspective that was dictated by its own ambivalent post-colonial identity. The critical consensus that IDE was not "as good as" English plays from the west clearly shows the critical bias towards a borrowed dramatic model. An audience bred on Broadway and West End classics found the efforts of Indian playwrights clumsy and embarrassing and simply stayed away. In the absence of support from theatre groups that would read and rehearse the plays, and in the absence of a tradition of IDE that they could draw upon, most of the playwrights returned to their own isolated struggles with their many problems. Their attempts at constructing varieties of spoken English for the stage – a daunting task given the complicated position of English in India – were met with disapproval and scorn. Indian English was still new and unacceptable on the English stage.

The 1990s have seen IDE emerging from this no-man's land between regional drama and English language plays from abroad, and becoming a theatre closely in touch with its changing socio-economic and cultural context. There are playwrights, scripts, and theatre groups that in the diversity of their practice have opened up the field of Indian drama in English beyond questions of literary quality to critical questions of identity and culture, questions that are vital for anyone trying to understand urban India today.

IDE has certainly become more visible. Some of the plays of Mahesh Dattani have been included in the curriculum by university departments in India and abroad (e.g. Calicut University, New York University). Dattani continues to be the only playwright to have won both critical acclaim – the Sahitya Akademi award in 2000 – and popularity. Similarly, Manjula Padmanabhan's first prize in the Alexander S Onassis International Cultural Competitions in 1999, which brought her an impressive cash prize and a production in Greece, brought widespread public attention to IDE.

There are more performances of IDE now than ever before. In his 1987 study Krishna Bhatta lists more than 400 plays written in the 100-odd years between the late nineteenth century and the 1970s. Very few of these were produced. Not more than half a dozen of these are performed or given rehearsed readings today (e.g. *Goa, Mister Behram, Larins Sahib, Doongaji House, Don't call It Suicide*). Compared to this, the prospect for contemporary scripts today is very encouraging. Of the 40 odd plays written in the last thirty years, almost all have been performed. If performance is taken to be one of the bases for judging visibility, it would appear that IDE has in recent years become more visible, and one of the reasons for this is the changing audience for IDE.

The audience for IDE comes from the English-speaking section of the middle class, which constitutes about 5% of the total population. Several sociological studies point out that the Indian middle class has seen unprecedented changes in the last three or four decades. There has been a significant growth in the size of the middle class, the new entrants coming from upwardly mobile peasant castes and members of several castes which had been associated with lowly and corrupting occupations. This upward mobility became possible for peasant castes, and some *dalit* castes and scheduled tribes, because of the land reforms and the green revolution, the reservation policies of the respective state governments, and liberalization. The result is that the middle class today is much more diverse in its origins than the earlier, upper-caste dominated middle class. As individuals from different castes and communities enter, they acquire new economic and political interests, and lifestyles, in common with the other members of that 'class'. There had always been a fundamental separation in Indian society between status and economic power. The pre-1970s educated, upper-class/caste elite had status and voice but little economic power. The new entrants to the middle class with their newly acquired economic power also made a bid for social status and cultural wealth. Several general features of this class have been pointed out. There is a trend towards secularization, one of the manifestations of which, as M.N. Srinivas says, is that "various aspects of society, economic, political, legal and moral, [become] increasingly discrete in relation to each other".[2] Secular criteria for "success" and a stress on education, especially in "English medium" schools and colleges, are offshoots of this process. A consumerist lifestyle – adopted not only because it is necessary in order to cope with modernization, but also because many of the symbols of this lifestyle confer social prestige – and the instrumentalist approach appear to suggest that the upwardly mobile individual may be less staunchly loyal to earlier notions of kinship with caste. Describing the self-centred and material pursuits of this class, Pavan Varma refers to the "siege mentality" of these "..parvenu elements" and their "cynical and deliberate withdrawal from a constructive interface with society"[3]. In an article provocatively titled "India: a nice place to get out of", Swapan Dasgupta identifies the chief goal of the affluent young in India today as personal advancement[4]. He suggests that they are impatient and irritated with India's third world status, and look for personal liberty and unlimited opportunities, thus embracing "these American values". The average Indian middle-class family aspires to send at least one member of the family abroad for higher studies, and perhaps to settle down there. According to Dasgupta, this generation has in some sense rejected the premise on which India has operated for the past fifty years or more.

At the same time, as Dasgupta points out, the "placidity of temperament ...conventionally ...associated with the middle class", the contentment born of predictable goals, security and certainty seems to be absent from the psyche of the Indian middle class today. The reasons lie in the uneasy co-existence of the past and the present. Sheth shows that while caste identity plays assuredly a less important role in the cultural practices of this class, it has not been completely erased. "Within this new middle class, caste identities of its members survive, but operating in conjunction with the new overarching identity of middle class, they acquire a different political and cultural meaning"[5]. There is a tendency to integrate at a higher level for economic and political gain. Sunil Khilnani describes how in the years following the imposition of Emergency rule in the country, "conflicts were arising among social groups where identities could be activated for political ends: religious, urban or rural, caste, language, class or ethnic origin."[6]. The world of the 1980s and the 1990s, according to Khilnani, is neither modern nor traditional, but simply "the world of politics" where "identities of caste and religion have bent the democratic ideal to their own purposes"[7]. Playwright Girish Karnad feels that the Indian bourgeoisie does not show a "faith in individualism as its ultimate value. 'Westernization' notwithstanding, Indians define themselves in terms of their relationships to the other members of their family, caste or class ..."[8]. Studies of popular cinema in recent years have shown the hidden ways in which caste consciousness informs our perceptions of occupation, skin colour, and our social behaviour[9].

Without a serious critique of the past, the "patchwork acceptance" of modernity by this class, says Varma, expresses itself in tensions and conflicts in everyday life. Thus, even in this "new ethos of acquisition and competition" there is a "hankering for the easy-paced securities and assurances of the past"[10]. Caste, for example, is rejected in theory, but continues to operate in rituals, marriage etc. Similarly, the working woman in the modern nuclear family bears unbelievable burdens as she struggles to balance the desire for economic independence with the yearning for the presumed security her mother enjoyed within the home. The oppression and violence practiced in overt and covert forms in many educated middle-class homes stem from deep-rooted prejudices and well-entrenched patriarchal social structures that continue to operate alongside the pursuit of modern lifestyles. The so-called traditional Indian veneration for authority, Ashis Nandy points out, very quickly gives way to anarchy and aggression because, "our traditional systems of child-rearing" do not emphasize "the slow training and controlled expression of one's aggressive drives", and so, "when aggression breaks out, it breaks out in a primitive, chaotic fashion"[11]. Thus, the contemporary urban Indian has to struggle with conflicting loyalties – modernity with tradition and orthodoxy, respect for authority versus a deep seated anarchic impulse, self interest against the desire to appear socially responsible. He has to confront, every day, the tensions created by his/her several fragmented identities of class, caste, gender and religion. These are the themes that appear and reappear in contemporary Indian drama in English. In particular, the family as a source of oppression and the breeding ground for social prejudice has been the subject of several Indian plays in English, including the plays of Mahesh Dattani, Cyrus Mistry, Poile Sengupta, Dina Mehta, and Gieve Patel. The responses to these plays in the different cities where IDE is performed shows that these themes strike a powerful chord in audiences.

The last few decades have also seen great changes in the role of English in Indian society. As Aijaz Ahmad says, "English is simply one of India's own languages now, and what is at issue at present is ... the mode of its assimilation into our social fabric, and the manner in which this language ... is used in the processes of class formation and social privilege..."[12]. Class and social privilege, as Ahmad points out, are inevitably linked to the use of English in India. Svati Joshi argues that in spite of "the emergence in some parts of the country of the rural, populist, provincial middle-class elite with increasing power that is not linked to English ... English remains the language that regulates access to higher education, and is linked to class interest, economic benefits and with the production and reproduction of major forms of social power and cultural privilege"[13]. The spread of English education has created increasing numbers of English-speaking people from intermediate and lower class/castes, with the result that there is a range of competence in English today, just as there are differing expectations from, and attitudes to, the language. The use of Indian English and of different varieties of Indian English has gained greater acceptance today, though varieties of English usage continue to be markers of class, caste, community etc. The IDE audience which is drawn from the English-speaking section of the urban middle class displays the great cultural heterogeneity that is the result of the differential social formations linked to the English language.

Increasing material prosperity, a desire to acquire cultural capital, a confident, almost aggressive pursuit of individual goals seen as a necessary attribute of modern life, lingering loyalties to traditional caste/community/gender identities, the recognition of English as the language of economic opportunity and power, ambivalent attitudes to the rapidly growing Indian forms of spoken English – these are some of the preoccupations of the new urban middle class, that have had an impact on the IDE audience, in the last two or three decades.

How have these changes affected the IDE audience?

The cultural profile of the English language theatre audience has changed. Bharat Dabholkar, whose sex comedies, revues and farces in the 1980s in Mumbai succeeded in creating their own audience, claims that after seeing a show of *Bottoms Up* a jam factory owner told him "This is the theatre I can understand" and a *paanwalla* declared that his "fear" of English theatre had vanished. With his contemporary themes and situations, satirical humour, and imaginative use of what has come to be called "Hinglish", Dabholkar had tapped a new audience for IDE – a much larger, and more heterogeneous audience than the earlier, mainstream ELT audience. Lillette Dubey, director of the Mumbai-based theatre group Prime Time, describes her Mumbai audience as "an amalgamation of the Gujarati, Marathi and other regional audiences" that had till now "been intimidated by the kind of English spoken on the stage"(personal interview, 2000). Aamir Raza Hussain, the director of the Delhi theatre group *Stagedoor* and producer of blockbuster shows like *Saare Jahan Se Achcha*, also found that his audience had expanded, and changed. There was a time when it was confined to "either a Delhi University student or an upwardly mobile executive in a private company", but now his mailing list has names and addresses "of people from Gurgaon, Meerut, Daryaganj and downtown localities like Suivala". That the audience base for English language plays has widened is reported by almost everyone, who has observed this theatre for some time. A common scene at the box office at Prithvi Theatre is a family of six or seven members approaching the counter and asking "Comedy kya?" ("Is it a comedy?") and then, "Story kya hai?" ("What's the story?"). If the fare promised an evening's entertainment, tickets would be bought for the entire family.

The increase in the numbers of the audience has led to the proliferation of new venues. One member of the audience at Prithvi Theatre told me that she had never been to an English play before, and that she had come that day with her husband "because it was so close" and so she could "afford the time".

Twenty or thirty years ago the audience for ELT used to be in the age group of 35-45 years or older. Theatre practitioners agree that there seems to be a greater percentage of the younger audiences now, between the ages of 25 and 35 years, than earlier. Many of these appear to be professionals who, as one senior actress said, "have money to throw around." An increasingly greater percentage of the audience consists of people with very little or no earlier exposure to English theatre. This has given young directors "more freedom ... to do the plays we want, in the way we want.... This theatre is more personal and relevant."[14].

IDE, for this audience, does not have to prove its "Indianness" by either drawing on Indian myths for its plots or borrowing dramatic conventions from Sanskrit drama. Besides, with the entry of satellite television into middle class homes, Indian productions of British or American plays aiming at "authentic" British or American accents are beginning to feel, look and sound a little strange, if not ridiculous.

An important element in the pleasure of going to the English theatre, prior to the 1970s, was the pleasure afforded by familiarity with the classics of the western stage – Shakespeare, Shaw, Ibsen, Stoppard – i.e. reading pleasure was remembered during performance. The spread of English education in India, the increasing number of Indians who can now speak, read and write English without the earlier familiarity with the classics of English literature, has changed this situation. Large sections of this new audience do not speak English at home, and use a mixture of English and the mother tongue for social communication, too. In the theatre, those who know the plays from reading perhaps feel additionally privileged. Some directors and actors feel that today's audiences do not have the kind of serious interest in theatre that earlier audiences used to have. "No longer can a production be expected to draw good houses on the strength of the name of the play or the playwright or the group" says BLT's Vijay Padaki[15]. He feels that heavy publicity and glitzy packaging attract an ignorant and gullible audience. In Mumbai there is a small degree of spillover from the regional theatre audiences. This is seen by many theatre persons as an expression of the social and cultural aspirations of a new middle class. "They are not comfortable speaking English, but they come to see English plays" says actress Sabira Merchant[16]. Cyrus Mistry had also noticed this, "Gujarati and Marathi theatre audiences are now wandering into English theatre... just for the heck of it... because there's money to spend..."[17]. This spillover also exists to some extent in Delhi, with a small percentage from Hindi and Punjabi theatres attending English plays. However, Bangalore shows almost no such mingling of the Kannada and the English theatre audiences, with the audiences and the practitioners of the two theatres remaining separate for the most part. The cultural exchange between English theatre and other audiences adds another dimension to the heterogeneity of the IDE audience.

Those who go to mainstream venues like the Chowdiah in Bangalore or the NCPA in Mumbai to see big budget productions like *Dance Like A Man* or *Final Solutions* are treated to an experience that combines the pleasures afforded by a combination of factors – an established theatre group known for high production standards, a famous play, and a venue with its own cultural value. The satisfaction that such an experience affords is necessarily different from what an audience expects or experiences at the smaller Prithvi Theatre watching Ramanathan's *The Boy Who Stopped Smiling*. The profiles of the play, the group and the venue demand different expectations. There may be some points of overlap – high production quality, for example. Generally, audiences seem to make the necessary adjustments in their expectations.

The shift in attitude to Indian English on the stage is an important development in IDE of the 1980s and the 1990s. The younger members of the audience, especially in Bangalore, are almost exclusively English speaking. They see English as their "mother tongue", or "simply the language we're comfortable in," and display an unwillingness to engage with the politics of the use of this language in India. In Delhi and Mumbai, too, where Hindi or Marathi or Gujarati may also be spoken along with English, varieties of Indian English seem to have been accepted on the stage. Consider the following instances. In 1972, Krishna Bhatta offers the following sentence as an example of bad English, 'What has happened has happened'. His objection to it is that it is a literal translation from a regional language and sounds awkward in English. In Sengupta's *Mangalam*, '*patti*' describes what makes good *payasam* – "the rice and the milk should not go searching for each other saying, 'Where are you? Where am I?'"[18] – an almost literal translation from the Tamil. During a performance of the play in 1999, the cosmopolitan Bangalore ELT audience responded to these lines with appreciation.

How is the IDE audience of today, not to be easily homogenized as the "English-speaking urban middle class", influencing developments in IDE? How is IDE responding to this changing audience? Let me present a case study to illustrate the participatory role of the IDE audience, and the possibilities that lie in such partnership.

Poile Sengupta's *Mangalam* deals with, among other things, the theme of domestic violence and reveals some ugly truths behind middle-class respectability, showing that 'educated' urban families can hide behind their sophisticated exteriors gruesome incidences of violence against women. While the first act of the play is set in a traditional, orthodox Tamil family, the second act more or less repeats the plot in a different setting, this time in a modern, urban family. Several reviewers pointed out the redundancy of the second act – it labours the point. Why did Sengupta feel the need to underline the message? Without the second act, perhaps Sengupta's urban audiences would have found it easier to distance the first half, to distance and dismiss the issue as not applicable to them, being more 'modern' and therefore 'liberated'.

The two families, apparently so different, share a lot of features that reflect the gender bias in society. The mother in Act 2 is unemployed, a factor that significantly affects the way a woman feels about herself and determines the power equations within the family. Though she is educated, and appears to be happy in the responsibilities of family, the facade is ripped off in the course of the play, when she discovers that her husband has been having an affair with another woman. Even if there had been no such dramatic skeleton in the cupboard, there are lots of other details in the play that point to a subordinate existence for the wife and mother. The playwright has used some powerful poetry as voice-over to reinforce the loneliness and hidden quality of much of women's experience. A play like *Mangalam* has the power to make a middle-class urban audience see how gender as a category of our existence cuts across class and caste, and at the same time takes on features peculiar to regions and communities that are also patriarchal in nature.

In July 1993, Dattani's *Final Solutions* was playing at the Guru Nanak Bhavan in Bangalore. It was the premiere show, and I was eager to see how this play, whose script I had read only a few days before, would work on stage. It had seemed like a powerful script in reading, and the performance at Guru Nanak was building up quite well to the moment of the confrontation, in Act III, between Smita, the 18year old college student and her mother Aruna. Smita accuses her mother of stifling her with her orthodox religious practices. Aruna is shocked because she had always regarded Smita as an ally in her constant battle against her rational and skeptical husband. Although shocked by this revelation, Aruna wants to understand her daughter, and asks, "Does being a Hindu stifle you?" and Smita replies, "No, living with one does." The mother, glancing beyond the rudeness, to the truth of the utterance, says, almost wonderingly, "I never knew I stifled you."

In the reading, the scene had come through as poignant and full of resonance for me personally. Subtle details were introduced that added complex layers to the characters even as the scene plays out what is commonly and simplistically termed "the generation gap". Aruna is deeply religious and assumes that her daughter, on account of being born a Hindu, has automatically inherited her beliefs. She is quite unprepared for the violence in her daughter's accusation, and her question shows both her bewilderment and hurt. But Aruna is not willing to run away from the confrontation, and sit nursing her wounded feelings. She stays to find out why her religion, that gives her so much strength, has failed her daughter.

This was an important scene in a play that attempted to link individual perceptions of religion to family, history and society, helping one see the ways in which "harmless" practices can turn oppressive. I thought the playwright had balanced very well the powerful emotional content of the scene and the sharp insights into character. This was also the first time that mother and daughter confront the truth about their relationship. In the production by Playpen, Dattani's theatre company, the character of Aruna was played with great finesse by Padmavathie Rao, a recognized name from Bangalore theatre. I was therefore not prepared for the laughter that I heard, during the performance of this scene, in some sections of the audience. I realized immediately that the laughter was a reaction to the "Gujarati" English that Aruna was speaking. The "convent"-educated Smita's spoken English approximated the variety of English most acceptable to the audience, and the mother's represented an Indian English still struggling for acceptance. In a scene that had only two characters, it was perhaps to be expected that the juxtaposition of two very different kinds of spoken English would have a comic effect. Later, talking to the playwright, who had directed this first production of *Final Solutions*, and the actress who had played the part of the mother, I realized that this performance could offer some valuable insights into some of the performance issues in IDE. Both Dattani and Padmavathie Rao, it appeared, had heard that laughter, and after the production, had considered changing Aruna's intonation pattern in order to make it more acceptable to the audience. Padmavathie, however, was convinced that she was being true to the character and was not willing to sacrifice that authenticity. Dattani had agreed, pointing out that such uneasy moments were bound to occur during performance until such time as audiences learnt to accept different, and authentic varieties of Indian English on the stage. Dattani and Padmavathie Rao saw no need to revise their earlier, important and sensitive decisions about characterization in reaction to the laughter, which they interpreted as a necessary part of the audience's learning experience.

Another important detail that Dattani pointed out, and both Padmavathie and I were able to corroborate this, is the fact that the laughter, among some sections of the audience, sounded like a nervous titter that was quickly suppressed. It looked as though even as they were laughing, these members of the audience were aware of, and uncomfortable with, the implications of their laughter. Our responses in the theatre, including, as in this instance, to the English used on stage, are often an accurate reflection of our responses in real life. In India references to regional accents very often evoke laughter, and exaggerated examples of these are usually exploited in advertisements for comic purposes. Thus, there are advertisements, which draw on a pan-Indian recognition of stereotypes of 'Madrasi' or Punjabi English. Directors often acknowledge the presence of regional prejudices in their audience. For example, Punjabi accents would definitely be more acceptable to a Delhi audience than Tamil. The section of the audience that laughed at Aruna's English at the *Final Solutions* show in Bangalore realized in the midst of their laughter that they were in a minority, and therefore quickly suppressed it.

The *Final Solutions* case might be analyzed further to recall three issues, raised earlier in this chapter, which are central to how audiences read contemporary IDE.

The moment of laughter and tension in the theatre reveals the ambivalences that mark attitudes to the use of English in real life as well as on the stage. Not only do different members of the audience respond differently to varieties of Indian English on the stage, the same set of members respond with deep ambivalences, as we saw in our case study. This reflects the uneasy relationship English-speaking Indians have with the language in real life. In most families today, one is likely to encounter the kind of generational difference in spoken English that the play uses. Those who are the 'present generation', often with a 'first language' relationship to English, find themselves having to acknowledge as parent or aunt or uncle, someone who's English 'betrays' strong traces of the mother tongue. Their responses to this in real life could vary from acceptance and indifference to amused tolerance to embarrassment and criticism.

In the case of IDE, the kind of English used on stage always gets noticed. Audiences and reviewers often refer to the accents of the actors, or the use of the vernacular in the script, or how close to or distanced from "real life" the language was, but seldom are these references pursued beyond casual comment. There is usually no attempt to read it, for example, as a class indicator, or to use it as a critical tool to analyze aspects of performance. The discussion between Dattani (who was also the director in this case) and Padmavathie Rao (the actress who played Aruna) that was referred to earlier, and their decision not to change the speech rhythms of Aruna, point to the possibility of other decisions. Ten years after that production of *Final Solutions*, the use of English on the IDE stage continues to resonate as a marker of class/caste privileges, and shapes our readings of language, – and gender-related cultural values.

IDE today is far from being cut off from an 'Indian' reality; on the contrary, it reproduces, in its aspects of performance, the shifting and constantly evolving plural realities of contemporary urban India.

## Notes

1. John McGrath, *A Good Night Out Popular Theatre: Audience, Class and Form*. Eyre Methuen, London, 1981, p. 6.

2. M.N. Panini, "The Political Economy of Caste", in *Caste: Its Twentieth Century Avatar*. (ed.) M.N. Srinivas. New Delhi: Penguin Books India, 1996, p. 52.

3. Pavan K. Varma, *The Great Indian Middle Class*. New Delhi: Penguin Books, 1998, p. 134.

4. Swapan Dasgupta, "India: A Nice Place to Get Out of" in *Seminar* 449 (1997), p. 24-25

5. D.L. Sheth, "Secularisation of caste and making of New Middle Class". *The Economic and Political Weekly*. Special Articles. August 21-28 (1999) n.pag.online.

6. Sunil Khilnani, *The Idea of India*. New Delhi: Penguin Books, 1999, p. 49-50.

7. *Ibid.*, p. 55.

8. Girish Karnad, *Introduction Three Plays*, New Delhi: OUP, 1995, p. 9.

9. Two studies of Indian cinema that might be useful in this context are: Ashis Nandy, *The Secret Politics of Our Desire: Innocence, Culpability and Indian Popular Cinema.* New Delhi: OUP, 1998, and Ravi S. Vasudevan. Ed. *Making Meaning in Indian Cinema.* New Delhi: OUP, 2000.

10. Pavan K. Varma, *Supra* note iii, p. 167.

11. Ashis Nandy, *At the Edge of Psychology.* New Delhi: Oxford India Paperbacks,1990, p. 108.

12. Aijaz Ahmad, "Disciplinary English: Third Worldism and Literature". *Rethinking English: Essays in Literature, Language, History.* Ed. Svati Joshi. Delhi: OUP, 1994. 206-263, 1994, p. 77.

13. Svati Joshi, ed. *Rethinking English: Essays in Literature, Language, History.* Delhi: OUP, 1994, p. 2.

14. Preetam Koilpillai, personal interview,2000, cited in Radha Ramaswamy, Unpublished thesis titled *"Aspects of Performance in Contemporary Indian Drama In English"*submitted to the University of Bangalore, June 2002.

15. Vijay Padaki, personal interview, 2000. Cited in Ramaswamy, *supra* note xiv.

16. Sabira Merchant, personal interview, 2000. *Supra* note xiv.

17. Cyrus Mistry, personal interview, 1999. *Supra* note xiv.

18. Poile Sengupta, Mangalam. In *BODY BLOWS: Women, Violence and Survival. Three Plays,* Calcutta. Seagull Books, 2000, p. 18.

# 29

# Identity Crisis in Multicultural Society

## The Case of Parsi Theatre

**Ranbir Sinh**

In its ancient days India has always had a multicultural society. It imbibed the cultures of different races, the Aryans, the Huns, the Muslims, the Hindus and at a later period, the Sikhs and the Christians. It honoured the ethos of different religions, such as Buddhism, Jainism, Hinduism, Islam and others. The social contacts and the conflicts among these races and religion gave birth to a new social system, in which, according to K.M. Munshi, "the customs and beliefs were adjusted, it imparted the understanding of each others' religion, and produced the fusion of politics, social, economic and cultural forces."[1] It provided a wider vision and understanding of 'coexistence'. It developed amongst the people, the strength and tenacity to adjust and make progress and most importantly the vitality to protect the identity and the national culture. This assimilation of cultures of different races weaved the society in a closely-knit fabric and provided the unity among all despite of several diversities. It is this peaceful coexistence, which in times of need became the inherent strength of the Indian society that enabled it to weather many a cultural storm. After the mass movement of 1857, when the British decided to take the reins of power in India, the system of 'colonization' began in, a system by which, the Super Powers dominated and governed other weaker countries, for their selfish interests. The imperial masters started controlling the political, economic, cultural, social order and above all the psyche of the people, which still persists amidst them. Based on doubt, loss of identity, and absence of the vital 'spirit of nationality' as foreigners who forever remained aliens governed it. The first and foremost principle of colonization is to manipulate and dominate the people. Complete subjugation of the innocent race was cleverly achieved by controlling the minds of the people. By which, they lose the capacity to think and reason. They only believe in what they are told. They see whatever is shown to them. Nationalism becomes meaningless and they look upon with reverence at the country of these imperialists accepting them to be the superior race. It was in this atmosphere when millions of Indian were being "skillfully injected with fears, complexes, trepidations, servility, despair and abasement,"[2] that Parsi Theatre came in as a ray of hope to the millions who had no more faith left in there hearts or dreams in their minds.

It is important that the entire theatre movement in India, which came up under the colonial rule around 1870 was based on the system of the Victorian theatre. The theatres of Marathi, Bengali, Kannada, Tamil, Telgu and several others named after their own regional languages, but the Parsi theatre, which in fact used Hindi/Urdu as its language, instead of being known as Hindustani Theatre was popularly known as Parsi Theatre after its ownership. It was also known as Company theatre because various theatre companies managed it.

The British wanted to transform Indian society through English education, and thus it demanded the adaptation of McCauley's education policy by which was aimed to "form a class of person, Indian in blood and in colour, but English in tastes, in opinion and in morals and intellect."[3]

This policy served the difficult task of the colonial masters to fulfill their double mission, one to destroy the social and cultural fabric of the society, by brain-washing them and creating a class conflict, winning over their friendship and using them as buffer against all opposition. But at the same time trying to causing them a great deal of harm at the hands of several such educational, cultural, and social institutions that caused them irreparable loss. Theatre was one of them. The English plays being staged by the university students set a modern trend in Indian theatre. The Parsi community was outrightly a business community and thus realized the potentials of Shaw business and instituted theatrical companies. Seth Pestonji Framji being the pioneer who founded the Original Theatrical Company in 1870. Later several theatrical companies came into being, which were known as Parsi Theatre, or Company theatre. Similarly several theatrical companies were made, The Great National Company in Bengal, Kirloskar Sangeet Natak Mandal in Maharashtra, Gubbi Theatre Company in Karnataka, and in other regional languages. It is indeed interesting to note that the Parsi theatre, as the Indian theatre was Victorian in character but Indian in spirit.

Theatre has been a social weapon initiating change, progress, and betterment of society and man. Whether the society initiates theatre or the theatre initiates society is an unanswerable question. But one thing is clear, that the effort is a must. Before colonial rule India was governed like one large family. Society was closely knit. But under colonialism society was oppressed, was forced into servitude, was divided into different ethnic units, the master race imposed its own culture, the people were made to lose their identity, the spirit of nationalism was lost, the very essence of multiculturalism was being destroyed. Theatre has always accepted the challenge and took up the task of tutoring the society. Parsi theatre also joined in hands to face the "slings and arrests" of the foreign oppression.

Here I would like to make it clear that I would widen my scope and speak about the Indian theatre as a whole, because I feel that the entire Indian theatre at that time was influenced by Parsi theatre, and one cannot isolate Parsi theatre from the rest.

Jomo Kenyatta said, "When the white man came to Africa he had the Bible and we had the land. And now? We have the Bible and he has the land."[4] The Indian theatre recognized this danger posed by imperial penetration and colonization, and Satyendra Nath Tagore communicated it to the people through his play, *Bharat Mater Bilap* (The Sorrows of Mother India), which was staged on 15 February 1873[5], by Great National Theatre at Calcutta. In one of the scene the beautiful hands of Mother India, instead of being adorned by jewels, were handcuffed. Her moon-like face was sad, her hair disheveled and she was dressed in rags. Her starving sons who were reduced to skeletons were almost lifeless, lying at her feet. Mother India after several efforts succeeded in awakening them, she informed them that the Queen who lives in a palace by the sea robbed everything they possessed when they were asleep. The oppressive colonial rule had not only robbed them of their national wealth, but their identity as well. But this had no effect on her lazy, worthless sons, and they start singing *God Save the Queen*. Mother

India, disappointed and ashamed, prays that God almighty might help her children with strength and courage to fight for their rights and freedom.

In order to subjugate the people it becomes absolutely essential to tear apart the society and cut down the unity of its people. 'Unity' turned out to be the matter of prime importance under the colonial rule unfortunately as an aftermath of the same colonial rule, and also because of the corrupting influence of the fundamentalists, it still persists to be.

The Indian theatre taking the leaf from history propagated the need for unity. Jyotindra Nath Tagore in his play *Purvuvikram*, Porus on the battlefield against Alexander the Great, in a speech to his people tells them that they are weak because they stand 'divided'. He reminds them that united they are a force to reckon with.

> Why do you fear the enemy?
> Virtuous always tread on virtue's path.
> Your divided strength has made you weak
> But united you will grow strong.[6]

In another speech, Porus inspire his men to rise and oppose the Invaders. He tells them that it is better to die than to live as slaves.

> Awake, Arise
> Look, the cruel Yavans
> Trespass into your home.
> Be of one mind
> Liberate the Mother India
> Delay is intolerable
> Advance with banners of victory in your hand
> What is life without freedom?
> Fire on them who wish to live
> Being robbed of his liberty.
> It is better to die
> But let liberty and honour pervade this land.
> Come and swear
> Either must win or must die
> Either kill the Yavans
> Or, follow death yourself.[7]

After 1857 the British had come to realize that they "were an imperial race, holding their own on a conquered soil by dent of velour and foresight"[8] Thus they could not bear to have any kind of human relationship with the Indians, as they never thought Indians to be human beings. The relationship itself was based on discrimination. This was the main cause of the conflict at the Indigo plantations. According to Charles Kingslay, the relation between planters and the labourers was of the "meanest and the weakest of bonds."[9] The labourers at the indigo plantations were not treated as human beings. They were fully exploited and the oppression of the planters had reached its climax, which in the words of Rev. James Lang was a "reign of terror". Harish Chandra Mukherjee, editor of Hindu Patriot wrote exclusively about the plight and miseries of the labourers. Though unbelievable, it was customary for the labourers to present their bride on the first night to the manager. Dinbandhu Mitra who belonged to the Nudea district and had ample opportunity to closely watch and hate the doings of the planters, in order to express the feelings of the labourers and make the society aware of the cruelties of the planters and the miseries of the labourers, decided to write a play. Being a government servant he remained anonymous. The play in question is *Neel Darpan* (Indigo Mirror), which was performed at Dhaka in 1961. The play was based on a real incident. Kheshtramani, the young daughter in the play was none other but Haramani, a peasant girl of Nudea, who was known for her beauty. One day she was abducted and taken to the house of the Manager where she was kept until the late in the night and was raped by the Manager.[10]

The effect of the performance of *Neel Darpan* was provoking and it raised a wave of indignation through the length and breadth of the country. This harbored a political, social and literary atmosphere. It was the first play, which was indicted at Calcutta High Court, but the play succeeded in stopping the oppression of the Indigo planters and provided the social rights and identity to those victimized indigo labourers. After several years later *Neel Darpan* in 1873 under the leadership of Girish Ghosh, when Great National Theatre staged it at Lucknow, it created a political stir. Scenes of oppression enacted by Wood (Ardhendu Sarkar) and Rose (Nirmal Chandra Kar) created great sensation among the audience. In the scene, when Rose, the manager catches the hand of Kheshtramani, who was pregnant, with heinous intentions, the poor girl piteously begs like Lucrece to be released but in vain. Helpless and in tears she pleaded, "Saheb I am like your daughter, leave me." But Rose dragged her saying, "I wish to be the father of your child." It was at this time that Trap and Navin Madhav entered the scene, rescuing Kheshtramani. Trap takes her away, but Rose and Navin Madhav proposes to fight. The outrageous Europeans in the audience rushed to the stage to stop the performance and riots took place. The District Magistrate banned the performances of the play. The company was asked to go back to Calcutta and the Dramatic Performance Act was imposed throughout the country under which the plays were censured.

The 20th century was the era of nationalism. The colonial masters were posed with the rise of the nationalistic forces. As a policy to have complete authority on the people, they imposed upon them the culture and the language of the superior race. They created an inferiority complex in their minds. They drove a wedge in society to disrupt the unity among the people on social, economic, and religious. It led to a loss of identity and the people started aping the so-called superior race of the British. National feeling was getting evaded. People naively believed that the foreign imperialist rule was benevolent. Even the term 'Ethnicity' hitherto unknown became the malice of the society. Parsi theatre was faced with this problem and realizing their duty took up theatre as a social weapon to challenge the colonial rule. Because of the Dramatic Performance Act, they could not openly express whatever they wanted to. So they turned to history and mythology, just as Sartre did in his plays *The Flies*, which was staged in Paris against the Nazi occupation and Aspajia, the Latvian playwright with her play *The Serpents Pride*, in which she propagated the quintessence of national feeling.

Agha Hashra Kashmiri, one of the leading playwright of Parsi theatre in Act II, Sc. III of his famous play *Yahudi Ki Ladki* (Daughter of the Jew) directly points out the difference of social status between the higher and lower class of society, which was manipulatively created by the colonial masters. There was a wide difference between the classes and the masses. It spoke about the relationship based on inequality and difference between 'the ruler' and 'the ruled'. In the court scene when Rahel, Uzra, Marcus and Brutus are prosecuted before the King, Rahel, a Jew, pleads about her love for Marcus, the Roman prince, Brutus objects that marriage cannot take place, as Rahel is a daughter of a poor Jew and Marcus is a Prince. Here Agha Hashra through his dialogues

underlines the distinction made by the imperial class, and their intolerable behaviour towards the people of India. Uzra's speech is directed
towards the king – but in fact it was meant for the race of English
imperial masters. He says:

> Your sorrows are sorrows, sorrows of a poor are but a story;
> Your luxury are luxurious, ours is mere pigmentation of mind;
> Our childhood is old age; your old age is youth;
> Your blood is blood and our blood is water.

When the freedom movement was at its peak, it was the unity of
the people, which was subjected to the unappreciable behaviour of the
imperialists. Agha Hashra, in his play *Bharat Ki Pukaar* (The Voice of
India) reminds people to stand united, and at the same time warns the
colonizers that they should keep their hands off as India belongs to
Indians. This land is sacred and pious as the great Ganga kisses the holy
hands of Kashi, where Mandir (temple) and Masjid (mosque) stand
together, symbolizing the ethical unity of the nation.

Parsi theatre played a very important role in emphasizing the
unity of Hindus and Muslims. The essence of composite culture, the
respect of each other's religion, the feeling of nationality is underlined
by B.C. Madhur, another playwright of Parsi theatre in his play *Jago
Bahut Soye* (Wake up! You Have Slept For Long). A poor man's house
is being auctioned. European wants to buy the idol of Lord Krishna, to
which a Muslim objects. The European is surprised at this and asks him
that you are not an idol worshipper, what will you do with it? To this
the Muslim replies, I may not be idol worshipper but I am an India. To
me Ram and Rahim are the same. Krishna is as much mine as any
Hindu. I will not permit any foreigner even to put his hands on
Krishna.

Indian society has always had the problem of untouchability. The
playwrights of Parsi theatre always brought out these issues through its
plays. Agha Hashra in his play *Sita Banwas* (Exile of Sita) discusses the
issue of untouchability very cleverly. Through the character of Ram he
supports the cause of the untouchables in Indian society. In Act I, Sc.VI
Bharat, the younger brother of Ram, that a Dhoby, a washerman, who
belongs to the lower class has no right whatsoever to condemn the
Queen, Sita, who is also Ram's wife, after all he is an untouchable from
the lower strata of society, not by a Brahmin or a Kshatriya. To this
Ram replies:

Ram:         Is he not my subject?

Shatrughan:  He is an untouchable, and society does not accept him as a human being. If he is not considered to be a human being then his voice has no value.

Ram:         Do not the untouchables take birth in the same way as Brahmins and Kshatriya? The untouchables posses the same faculties of understanding, and wisdom. Only they are not educated. When the roots of a tree are rotten, the pillars, which support the roof, are weak, the foundation of the building is weak, when a handful of higher caste of society treats the weaker section with hatred, they want to subjugate them and inflict upon them the miseries and atrocities, I am afraid, that nation cannot exist with pride and head held high. Therefore learn to treat the untouchables as human beings and understand their voice.[11]

The kingship in Indian society itself was the fountainhead of multicultural environment. It respected equally all the cultures and religions. The noted playwhright of the Parsi theatre underlines the duties of the Raja or the King know as Rajdharam in *Sita Banwas*, when Ram says that the king for his actions is accountable to God and to his public, for him duty is higher than love and consideration of his brothers, sons, wife, his self interests, religion or any other emotion or relation or even temptation

Narayan Prasad Betaab, another well-known playwright of Parsi theatre introduced the character of Chet Chamar in his play *Mahabharata*. The scene was deliberately introduced as a protest against the treatment, which was being meted out to the low caste or the down trodden. Not only Betaab opposed the Brahmans, the so-called beholders of knowledge, but he also condemns the arrogance and the false pride of the Kshatriyas. In the scene when Dronacharya hears Cheta Chamar and his followers singing the Bhajans, he in rage rebukes them saying that they are untouchables and do not have the social rights to take the name of Gods. He asks Cheta, 'Who gave you permission to do this?' Cheta replies, "Learned people like you. The water from various underground sources comes into the well. From where it is drawn out by a bucket, from the bucket people bathe and wash their clothes, the same water travels through the outlet to the drain, where poor animals quench their thirst. In the same way Veda transmitted the knowledge to the Rishis, they in turn passed it on to mankind and a poor untouchable like me secretly heard it."[12]

Betaab, in the same scene of the play also attacks the Brahamins who for centuries became the custodians of knowledge and usurped the highest social status in the society, but the Kshatriyas, the royalty who from ancient times always exploited their pageantry, the flags and insignias, which had become their false ego and identity. Nobody else was allowed to use flags. Duryodhana when he sees the flag of Cheta, he is furious and demands to remove it and wants to know as to what was written on it. Cheta recites the shloka of Yajurveda. Both Dronacharya and Duryodhana question his rights of displaying the flag and reciting the shloka. Cheta bravely replies that the freedom of speech to every individual of society is permitted by this very shloka to do so. In this way Parsi theatre and its playwrights propagated the cause of social and cultural rights, the dignity and identity of every individual in this multicultural society.

In the year 1927 Miss Katherine Mayo's book *Mother India* was published. It was based on her experiences that she had on her visit to India. The purpose of her visit to India and writing the book is not defined. In the book she says that she wished to know about India because of "self intelligence and self protection." Yet the purpose for such enhancement of intellect and the desire of self-protection from remains vague. She supports the cause of her visit in her own words saying "as a volunteer to unsubsidized, uncommitted and unattended to observe the daily life of the people."[13]

Thus it seems to be a visit without purpose to state that was reduced to the mere status of a colony, she did not have anything particular in her mind. She was only gathering superfluous facts to be presented to the people of America. Though it seems that if this was her purpose, then she perhaps had a special eye, for the bad side of the society. She attacked every social institution and defamed them. The book presented a meticulous and defaming account of India and Indians. It is no wonder that Lal Lajpat Rai, one of the great political and social leader, called it as the "Drain Inspector's Report". Narayan Prasad Betaab wrote a play *Kinnar Kumari* as a reply to this book. The play was staged at the annual conference of Indian National Congress at Calcutta, which was presided by Moti Lal Nehru. The play was an outspoken reply. In one of his songs he said, "It is the Bulbul, which is happy to see a splendid garden and the vultures always spot the dead bodies and filth. Likewise the drain inspector does not inspect the places of worship or anything good, but only the heaps of dirt. There were temples and mosques where doors were open, but Kinnar Kumari (meaning Miss Mayo) was afraid to go there." Probably this was the first time that a play was written as a reply to malicious and slanderous report. Through his play Narayan Prasad Betaab as a playwright fulfilled his responsibility of defending the dignity of every individual Indian.

History and mythology were the two subjects, which provided the subject matter for the plays, the bravery of the past heroes, unity among the people, the brave opposition offered to the foreigners, their rule of oppression and the desire to achieve freedom. The plays written on historical and mythological themes were cleverly interpreted to avoid censorship. It was undoubtedly the glorious period of Indian theatre, when the entire theatre of India, Bengali, Marathi, Kannada, and others, besides Parsi theatre joined hands to oppose the foreign rule of the British. I strongly feel that I will be shirking from my responsibility if I do not mention the role of Bengali, Marathi and other regional theatres, because I feel that all of them were a part of the tradition of Parsi theatre.

Bengali theatre was definitely the forerunner. Girish Ghosh adapted the famous novel *Sita Ram* written by Bankim Chandra and staged it in 1884, and in 1904 he produced *Satnam*. Both the plays propagated Hindu-Muslim unity. Historical plays based on the lives of *Sirajuddaulah, Mir Kasim, Nand Kumar, Chhatrapati Shivaji*, were successfully staged. At the same time a playwright by the name of D.L. Roy appeared on the scene of Bengali theatre. His plays *Rana Pratap, Aurangzeb, Mewar Patan, Alamgir, Shahjahan* were not only staged in Bengali but they were translated in almost every regional language and successfully staged all over India. The central theme of all his plays was unity amongst Indians and to attain freedom. In his play *Durgadas* in Act V, Sc.IV, he makes Diler Khan one of the commanders of Aurangzeb talk about Hindu-Muslim unity, and very subtly reminds the people that if they unite together they will have one government, which will rule India from one end to the other. Diler Khan tells Aurangzeb that it is necessary that the hearts of Hindu and Muslim should unite, they should have the freedom to worship in temples and mosques, the sound of azan (prayers) and shlokas at the same time should resound under the same sky. Hinds and Muslims should embrace each other as brothers. The day this happens such a government will be installed which will govern India from one end to the other and it will be the most powerful government in the world. In almost all historical plays unity and freedom from foreign rule was the central theme, and these plays played an important role in creating the national feeling amidst the people and helped the nationalistic forces in their movement of independence.

Manmath Roy depicted the cruelties committed by the British, the indignity suffered by the people, in his play *Karagaar* (Prison) taking its theme from mythology. Kansa, the ruler of Mathura symbolized British and the brutalities of the colonial rule were shown. Krishna was born in prison and he was the redeemer of the people of Mathura, thus the name of the play as in the play Krishna is shown as the redeemer of the people of India. Qazi Nazrul Islam, the revolutionary poet, wrote the patriotic songs. The popularity of the play forced the British government to ban the play, but the songs by then had become popular and liked by every Indian.

Marathi theatre has been very fortunate as it has always received the blessings of the enlightened political and social leadership, like that of Lokmanya Tilak. He was so fond of theatre that when he was released from prison, the first thing that he asked was, how is Kirloskar Natak Mandali doing. Inspired by him many of his associates K.P. Khadilakar, N.C. Kelkar, Veer Vaman Rao Joshi and many others wrote plays on several burning political and social issues. When Lord Curzon, the Viceroy of India, partitioned Bengal in two halves, the fire of agitation, which was lighted at Bengal reached Maharashtra, K.P. Khadilkar wrote his famous play "*Keechak Vadha*". Maharashtra Natak Mandali staged the play on 23 February 1907.

Khadilakar based his play on an incident from *Mahabharata*. The return of Keechak to Viratnagar and his passion for Draupadi, in disguise, as Sairandhari, was serving the Queen. Khadilkar cleverly weaves the plot and as the play progresses the inner meaning of the play becomes clear to the audience. They identified Keechak as Lord Curzon, Draupadi as India, Yudhisthar as the moderate group of Indian National Congress Party who favoured the constitutional means and ways to achieve independence, and Bhima represented the extremist group of the Congress party who wanted action, even if they have to adopt violence to free India from the shackles of bondage. Khadilkar succeeded in communicating the idea to the people that a weak government in London represented by an arrogant Viceroy, who had usurped power in his hands and used it to humiliate and insult the people of India, partitioned Bengal in two halves. Khadilkar advocates violent means to achieve freedom.

Khadilkar used many lines from the speech of Lord Curzon as in Act II, Sc. IV when Keechak says, "We must always remember that slaves are slaves and can never equal rulers." In Act III, Sc. II Keechak advises his followers that, "Never speak softly and nicely to your slaves. If we use such words for a moment, they think they are on equal footing. They then envy our happiness and call our rule oppressive". These were the statements, which Lord Curzon had made in his official speeches. One of the most meaningful speeches of the play, which expresses the sorrows and helplessness of India who has been tolerating and suffering the foreign oppression for so many years is delivered by Sairandhri who represents India. Sairandhri narrating her sad experience of leading a life of a slave to Kankubhat (Yudhisthara) in Act I, Sc. III says: If one accustomed to enjoy freedom, voluntarily passes same days of servitude, his mind becomes weak and he fails to distinguish between honour and dishonour. He thinks it virtuous to put up with disrespect and to forget the bygone days". This was the real picture of India where people under the dominion forgot themselves; they lost their identity and as time passed by they willingly and silently subdued to the evils and humiliations of the British rule. In the words of Ngugi Wa Thiango, "It is the final triumph of a system of domination when the dominated start singing its virtues."[14]

In this way Khadilkar reminded the people of their identity, their dignity and honour and inspired them to take action. The play had its required effect. Mr. Morrison, the Commissioner of Bombay did not even doubt that the murder of Keechak was a very cleverly veiled incitement to murder of European officials. This was substantiated by the murder of Jackson, a British official. The play was officially deemed seditious and was banned, and Khadilkar was imprisoned.

Khadilkar's second play was *Bhau Bandki*, staged by Maharashtra Natak Mandali at Sholapur on 18 September 1909. He based his play on a historical incident, which occurred during the Peshwa rule. At the time the play was staged Tilak was serving his sentence in Mandlay (Burma). Khadilkar cleverly infused patriotic fervour by modeling the character of Ram Shastri, the fearless judge of the Peshwa Court after that of Tilak. Raghoba who was aspiring for the throne asked Ram

Shastri that he should declare him as the Peshwa. Honest and fearless Ram Shastri refused to do so. Anandi Bai, the wife of Raghoba then threatened to have him beheaded. Ram Shastri refused to obey the orders and required speaking the famous lines of Tilak, which he delivered during his trial of sedation in 1908 at the Court of Mandlay, "All I wish to say is, that in spite of the verdict of the jury I maintain that I am innocent. There are higher powers that rule the destiny of things and it may be the will of Providence that the cause that I represent may prosper more by my suffering than by my remaining free." The purpose of Khadilkar was to tell the people of India that to achieve freedom from foreign rule one had to be fearless.

*Ran Dundubhi*, a play written by Veer Vamanrao Joshi was another one in which the playwright inspired the people to rise and free themselves from the shackles of bondage of foreign rule. In one of his songs he points a vivid picture of the oppression of the foreign rule when people are forced to live in their own country as slaves. The song was worded as:

> When the noose of slavery is put round one's neck, one is forced to live a life of a slave. He lashes his self-respect and although alive but to all-purpose he is a dead man. He is treated as a thief in his own house. He slaves and labours but his master enjoys the luxuries of life. He is an unfortunate being who is forced to live in his motherland which is shackled by the chains of bondage and becomes a prison to him."

This was the subtle manner in which the playwrights of Parsi theatre used to provoke the British authorities and yet communicate their message to the people. The songs in the plays did a great job as they reached each and every home and were sung by everybody, even at the teashops and in the streets as well. The playwrights of Parsi theatre had become a major concern for the British government. Many plays in Hindi, Urdu and in regional languages lead to several political riots. Theatre had become a major threat to the British government. The British had realized the power that drama exercised over the minds of the people. As Hobbhouse, member of the Legislative Council of Viceroy had said, "No greater stimulus could be supplied to excite the passion of mankind than that supplied by means of drama, and no feat was too difficult for a dramatist who could produce any effect to please the minds of spectator." The Dramatic Performance Act did not affect the popularity of Parsi theatre as it continued to affect the minds of the people. The colonial masters played the clever game of classification. As they had succeeded in classifying society and divided it into sections, they tried to classify cultures well. Parsi theatre being more approachable reached almost all the corners of the country and became the most popular among all the other existing regional theatres and therefore deliberately was underestimated as vulgar and cheap. The government took up administrative measures and did not permit the theatre companies of Parsi theatre to build makeshift stages when they travelled to the small towns. The theatres in the cities were turned into cinema houses. The death knell sounded close at hand and the glorious era of Indian theatre came to an end.

Multicultural society no doubt has the inbuilt strength of unity, but at the same time its strength of being multicultural becomes its weakness, and in the name of culture and religion the fundamentalists fully exploit it to their own advantage. It therefore becomes the prime duty of theatre to preserve the unity and strength of society through its plays. Friends, in the time that we are living our responsibility have become greater, and we all must do our best to save mankind from the fundamentalist neo-imperialism and other evils.

## Notes

1. Munshi, K.M., Foreword in *The Vedic Age* (ed.), Bhartiya Vidya Bhawan, Bombay, 1988, p. 9.

2. Cesaire, Aimé, *Discourse sur le Colonialismel* [Franz Fanon, *Black Skin, White Masks*, Translated by Charles Lam Markmann, Grove Press: New York 1967, p. 7].

3. Phillips, C.H. (ed.), *The Correspondence of Lord William Bentinck*, Oxford University Press, Vol.II, 1977, p. 793.

4. Mazrui, Ali A., *Cultural Forces in World Politics*, Heinemann Educational Books. Inc, Northhampshire, 1990, p. 6.

5. Das Gupta, Hemendra Nath, *The Indian Stage Vol. II/III*, Metropolitan Printing and Publishing House Ltd., 1946, pp. 256-7.

6. Ibid., p. 260.

7. Ibid., p. 261 (The word *Yavan* is used for Greeks).

8. Metcalf, Thomas R.; *Ideologies of the Raj*, Cambridge University Press, 1998, p. 44.

9. Tinker, Hugh, *A New System of Slavery*, 1974, Oxford University Press, p. 184.

10. Das Gupta, Hemendra Nath, *The Indian Stage Vol. II/III*, Metropolitan Printing and Publishing House Ltd., 1946, p. 92.

11. Narang, Abdul Qudus, *Agha Hashra Aur Natak*, Sangit Natak Akadmi, Lucknow, 1978, p. 214.

12. Betaab, Narayan Prasad, *Mahabharata* (Play) Act ii, Sc.10, Betaab Pustakalaya, Delhi, 1961, p. 95.

13. Mayo, Katherine, *Mother India*, Johanthan Cape, London, 1930.

14. Thiango, Ngugi Wa., *Decolorizing the Mind*, James Curoy-Heinemann, London, 1994, p. 20.

# 30

# Subaltern Theatre

## Parallels in Jewish and Bengali Theatres

### Seth L. Wolitz

The names of Broadway playwrights and composers such as George Gershwin, Leonard Bernstein, Arthur Miller, Tony Kushner, not to mention Rodgers and Hammerstein or Stephen Sondheim and their American musicals are today well known in most theatrical circles in the world. These dramatists and composers are all Jewish-Americans and share their hybridic cultural realities. Most of the named had parents who did not speak English or were bi-lingual and had bi-focal cultural perspectives. Most of American Jewry descends from Eastern European Jewish ancestors who spoke mainly Yiddish and are the heirs to Jewish cultural traditions, both secular and religious, which were brought to America and flourished, especially Jewish theatre in Yiddish. In New York City alone, around 1900, "Second Avenue" was synonymous with Yiddish theatre where over twenty-two theatres produced not only many original plays but served as a raiding field for Broadway and Hollywood to garner playwrights, actors, choreographers, set designers, etc.

No one questions the presence of these people or their participation but they have given American theatre a perspective that in closer analysis reveals important sources of focus and styles directly related to the Jewish theatre and Jewish modern consciousness which goes straight back to Tsarist Russia.

This paper seeks to present the problematics of the establishment of a subaltern theatre, the first secular Jewish theatre in Eastern Europe constructed under the hegemony of the Russian Tsarist regime and the role of theatre in helping form a modern Jewish consciousness which affects to this day the cultural realities of the State of Israel, the life of Jewry in America and where ever descendants of Eastern European Jewry now reside – if they escaped the barbarism of the European Holocaust. The first secular Jewish theatre shares, in fact, remarkable parallels both in time and space with all the emergent secular Indian theatres as well as the same conditions of subalternity in relationship to hegemonic forces on the political, economic, social and cultural planes. They also reflect the same challenges to their theatrical existence and to their artistic expression and how they resorted to the same methods of resistance and adaptation to the given oppressive realities while being totally unaware of the other's existence.

The traditional Jewish culture shares with many other traditional cultures of monotheistic suasion that representation or performance reflects efforts to mimic the Creation and therefore falls into blasphemy. Christianity and Shiite Islam allow space for a "sacral drama" to be performed such as the Easter Passion plays and the performances about the seventh Imam. In Judaism, the European Rabbis permitted, during the joyous holiday of Purim, under the guise of the carnevalesque, a mummer's style of play based originally on the Book of Esther. This floating skit known as a *Purimshpil* became at times more elaborated and scenarios were published in the vernacular Yiddish especially in the 18th and early 19th centuries.[1] The *Purimshpil* can be compared to the popular *Yatra* folk theatre tradition in Bengal. They both were theatres of popular expression related to a religious holiday and celebrated with song, dance, witty dialogue-often of local reference- and performed only by males.[2] (The Jewish folk play, however, eschews love and uses lust as a source of disruption as opposed to celebrating the erotic delights of Lord Krishna in the *Yatra*.) Apart from this one day Purim play, any form of drama was considered sinful and forbidden!

But 2,000 years earlier, the Jews did create plays in Ptolemaic Egypt that followed Hellenic models and were composed in Greek for the Greek-speaking Jews of Alexandria. Only fragments subsist but one name, Ezekiel of Alexandria and 269 lines of his tragedy, *Exodus*, prove that Jews composed and participated in theatre.[3] Jews in Germany and

Russia at the beginning of the 19th century were totally ignorant of this past history, which only now is being brought to light.

In the Tsarist Empire of the 19th century, the Jews were essentially colonialized and lived under Russian hegemony. They sought at all costs to preserve their identity especially through their traditional religious cultural existence. They shared a parallel political and cultural condition as most subaltern peoples in the 19th century except that they dwelled inside the metropolitan imperial power. Esthetic culture, and especially theatre were foreign imports and held by the religion and the Jewish masses to be taboo. The development of modern Jewish secular esthetic culture and its aggregate, theatre, had no thespian tradition for these Jews unlike the Bengalis developing modern Indian theatre, in the same time frame, the 19th century, had both a living folk theatre tradition and the proud memory of Sanskrit theatre. If the English hegemony especially in Calcutta, provoked a cultural theatre renaissance ultimately in Bengali, affected by English and European Enlightenment cultural traditions, the Jewish Enlightenment movement, the *Haskala*, embracing European Enlightenment coming from Germany made little headway in the esthetic realm.

The Eastern European Jews were receptive to the philosophical concepts of human equality and humanistic ethics, the centrality of reason and the role of education, but they approached esthetic expression gingerly and theatre most warily. Those Jewish "modernists" found themselves in full combat with the traditionalists and the first efforts at establishing esthetic space as a field of expression or even as a site of resistance came first in satirical writings. There was no possibility of theatre. Nevertheless, by 1830, we have proof of a few plays being written and amateur theatrics performed in the privacy of a home. But these plays were never performed publicly nor published until the 20th century when Jewish scholars sought to recuperate the origins of modern Jewish theatre.

The English had introduced English language theatre in Calcutta by 1775 and it drew by 1840 a sizable population of Indians who understood English.[4] Russian theatre by 1840 existed throughout the areas where Jews were permitted to reside in the Tsarist Empire but few Jews ever went to see Russian or Ukrainian productions and few Jews, in any case, understood the imperial tongue. By contrast, the 'colonized but modernizing' Indians in Calcutta between 1831 and 1872 were busy adapting the classic Sanskrit plays into Bengali, absorbing the British theater, both the classics and the popular frivolities and putting on productions in Bengali in private theatres in homes.[5]

In Tsarist Russia, the few "enlightenment" Jews interested in theatre in this period could find only models in the Western world as literary texts, not as living theatre for what was performed in the provincial theatres were mainly contemporary vaudevilles, operettas and farces. Nevertheless, some modernizing Jews did attend local theatres with their traveling troupes, which acclimatized them to theatrical entertainment. Unlike the Bengali who knew English but for national consciousness wished to develop a national Theatre in the Bengali tongue, the Jews were caught in a linguistic battle between using Hebrew, the religious language and source of the old high culture like Sanskrit but unspoken for 2000 years, or the vernacular tongue, Yiddish which was despised by the Enlightenment Jews as a "jargon" and an embarrassment. Russian as a theatrical language only came into play at the beginning of the 20th century. Yiddish, however, would win the day in the 19th century because Jewish theatre would be come a popular medium.

In the second half of the 19th century the Jewish people felt increasingly under a two-pronged attack: (1) from without, state anti-Semitism and barely disguised Russification, the latter intention, a new policy from 1855-1881, which permitted a limited number of Jews to obtain secular education in Russian state schools but with the intention of Russification and conversion and; (2) from within the community, there were growing tensions between the modernizers and the traditionalists. The increasingly secular Enlightenment movement among the Jewish merchant class sought modernization not unlike in colonial India, where the same rising middle class sought a freer lifestyle and less religious observances.

At first, the 1860s and 1870s were a period of economic growth in Tsarist Russia and of some liberalizing under Tsar Alexander II and Jews sought to accommodate with the hope of obtaining co-equal citizenship individually and as a recognized community. Certainly a segment of the Jewish middle classes was adapting western educational ideas and western forms such as western dress and social customs and its concomitant interests in culture and theatre.

By the late sixties, secular Jewish popular culture developed beyond reworked folklore. Into this beginning secularizing milieu, a former seminarian, Abraham Goldfadn, (1840-1908), who received a partial secular education realized that a Jewish theatre could serve both as a source of entertainment and "enlightenment" by reaching a vast Jewish audience in its own spoken language, Yiddish, and not in its liturgical and traditionally high culture tongue, Hebrew. But that did not come over night. Goldfadn began as a poet reciting verse in 1876 in a *café chantant* setting and after many boos, learned to craft poems, songs and dialogue to reach a Jewish audience originally more underclass than middle class.

The playwright faced multiple problems, the hostility of the Rabbis, the indifference and fear of the broad traditional Jewish population, the absence of actors, theatres and any known theatrical tradition. Abraham Goldfadn, the father of modern Jewish theatre, faced all of these problems and successfully negotiated all these obstacles. He might best be compared to Moliére in the West and perhaps to Girishchandra Ghosh in Bengali theatre. He created himself *ex nihilo* as dramatist, actor, composer, stage manager, stage designer and trainer of actors. He created the plays, songs, stage sets and built a troupe around his repertoire. That he borrowed liberally may be too generous a term but plagiarized is far too cruel for he brilliantly "Judaized" whatever entered his eyes and ears. He was in fact functioning in an old and universal tradition. But overnight, he had taken young religious singers and made them secular actors and "Wandering Stars!" He sensed the time was ripe for introducing theatre in Yiddish to the Jewish public eager to taste and enter modern life.

Jewish theatre would become the bridge to modernity. Goldfadn enticed the Jewish masses into theatre by using Yiddish, choosing tableaux settings that carried affective cultural meanings and semiotic significances and introduced song melodies, which evoked both the synagogue and the home. People ignored the Rabbis and came to experience theatre. That he succeeded in making his audiences pay for a ticket makes him the first successful Jewish playwright and man of theatre. I am struck that in Calcutta, at almost the very same time, the first public theatre opened in 1872 and also charged for an entrance ticket.[6] Nor should we sneer at the commercial element in emerging subaltern theatre for a public willing to pay for a seat reflects the belief and acceptance not only of theatre itself but a compliment to the new self-conscious validation of reborn national expression. The parallels to the Bengali theatre or even the Marathi, Parsi and Urdu theatres in Bombay reveal a common development that underscores the shared subaltern conditions at the origins of their modern theatre.

Goldfadn began his theatrical output with small contemporary social satires using European vaudeville and melodrama genres imitated from the stage practices of the surrounding populations, the Ukrainians, Russians and Rumenians who themselves were totally dependent upon Western European models drawn from French vaudeville, Scribean *pièces bien faites*, German *Volkspiele* and the operetta tradition from Offenbach and Strauss. Goldfadn mentions in his *Autobiography* that he was well read in the German Theatre of Goethe and Schiller, the Russian theatre of Griboyedev, Shakespeare and Moliére but that he faced an audience that had no background whatsoever in secular culture and theatre and therefore had to wean his audience into basic esthetic expressions.[7]

Between 1877 and 1880 he introduced plays, which attended his agenda as a *maskil* or Enlightenment figure in the defense of individual rights and the importance of modern learning. The plays like *Shmendrik, the Grandma and her Grandchild*, the *Witch* and *the Fanatic* all treat the foibles of family, caste and class interests which are prepared to sacrifice the individual member at the cost of his or her happiness, particularly the young lovers who, because of patriarchal interests or religious traditions, must be separated. [I must point out that the introduction of the concept of Romantic love, a western concept, in marriage as the final arbiter of meaning between two consenting people goes to the heart of the Enlightenment movement affecting not only the Jews but all patriarchal traditional societies as a citizen of the Subcontinent is fully aware. Love places individual rights over the community and family which becomes a major source of conflict on and off stage in non-European theatre.] In fact, as Bengali theatre by 1872 was allowing female actresses on stage albeit from the Red Light districts and only before WWI did respectable ladies finally perform, Goldfadn's troupe began in the late seventies to permit Jewish women to perform only if they were married!

The presence of women on the stage was breaking a major ethical taboo of Jewish men allowed to watch females perform. The presence of women on stage may not have hastened the co-equality of men and women but the theatre by such an act entered directly into the dynamics of cultural conflict and change.

Goldfadn's early plays-adored by Soviet Jewish critics-defend the modernizers against the traditionalists. These traditional plot structures are always set in contemporary times in a provincial city or town, placed in a domestic situation, and plotted around a triangular conflict involving love, dowry money, enlightenment principles and religious fanaticism. The plays do reflect contemporary Jewish middle and lower class conditions but the situations, characters and plottings in close analysis reveal worn out templates and formulae re-worked from European popular theatre. The plot outline of Goldfadn's *Shmendrik* of 1878 seems a Jewish version of Smetana's opera libretto of *The Bartered Bride* written and composed ten years earlier and itself barrowed from a German folk play. The borrowings do reveal cultural cross-fertilization but the new theatrical expression permits a venting of communal identity and inner conflicts. The Menanderesque coda: a marriage ceremony is given a rousing Jewish sendoff with klezmer band music and raucous joyous wedding songs and dances lifted directly from contemporary life. Such scenes legitimate to the paying audience its identity, culture, values and distinctiveness while partaking in the universal form of esthetic delight, theatre!

The use of songs as concentrates of feeling proved to be very successful with the new Jewish audience and Goldfadn mentions that he even introduced one of his popular songs that were independent to please his audience. [See "Rozhinkes mit mandlen" in Act I of Goldfadn's *Shulames.*] Song was an essential ingredient from the first of his theatre, which emerged from the *Café Chantant* world with its satirical songs, humour songs and nostalgic ones. Jewish theatre was born, might I say ironically as a natural Wagnerian *Gesamtkunstwerk* for Goldfadn correctly recognized that his public wanted a full theatrical experience: in Diaghilev's term "to be astounded". Song in particular carried the cultural and emotional baggage, which the dramatist integrated more and more into his theatre works. Goldfadn melodies recalled the synagogue, the religious festivals and folksongs, introduced melodies barrowed from Italian and French operas, and reworked Slavic, Romenian and even Turkish folk songs. He joined the melodies to his verses and Judaised them. In the same manner, Goldfadn judaised European plot structures, reshaping them to fit Jewish sensibilities and developed Western themes into Jewish contexts. His lyric skills have proved to be his most enduring quality but his 19th century dramaturgy invented the modern Jewish theatre and drew a paying audience. All previous efforts at Jewish theatre in the 19th century remained closet dramas. With Abraham Goldfadn, Jewish theatre was alive and performed. The boundaries of the physical

Theatre, the esthetic space of the boards, suddenly made available to a people without a homeland a *lieu de mémoire* and a site of resistance.

Between 1877 and 1880, Goldfadn critiqued on the stage his contemporary Jewish society, its pettinesses and degraded condition, as did all the enlightenment writers who applauded the modernizers. But this comedic and melodramatic theatre proved too narrow for his larger desires and those of the new Jewish secular intelligentsia. If theatre was theorized in the West to serve the social good, this premise carried greater weight for the intelligentsia in colonized conditions that aspired to see theatre restore a past and regenerate a people with a vision of the future.

By 1880, Goldfadn traveling with his troupe performed to great success throughout Western Russia (the Pale of Settlement, where Jews by Russian law were restricted to live). His company and new rival troupes – made up of actors who abandoned his troupe and set up their own – had overnight built a public that attended theatre with hot enthusiasm. Unlike Bengali theatre, which could build a permanent base in Calcutta, this Yiddish theatre was peripatetic and more in line with traveling Urdu and Parsi troupes in India. The new Jewish companies with their matinee idols and dramatists re-working Goldfadn's plays or imitating his style quickly moved out of restrictive Tsarist Russia and established themselves in Warsaw, London – where the best actors were found in the 1880's and in New York City where the fullest theatrical freedoms existed.

This traveling Jewish theatre knitted the widespread Jewish communities together linguistically, culturally, ideologically and ultimately politically. Jewish Theatre became one of their first modes of shared modern secular activity that actualized the Jews as modern participants in history with their own theatre, It was soon followed by literature and the plastic arts transmogrifying a passive traditional religious Jewish world, a *Gemeinschaft*, in Toennies terminology, into a living corporate presence. The emergence of Jewish theatre parallels the urge, in the same time frame and manner, in Indian theatres to find a modern esthetic space within which to celebrate the ethnic inheritance, its history with its high and low points, and find the means to express, if not protest, the contemporary conditions of their subalternity and project an alternative vision.

By 1880 Goldfadn was aware and encouraged by the Jewish intelligentsia to deepen Jewish theatre by extending the range and subject matter and he followed the nationalist trend by moving back to the distant past. He chose post-Biblical material first, which was well known and safe, both for his public to assimilate and not to threaten the Tsarist censors, which was far harsher than the British. By choosing a post-Biblical play, Goldfadn careful distinguished between 'sacral history" inside the Bible [Old Testament for Christians] and secular history, in linear time in order to place Jewry in modern linear history and not in sacral time and religious circularity. By choosing settings as close to the Biblical Age as possible, he underscored the ancient continuity and longevity of Jewry not unlike the Bengali theatre using mythic themes first and then progressing into its own history.

His most successful Biblical play, Shulamith [*Shulames* in Yiddish], 1880, is almost a "number opera" [pre-Wagnerian structuring] in five acts and multiple sets [*bilder*] with alternating grand choral scenes and intimate ones joined by marches and fanfares, love songs, lamentations and even dancing. From communal typological figures, Goldfadn moved to greater individualization, and psychological portraiture – a sign of the influence of the Enlightenment – and intensified the love conflict and allied it to the larger implications of full nationhood restored. By using ancient sovereign Israel as the backdrop, he recuperated the historical past not as a mythic a-historical setting as in Purim plays, but forced the Jews to witness scenes of Jewish fullness regenerated on the stage providing a restored linear past. Israel could be and was restored, alive, a free full-blooded sovereign people with a retrievable past that could be harnessed again in the future.

In reverse order, Bengali Theatre began with mythic plays drawn from Sanskrit classical plays and the great epics with their panoply of gods in an a-historical context as in Jewish Purim plays. When the present time is represented on stage both young theatres chose to satirize the provincial middle class usually in its boorish upward mobile family settings. Lacking the conscious theatrical past, Jewish theatre necessarily chose first, the present, with its typological figures in comedic settings, and moved back in time cautiously to the mythic aura proffered by the Bible carefully drawing the Jews back into modern linear time by eventually treating historical figures.

Goldfadn's most successful play, *Bar Kokhba*, deals with the last leader of the revolt of the Jews against Rome in 163A.D. and the destruction of the Jewish State and its sovereignty for two thousand years. This play appeared in 1883 at a period of savage political and social repression, for the Tsar Alexander II had been assassinated in 1881. Those who scapegoated the Jews in particular, sponsored programmes against them and introduced special repressive legislation known as the May Laws instigated in 1882.

This play can be read in numerous ways: as a piece of romantic history using the Italian number opera libretto structure fusing a multiple love rivalry, which swirls around the fate of an Israel. It can be seen as an allegory with Russia represented by Rome crushing the Jews and with an implicit proto-Zionist appeals for a resuscitated Israel. Whatever reading chosen, the historical figure of Bar Kokhba looms over the play as a full Jewish hero, even if a tragic figure, who proffers for the first time a full blooded Jewish warrior, lover, fighting for his people and national rights. Here was the Jewish Arjuna who lacked only the Pasupata.

The presence of a newly minted Jewish hero on stage with all the attributes of a normal Gentile hegemonic type forced the Jewish audience into a modern consciousness that it could take responsibility for changing its condition. Goldfadn had forced the Jews to see themselves in the past as a normal people with Kings and aristocrats, landowners and peasants [in Russia Jews were forbidden to own land!], in short, to be sovereign once more. Against the present reality, their condition was subaltern, a mutilated nation in exile. Bar Kokhba the hero must lose against the overwhelming might of Rome and Israelite betrayers but his message is clear: Israel is! The stage restituted Israel whole again to the Jewish audience and the theatre itself had become a microcosmic representation of Israel, a new secular Israel. The synagogue remains sacral still but the new Jewish theatre established a site of modern Jewish consciousness, a place where esthetics renewed a sovereign nation again. Jews, traditionally, were supposed to be passive and await the call of return but theatre proffered other solutions.

The play was swiftly banned and a Ukase in 1883 from Saint Petersburg closed down all Yiddish theatre in Russia. In comparison, Bengali theatre far more swiftly dared to treat "purposive plays" or modern problem plays. The most famous of these plays on the exploitation of the Indians by the British indigo farmers, *Nildurpan* [1872] by Dinabandhu Mitra (1830-1873) was actually produced several times inspite of British colonial agitation and intervention.[8] Censorship was imposed in 1876 by the British Raj but Bengali theatre was never banned outright like Yiddish theatre in Tsarist Russia! (There are even differences in colonial masters!) These types of Biblical, Post-biblical hero plays would find a large development in the freedom of the New York Yiddish Theatre. Such historical plays reenforced the nationalist political dreams and the growth of modern Jewish culture and consciousness. Interestingly, Bengali theatre arrived at historical plays after passing first through gods and epic figures, contemporary domestic types, contemporary problem plays and finally staging historical figures such as Rana, Pratap and Siraj-ud-Doula. D.L. Roy [1863-1913] specialized in historical plays placing Rajput heroes and Moghul Kings on display and can be compared to Goldfadn's historical plays who would have agreed with Roy that "nationalism is not enough," we need "regeneration" – a term most likely borrowed from Max Nordau who developed this concept of national regeneration.[9]

A few years later, Goldfadn was able to perform in Tsarist Russia under the guise of performing "German" theatre and bribing local officials to permit the Jewish plays in Yiddish. But Warsaw, still in the Empire but governed differently, permitted a heavily censored Yiddish theatre.

By this time in the late eighties, modern Jewish culture was surging whether written in Yiddish, Hebrew or even Gentile languages, and following supinely developments in European capitals. The audiences were more sophisticated but Goldfadn's various plays remained popular ironically because they seemed to define diasporic Jewry of an earlier era – even if only ten years earlier! The new Jewish consciousness was oriented toward more complex plays and serious drama by the 1890's. The centre of Yiddish theatre had moved to New York by 1900 and, following the Jewish masses, even Goldfadn settled in New York. Goldfadn found all his former actors now impresarios, leading actors and playwrights who honoured him but kept him out of their theatres. His end was tragic: honoured as The Father of Yiddish Theatre, his songs, performed all over, his plays, brutally adapted with no royalties, he died in poverty but given a hero's funeral by 100,000 Jewish immigrants.

Yankev Gordin was the new serious playwright influenced by Russian theatre who also Judaized Shakespeare, re-making *King Lear* into a contemporary matriarch with the inevitable consequences. In fact Yiddish theatre produced many adaptations of Shakespeare probably inferior to Bengali adaptations for New York Jewish impresarios believed in the thesis called: "translate and improve the play!" Actually Yiddish theatre audiences were scorned as not being sufficiently sophisticated but the Yiddish theatre In New York produced Russian symbolist plays and German expressionist plays before they were performed on Broadway in English. And Yiddish theatre in New York had its own Art Theatre in imitation of the Moscow Art Theatre in Moscow and the Theatre de Lugné Poe in Paris where serious plays were produced for an audience with a full secular modern consciousness. By 1914, Yiddish theatre had helped create a Jewish public receptive to esthetic accomplishment and alert to modern political, social and economic realities in fully western terms and perspectives.

Single-handedly Goldfadn had built a Jewish theatre with a devoted audience, a repertory of plays and a sense of a new secular and esthetic culture and a politically conscious people determined to change their condition. Jewish theatre is one of the most successful examples of a 19th century ethnicity able to transcend its sclerotic religious inhibitions to representation and performance, to create pride in its scorned identity and establish a body of playwrights and actors who in themselves became symbols of the renovating nation. Theatre became the mediator by which a people were able to pass from tradition to modernity, able to witness on stage a restored Israel and people, to remember and recover its past, to recuperate its inheritance and to forge a new template for a new existence. Strikingly it functioned under harsh Russian hegemonic censorship and all political or ideological allusions were necessarily Aesopean. If Jewish theatre reveals its derivative generic forms from the West, and even its thematic concerns, its illustrations and perspective are distinctly its own having preceded the West by two thousand years and therefore makes it one of the originary cultures of the world in its new sari! Indeed, one can say, it has returned to a period when in Alexandria of the first century, Jews were attending Jewish plays in Greek written by Jews.

In this way, the Jews share with the Indians a hoary past of high points and sad points of history and in which its very cultures have gone through vast changes. The return of the Jews to representation performs a défi to the world that the Jews are alive and exist! But more significantly, for themselves they experience a sense of renewal, having recovered an esthetic space to create and challenge themselves to perform visions of their past and future. This is not ethnocentric theatre at all, its structures are hybridic and its vision is universal passing through the particular of the legitimacy of the historical nation to exist and perform its inheritance.

From Moscow to Buenos Aires, from Shanghai, Melbourne to Johannesburg, Yiddish theatre flourished until the Holocaust. But the descendants of Yiddish theatre now carry on in Hebrew, English, French, Spanish and Russian creating a modern Jewish hybridic culture and consciousness. Jewish theatre shares with the various theatres of India and the other great civilizations the joy of regeneration, from one renaissance to the next renaissance.

## Notes

1. For a general overview of Eastern European Jewry, both historical and cultural in English, see Zvi Gitelman. *A Century of Ambivalence: The Jews of Russia and the Soviet Union, 1881-to the Present* (2nd Edition). YIVO Institute of Jewish Research (Bloomington, Indiana: Indiana University Press, 2001.) [The photographs are invaluable.] For an overview of Yiddish Theatre in English, see Nahma Sandrow. *Vagabond Stars: A World History of Yiddish Theater* (New York: Harper and Row, 1977). [multiple editions] For a rapid view of the Purim Play and Yiddish theatre and culture in general, see articles in *Encyclopedia Judaica*. (New York: Macmillan, 1971-72).

2. Yajnik, R.K. *The Indian Theatre*. (New York: E.P. Dutton & Co., 19504, pp. 54-55; Raha, Kironmoy. *Bengali Theatre*. (New Delhi: National Book Trust, 1978), p. 7.

3. Ezekiel of Alexandria (2nd Century, B.C.). *Exodus*. Berlin: J.A. List, 1830. [There are many later editions.]

4. *Bengali Theatre: 200 years.* ed. Utpol K. Banerjee (New Delhi: Publications Division, Ministry of Information and Broadcasting, 1999), p. 257; Yajnik. *op. cit.*, p. 86.

5. Raha, *op. cit.*, p. 16; Rangacharya, Adya. *The Indian Theatre* (New Delhi: National Book Trust, 1971), p. 95.

6. Raha, *ibid.*, p. 23.

7. The *Autobiography* of Abraham Goldfadn is not published in book form but printed only in scattered parts. The best place to read the material alluded to in this article must be in the Yiddish original in the Goldfadn

volume: *Oysgeklibene Shriftn [fun] Avraham Goldfaden*; [the plays, *Shulames* and *Bar Kokhba]*[araynfir un redakts'ye fun Shmu'el Razshanski] (Bu'enos Ayres: Yosef Lifshits-Fund fun der Literatur Gezelshaft baym YIVO, 1963). Autobiography in the volume: "Fun Shmendrik biz Ben Ami: 30 yeriker Epokhe-Gang in der Antviklung fun mayn Yidishn Te'ater-Kind"/Avraham Goldfaden; p. 240-254. Di Muzik fun mayne Gezangshpiln/ Avraham Goldfaden; p. 255-261.No English translations of his plays exist.

8. Raha, *op. cit.*, p. 27.

9. Ibid., p. 64.

# Part V

Subjugation of Identities and Ethnic Icons

# 31

# Tehrik-e-Niswan

## Theatre of Identity

### Asma Mundrawala

Theatre for the community is a phenomenon practised world wide, manifesting itself in a variety of guises and forms. What unifies the diversity, though, is the common emphasis on the personal; stories drawn from the lives of the individual, group or community that street theatre reaches out to. Within its range of practices, street theatre has essentially aimed towards the development of a community and has remained distinguished from high art, commercial mass culture and avant garde theatre.

In lesser developed countries theatre companies and playwrights have often engaged head-on with the establishment in their views on government, reforms, etc. The response of the state has come in the shape of censorship policies, banning, and deliberate measures to control the promotion of critical theatrical activities for reform. The impact of cultural interventions can never be clearly measured and this "[...] is one reason why politicians, economists and various types of development agencies, who usually have control of the purse strings, are so often reluctant, worldwide, to fund cultural expression. [...] (These) agencies may at times fear the uncontrollable nature of creative expression and so, again, be reluctant to support the arts".[1]

The scope of this paper is to look at the practice of a single theatre group from Karachi, the *Tehrik-e-Niswan* (The Women's Movement) in the context of Paulo Freire's theory of conscientization and his ideas on education that encourages dialogue. These theories in turn influenced the work of Augusto Boal[2] who incorporated Freire's ideas into his revolutionary theatre practices. Boal and Freire both belong to Brazil and their concerns are similar to those in other lesser-developed countries like India and Pakistan. Both theorists argue that in order to emancipate the oppressed it is essential to make them part of a dialogue that allows them to critically reflect upon their conditions. While the work of *Tehrik-e-Niswan* does not involve direct participation in the manner Boal advocates, the reasons for this are complex and multi faceted. State oppression towards the promulgation of culture, and social and political biases, have all combined to create setbacks for theatre in Pakistan. *Tehrik-e-Niswan's* practice then, does not include direct participation on the part of the audience, but its plays aim to build a platform that allows an audience to think about the issues that are raised.

There is evidence of considerable theatrical activity in (what is now) Pakistan in the pre-partition years. Apart from the folk tradition of singers and storytellers performing in villages and fairs around the rural areas of the region, there existed a western-influenced theatre inherited from the British colonisers which existed here since the 19th century. One of its manifestations was the Parsi[3] theatre, described as a confluence of Victorian melodrama and indigenous music and dance,[4] that drew on an old repertoire of Indian classics in addition to new social dramas and western imports, especially popularised versions of Shakespeare. After the collapse of Muslim rule in India, and the disappearance of the court as a social institution, the means of sustaining dramatic activity became concentrated in the economic networks for entertainment that were developing in the cities. The Parsi theatre was the foremost in these activities. The English-style playhouses erected by the British in Bombay and Calcutta were later used by the Parsi companies that took over the material culture of European theatre. Using the proscenium set-up with western furniture, props, costumes and a variety of mechanical devices to create special effects, the Parsi theatre embraced all things European, yet simultaneously revealed a distinct Indian characteristic, employing song and dance, and using Indian subject matter for its plays. In their widespread travels, Parsi theatre groups travelled across India between Bombay, Lahore, Karachi, Peshawar, Delhi, Calcutta and Madras.

In the 1930s one of the developments that had a significant impact on the development of theatre in Pakistan was the founding of the Indian People's Theatre Association (IPTA). This left-wing group encouraged dramatic writing in a more European style. It promoted a more socially rooted culture and had branches across the subcontinent, including Karachi and Lahore. Through its plays IPTA encouraged the continuing struggles for independence from the British. The plays were performed indoors as well as in streets or parks. With independence in 1947, most Hindu or non-Muslim IPTA members left Karachi and Lahore taking most of the serious theatre with them. However one of them, Safdar Mir, who had left Lahore in 1945, returned to Pakistan in 1948 and reorganised the Drama Club at the Government College in 1951. The GCDC introduced the seriousness of the IPTA group to many young students, and some of them subsequently made significant contributions to modern theatre in Pakistan.[5] While there were exponents of theatre in Karachi who did a lot for its promotion in the 50s and 60s,[6] their efforts did not continue after their deaths and theatre never really established itself as an institution in Pakistan. In the 70s, colleges and universities maintained some theatrical activity. This cannot be attributed to the failure of the medium, because theatre still exists in the folk traditions in rural areas of the country. Its failure can be looked at in view of the cultural decay that set in gradually with the inception of Pakistan as an independent country.

When Martial Law was enforced by General Zia-ul-Haque in 1977, there existed two kinds of theatre in Karachi; the commercial slapstick comedy, and the elite theatre that catered to an upper middle-class audience.[7] The only socially conscious theatre that existed then was headed by Ali Ahmed, whose group NATAK (National Academy of Theatrical Arts Karachi) (translated as "play"), was partially funded by the Bhutto regime. With the fall of that regime, and the group's patronage and support removed, it gradually disintegrated under the pressures of the Martial Law era. In the wake of this polarisation between the slapstick theatre and the anglicised elite theatre, another tradition of theatre emerged in the 80s, established by people who were political agitators. In 1981, a group called *Dastak* was formed, and this was also the time when *Tehrik-e-Niswan* was established by Khalid Ahmad and Sheema Kermani. It was *Dastak* that proved to be the turning point in Karachi's theatre history. Due to its political background, *Dastak* attracted many political activists, and its low priced tickets made it accessible to many political workers. *Tehrik-e-Niswan* joined in with plays that were politically relevant, and dealt primarily with women's issues. The Martial Law era in fact created an atmosphere for dissent through theatre and at the time of Zia's death there were at least eight theatre groups in Karachi, only two of which existed from pre Martial Law days.[8]

*Tehrik-e-Niswan's* role can be seen as adapting a cultural form that allows disenfranchised people to raise their voices. It must be made clear here that while the term "street theatre" may imply that the plays are performed unannounced in the streets of Karachi, this is a condition that the group cannot adhere to given the political nature of the plays and lack of state support to theatre activities which makes such a performance impossible. The group works very methodically with other NGOs in low-income community areas and is invited to perform on predetermined dates. *Tehrik-e-Niswan* prefers to call its form of theatre *mobile theatre.*

*Tehrik-e-Niswan* was formed in 1980 as a response to the anti-women laws passed by the Zia-ul-Haque regime and the conse-quent encroachments it had on women's rights. These highly discriminatory laws against women singled them out for attack and degraded their status in an already patriarchal society. The idea behind *TN* was to create a dialogue and awareness about women and their status in society in such circumstances.

Establishing a movement focussing on women's rights was relevant to its members in light of the repressive conditions that emerged in the time of General Zia-ul-Haque's regime. *TN*'s launch was simultaneous to the beginning of the Women's Movement in Pakistan, which came into being in 1979 after discriminatory laws against women were promulgated. The so-called Islamisation[9] process was directed towards making women and minorities second-class citizens of Pakistan. For instance, " [...] the evidence of two women was considered to be equal to that of one man. The testimony of four adult Muslim males was required for the *hudd*[10] punishment. A female victim received only half the compensation as that of a male and women and members of minority faiths were disallowed from being appointed judges."[11] The overall impact of these laws was more intense. Apart from reinforcing the patriarchal bent of the society, they encouraged the Islamic clergy and religious parties to create the space for an anti-women environment.

In 1979, the Hudood Ordinance was promulgated as a first step in Zia's so-called Islamisation process. The Ordinance covered adultery, fornication, rape and prostitution (*Zina*)[12], bearing false testimony (*Qazf*), theft and drinking alcoholic beverages. It contained a section relating to the manner in which punishments were to be executed. The implications of this ordinance were not to come to light until 1981 when a session's judge sentenced a man and a woman to being stoned to death and a hundred lashes respectively under the provisions of this Ordinance. Amongst the educated section of the society, the reaction of women to this was that of outrage.[13]

This onslaught was challenged by the formation of Women's Action Forum in 1981 in Karachi, with Lahore and Islamabad consequently following suit. *Tehrik-e-Niswan* then, under whose banner plays about the plight of women began to be staged, in a sense, became the cultural wing of the women's movement in Pakistan. It was in this background that *Tehrik's* first play, *Dard Kay Faaslay* (Distances of Pain), was performed in 1981 for an all-women audience in a shopping centre in one of Karachi's populous middle-class areas. Despite the active atmosphere of the market, the play drew a gripped audience, moved by the issues that it found close to its lives. The play adapted from a short story by the playwright Amrita Pritam, revolves around the laws of the land and how they affect the women who live in it. The positive response the play received convinced the members of *TN* that performing arts was in fact a powerful medium to convey ideas, and strengthened their belief in the effectiveness of the medium for communication and consciousness raising.[14]

Since 1981, *TN* has been presenting plays under its Mobile Theatre Programme, in middle-class and low-income areas of Karachi. A team of performers travels to different areas at the request of various Non-Government Organisations (NGOs) working specifically in those localities. In meeting its aim to work for the attainment of rights denied to women, *TN* focuses first towards the comprehension of these problems, bringing out amongst all sections of society an awareness of women's rights. This presents a two-fold struggle for the group. Apart from some cultural barriers that the notion of performance holds as a result of social and religious reasons, and the discouraging environment towards the arts in the country, there is a general lack of education that is prevalent in the population at large and specifically amongst women. However this illiteracy determines and aids *TN's* method of spreading consciousness, and the employment of an artistic means becomes mainly practical as opposed to the use of seminars and lectures for a largely uneducated audience.

The audience of the mobile plays in these low-income areas is predominantly female, and the work-force here comprises of industrial workers or people doing small jobs in various service sectors. The performances, which are held free of cost, are of short duration (usually between 30 to 50 minutes) and are often based around real life issues drawn from the lives of people of these localities. The productions are devised to remain simple so that they may be performed conveniently in small spaces at short notice. The aspect of entertainment remains an important feature of the *TN* plays that face strong competition from television, cable TV and video, all easily accessible within homes. Meaningful theatre then presents quite a challenge that can only be met by making the form and presentation of the play entertaining. Traditional story telling techniques and conventions borrowed from the sub-continental folk traditions of *Yatra*, *Nautanki* and *Tamasha* are incorporated using song and dance as part of the narrative.

One of the important aspects of these performances is a post-performance discussion that is held between the audience, the cast and *TN* members each time. While these discussions vary from area to area and depend more on the nature of the audience, there is often a general reluctance to speak up initially. This response stems from a number of reasons pertaining to the place theatre and other performing arts have in Pakistani culture, and the general inhibition Pakistani society imposes on women. This inhibition is essentially a part of the oppression women experience at the hands of the patriarchal system that renders them fearful of protest.

*Tehrik-e-Niswan's* work and the response to it are often affected because of the general approach towards culture in the society, a matter that stems from a multiple of reasons. One of the problems is rooted in the composition of the ruling classes that have governed Pakistan since 1947.[15] Of its near fifty-five year history, Pakistan has been ruled by military dictatorships for nearly twenty-seven years.[16] The brief interludes of civilian rule have been dominated by people from feudal backgrounds. Neither of these set-ups could look at serious cultural activities with any sense of security because of their potential power to challenge and question. The hostile attitude of each successive government manifested itself in the form of obstacles such as the imposition of police and excise clearance, censorship policies (every script of a staged play is required to be sent for scrutiny before obtaining clearance), and the procurement of a No Objection Certificate.

Interestingly enough, founding member Khalid Ahmad purports the idea that a major hurdle in the path of the development of theatre specifically and of all the performing arts at large, stems from the establishment's efforts to ascertain a cultural identity that is totally distinct from that of India. Years of combined history are swept aside along with everything that may be part of a combined heritage. "The arts suffered the most through this policy because everything that was being done on the other side of the border was discarded as being 'Indian' or 'Hindu'."[17] Being a theatre practitioner himself, Ahmad resents the parallel availability of Indian movie videos and the accessibility of Indian satellite channels to the population at large, and sees it as a deliberate overall policy to discourage serious challenging activities. This is further substantiated by the in-built prejudices that the middle class society has towards the performing arts. This stems partly from the fact that in the pre-partition days, theatre was promoted by the Hindu middle classes that lived along with the Muslims in Sindh.[18] The cultural scenario was determined largely by them until Partition, when they migrated to India. The Muslim middle class in the region regarded the performing arts with disdain and considered participation in it unworthy of middle class respectability.[19] As a result of the strict biases against cultural activities that prevail in society, especially against the performing arts, theatre faces resistance from society in general. Singers, musicians, actors and dancers are derided and often reduced to the status of mere entertainers. It would be important to note here that while the English press in Pakistan covers theatre on a regular basis, the Urdu press ignores it completely. Founding member Kermani points out that while these cultural missions are set up in Pakistan with the objective to raise awareness and promote their own cultural heritage, they are the only institutions that are doing anything to serve culture in the cities.[20] It goes without saying that in these circumstances theatre does not exist as an institution in Pakistan. In the absence of venues or schools for performing arts, there are no full-time actors or people specialising in other areas of a production.

Given the setbacks *TN* faces in using theatre as a tool for social development, its task is indeed a challenging one. However it is through this very medium that openings are created in the minds of the audience. By bringing issues close to the lives of the audience, serious reflection towards their situation is encouraged, and there is an opening of direct involvement through the process of discussion and debate. While Freire believes that critical dialogue must be carried on with the oppressed at every stage, it should not be substituted by monologue, slogans or communiqués, because this in effect is an attempt to liberate the oppressed with the instruments of domestication.[21]

The fact that *TN* uses its plays to bring forth issues would not have been enough for the audience it wishes to engage with. The plays without their post-performance discussions would have substituted the monologues Freire speaks of. It is the engaging of the audience with the issues during and after that encourage the serious reflection deemed necessary towards the act of liberation.

Given the complexities faced by *TN* in taking plays to various localities, the group finds it essential to first build up a relationship of trust with the communities and the locals before venturing to take a theatre performance there. In view of the general environment created for theatre in the country *TN* is unable to spontaneously stage unscheduled performances in public areas and there is a lot of fieldwork and preparation involved before a play is taken to a locality. This may include going into these areas, talking to the community members, to the women, maybe about their problems too, essentially building up a relationship that goes beyond a performance.

Since 1997 *TN* has reviewed its Mobile Theatre policy by focussing on a limited number of communities, which are visited on a regular basis, rather than a wide range of community visits. This has created a relationship with the audience and inhabitants of the community so that audience participation in discussions has gradually grown to a more comfortable level and has allowed the group to assess the impact of its work in a more effective way.

*Tehrik-e-Niswan* first gets in touch with a Non-Government Organisation that assists it in getting in touch with Community Based Organisations that may be working under the umbrella of the larger NGO. The CBO's and smaller NGO's are the groups that are involved in working directly with communities, running schools, health centres, adult literacy centres etc in various low income areas. Since these are the people who are in direct touch with the communities, they are able to provide a Community Focal Person to act as a mediator between *TN* and the community. They provide assistance from setting up initial meetings to identifying or providing performance spaces either in their own premises, in private homes of people in the community or in other non formal spaces like halls, churches, courtyards of buildings etc.

One of the communities *TN* has worked with chiefly consists primarily of second and third generation migrants from India. Located near the peripheries of the city, Orangi is the largest unplanned settlement in Karachi since 1965, and is home to immigrant groups from India, Bangladesh, the Punjab, and Northern areas of Pakistan.[22] The Orangi Welfare Project is the link for *TN* in this area and is a team of people who work for the social reform of society in Orangi.

The endeavour to make an audience participate has not been an easy task initially. It has required the efforts of the CBOs as well as the theatre group to create an atmosphere of trust in the first place. The very fact that women are able to collect in one place for an event is an encouraging sign for the NGOs working in the communities. Working with communities has had its own series of setbacks. There have been occasions when a lot of field preparation work has gone to waste because a certain community is not prepared to welcome a theatre group in its midst. Such a conservative response may come in the form of objections put forth by the male members of a community who do not wish to allow their women go to a play. This reluctance usually stems from traditional ideas of not allowing women to step out of the house, rather than fearing the content of the plays. One such community, which is also one of *TN*'s target focus areas, is the Qasba Colony. Situated a little further north of Orangi, its population comprises mainly of migrant Pathans[23] and is largely uneducated. The CBO for this area is a group of fifty individuals working under the name BRIGHT. Despite the efforts of BRIGHT to create an opening in the area for *TN*, no headway was made because of the conservative mentality of the Pathan members. It was often the case that a certain performance was held at first for the male members to convince them of the harmlessness of such an activity and another was held later for women after it was met with the approval of the men. On one occasion, a performance in Qasba was held for both men and women with a tent pulled in the centre of the audience to segregate it. The breakthrough was considered to be a starting point for *TN* to show more plays in this locality. This however was a difficult task as *TN* met with resistance and stopped performing there subsequently.

Despite these hurdles an unmistakable attitudinal change is seen as many women break free of their shackles and speak out against deeply entrenched male chauvinism. The plays in *TN's* repertoire focus on the marginalized lives of the women, with subtle political undertones, questioning officially prescribed gender roles and a lop-sided moral system.[24] "After each performance there is an interaction with the people who are watching so that we can find out how they have felt about the [...] issues raised. (Through the discussion) We try to locate more issues so that we can try them in our next plays."[25] As a result, many women raise issues that not only question the system around them but their own conforming nature towards it. At one particular performance in Orangi where I was present as a performer, one woman profoundly brought to attention the fact that women themselves were responsible for the chauvinistic attitude of men in their families because of the way they were raised by the women, empowering them at the disadvantage of their own daughters.

The strength of community theatre lies in the fact that it brings forth issues that are close to the hearts of the audience. However *TN* believes that this in itself is not enough to capture the attention of the audience. In order to contest with the culture of television and video, the content, form, and presentation of its plays have to be powerful. Apart from a strong emphasis on the design aspect of each production, a great deal of attention is given to the quality of writing of each script. Careful consideration is devoted to the colour coordination of the costumes to reflect the mood of the plays and props are designed not only to facilitate the narrative but also support the form of the play. In the presentation of its plays, the *TN* "employs a whole range of theatrical devices, borrowing freely from sub continental traditions such as the *Yatra, Nautanki and Tamasha*"[26] and its plays are a devised mixture of song-dance, story telling techniques juxtaposed with the use of colourful costumes to appeal to the audience.[27] The presence of the storyteller brings the audience closer to the narrative and its participants as he acts as a mediator between the two.

While the ultimate aim of *Tehrik-e-Niswan* is to encourage members of a community to form their own theatre groups and produce plays based on their issues, it seems an arduous task in the circumstances described previously. Where the group faces difficulties in some circumstances to simply draw the women out of the homes to view a play, it is optimistic to think that they might be ready after a few performances to participate in the activity themselves. Given that Orangi was one area where a lot of work had been devoted towards building a relationship with the community, *TN* tried to initiate a workshop for the women. However the attempts were unsuccessful when the women were not allowed to participate in theatre workshops due to family restraints.[28]

The apprehension towards the performing arts may partially stem from the conservative nature of the lower middle-class societies. This along with some religious biases against song and dance makes the entire idea of participation in performance at any level problematic for the majority of the population. Yet on another level, the city of Karachi offers a rich array of visual elements on a popular level where there is a common interest in decoration, graffiti, which infiltrates the lives of people at every level. The highly decorated trucks and other modes of transport that ply the country and the instinctual response to a rich visual vocabulary is inescapable in any part of Pakistan. The rural areas of Sindh are rich with traditions of the Sufic culture, where there is an extreme reverence of saints throughout the province. Traditions of song and performance are part of the Sufic traditions. Essentially there has been evidence of less inhibition towards performance in the rural areas compared to the city where *TN* visits its audiences.

This is evident in the example of a rural group of performers in Sindh, who members of *TN* worked with for theatre workshops. The NGO – LSRDA (Lower Sindh Rural Development Association) in Mirpur Khas – is a vivid example of the contrast of response to theatre workshops and mobile performances in the city and the villages. Working with farmers since 1975, the group reaches out to underdeveloped villages that sometimes have no electricity. While the initial mode of operation was for the group leader to take video recordings of programmes on farming to the villages, he found that the method was not interesting enough to capture the attention of the villagers. Funded by the NGO Church World Services, LSRDA invited *TN* practitioners including Kermani and Ahmad to conduct workshops with its members. The theatre group that evolved in 1999 from this consists of the local people and their families, ranging from ages 8 to 25. Their plays are about the common problems that the farmers face, including suicide, population, and the environment. The plays attract an entire village, sometimes reaching up to 600 people. The response of the audience is evident of the form's acceptability. There is no resistance or suspicion towards the plays, as compared to the varied response to *TN*'s mobile plays in the city. By bringing these issues to the villagers in a language they can relate to, the medium becomes increasingly effective. The script is developed by the group members based on the problems of the villagers. Songs that are inserted were initially drawn from films but are now written by the group. In the last three years, the group has developed ten plays on a range of issues.[29]

For the moment *TN* has turned it attention towards community theatre workshops for the workers and leaders of the Community Based Organisations that it works with. The aim of these workshops is to introduce participants to various elements of theatre, and evolve plays around improvisation and role-play. These workshops help the CBO and NGO workers to integrate theatre techniques into their everyday work, to ease communication and help break down barriers.[30]

The use of theatre in community development has several aspects. Apart from raising awareness, it is a means of collective self-reflection. Since the plays that result in such workshops are created by the community members/workers themselves, it is a process of tapping into their creative energies. It allows for the members to draw upon their own resources for stories. The potential for collective creativity offers immense possibilities of breaking down inhibitions, leading to heightened communication and a harmonious working atmosphere.

In its assessment of the impact of its work since 1997, *Tehrik-e-Niswan* has found a growing acceptance of its cultural work. This is reflected by the fact that today *TN* collaborates with thirty-five organisations that regularly invite it to complement their development work by introducing the cultural aspect. Compared to its early years of work, *TN* now sees many NGO's and development agencies that it can collaborate with and that seem convinced of this method of approach. "[...] Evaluating the impact of cultural work [...] and bringing about a change in people's thinking and behaviour though cultural interventions is very different from all other material development work in that, unlike the latter, the effect of the former is not easily quantifiable. It is a process of changing minds and values which works in imperceptible ways and it is difficult to say [...] in which manner cultural experiences affect the people."[31] Yet it is seen that in certain communities, where *TN* has established a regular presence through its Mobile Theatre Programme, there is a change in the attitude of the audience, especially that of women. They seem more outspoken and vocal in the postproduction discussions. "*TN* has forged a great rapport with the *khaddi* (loom) weaver women in Lyari (Karachi). Some of the teachers from the Orangi School talk to us very uninhibitedly about themselves and their problems."[32] There has been a steady increase of demand for *TN's* work by NGO's working at grassroots, and its receptivity has increased over the years. Through its Community Theatre Programme and workshops, *TN* has reached out to teachers, health workers, and community workers at large who are now using the tools introduced by *TN* to work in their own communities.[33] Freire suggests that the task of revolutionary leaders is not to go to the people with a message of salvation, but rather to come to understand through dialogue with them both their objective situation and their awareness of it. Positive results cannot be expected from any political/educational/cultural action programme which fails to recognise and respect the particular worldview of the world held by the people it reaches out to. Such a programme, no matter how well intentioned, can only be referred to as cultural invasion.[34] By collaborating with the community workers who often come from the communities they serve, *TN* tries to understand and draw from their world view in order to model its own understanding of the people it works with.

It has been a long battle of struggle for *Tehrik-e-Niswan* against the state, against attitudes, and cultural and religious biases. While it may yet find itself in the first stage of this struggle, it has sustained itself through these complex situations over the last twenty years and evolved according to the changing nature of the society it works with, gradually and subtly making its voice heard.

## Notes

1. Richard Boon and Jane Plastow (eds.), *Theatre Matters, Performance and Culture on World Stage*, Cambridge University Press, UK, 1998, p. 2.

2. A theatre practitioner who in the late sixties worked with Freire's literacy campaigns and incorporated the ideas into his theatre practice.

3. The Parsis practice the pre-Islamic Persian religion founded by Zoroaster. They emigrated from Iran to Gujarat in the 8th century and settled in Bombay under British encouragement after 1660. In the 19th century they achieved prominence in law, education, business and became one of the more westernised communities of India. Cited in Kathryn Hansen,

*Grounds for play. The Nautanki Theatre of India.* University of California Press, 1992, pp. 321-22.

4. Khalid Ahmad, "The Story So Far", *Tuesday Review*, Karachi, 25 February-3 March 1997, p. 4.

5. Don Rubin, *The World Encyclopaedia of Contemporary Theatre*, Volume 5, Asia Pacific, Routledge. London and New York, 2000, p. 357.

6. In 1948 in Lahore, a privately operated Pakistan Arts Council was created for the promotion of the arts, since the government was preoccupied with establishing other national institutions. Its founders included the poet Faiz Ahmed Faiz, writer Imtiaz Ali Taj, and the painter A.R. Chughtai. Its first play *Mera Qatil* (My Killer) was produced in 1955 and very soon the PAC was the centre of theatrical activity in Lahore. In Karachi the Drama Guild was founded in 1952 by writer – director Khwaja Moenuddin, whose plays dealt with the problems of the migrants from India and attacked the lack of any real change in the values and attitudes in the new Pakistan. His play *Naya Nishan* (New Mark) in 1954 referred to the situation in Kashmir and was written during the negotiations between India and Pakistan about Kashmir's future. It was banned by the then government. Also in the 1950s, a totally non-professional group appeared in Peshawar as part of several "Islamic" theatre groups. The Socrates Dramatic Club staged productions each year on themes of significance to Islam and national pride. In the late 60s there was a popular movement for democracy, which saw the creation of a number of plays. A leftist leader Major Ishaq Mohammed wrote *Mussali* (Sweeper) in Punjabi. The play was performed in lower class neighbourhoods in Punjab, which included several performances by the sweepers themselves. Another writer, Sarmad Sehbai wrote several plays in this period that depicted the spirit of rebellion that characterised these times. Rubin, ibid., p. 358.

7. Imran Shirvanee, "The Emergence of the Third Force", *The News International*, Karachi, 22 July 1994.

8. Shirvanee, ibid.

9. General Zia ul Haque imposed Martial Law in Pakistan in July 1977. Drawing from his own takeover speech at that point Islam did not seem to be in any particular danger. On the contrary Martial Law had been imposed to 'avert a national crisis' with a promise to hold elections in 90 days. Instead, nine months after assuming power, Zia ul Haque voiced his intentions to Islamise the penal code of Pakistan as a first step towards establishing a truly Islamic state. It became evident suddenly in his speeches that Zia considered that Islam was endangered and it was imperative to first ensure the supremacy of the religion before the country could be entrusted to civilian rule. Islam was being used to justify Martial Law while most

political parties were against it. Having assumed power without authority, the army was now looking for means to prolong its rule and found the perfect excuse in Islam. Zia revitalised the Council of Islamic Ideology, which under the 1973 Constitution had the mandate to review existing laws and make recommendations for bringing them in line with Islam. The Council was expanded, and packed with conservative members of the clergy. Subsequently, the most reactionary suggestions especially regarding women came from this body.

Khawar Mumtaz and Fareeda Shaheed (eds.),"Zia and the Creation of WAF", *Women of Pakistan. Two Steps Forward, One Step Back,* London and New Jersey, Zed Books Ltd., 1987, pp. 15-17.

10. Means literally, *the limit,* and is used in Muslim jurisprudence to denote that punishment which has been prescribed in the Quran for a particular crime and is therefore deemed the maximum punishment awardable.

11. Anis Haroon, "Time for Reassessment", *Books and Authors, DAWN newspaper*, Karachi, 3 March 2000, p. 1.

12. The Hudood ordinance made *zina* an offence against the state, unlike the British law hitherto in force, which considered adultery a matter of personal offence against the husband.

13. Mumtaz and Shaheed (eds.), ibid., p. 73.

14. *Tehrik-e-Niswan Cultural Action Group. Women's Development through Theatre and Television. TN* Publicity Brochure.

15. Khalid Ahmad, ibid, p. 5.

16. The Military dictatorships in Pakistan are as follows: Ayub Khan, October'58–April'69, Yahya Khan, April'69–December'71, Zia-ul-Haque, July'77–Aug.'88, Pervaiz Musharraf, October.'99–present.

17. Ahmad, ibid., p. 6.

18. One of four provinces of Pakistan. Karachi is the capital of Sindh.

19. Ahmad, ibid., p. 6.

20. Rizwan Tufail, "Spotlight on Theatre. Sheema Kermani", *Tuesday Review,* Karachi, 25 February-3 March 1997.

21. Paulo Freire, *Pedagogy of the Oppressed*, translated by Myra Bergman Ramos, Penguin Books, 1996, p. 47.

22. *Tehrik-e-Niswan Mobile Theatre Report*, Quarter II, yr I, April–June 2000.

23. A tribe from the North West Frontier Province of Pakistan.

24. Adnan Sattar, "All the Street's a Stage", *The News on Sunday*, Karachi, 30 April 2000.

25. Sheema Kermani, Founder Member, *Tehrik-e-Niswan*, in discussion, Documentary "Mobile Theatre, *Tehrik-e-Niswan*", 30 minutes, 2000, colour. Produced by *Tehrik-e-Niswan.*

26. Khusro Mumtaz, "More Please", *The Friday Times*, Pakistan, 15-21 December 1994, p. 16.

27. *TN* Documentary, ibid.

28. *Tehrik-e-Niswan Mobile Theatre Report*, Quarter II, year I, April-June 2000.

29. Salman Rashid, "Desert Drama", www.jang.com.pk/thenews accessed 9 June 02.

30. *Tehrik-e-Niswan. Community Theatre and Creative Expression for Women's Development, 3-Year Project Report*, December 1996–February 2000, Karachi.

31. "*Tehrik-e-Niswan*'s Three year Project: An Overview". *Tehrik-e-Niswan. Community Theatre and Creative Expression for Women's Development, 3 Year Project Report*, Dec 1996–Feb 2000, Karachi.

32. Kermani, e-mail interview, 1 June 02–6 June 02.

33. *Tehrik-e-Niswan. Community Theatre and Creative Expression for Women's Development, 3-Year Project Report*, December 1996–February 2000, Karachi, ibid.

# 32

## Emptying the Sea by the Bucketful

### A Difficult Phase in Cambodian Theatre or the Creation of a Culture of Dependency[1]

#### Catherine Diamond

At the Royal University of Performing Arts in Phnom Penh[2] the cars slowly roll up the main drive heading straight to the pavilion where the performers of the Cambodian classical dance train.[3] On either side of the road, the other theatre forms are bypassed with nary a glance – *yike*, the traditional dance drama; *bassac*, the Sino-Vietnamese musical drama, and *lakhaoun niyeay*,[4] the spoken or modern drama.[5] The teachers and students alike look longingly at the cars bearing "rich foreign sponsors" as they arrive and leave without acknowledging their existence.

The theatre performers contend that the country is now too poor to support them and that their local community base, devastated by the Khmer Rouge, has not recovered under the present government. They see foreign support as their only hope and live in expectation of its eventual arrival rather than developing a self-reliant approach. Since 1991, Cambodia has received more international aid than any other Asian country. Why, after receiving so many millions of dollars, do Cambodians seem poorer than they were in 1989 when the caretaker Vietnamese rule pulled out of their country? Why do the artists seem to show so little initiative and passively wait for outside help? Is it possible for once-popular arts to develop while relying so heavily on foreign direction, collaboration, and aid, or have foreign donors, despite the best of intentions, been in some way responsible for creating and continuing a culture of dependency?

Western interest in the classical dance over and above the other dramatic forms is not new. Ever since 1906, when King Sisowath was brought to France with an entourage of forty dancers in order to lend authenticity to the spectacular replica of the royal palace at the Colonial Exhibition in Marseille, the court dancers have sustained an exotic image in the occidental mind.[6] The dancers, along with Angkor Wat, are not only the most enduring images of Cambodia, but also have continued to be of supreme national significance. The temples are currently its greatest, and virtually only, money earner (except for foreign aid) and the classical dance, too, is both an important attraction within the country and an export commodity.

Although Cambodians from all walks of life suffered under the Pol Pot regime, the particular decimation of the court dance inspired outside donors to contribute to its restoration, which would not only elevate Cambodia's international prestige, but would also resurrect a desired image formerly cultivated by both the Cambodian kings and the French colonial protectorate. Elegant and subtle, it represents only one aspect of Cambodian culture, and one distant from the majority of the population. Moreover, requiring no language, the dance can be appreciated for its own aesthetic value or adapted to a familiar text, such as *Othello*, for foreign touring.[7] This promotion of an ancient and courtly art at the expense of stimulating a contemporary artistic impulse from the (once) popular arts might leave the country more culturally bereft than if no aid was given at all. The exclusive support for the dance might perpetuate a backward glance rather than encourage a forward vision.

*Yike*, as the oldest of the three theatre forms, has also been at pains to stress its antiquity, claiming that its origins date from *before* the Angkor period. Legend, however, maintains that it gained its most characteristic attribute, the frame drum, from the Angkor King Jayavarman It's ninth century trip to Java. Other scholars contend that *yike* was not known in Cambodia until 1876. Initially a presentation of dance and song with specific gestures, *yike* developed narration and plotted dialogue based on regional legends. Though it shares some characteristics with the Malay *jikey* and the Thai *likay*, *yike* is set apart from other Cambodian forms by the dominating pulse of the drum.

*Yike* always begins with the *ham ron*, a song and dance paean to past teachers and masters of the art. Described as "soft" by its proponents, *yike* stresses gentleness, so that even the scenes with struggles or fights are so highly stylized that the violence is minimal. The story proper often involves court figures of both local and foreign lands, but common people are also represented in the chorus. Nearly as important as the male and female leads are the two clowns who constitute a funny man-straight man combo. They often play servants within the story, but also step outside of their dramatic roles to deliver purely comic shtick.

*Yike* is primarily emotion and spectacle. While song and gestural movement dominate the style, the longer portions of spoken dialogue are in verse and short conversations are colloquial and open to improvisation. In the past, *yike* took its plots from stories about mythological relations with nature, historical events or personages, and well-known legends. *Tum and Teav* (Tum Teav) is perhaps the most popular *yike*. Based on a sixteenth-century love story, it is considered the Cambodian *Romeo and Juliet*. Tum, a poor monk, loves Teav, a girl from a wealthy home. Although he is a brilliant poet, the girl's mother who wants her to marry a rich man, prevents their union. *Yike* performers also have adapted modern themes. They keep the traditional tunes and stylized movement, but incorporate contemporary dialogue when the material concerns such social issues as the story of a girl from the countryside being sold into prostitution to work at the Thai border. It was during the PRK years (1979-89) that *yike* performers were first put to use disseminating populist messages and communist propaganda. Many performers now look back at that period as a golden one of activity, popularity and integration into the social structure. In the current period of political instability caused by rival politicians who collaborate with members of the Khmer Rouge and by lack of governmental support, they have not been able to recapture a sustained local following.

In the early twentieth century a new form, *bassac*, challenged *yike*'s popularity. Originating in the Bassac river basin it is derived from *hat boi*, the Vietnamese adaptation of Chinese theatre that supposedly entered Vietnam during the Mongol Yuan dynasty (1279-1368). Both *bassac* and *hat boi* are characterized by modified versions of Chinese face painting, martial art (*kabat*), acrobatic movement (*hun*), and the musical accompaniment of drums, chimes, gongs and wood blocks. In the same period when *bassac* was gaining popularity, all traditional forms began borrowing the French concept of "set" or "*decors*" from the emerging spoken drama and *bassac* and *yike* continue today to use canvas backdrops.

One of *bassac*'s developments was that the actors themselves sang rather than depending on an offstage chorus and a speaking narrator to describe the action before it was performed. But the present inclusion of the offstage chorus and narrator demonstrates how much it has merged with *yike*. *Bassac* also allowed for more naturalistic and strong movement on stage compared with the slow-flowing *yike*. Performers often traveled to give all-night shows at temple festivals but this source of income has nearly dried up. While a single story could last a week or a month, once lodged in permanent buildings, performances became shorter and were popular with urban working classes. Drawing upon legends common to the whole region and folk philosophy, its plots and characters were adapted to local tastes. While in Vietnamese *hat boi* villains are often Chinese, in bassac, they are Vietnamese.

Initially *bassac* did not attract the upper classes or the intellectuals, who were more drawn to the spoken drama. But *bassac* enjoyed a short revival in 1986 when Cheng Pon, the then Minister of Culture and Fine Arts staged a performance of *Saing Selchey*, an epic story based on a *jataka* – Buddhist rebirth stories. *Saing Selchey* involves three brothers who had been forced into exile because of their unusual attributes: one is half-human, half-elephant; another half-human and half-snail, and the third is a boy born with a bow and arrow in his hands. When the king's sister is abducted by the ogre king, the exiled brothers are called to the rescue. However, unlike Sita in the *Ramayana*, the abducted woman has had a child and appears to be content with her ogre husband. Still she is forced by the brothers to return to her homeland or face decapitation. Frequently such "happy endings" seem only to consider a male point of view.[8] *Bassac* performances are shown every Saturday afternoon on television but all the former *bassac* theatres have been destroyed and there is no regular live performance.

Spoken drama in Cambodia, as elsewhere in Asia, is primarily the result of contact with Western-style realism in the early twentieth century, and while it does not have deep roots in the rural population, it is an important reflection of the nationalistic aspirations of the educated urban populace. Spoken drama's emphasis on the dissemination of ideas, principally ideas critical of some aspect of the status quo, make it the mouthpiece of intellectuals and an activity eyed with suspicion by the authorities when not under their control. In the 1930s, the actors, mostly students and teachers, experimented with, translated and adapted works of Molière, Chekhov, and Shakespeare. But when *lakhaoun niyeay* took contemporary life as its subject, it almost inevitably came into conflict with the authorities.

A common device for the theatre was to draw from the reserve of local folk tales but rewrite the moral message to provoke thought from the audience. A spoken version of *Tum and Teav* became a more obvious social critique about the discrepancy between rich and poor. Another drama adapted a folk tale that relates how an impoverished couple who, desiring the treasures they believe exist at the bottom of the sea, begin to empty it bucketful by bucketful. This example of Herculean silliness that originally attacked greed and simplicity was exploited in the new version to suggest a means to overcoming obstacles. The Naga king ruling under the water, being as foolish as the couple, fears that they might actually succeed in draining the sea and offers them some pearls to cease their labors. So, in fact, they do gain the treasures they were seeking. Thus a story that once ridiculed their action had been revised to suggest that although one's dream might appear foolish, if pursued with conviction it might become reality, thereby encouraging initiative and pursuit of one's goal in adversity.[9]

However, the greatest support for modern drama remains foreign embassies and various NGOs who know theatre to be a useful vehicle for social messages. One important recent example is *A Wounded Life*, written by three teachers at the university. Created in collaboration with the Women's Media Center of Cambodia and the Cambodian Women's Crisis Center, sponsored by U.S.A.I.D. (an agency of the American State Department) working through The Asia Foundation and in collaboration with UNESCO, the play deals with the trafficking in women. It focuses particularly on the deception practiced in the villages in order to entice girls into prostitution through a well-known and trusted "auntie". The script contains little in the way of creativity or innovation, and follows the model of the melodramatic socialist realist play, complete with victimized drug-addicted girls, corrupt local police, and a "heroic" rescue team stressing the assistance and cooperation of concerned family, friends, authorities, and the relevant NGOs.[10]

Today spoken drama addresses such social ills rather than attacks political corruption and ineptitude as it once did. In that the current government manipulates its policies in order to continue to take advantage of foreign aid, it is not surprising that artists attempt to operate similarly especially since they see few alternatives. Performers talk about needing help in marketing their art, in having access to NGOs and other potential sponsors. Early exponents are critical of their younger colleagues for not possessing the passion necessary to overcome obstacles and thinking only of money rather than their art. Nonetheless, they must sense the reason for the compromised enthusiasm of this generation. In a post-Khmer Rouge society in which the perpetrators of the massacres still operate with impunity, socially conscious theatre is overwhelmed and rendered superfluous by the magnitude of death and destruction.

Despite being confronted with major external obstacles and the internal erosion of confidence and purpose, a few dramatists have shown exceptional dedication and individual initiative. Mann Kosal, a self-taught master puppeteer and the cofounder of Sovanna Phum (Golden Village)[11] Association, a community-based art centre in Phnom Penh, has managed not only to survive on his art but also to help promote other artists. Born into a family of farmers, trained as a *bassac* performer, Kosal carefully attends to every aspect of making the puppet, taking his time, and only performing with those puppets that pass his own standards of excellence. This would not seem so exceptional were it not for the context of isolation, the lack of a continuous tradition to imbibe, and the lack of a master to imitate or consult. Kosal has had to piece together remnants of a broken tradition and follow his own intuition.

In 1995, when Kosal had perfected his first six working puppets, he began making up new stories and taking them out into the countryside where he continues to get an enthusiastic reception. His excursions have inspired others. A young man from Siem Reap, and later his sister, joined him in Phnom Penh to transform tradition by becoming the first woman puppet-maker.

Kosal's love for his art is conveyed to both audiences and potential apprentices. His hands-on "just do it" approach seems not even to acknowledge obstacles because he loves his puppets so much. The core artists of the association no longer have to have outside jobs and are now financially self-sufficient.[12] In 2002, they were building a new theatre while most of the city theatres remained dormant or in ruin. Perhaps Kosal is offering a significant alternative for other performing artists alongside the resurrection of the classical dance. His self-sufficiency has allowed him to pursue his art regardless of whether aid was forthcoming or not. Cambodia's performing artists face a sea of troubles, but Mann Kosal is one man who has begun to empty it with his own bucket.

## Notes

1. This article has been published with the kind permission of the University of Hawaii' Press. The more extensive and complete version of it was first published under the title "Emptying the Sea by the Bucketful: The Dilemma in Cambodian Theatre" in *Asian Theatre Journal*, Vol. 20, No. 2 (Fall 2003), pp. 147-178.

2. The university was first formally known as École Nationale du Théâtre, or *Sala Cheat Phneak Lakhaoun Niyeay* (The National School of Spoken Theatre) in 1958. In 1965, it became the Royal University of Fine Arts and then in 1970 was renamed the University of Fine Arts. "Royal" was restored when Norodom Sihanouk became king again in 1993.

3. The court dance was referred to by various terms, including *lakhaoun hlong*, the royal or king's dance-drama, and *lakhaoun preah reach troap*, "drama of the royal heritage." In 1970 with the Lon Nol coup, "royal" was dropped and it became the present "ancient dance."

4. I have opted for the rather unusual spelling of "lakhaoun niyeay" because it most closely approximates the sound in Khmer. Moreover, the word is derived from the Thai word "lakon", and in order to distinguish the two I use the spelling chosen by the authors of the most recent and thorough book on the subject, *Cultures of Independence* by Ly Daravuth and Ingrid Muan, (Phnom Penh: Reyum, 2001).

5. Pich Tum Kravel lists many more types of Cambodian theatre, a good number of which are hybrids, adaptations of court developments, or local versions of a form originating elsewhere. Some no longer exist but their attributes have been incorporated in current performances. He identifies *paol srey, bamaothai, apei, kaen, bauek bot, pleing kar, takkata, chamroh* and *lakhon kamnap*. See Pich Tum Kravel, *Khmer Dances* (Phnom Penh: Toyota Foundation, 2001), p. 8. Ly Theam Teng discusses even more hybrids that existed at the beginning of the twentieth century. See Ly in Daravuth and Muan, p. 94.

6. The dancers also appeared at the ensuing expositions in 1922 and 1931. Much of the current Royal Palace was also built by the French. It was they who insisted it become the primary residence of King Norodom, who preferred the older palace in Oudong. The expansion was carried out during the reign of Sisowath in 1913-1914 after his successful trip to France, and includes the Chanchhaya pavilion where the dancers perform for guests of the king. See Nicola Cooper, *France in Indochina; Colonial Encounters* (Oxford: Berg, 2001, pp. 65-90).

7. The dance version of *Othello* was entitled *Samritechak*. It was conceived and choreographed by Sophiline Cheam Shapiro, who graduated from the university and now resides in Los Angeles. The main character, Samritechak, is portrayed as a Naga, half-man, half-demon. The Iago character is represented by the monkey, Virul, performed by the one male dancer in the production. Inspired by the similarities she saw between Desdemona's plight and the miserable fate of most female characters in Cambodian stories, Shapiro had to find appropriate ways to reinscribe the Shakespearean tragedy into Cambodian aesthetics, which, for example, do not permit showing a death on stage. In addition, she had to face negative Cambodian reactions to a great general's killing himself for a woman. Email interview with Sophiline Cheam Shapiro, 26 March 2002.

8. See Zeman McCreadie, Zeman. "The Rekindling of the Bassac Theatre." *Principal*, October 1999.

9. The tale is well known. See Judith M. Jacob, "The Short Stories of Cambodian Popular Tradition" in *The Short Story in Southeast Asia*. Edited by J.H. Davidson and H. Cordell. (London: University of London, 1982) pp. 37-61.

10. Interview with Sithan Hout, 12 February 2002. *A Wounded Life*. Publication sponsored by U.S.A.I.D.; translated by The Asia Foundation.

11. The Association also makes a connection with Cambodian antiquity. "Sovanna Phum" refers to the "golden regions," the name for the Khmer community in 309 BC before the advent of Buddhism and Brahmanism in the area. (See Pich Tum Kravel, *Khmer Dances*. (Phnom Penh: Toyota Foundation, 2001), p. 21.

12. Interview with Delphine Kassam and Mann Kosal, 15 February 2002.

# 33

# Performing Taiwan

## The Taipei Theatre in New York and Cultural Propaganda

### Chia-Hsin Chou

The Taipei Theatre, located in midtown Manhattan, New York City, served as a vehicle to promote Taiwanese culture through the performing arts in the United States. Opened on 14 August 1991, this non-profit performance space, sponsored by the Taiwan Government, labeled itself as a crossroad of Western and Eastern cultures, but its work was often treated as propaganda by both the Taiwanese and the American public. As a result of a dramatic rise in the rent, the Taiwan government ended the project on 28 June 2002. The shutting down of the Taipei Theatre raises paradoxical questions: is it acceptable to show the flag of art for diplomatic means? Does official involvement violate the freedom of artistic expression in a democratic state?

In this paper, I argue that a playhouse under the wing of cultural propaganda attempts to conform with the accepted values and power symbols of a given authority, concealing its overt purpose. But it also spontaneously reproduces images and perceptions that undermine its purpose. The Taipei Theatre inevitably embodied political power in negotiating its identity in a complicated political diplomatic situation (the Taiwan government cannot use the names either Taiwan or the Republic of China in terms of the unsettled relationship with the People's Republic of China) But it also resisted the stereotypical representations of Taiwanese performing arts in New York.

Walking to the Avenue of the Americas and Forty-Ninth Street, gigantic skyscrapers lifted up toward heaven, the city spectator would encounter a black signpost reading "Taipei Theatre." Administered by the Chinese Information and Culture Centre (CICC), the chamber playhouse existed deep down in the McGraw-Hill Building. Remodeled from a Sony movie theatre, the Taipei Theatre was a product hastily created to present Taiwan on the world stage as a cultural contribution to the government's attempt to resolve the two-China diplomatic embarrassment. The performance space became the diplomatic extension of Taiwan's territory dislocating in New York and was expected to capture the imagination of the world superpower (the American public) and to reflect glory back home. Designed by Chinese American architect Lee Shi, a semi-circular stage faced 234 seats spreading out in eight semi-circular rows. This performance space incorporated and signified complicated ideologies of Taiwaneseness and Chineseness backed up by nationalism. For example, the circular units of the stage and seats denoted the traditional Chinese architectural ideal; the presence of the National flags symbolized the national power; worshipping the sacred statute of Peking Opera God in the theatre derived from a Taiwanese civil custom for the well-being of the playhouse.

I investigated the Taipei Theatre in March 2002. My ethnographic curiosity quickly alerted the CICC staff's political sensitivity because they were puzzled as to why I was interested in such a small theatre, which impressed upon almost nobody. Some of them suspected that I might be a journalist looking for headlines, or a spy from mainland China hoping to dig out scandal to damage Taiwan's image and to get them into trouble. Then tried to persuade me to abandon the project because the Taipei Theatre was too unsuccessful to write about. In 1996, *New York Times* also questioned this kind of cultural exchange, which spent "so much money to stage lavish productions abroad for a relatively small audience." The two venues consolidate the political complications of a diplomatic cultural agency.

Cultural propaganda is a form of manipulation and does not often come marching toward the receiver chanting its packaged message. Mieke Bal suggests that to understand the function of manipulation we must focus on *the context*: "manipulation is not only an instance of (ideological) agency, but also of the historical embeddedness of that agency."[1] The Taipei Theatre failed to prove the power of its marginalized political autonomy in New York; however, its failure implies a cultural rupture and historical discontinuation while a performance agency is dis/relocated in a foreign context.

A senior employee of CICC complained of the difficulty for a governmental organization to "make friends" with the New York media and other theatrical entities, which seems to echo *New York Times'* report of Americans' aversion to official involvement and bureaucratic control over the arts: federal support of culture has often set off heated debates in America from the Depression-era Works Projects Administration to the more recent controversies over the National Endowment for the Arts.[2] Therefore, it was not surprising that the Taipei Theatre was merely marked as "the public forum for a country's enthusiastic salesmanship on behalf of its arts."[3] The Taipei Theatre specifically demonstrated a politics that conflated nationalism with capitalism. The CICC staff mocked themselves that "The government serves the original, but the Americans prefer sour spicy General Tao's chicken." The statement perfectly depicts the embarrassment of the Taipei Theatre of attracting an American audience: the Taiwanese authorities passionately brought a lot of products without understanding the American appetite.

A space, as Michel de Certeau conceptualizes in *The Practice of Everyday Life* (1984), is like a visual simulacrum in a planned text for political and socioeconomic measures. The rejected "waste products" in process of modernity are transformed into products that can fit into the machinery of order, but importantly it repeatedly produces effects contrary to those at its aims in the multiple forms of *waste* inside it. De Certeau's waste is *a loss* in the profit system and constantly transforms its production into "expenditure."[4]

The Taipei Theatre was a "waste", but its journey invoked an indexical agency to write a performance text. If propaganda may be interpreted as a dramatic illustration between sign-vehicle and object, the act of propaganda *in motion* importantly performs a mode of cultural action, although accommodating an agenda, functioning as webs of signification within which experiences and meanings are constituted and invented. Thus, the discursive waste narratives are capable of disrupting the fixed political status of the Taipei Theatre and allow the indexical agency to re-enter the discourse through its transgression of the rational signification. The Taipei Theatre was not only a space for the game of power *by contiguity*, but also a disquieting borderland of a marginalized Third-World autonomy struggling to channel a political language and identity through performance energies in its First-World host.

The Taipei Theatre under the wing of cultural propaganda reproduces the desired perceptions, but also undermines them. The Council for Cultural Affairs on Taiwan annually selected ten to twelve "well-received" productions for this theatre; the standards and process of selection were always controversial and sometimes scandalous on the island. The Taiwanese artists often hoped that their works might attract international attention through the Taipei Theatre. Yet, analyzing the productions presented, we realize that over the course of its life more than one hundred performances condensed, dramatized, or attempted to respond to the changes of Taiwan's internal and external political conditions, the people's identity, or collective memory in New York. For example, the soaring productions of Taiwanese Opera, modern dance, and contemporary experimental theatre, and the declining number of the Chinese Opera productions, reflected that the people in Taiwan were/are searching for a national identity and lost cultural roots in the post-colonial situation.

By contrast, *the New York Times'* reviews of the productions for the past twelve years systematically favoured the images of the productions with a touch of the Chinese (such as *The Monkey King*) and the Taiwanese (the dance of Formosa Aboriginal Dance Troupe was a great example) to satisfy the New Yorkers' orientalist fantasy and to serve as a contrasting model for the occidental stage in contiguity although the traditional kind of productions were less approachable for Westerners. The Taipei Theatre was ironically celebrated as a place to export "varieties of traditional Chinese opera,"[5] which reinforced the mystified and exotic image of the Orient.

The disparities of representation and reception of the Taipei Theatre and the media provided an alternative scenario of the power of performance. In channelling the energies of performance, the Taipei Theatre Stage often undermined the very intention of its representations: the productions constantly redefined what a "Taiwanese" performance should be and not every performance from the Orient could conveniently fit into a simple category, such as Chinese Opera. The termination of the Taipei Theatre provides an opportunity for the Taiwanese to rethink the relationship of cultural propaganda and theatre: is art expression an efficient tool for diplomatic survival?

However, will the performers from the margin with or without official support be continuing to change and to attribute values to artistic entities, marking their own identities and communicating with local spectators without reclaiming their cultural roots in the age of globalization, or specifically of Americanization?

I do not know.

## Notes

1. See Mieke Bal, "Reading the Gaze: The Construction of Gender in 'Rembrandt'," *Vision and Textuality* edited by Stephen Melville and Bill Readings, North Carolina: Duke University Press, 1995, p. 148.

2. See Michael Z. Wise, "Showing the Flag of Culture (or Not)," *New York Times*, 14 April 2002, sec. 2, p. 1.

3. See Bernard Holland, "From Taiwan, More Than Meets the Ear," *New York Times*, 24 August 1991, sec. 1, p. 15.

4. Michel de Certeau, *The Practice of Everyday Life*, trans. Steven Rendall, Berkeley: University of California Press, 1984, pp. 91-110.

5. See James R. Oestreich, "Hsin-Chuan Taiwanese Opera Troup," *New York Times*, 12 March 1994, sec. 1, p. 12.

# 34

## A Breathing Space Where Anything Can Happen...

Travelling Theatre in Japan, China, India and Bangladesh
in a Contextual Perspective

**Christina Nygren**

An actor in a Japanese travelling theatre group once told me "We do not *play* theatre, we *live* theatre". Though this statement radically challenges the accepted concept of theatre as something that is not real, I think it gives a good illustration of the role the travelling actor has or believes he has in society. It also indirectly sheds light on the expectations of the audience. On the other hand this actor's declaration sheds light on an interesting paradox, exemplified in Japan's popular theatre where well-known and popular *enka*-songs, not inherently part of the plays, are incorporated to comment on the content and to set an atmosphere. These songs tell about *Yume no shibai* (Theatre in dreams) and *Jinsei gekijô* (Life on stage, or a more literary translation, The stage of life) becoming a mirror of the plot of the play as well as of the actors' actual lives. The identification and recognition of this by the audience is, together with creating a sense of community, as important as any artistic/aesthetic achievement or experience of artistry.

In the latter part of this paper I will come back to the controversial definition of "popular theatre", but at the moment I think it is enough to say that I regard the popular theatre, performed by travelling theatre groups, as inseparable from the society and from the social, human or divine context where it is performed, and it should therefore not be seen as an isolated work of art. Consequently, in order not to be limited by the restrictions of a strict performance analysis I am primarily looking at the context, letting the stage art take a subsidiary role and emphasizing the "common" rather than the "unique".

So, that said, please let me share with you a few situations from the countries where I have been working for quite a few years. The "situations" or "events" I will tell about are chosen from hundreds of such experiences, and I have intentionally selected very different contexts in order to give a broad perspective for my later discussion. Let's travel with the groups, then, starting in Japan, then moving to China and further south to Bangladesh, ending our journey in the Indian province of West Bengal.

We are at a huge hot spring resort in Kyushû in Southern Japan. It is early in the afternoon and the approximately 250 men and women in the audience arrived already in the morning to this palace of joy and delight, alone or in small groups. The entrance fee is low enough to let in even the less privileged citizens and does not only include unlimited bathing in numerous pools with a selection of rejuvenating waters, but also admittance to afternoon and evening performances of theatre, song and dance.

The first of two daily performances has just started. The stage is dark, a popular *enka*-song is blaring from the loudspeakers, setting the atmosphere for the first scene of the play *Tokujirô Shigure* (Drizzling Rain over Tokujirô), a story about a married woman who is secretly having an affair with a gangster and becomes pregnant by him. The well-known song is not a part of the play, but conveys in sentimental words and easily accessible music the emotions of the upcoming performance. The music becomes more subdued, the stage brightens and a man who is quite obviously looking for someone appears. He talks with the audience, chatting and joking with them to build up an intimate rapport with the spectators.

One by one the audience has been entering the auditorium, taking their seats on the cushions placed on the floor. They are all dressed in cotton bathrobes patterned with seawaves and provided at the resort. Many are nibbling from small lunchboxes filled with a variety of foods. Most of them fill their cups with tea from big thermos flasks, while a few sip beer or *sake*. As a billowing blue and white sea, the spectators newly emerged from the baths, refreshed and fragrant with soap and dressed alike, find transient affinity in the expectant atmosphere.

On stage the introductory chat has ended and the play has moved on. The acting is fragmented, improvised and unpretentious but strongly melodramatic. The simple stage set does not change, and with only the lines of the actors the audience is enticed to imagine time and space. The play proceeds, with an air of despair and abject misery, when the husband finds out his wife's well kept secret concerning the boy, whom he has always regarded as his own son. His inner feelings are again conveyed to the audience through a well known *enka*, loudly accompanying his changing of clothes on stage – an outer manifestation of his inner change, while the prerecorded song fills the air.

With strongly exaggerated gestures, first hesitating and then resolute, with distanced but expressive inner acting he forces himself out the door, accompanied by the song:

*...playing games of life and death...tearful....I am leaving, I am leaving...*

He turns his head back, looking at the closed door to the home he is leaving, then lifting his eyes to an imaginary sky, performs a powerful and carefully choreographed pattern of movements with a final frozen pose. He then continues his bitter walk on the narrow bridge extending the stage to the left. The audience gasps for breath, applauds and crys out its admiration for both the hero *Tokujirô* and the actor *Momotarô*.

*...My tears carry the love, in despair...despair...despair...*

The onlookers, now with their eyes filled with tears, sigh and sob together with the hero. With sword in hand he decides to spare the unfaithful wife's life at the very last minute and the audience shows its support with a storm of applause. The hero, now standing in solitary reflection crys out his grief and despair. He poses under a crimson umbrella, with costume half open letting his pale, soft shoulder lay bare and displaying the white edging of his pants.

With an agonized moan he throws himself to the floor but manages to finish in another beautiful pose. The curtain closes slowly and *Sadamegawa* (River of Fate) is played at full volume.

*...Looking for a place, a road for tomorrow...but my eyes see nothing...River of Fate...*

Everybody has had their share of sentimental grief; the painful atmosphere is broken by an elderly man dressed as an old woman carrying a baby on her back. He walks around in the audience, commenting on trivial events and spreading pictures of the actors. At the same time he is also presenting the artists and re-introducing the different scenes during the latter part of the performance.

Soon, a lovely woman dressed in white silk kimono with her head covered by a silken veil slowly moves through the audience. The hero from the play has been transformed into an *onnagata* – a male impersonator of women. Graceful and with well-balanced gestures, she dances with a traditional touch to another prerecorded, well known *enka*-song. A sudden sparkling smile reveals a glittering jewel affixed to one of her front teeth. It is erotically enticing, suggestive of passion but still pleasantly beautiful, attainable yet unattainable at the same time. Some women from here and there in the audience run up to the *onnagata*, tucking envelopes with money inside his costume and then crouching and returning to their seats, giggling.

He is admired and has a close, almost familiar contact with the viewers, sometimes shocking them by unconventional, unexpected moves like jumping with both feet together from the stage and running into the audience with a masculine shout, "*Irasshai!*", Welcome! At the end of his *onnagata* dance performance he sometimes first thanks the audience in a soft, feminine manner – then hoists his skirt, trotting off the stage with masculine steps. An illusion so perfected that he boldly dares to puncture it!

The situation I've just described is representative of the vast majority of performances regularly given by travelling troupes in Japan, *tabi shibai*. *Tabi* means travel or journey and *shibai* is one of the words applied to theatre or plays hence – "travelling theatre". Today, more than a hundred troupes have joined three main organizations and in addition to this there are roughly some two hundred non-member groups of varying sizes and structures. *Tabi shibai* has a low status in the established theatre world, and is usually performed at simple and often quite shabby theatres for periods of two to four weeks. Over the past few decades these kinds of theatre buildings have decreased, while recreation centres and hot spring resorts with built-in theatre stages, like the one I just described, are increasing in number. Even if we only count the number of performances given by the organized groups and keep to a low average rate of 45 per month for each troupe (they normally perform twice a day), it makes some 55,000 events per year, and these rarely included or even mentioned in the outlines of Japanese theatre.

Now let's travel further southward to China, the hugely expansive country that like India should rather be defined culturally as a continent than a country. The travelling troupes in China mostly perform *difangxi* (regional theatre) in the countryside and do so under greatly varying working conditions. Due to the vast size of the country and the many different dialects, languages, musical traditions, lifestyles, etc., the travelling groups enjoy the most success within the area where the language of their particular type of theatre is spoken. There are more than 300 clearly distinguishable types of local theatre, differing from one another in terms of music, language, structure and content. The *difangxi* are traditional forms of theatre with strong ties to the community. The performances are based on a blend of dialogue, songs, music, acrobatics, juggling and marshal arts, with historical and mythological content.

In former years the authorities often told me that private travelling theatre troupes no longer existed in the country, but with a bit of pressing, I was able to meet several such troupes. Then once I started to search in seriousness for evidence of a continuing vibrant popular theatre tradition in the countryside, I learned of hundreds more of them. Due to the economic and social changes that have occurred in China in recent years, theatre has again become a commercially viable alternative to other forms of enterprise, and private theatre groups are being tolerated. The political slogans have gone from the theatre, and these days, mainly historical plays are performed in addition to the mythical stories and older pieces based on folk tales.

The official statistics, which are probably not even accurate for state-supported groups, do not include the collective and private theatre groups that mainly tour in the rural areas. Three years ago, the leader of one theatre group in the not very wealthy, Northern Shanxi province, estimated the number of private or collective travelling theatre groups in that particular province alone to be about 300. Knowing that China has 22 provinces and 5 autonomous regions, we can only guess that the actual number of groups are in the thousands, as no reliable statistics are available. Again, these performances or troupes are rarely mentioned in discussions or outlines of Chinese theatre.

Now it is February and I find myself right in the heart of a performance in a remote village of the Northern Shanxi province. There is no regular transportation such as buses or trains, and facilities for food and accommodation are non-existent, factors which make this a *bu kaifang* (not open) area, meaning that foreigners are officially not allowed to stay here. It is already eight in the evening, 14 degrees below zero (Celsius) and thousands of stars are visible in the clear, ebony sky. In mid-winter no agricultural work can be carried out and the villagers are enjoying a long-awaited reprieve from their hard labour. Many of them have been waiting for hours, standing in front of the outdoor stage, dressed in rough cotton-padded clothes and woollen or fur caps. Some of them are holding small children, wrapped in padded sacks and woollen blankets.

Finally, the sound of a wooden *bangzi*-clapper announces the beginning of the performance, the hollow rhythmic clap mingling with the metallic beat of a drum, giving a hint to the spectators that the play will start very soon. Before the first performance of this group's five-day visit, after which a program totalling nine plays will have been performed, the event must be suitably celebrated. A selected villager enters the stage to set off long strings of fire crackers, a custom from long ago, performed to frighten away evil spirits. Solemn and ceremonious, the man takes his position at the front of the stage and sets the air burning and flashing until the audience applauds and shouts with joy. The yearly intensive period of theatre performances has commenced in traditional fashion.

The play starts with song, music and dialogue, dance and acrobatics, colourful costumes and heavy, mask-like make up. As in all other kinds of traditional Chinese theatre these components jointly give the performance its character and attraction. The music of this local theatre form, called *shangdang bangzi*, is intensive and is led by a rythmic wooden clapper, reinforced by percussion instruments to underline the special activity in the story line. The piercing style of song supports the drama and conveys a tense atmosphere of excitement and beauty in the sad, sometimes bitter-sweet stories.

Tonight's play is a sequence of the long historical drama about The Women Generals of the Yang Family. The audience follows the play attentively, standing in front of the stage with their hands stuffed inside the arms of their coats like makeshift mufflers. As the actors and the audience breathe, traces of mist rise as though they are exhaling smoke, due to the freezing temperatures. Sometimes one or two of the spectators drift away to find warmth, sadly shaking their heads at the severely cold weather, but many still remain. When a part of the stage set falls to the floor, a murmur of disappointment goes through the audience, but as no one expects realism on the stage, the incident is forgotten as soon as the piece is put back in it's original position.

Just before midnight, the performance ends abruptly, without conclusion or applause. The spectators rush home in the dark without uttering a word. The actors scurry around each other. Withdrawn and shivering they wait for a free washbowl and hot water from thermos flasks to wash off their oily make up. The costumes are folded, quickly and efficiently, shoes are put in their places, hats and caps are put on the right shelf or in one of the 65 big green boxes in which all the group's belongings are kept. With stiff hands, the musicians pack their instruments into the proper wooden boxes, and in a few minutes both the stage and the spectator's area are eerily empty and quiet. The set design, curtains and back drops have been secured with wires or knotted together to prevent the wind that is howling through the stage opening, blowing through the glass-less windows and the door-less entrances and exits, to destroy anything during the night. Everybody is in a hurry to reach the place in the village they have been allotted to stay. The leader of the troupe will sleep in a villager's kitchen, his wife in a small space in an entrance hall nearby. An actress who has fallen ill is lent the tiny gatekeeper's room of the school, with only a candle to keep warm. Two of the elder actors have found an empty classroom in the village school, with some desks to put together to serve as beds. The youngsters have spread their tarpaulin clad sleeping bags side by side on the earth floor in another empty classroom, where a coal heater gives off lots of smoke and a minimum of warmth. I am taken, walking between dark and already silent houses, to a peasant family on the outskirts of the village. They have given me the use of a small room with a coal heater, and I share the space with a motor bike, two bicycles and a pigeon in a cage.

While sitting there, huddled in borrowed blankets reflecting over the performance and the hardships experienced by the travelling theatre group, as well as the strong appreciation shown to them by the villagers who so sincerely enjoyed their longed-for, once-a-year entertainment, I could not help comparing this genuine and powerful situation with a very different experience I had had a few years earlier.

It was also in Chinese village, far away from the big cities, and also prohibited to foreigners. An old man shared with me his wisdom, and his observations, which put the discussion of theatre in yet another light. It was during a "New Year performance" staged out of context, two months after the actual Chinese new year, as a part of a conference program for about hundred Chinese delegates and a handful of foreign so-called experts. We had obtained a special permission to visit the village and arrived, escorted by police, in the early morning by a rented bus. The performance was supposed to address and honour the local gods with plays, music, song and dance but did also include animal offerings and different kinds of food and drinks. The old man I just mentioned, puffed his pipe and smiled gently when he told me "*Shen bu xia*" – "The gods will not descend", nodding and following the crowds of visitors with his eyes. Or maybe he said "The gods are not blind", the difference between the two statements being only whether the last word is pronounced in an even or a falling tone. Either meaning would have been suited for the situation. For the villagers, we – the foreigners and researchers – were the attraction and their own ceremonies an empty shell of insignificant codes. In an ironically reversed situation, the surprised and amused village people and their gods were observing the restless and enthusiastic "experts" circulating with their cameras and notebooks, trying to "experience" the artificial imitations of what was usually a deeply significant event.

From China now let's move further South to Bangladesh in order to attend a performance of *yatra* performed by a travelling troupe in a small village. *Yatra* means "travel" or "procession" and is the most popular and widespread form of theatre in Bangladesh as well as in the Indian West Bengal area. *Yatra* is also appreciated in the border areas like Orissa and Bihar. The former province of Bengal was divided in 1947 into the Indian West Bengal and East Pakistan, which in 1971, after a devastating war of resistance against Pakistan, became Bangladesh. Since the division *yatra* has been politically and religiously controversial in Bangladesh, but still it has managed to survive through the dedication of hundreds of travelling theatre groups. The number of these groups however, has been constantly diminishing over the past few years.

This village is situated in the South of Bangladesh, not far from the huge mangrove forest called the Sundarbans. On a riverbank a *pendel*, which is the name for the performance space, has been constructed of bamboo poles and covered by a huge tent. It is late evening. The audience that started to arrive hours ago take their seats on the ground close to each other. The spectators surround the square, raised stage platform. A soiled piece of cloth is only scantily hiding the coarse wooden stage enclosed by a fence. The platform is placed in the middle of the tent and has an earthen pathway, sloping downwards to the green room, hidden behind a curtain. Though it is rather hot and humid, the spectators are all wrapped in shawls as protection from the heavy dew that they know will fall far into the night. On two sides of the square platform are raised benches where the musicians are already sitting, in an unconcerned and relaxed manner, playing the well known tunes of the *yatra* musical accompainment.

The play is preceded by young girls singing a patriotic song, followed by scantily clad women showing their bellies and long, loose hair, while dancing to the latest popular songs from Mumbay or Bengali films. The young men of the audience shout with joy, standing up dancing with jerky movements while the very small group of female spectators keep close together, hiding their faces behind their shawls. After a few dances the performance continues with a traditional play, *Komolar bonobash*, or "Komola's exile in the forest". The dramatic and sad story, full of both unfaithful intrigues and heroic behaviour, is presented through dialogue, intensive music and singing and melodramatic acting. The roles are taken by both female and male actors who follow an expressive tradition of well-known movement patterns, aiming to reach all spectators on the four sides of the stage. The performance continues until dawn, and during the night the play is stopped twice for shorter interludes with dance and popular songs performed by specially engaged female dancers and singers.

When *azan*, the call for morning prayer, is suddenly heard in the distance, it, together with the dazzling light catch us anawares. Within a minute we are deprived of the illusion, the dream-world where deep love and honesty overcome any evil conspirations, and where the inhabitants show their strong emotions of life and death in full coloured beauty and awkwardness. Now, the rough wooden stage, the actor's worn and somewhat soiled costumes and heavy make up brings us back to reality, from the bewitchment of the dim, damp light – the spell is broken. Everybody feels sleepy in the raw morning cold and in haste the *yatra* artists are served one of their two free daily meals on the grounds behind the combined greenroom and sleeping tent. In a couple of minutes they eat their rice and withdraw in silence to their mosquito net covered mattresses spread on the ground.

The teacher of the village school who has been sitting among the audience speaks up, as if he would like to make an excuse to the foreigner to smooth over the vulgarity, triteness and poverty. "Madam....*yatra* is a health resort for the Bangladeshis...we don't have any night clubs or dance palaces..."

Some young men are standing around us, nodding and wanting me to understand their appreciation for *yatra* that has been the most popular theatrical entertainment since their childhood. Nowadays, however, the theatre form is often deprived of it is full value, not only by religious fundamentalists but also by intellectuals, the highly educated and the representatives for highbrow performing arts. From these groups of the society I have heard the jingle-like taunt, "*Yatra dekhe, fatra loke*" – "The one who look at *yatra* is a silly idiot." The growing contempt and mistrust in which *yatra* and the travelling troupes that perform them are held, has during the last decades opened an opportunity for private organizers and producers to exploit the situation. To bring in extra money, gambling (which is prohibited in Bangladesh) and strip dancing are attached to the *pendels*, additions which further reduces the respectability of these events and play *yatra* into the hands of its critics.

Not very far westwards, after crossing the border between Bangladesh and India we reach Kolkata, the provincial capital of West Bengal. As I've mentioned already, *yatra* is widely spread in the West Bengal as well, though its development differs considerably from Bangladesh during the last centuries. While Bangladesh has kept much of the original music, acting styles and mythological or social content of the plays, in West Bengal themes from modern history and political/social life as well as a modernized form of music have been incorporated. During the last century the acting style has been strongly influenced by Western theatre and film and incorporated a commercial booking system with an extended star cult. In the cultural melting pot of Kolkata, a rich and lively theatre life existed with popular theatre being performed at several commercial theatres until recent years when these performances seem to have lost their attraction. On the other hand, migrant, less prestigious theatre groups performing *yatra* as well as other theatre forms are still keeping the tradition vibrant, especially during *puja* seasons.

We have come to meet a travelling troupe who has been invited to one of the many red light districts of Kolkata. It is early May and traditionally the time to worship Shitola, the goddess who helps ward off diseases like smallpox and chickenpox. The community of sex workers and their children have invited one of the about 30 theatre groups in the region performing another traditional theatre form, *tonsha* to perform in front of the Shitola shrine situated in a small square surrounded by narrow alleys, with cramped, combined living quarters and space for the women to receive their visitors. The 20 members of the theatre group are dressing, making up and having a light meal before the performance in a tiny cellar room while neighbouring children are jostling one other in the doorway to get a glimpse of the actors. At the small square in front of the shrine, a wooden platform stage has been built and is covered in white cloth. The stage faces the Shitola shrine and the audience is to sit on the ground in between. The performance begins with a ceremonial prayer to the goddess and continues with the play, an episode from *Mahabharata* in which the great King Virata refuses to recognise the goddess Shitola. She manifests herself in ten different aspects appearing for example as Kali and as Durgha threatening to destroy the whole country before King Virata finally accepts her. Accordingly Shitola is both the main character on stage and the subject for worship in the shrine, letting the spectators get both an experience of the divinity impersonated, and take part as worshippers together with the theatre group.

Initially the audience is mostly children and a few men and women but as time passes more and more women finish their tasks and join as spectators, enjoying the colourful and sometimes noisy play. The goddess Shitola, as well as some other female roles are performed by male impersonators of women. Around three o clock in the morning the performance finishes and we are slowly leaving the square. A middle aged woman approaches me, stretches out her hand and touches me lightly.

– Sister, why did you come here?

She wants to talk about her life, and stresses the importance of *puja* and these kinds of performances by travelling troupes. Few other groups would bother to come to perform in this area of the city. When we say goodbye she takes my hand, this time without hesitation, and adds:

– Please understand that except for these occasions of celebration, our life is only sex and liquor.

These examples from different "situations" or "events" that I have shared with you have many similarities, though the differences in context are also clearly visible. Before I elaborate a little further on these experiences I would like to summarize my view on some commonly accepted definitions and terminology.

The concept of "popular" theatre has been discussed intensively in certain academic circles, and popular or "low brow" culture in relation to "high brow"/elite culture has been the focus of much debate, though the boundaries still today are not always clearly defined. In my work I define the term "popular" in its broadest sense, including intersections with mass culture and folk culture, and with two sub-divisions, i.e. popular theatre and folk theatre, depending on the venue, purpose and/or function.

*Popular theatre* refers to performances that are created to be performed for a wide audience, often in cities and particularly in major cities, or for extensive touring. It includes comedic or sentimental performances in the entertainment districts of cities or at venues that offer various forms of entertainment. I cannot, however, identify any obvious delineation between the theatrical structure of popular theatre/lowbrow theatre and elite theatre/highbrow theatre. (There are often links between popular theatre, lowbrow films, and popular music and songs. The audience members are observers and do not physically participate.)

I use the term *folk theatre* to indicate theatre and dance that is provincial and linked to traditions, customs and patterns of behaviour in defined geographical locations. This form of theatre is particularly useful for teaching people about religion, history and moral values, and has long been an integral part of the lives of people in the provinces. In recent years it has had stiff competition from television. Performances are often linked to a broad festival tradition. (The audience tend to participate in the event, either directly by dancing, speaking or singing, or by merely being present, feeling like participants in sacrificial rites, thanksgiving ceremonies or purification rituals.)

Discussions about the issue of highbrow and lowbrow culture seems fruitless if we limit ourselves to mere aesthetic and/or theoretical classifications and if we do not take into account the significance of social, religious, economical and political differences. The crux of the matter, in my opinion, is the fact that the definitions are formulated based on the standpoint of elite culture, often assuming that highbrow culture is the most desirable kind.

Lowbrow culture, "popular" or unofficial culture is disdained by society's "taste judges", overlooked in the cultural sections of newspapers, does not receive prizes or distinctions, and is not supposed to be taught about in schools. Nevertheless, from a quantitative perspective, this is the culture that dominates. Highbrow culture, on the other hand, tends to be regarded as the "serious", official culture; the kind that is often considered our "cultural heritage" in text books and historical accounts, the kind that might receive funds from the National Council of Cultural Affairs, and its authors/producers are members of academies and societies and are rewarded scholarships and prizes. This is the world of a small but important minority: the group of individuals who, by virtue of their cultural position, have the power to mould public taste. Political and economic resources are focussed on getting people to see "serious" theatre, listen to "fine" music and read "good" literature. Serious, fine and good for whom?

This situation is in no way confined to Sweden or to Western countries. During my extended periods of study and research abroad over the last 20 years, with bilateral support or with local educational grants from the countries I have visited, it was taken for granted that I would study elite culture. Over the years I have noted a strong unwillingness among researchers of the academic world and also among many established artists to discuss the popular theatre, and I have found all the more disregard when it comes to the appreciation of the theatre performed by travelling companies, the existence of which is sometimes even considered non-existant.

There is another problematic point when we are discussing the so-called popular theatre and the travelling theatre groups in four different countries of Asia using the English language. Definitions in each indigenous language would have a slightly different conception. For example in Japan we would use the term *taishu engeki*, "theatre for the general public", corresponding to the English term "low brow theatre". In China it would be natural to talk about *dazhongxi*, theatre popular among the masses, or *tongsuxi* meaning uncomplicated theatre popular among the commoners. Again in Bangla, the common language between Bangladesh and West Bengal, the correspondent word would be *loko natok*, "theatre for the people or"*jonoprio natok*, theatre that is popular or famous among the masses. The understanding of these terms in each region is different and depends on each context. Actually, in trying to define the commonly used English terms "highbrow" and "lowbrow", I find I must regard them as extremes on either side of an overlapping middle zone, where the differences are not clearly visible. However, I do not find it necessary to take a forceful stand on rigid distinctions as this tends to block the view rather than shed light on the theatrical event. The context becomes a handy tool to see the role and position of popular theatre performed by the sometimes "non-visible" travelling troupes.

In Japan, for example, the numbers of audiences that gladly frequent these performances, even in its most cleaned-up version on the grand stages of big cities, tend to avoid speaking about their preferences. In China, popular culture and mass culture were used for political ends in the 1900s when the regime's agents carefully selected commercial forms of dance and theatre and used them to mobilize the masses. The concepts of popular and lowbrow, elite and high culture cannot be defined using Western norms. Chinese people today prefer to talk about the difference between new/modern and old/traditional, and the discussion includes references to the general process of the past decades. The entertainment available to the general public is still controlled by the country's leaders, although now market forces are at work instead of political slogans. Traditional art is frequently looked down upon and is often portrayed as the antithesis of the desirable economic development.

Let's go on a final trip to a *yatra* performance in West Bengal. We are driving north of Kolkata on gravelled roads in the darkness, the velvety black pierced by stars and the glow of a full moon. Two roads intersect in the city of Satgarchia and it is just there where the stage has been built. Thousands of spectators are crouched, sitting on the road and around the square platform. The air is humid and I make my way through the masses of men, women and children silently watching the play *Ganga tumi moila keno?* (Ganga why are you so dirty?). The drama is posing an ambiguous question, both to the mighty river Ganga and to an exploited and humiliated woman in the play. The play goes on with dialogue and music, passionate or pleasantly melodious. The tempo is high and beads of moisture are visible on the actors heavily made up faces. But, suddenly an unrestfulness is felt, first only as a vague misgiving and then with a recognisable sound that creates an impalpable frenzy.

Watch out for the ambulance!

The already dense mass of people crowd even closer together. Leaping to their feet, serious and silent. The siren is ear-splitting. Cautious but intractable it cuts an open swathe through the crowd, skirting around the stage then driving to the South. This immediate encounter between reality and fiction, emphasizes the disparity between reality and the dreamlike feeling. The sound of the sirens slowly fades. The spectators are sinking back into their places. The play continues. The theatre gave life a chance – the encounter is unforgettable.

In my experience, the integration of popular theatre in society and in people's everyday lives is merely an aesthetic experience and a form of entertainment. The performances also often have an important function in creating a sense of community, and are a unifying force in groups within the social structure. Amateur theatre activity gives professional drama a firm place in society, both by keeping interest in theatre alive and by helping to create a knowledgeable audience. Traditions are passed down through families or through the knowledge and wisdom of masters or elders, and are proudly kept alive by the general public.

The theatre we have been talking about does not necessarily reflect the modern reality in which the audience lives. Historical and mythological figures and roles are portrayed in theatre and dance, bringing mythological beings, gods and ancestors to life through inspiring and awakening the spectators' emotions and imaginations, hopes and desires.

The performing arts do create a platform linking reality and fantasy, where it is possible to confront things that are otherwise unattainable or frightening in the same manner as our own dreams. Everyday life has no real place in performances of the travelling groups or in the dramatic art of popular theatre. Rather, these performances provide a breathing space where anything can happen.

# 35

## Modernity vs. Tradition

### A Case Study of Wu Hsing-Kuo's Stage Presentation

### Li, Ruru

My paper focuses on a solo performance based on both *King Lear* and *jingju* that has been known as Peking Opera or Chinese Opera outside of China. The title is *Li Er zai ci, Wu Hsing-Kuo Meets Shakespeare*,[1] which is produced by Contemporary Legend Theatre in Taiwan. In this work Wu performed ten roles covering five conventional character types of *wusheng* (male warrior), *laosheng* (singing male role), *qingyi* (singing female role), *huadan* (vivacious female role) and *chou* (the clown). What is the artistic intension behind this bold and experimental production? Before we try to answer this question, we should first have a quick look at the performance itself.

Instead of following the original plot as most Chinese operatic Shakespeare productions do, or as Wu did in his earlier adaptation of *Macbeth*, Wu's reading of *King Lear* and his empathy with the character cut to the most dramatic scene of the original. This adaptation starts from the mad king in the storm. Following the *jingju* convention, there is a self-introduction aria in this act, telling audiences who this character is and why he is suffering this unusual mad state.

In Act One in the adaptation, while the story of the mad King Li Er in the storm is unfolding, the narration of Wu Hsing-Kuo and his acting career starts to intertwine with the main plot. Towards the end of act one, Wu took off his headdress, long beard and armour; the traditional undercoat for a male warrior was revealed. He started with the lines:

> I am back!
> This decision was very difficult to make, more difficult than deciding to be a monk.
> *Looking at the beard in his hand.* Who is he?
> *To audiences.* Does any one know him?
> *Looking at the beard again.* This is not Li Er.
> *Standing up.* Then where is Li Er?
> Is this Li Er walking?
> Is this Li Er speaking?
> *Looking at the beard, slowly walking forestage, touching his own face and eyes.* Where are his eyes?[2]

While talking, Wu, using his right hand, spread the reddish-brown colour of his facial pattern (as a King) onto the whole of his face, completing the transformation from King Li Er to Wu Hsing-Kuo. By removing the costume and make-up in front of the audience, Wu changed his image of a noble aristocrat to that of a contemporary actor standing on the stage. Audiences were astonished by the quick transformation and were amazed by the contrast of an excellent and unique display of martial arts, and an ordinary human being like any passer-by in the street. Such astonishment naturally led audiences to the inner world of Wu Hsing-Kuo, who invited them to share the conflict and confusion he experienced:

> *Mixing the facial paint clockwise.* Is he confused?
> *Mixing the facial paint anti-clockwise.* Is he numb?
> *Mixing the facial paint to his neck.* Is he awake?
> *Slowly taking his hands off his face.* Who can tell me? Who am I?
> I want to make sure who I am.
> *Kneeling down, folding the armour.* My state, my wisdom and my power all cheated me,
> They all want me to believe that I am from here.
> *Picking up the folded-armour.* I'm back! ... I have returned to my profession.
> This break-up is more noble than becoming a monk.

In the video, an enthusiastic round of applause from the auditorium could be heard after the above lines, and this was the most touching moment of this performance, when the stage was clearly associated with the reality. Wu's honest confession of how difficult for him to return to a *jingju* career genuinely moved the audience, as they had been worried that Wu and his Contemporary Legend Theatre might disappear from Taiwan for ever. From the depth of their hearts, they gave the actor their sincere support. Wu bowed, and bent his body extremely low for a long time. Then suddenly he 'jumped' back to the story on the stage:

I'm back again. Just now ... did Li Er dream? Then I ...? Am I ...?
Am I ... the ghost of Li Er, the shadow of Li Er, the other half of Li Er? No, no, no, I am telling Li Er's story.
Why is it Li Er?
Who is Li Er?
I'm the real Li Er!
Each inch of my skin is Li Er. I've been Li Er since I was a child. I'm fated to be Li Er.

In this long speech, 'he', 'King Li Er' and 'I' were mixed up and audiences, led on by the performer, happily and excitedly 'travelled' between the two roles.

Having prepared his audiences for the frequent exchanging roles between King Lear and a *jingju* performer, Wu decided to make the audience 'jump' with him in a faster pace, and further stretched audiences' ability of crossing between reality and the illusion on the stage. He first called out his colleagues' names to prepare the performance, but immediately, without a cue, he shouted the names of the characters in the Li Er story:

I'm back. The Performance is to start! Brother Liu, Guanqiang, and Xiao Bao [names of his colleagues]!
Where are the people?
Weimin, Anli, Aliao [names of more colleagues]!
Where are the men of our orchestra?
*Enter members of the orchestra.* Why are there so few people? Where are my men? My men?
Goneril, Regan, Cordelia, my loyal minister Kent, Gloucester,

Edmund, Edgar! My one hundred guards! My soldiers! Come, my men! Come over!

Where is my magnificent palace? Where is my vast land? Where is everything I have owned? Where have they gone? How could it be only me that is left?

The roaring thunder and the dazzling lighting helped the performer to bring his audiences back to Li Er's story.

Act Two starts with Wu as Li Er's fool. His facial make-up changed to a clown's pattern codified by a white patch on his nose. In this act, Wu played nine roles, including the Fool, Kent, Lear, the three daughters, Gloucester, Edmond and Edgar, covering a wide range of the character types in the *jingju* form. The switching of different roles was mainly achieved by exhibiting differing character types, the corresponding singing voice and style, and the different acting, including gestures, body movements and steps. It was also assisted with some small props and the costuming. For example, the three daughters were acted according to the three different female acting schools. The Chinese Regan used a handkerchief and specific *huadan* [or 'flowery female part'] steps of the Xun School to distinguish herself from the other two women. The most interesting part of this transformation is that Wu still kept his clown facial pattern while he played all the other eight roles. But I, as a viewer, focussed on his acting and singing, completely ignored the incongruent make-up.

The best episode in this act is the scene where Edgar agrees to guide Gloucester to Dover. A stick, which is used by Gloucester as he is blind, and is also used by Edgar when living in the wilds, plays the magic wand in this frequent role-exchange scene. Both roles sang and Wu on his own managed to present a beautiful dance duet. Apart from the different steps and gestures Wu used to represent Gloucester and Edgar, he also set up a definite coding system on the stage: when he was Edgar, he used one end of the stick as if he were leading a person forward. While playing Gloucester, apart from closing his eyes to show his blindness, he also acted as if he were led by an invisible figure.

The core of Act Three is a thirty-five-line aria, in which Wu sang as Li Er and as himself. The performance ended when Li Er/Wu Hsing-Kuo was lifted by the stage mechanism. The essential idea in this aria is the identity that brings Shakespeare's King Lear and a contemporary *jingju* actor together. 'Who am I', the question asked in Act One when the mad king asks in the storm is also a puzzle that Wu attempts to figure out. As observed in *Adaptations of Shakespeare*: 'Shakespeare is, here, now, always, what is currently being made of him.'[3] Wu Hsing-Kuo, the creator of this solo performance, visualized himself as the central figure of the foreign tale of an ancient British king, and his adaptation was made to vent his inmost emotions and personality. Wu claimed that *King Lear* was the only play that could assist him to 'utter and display [my] loneliness, and further get rid of it'.[4]

Like every *jingju* performer, Wu has a master. So what is the goal of his career? Should he try to imitate his master or should he try to create his own image? This question also goes beyond the personal relationship. What should an old theatrical form do in the twenty-first century? Should it try to remain as it was hundreds years ago or should it try to develop? Is tradition definitely contradictory to modernity? This is the backbone behind this bold solo performance. This is the laboratory work that Wu intended to apply his own theory of *Chuancheng*, which means handing-down and carrying-on.

'Handing-down' is from a master's point of view, while 'carrying-on' is what a disciple is expected to do with the knowledge and skills a master has handed down to him. However, *Li Er zai ci* illuminates Wu's own interpretation of this concept: 'We may have to destroy the existing form in order to bring forth new ideas. But the purpose of bringing out the new is for 'handing-down' and 'carrying-on'. Thus 'carrying-on' is not an entirely follow-up of the old. It will exterminate first, but the 'extermination' will then be followed by [a real sense of] 'carrying-on'.' Like *yin* and *yang* in the Chinese philosophy, Wu's concept of handing-down and carrying-on (*chuancheng*) is based on the destroy and innovation. To him, only by destroying and innovating the old, will the tradition then be able to continue. As the English translation shows, this word itself consists of two associated aspects and indicates continuity, expressing Wu's artistic pursuit.

Guided by the idea of 'handing-down' and 'carrying-on', the three acts in *Li Er zai ci* set up a system in which two parallel stories develop at the same time: Wu Hsing-Kuo explores and attempts to understand Lear, a contemporary Taiwanese meets and talks to Shakespeare, and a twenty-first century *jingju* actor wrestles with the old theatrical form.

# Notes

1. In this paper, I use Taiwanese spelling for people and institutions based in Taiwan.

2. The quotation is from the stage script kindly given to me by Wu Hsing-Kuo.

3. Fischlin, Daniel and Fortier, Mark, *Adaptations of Shakespeare*, Routledge, New York and London, 2000.

4. Programme Note Li Er zai ci, (Taipei, 2001).

# 36

# Wayang Kulit as Contact Zone

## Tradition in Global Flux

### Matthew Issac Cohen

"Theatre and its thought are possible only within a *polis*", writes Alan Read, but much recent scholarship on global theatre and performance has argued that the site of integration where meaning and significance are articulated and negotiated is not so easily located in a distinct and definite political terrain.[1] A particular performance might be enacted against the backdrop of a political regime or polity, but that is not to say that a theatre's apparatus, dramaturgical structure, content and associated horizons of interpretation can be comprehensively explained in terms of the ideological, economic and social contingencies operative in a given time-space. Theatre travels both across space as well as time. Theatre as a performative art also involves a restoration of behaviour, in which texts, images, movements, sounds, and psychophysical states from the past are evoked and re-presented in the present.[2] Actors and spectators from different backgrounds converge in performance momentarily, collectively constituting a unique social constellation. Sometimes, the participants in a theatrical event are drawn from a single community of location; this is the case for much folk theatre world wide, from traditional mumming in Ireland to Pandav Lila in North India to Rangda-Barong trance dance in Bali. But oftentimes the excitement of a spectacle attracts people from far and wide, bringing together individuals and clusters of people, who would not ordinarily come into direct contact.

Theatre is in this sense a contact zone, "the space in which peoples geographically and historically separated come into contact with each other and establish ongoing relations, usually involving conditions of coercion, radical inequality, and intractable conflict". A contact zone "emphasizes... how such subjects are constituted in their relations to each other; [and] stresses co-presence, interaction, interlocking understandings and practices... within radically asymmetrical relations of power".[3]

It is not hard to understand why the two most critiqued global theatrical spectacles of the 1980s, Robert Wilson's *The Civil Wars* and Peter Brook's *The Mahabharata*, might be suitable for analysis as a contact zone. Likewise, much of the work of Ariane Mnouchkine and Julie Taymor's *The Lion King*. Much contemporary theatre and performance, including notably the work of Robert Lepage, Ong Keng Sen and Guillermo Gómez-Pena, thematises and interrogates difference and asymmetry that emerge in performative situations. My concern here is not with these much theorised global artists and productions, however, but with *wayang kulit* (shadow puppet theatre) in Java (Indonesia) and elsewhere.

Studies of *wayang kulit*, the pre-eminent theatrical form of Java, have to date mostly focussed on its grounding in the local. This is true, I should add, of most so-called traditional and folk theatrical forms of Asia and Africa. Dimensions of belonging, community and ethos are routinely emphasised over world-view, extra-communal awareness and negotiation with others. *Wayang kulit* has long been identified as a central cultural icon of Java and a repository, a sort of performative encyclopaedia if you will, of everything Javanese. Javanese students of theosophy, for example, identified the essence of the Javanese self in the performative processes of *wayang kulit* – an understanding both amplified and modulated by Ward Keeler in an exemplary performance ethnography.[4] The carved and chiselled hide puppets are made from the skin and horn of the water buffalo, a domesticated animal of central importance for labour and transportation in traditional Java, as well as an important source of protein in a Javanese diet. (Puppeteers often joke about converting old puppets to buffalo skin *krupuk* wafers.) Performances are a ritual "journey through the night", perfectly attuned to the different feelings of night in the dry season of Java's tropical clime.[5] The musical overture and lengthy narration and formulaic displays of etiquette during the warm hours of the early evening are a means of separation from the everyday and an entrance into the shadow world; the furious battles and humorous escapades of the night's middle are liminal enactments of disorder and inversion in the cool darkness; the philosophising, rapid reversals of fortune and unmaskings of the hours before dawn serve to aggregate, resolve and integrate in the approaching light of dawn. *Wayang kulit* performances always involve a careful co-ordination of artistic and manual labour with material culture, deeply integrated with localised systems of trans-portation, apparatus manufacture and equipment rental. The theatre is in all these noetic and ecological respects thoroughly Javanese.

The popularity of *wayang kulit*, with its stories of Hindu gods and heroes performed in a predominantly Islamic society, is sometimes taken as 'proof' of an essential Javanese religious 'syncretism'.[6] This culturalist interpretation, supported by indigenous and foreign exegetes and scholars alike, is an overly partial view of a 'performatively poly-' art form[7] that has mediated and re-presented relations across commu-nities of religion, ethnicity, race and nationality for centuries. *Wayang kulit* allows for creative juxtapositions and synthesis of materials of social reality that cannot ordinarily be crossed. It is not homologous with the everyday world, but a fantastic world of play. Realms cross as Hindu gods cite Koranic passages, Indonesian educational policy is debated by ancestral heroes, definitions of self and other are articulated and local gossip is indexed. Participating in this play world as performer or interested spectator does not necessitate a commitment to a particular ideological or religious position (even a position as loosely defined as 'syncretism'). Participating in *wayang kulit* however, does indicate a willingness to experiment with identity and its relations in a socially sanctioned forum for dialogue across boundaries of time, space and community. This paper surveys historical and contemporary aspects of *wayang kulit* in this intercultural/global light.

## The Example of a *wali*

Let me start by quoting at length from an early nineteenth-century manuscript dealing principally with the history of the coastal sultanate of Cirebon and the exemplary semi-legendary 'friends of God' (*waliullah*; *wali*), who are credited with introducing Islam to Java in the fifteenth and sixteenth centuries.[8] The wali most closely linked to *wayang kulit* is Sunan Kalijaga, a cultural mediator par excellence and an apical ancestor for many Cirebonese performers (particularly shadow puppeteers and *topeng* mask-dancers).

One night after the evening prayers, Kalijaga said to his two disciples, "Let us go and watch a wayang performance."

His two disciples asked, "Master, where is the wayang being performed?"

The prince answered, "It is taking place in the city of Demak. If you do not believe me, just look over there: there's the wayang performance. There's the light, you can see it from here."

The two disciples answered promptly. "It is true that the light is visible from here, but because the city of Demak is far away, the wayang performance will surely be over by the time we arrive."

With a smile, Suhunan Kali Jaga said, "Very well, both of you hold on to the corner of my shirt. But don't even blink. Close your eyes tightly until we reach the city of Demak."

They set out and in less than a blink of an eye had already arrived at the city of Demak. The two disciples were amazed and surprised beyond words by the God given powers of their teacher. They reached the city of Demak so quickly that when they arrived the puppeteer had not even begun to perform.

Dawn was approaching when Kalijaga spoke again to his students, "Let us return to Cerbon. If not we will perhaps be found out by the locals as we are not native to Demak."

One of the disciples replied, "Forgive me, master. I would like to know how the story ends."

The prince said, "If that is the case, I will leave you here by yourself." In a blink of an eye, Suhunan Kali Jaga and his second disciple arrived at their residence, at the bank of the Kali Jaga river.

In the morning, the disciple who was left behind was apprehended and the people of Demak were in an uproar. They then interrogated the disciple. They asked, "Where is your master from?"

The disciple replied, "I am from the nation of Cerbon. I accompanied my teacher to watch this wayang performance. At around dawn, my teacher returned to Cerbon. I did not go home with him because I really enjoyed the wayang performance."

Eventually the disciple is brought before the Sultan of Demak and he informs the sultan that he is a student of Kalijaga, the great 'friend of God'. In the end, the Sultan sends his son to find out more about Kalijaga. Kalijaga in turn sends the prince to Syarif Hidayatullah, the

Sultan of Cerbon and the *insan kamil* or Perfect Man of his time according to Cerbonese belief. The prince ends up studying Islamic mysticism with Syarif Hidayatullah, thus cementing a political relationship between the two polities.

Like most tales about the friends of God, this story is meant to be instructive. This tale, like others, presents a model of and for how to view *wayang kulit*. I would like to elucidate a few aspects of this textual modelling. A *wayang kulit* performance is seized by Kalijaga as an opportunity to form an alliance between the rival city-states of Cerbon and Demak. The performance-event is a social invitation: its light beckons Kalijaga and his disciples across the 250 mile (400 kilometre) distance and political barriers that separate Cirebon and the rival city-state of Demak. One finds this sense of performance as instrumental in creating and solidifying social bonds reflected in the song texts of the female vocalist (*sinden*) sung at *wayang kulit* performances in Cirebon today.

*Seni mung kanggo hiburan; sing penting rapetaken seduluran* – art for entertainment's sake, what is important is consolidating social/familial relations.

*Dari jauh-jauh datang kemari, bukan maksud cari lawan, melainkan cari kawan* – from far away to come here, not to look for enemies but to look for friends.

The *wayang kulit* performance takes place in Demak, but its importance as an event lies in its relation to the world outside Demak.

Note as well the tale's careful play of agency. Kalijaga does not approach Demak's potentate directly, but allows his *wayang kulit* enthralled disciple to act as an intermediary. He intentionally traps his clownish sidekick in the magical snare of *wayang kulit*. Kalijaga knows fully well that his disciple will be seduced by the *wayang kulit* performance, and will be unable to disentangle himself from the story's siren call, though it will mean being found out when the performance is over at dawn and a spectator's anonymity is removed by the Sun's rays. What makes this move particularly interesting is that it is the mythical story that the disciple needs to see to completion: *wayang kulit*'s fictional intrigues of ancient princes, hermits and gods generates an actual political shift.

Tales similar to this episode, in which *wayang kulit* strategically mediates across distances, abound in Javanese oral and written literature. A powerful puppeteer's performances in the hagiographic literature can be seen from great distances away – like television today, say contemporary pundits. A performance might be taking place in one locale, and its 'essential audience' might be far away, as for example in certain *wayang kulit* ritual dramas when the unseen spirits that occupy other dimensions observe their exploits being enacted by their shadowy doubles upon the screen.

## Intentional Dialectical Hybridity in Cirebonese *Wayang Kulit*

*Wayang kulit* not only serves to attract a variegated audience, it is itself a hybrid performance form, integrating tales of Hindu gods and heroes, Islamic Javanese philosophy, contemporary political and social issues and the latest fashions and trends in popular art. The hybridity of *wayang kulit* is perhaps most evident in the linguistic realm. Its language of performance is simultaneously organic as well as intentionally hybrid, in Bakhtin's terms.[9] It involves unmediated mixtures of speech styles and linguistic codes that are characteristic of everyday Javanese. There are the normal word borrowings from Indonesian, English, Dutch and many other languages which have pollinated Javanese. But there are also the extraordinary moments of aesthetic virtuosity, when different linguistic forms collide and serve to mutually illuminate each other. Admixture is governed by a traditional sense of decorum of what is considered proper in *wayang kulit*, but a good puppeteer makes a name for himself by bending or changing rules, introducing new elements and ratios to the mixture. This too is sanctioned by the hagiographic texts dealing with Sunan Kalijaga, who when performing as an artist himself was said to 'have delighted in composing performance texts by mixing things *up*' *(karemene asusunan/lampahe nyampur anyambri)*.[10]

Different dialects known in and around Cirebon are stratified among the different puppet characters, in a way similar to *commedia dell'arte's* stratification of Italian dialects associated with different city-states of the peninsula. (Commedia is an example cited by Bakhtin as an intentional dialectical hybrid.) Thus, among the clown servants, Bagong typically speaks in Sundanese and Duwala in Betawi Malay (or sometimes Chinese Malay). In the Gegesik sub-variant of Cirebonese puppetry, Gareng speaks in a dialect associated with a neighbouring village (Jagapura or Bayalangu). Togog speaks in a rough imitation of Central Javanese, replete with back-rounded 'a' sounds and Central Javanese lexical items (e.g., the deictic '*kuwi*'). Puppeteers and spectators are conscious of the distribution of these linguistic types across a range of *wayang kulit* characters, and take this as a commentary on both the variety of language, as well as on certain sorts of people. It is not accidental, for example, that Togog, 'attracted to wealth like an ant is to sweets' and thus associated with negative, 'left-hand' characters, serving wealthy masters such as the rapacious Rahwana, is represented as a Central Javanese. During the colonial period, Central Javanese often served as mid-level agents in the colonial bureaucracy in Cirebon and elsewhere in western Java, and are consequently symbolically associated with a position of servitude under repressive masters.

Old Javanese texts in Cirebonese traditions of *wayang kulit* are not only sung by puppeteers as 'mood songs' (*suluk*), they are also translated or 'illuminated' (*dicandrakaken*) by the puppeteer at critical moments of performances. *Sloka*, or archaic aphorisms and expressions, also pepper narration and dialogue; it is always incumbent upon a Cirebonese puppeteer to not only cite a *sloka*, but also to translate and explain its meaning. 'The gods descended to earth from Suralaya like *sela blekiti. Sela* means stone; *blekiti* are ants. They were like ants marching over a stone, in ranks and columns'.[11] These devices are traditional and are part of the basic rhetorical equipment that defines performative competence.

Puppeteers today, are not only expected to preserve oral and written traditions, but also to cite and comment upon a more recent linguistic code. This code is sometimes referred to as *bahasa intelek* (intellectual language) by rural puppeteers from the Cirebon area. It is the sort of neologism and acronym-inflected language, villagers hear at cultural seminars and government-sponsored meetings and (for those that read) encounter in newspapers and books. It is basically a form of educated Indonesian (as opposed to colloquial Malay) with a heavy admixture of English words and loan words. (A special subset of this code is referred to as *bahasa internasional*, or 'international language', meaning basically English words or their Indonesian derivatives.)

In traditional Cirebonese *wayang kulit*, Malay is spoken by characters from overseas kingdoms and 'the lands above the winds', above all by the covetous king of Alengka, Rahwana.

"*Ladala, kurang ajar ya, hait brenti. Ya, siapa kamu he! Kamu ketek yang berbulu putih siapa he? Saya kira aku pernah melihat kau*" (Hey, stop you ill-mannered wretch. Who are you? Who are you white-haired monkey? I think I've seen you before).[12]

Malay, thus, tends to have markedly negative associations, due to the nature of characters associated with it in *wayang kulit*. In contrast, *bahasa intelek* tends to be used by virtuous characters more, above all Kresna, the Pendhawa's trusted advisor, who regularly drops *intelek* words and phrases (underlined below) into his Javanese utterances.

> *Selaku Dewa Kemanusan iki ngatasi ngurus manusa dhateng jagat madyapada niku diatur sedemikian rupa supaya takwa supaya bener. Mangka ngadhepi siluman iki pripun rama? Sehingga kula niki nimbulaken gagasan enggal perlu kangge nganakena persatuan lan kesatuan kelayan rayi Arjuna. Manunggaleng dwifungsi di antara Arjuna kelayan Kresna* (As the god of humanity, my concern is to provide guidance for all people of the earthly plane. People should be guided by whatever means necessary so that they are religiously devout and righteous. But in what manner should we confront these *silmuan* father? It has come to the point, where I have devised a new idea. There needs to be unity and integrity between Arjuna and myself. The dual functions need to merge into one).[13]

An overuse of *bahasa intelek* by the college-educated puppeteer Purjadi in a 1993 radio broadcast, early in his career, resulted in a direct critique by Asli, the widow of Akirna Hadiwekasan, Purjadi's favourite puppeteer. '*Ari ngomongaken wayang, aja dipai litas-litas*' – when your puppets speak, don't use words like 'litas' – Asli's pronunciation of *prioritas*, a loan word meaning 'priority'. Purjadi took this criticism to heart and assiduously avoided such words and phrases for a year or so. These words were part of his own day-to-day conversational discourse, but he realised they were unfamiliar to many villagers, who might experience them as jarring and out of place. Such words began slowly to creep back in, however, as Purjadi's confidence as a puppeteer grew. In a May 1995 show, I recorded and transcribed with Purjadi, the clown-servant Cungkring demands to see his uncle Bethara Guru (the Javanese version of the high god Shiva) on the basis of his sanguinal relation. '*Dadi ya, ya nyuwun supados ya jare jaman kiyan sih njaluk diprioritasenang, lah konon*' (so that's why I would you know, as they put it these days you know, I would like to be prioritised, that's right). Purjadi told me that the hedge 'as they put it these days' was meant to signal to members of the audience that he was using the word 'intentionally' (*sengaja*) and not due to a lack of knowledge of the linguistic decorum of *wayang kulit*.

When I asked Purjadi, half tongue in cheek, where Cungkring would have learned such a word as *prioritas*, he supplied the only logical answer: he didn't know for sure, but perhaps Cungkring reads newspapers.

## Performing *Wayang Kulit* in Scotland

So far, I've explored how *wayang kulit* as a social event in Java draws diverse spectators into its performative arena and has the capacity to generate new social relations. I have conveyed the sense that *wayang kulit* might also be usefully understood in Bakhtin's terms as an intentional hybrid, allowing a linguistic consciousness to cast new light upon another, creating an opportunity for reflection and contemplation of the multifarious nature of contemporary existence. These aspects of performance are traditional, and part of what defines *wayang kulit* as it exists in the world. There are no precise relations of homology among setting, participants and dramaturgy. Within the 'traditional' framework of *wayang kulit*, transformation and revaluation are of paramount importance in the determination of whether a performance-event is deemed significant, meaningful or exciting.

I would now like to turn to the issue of *wayang kulit* as an international performing art form, which has been modified, adjusted, adapted and appropriated in various performative circumstances. This, too, I would suggest must be conceived as an essential part of understanding what *wayang kulit* is. For an artistic style can only achieve coherence by identifying itself dialectically as what it is not.[14] It is at the border lines that *wayang kulit* either triumphantly establishes itself as a vital artistic form or is dominated by other interests or forms.

Many historical surveys fetishize the appropriative moment when European and American practitioners from Voltaire and Goethe to Peter Brook and Ariane Mnouchkine first encountered Asian theatrical texts on the page and the stage. Asian theatre is deemed important in terms of the impact it has made on Western theatrical practice. A survey of the intercultural history of *wayang kulit* from this ethnocentric frame would prioritise practitioners, such as Henri Rivière, Edward Gordon Craig, Lotte Reininger and Julie Taymor. For many of these theatre artists, *wayang kulit* served as a sort of 'found object', upon which they mapped their own desires and conceptions. Attending to these practitioners presents the danger of effacement of another intercultural history, the history of transmission and circulation of puppets and puppeteers from India to Java, and from Java to the islands of western Indonesia as well as the Malay peninsula and Thailand. It would also possibly efface the efforts of numerous Javanese practitioners, who have individually and collaboratively adapted *wayang kulit* to fit the needs and demands of European, American and other sponsors. Some sponsors, like Richard Schechner at NYU, have called for 'authentic' reproductions of the Javanese experience.[15] Others, such as the organisers of the Hague's annual Pasar Malam Besar cultural fair, want to provide a nostalgic half-hour 'taster'. Some sponsors object to the patriarchal values imbedded in Javanese *wayang kulit* and demand 'rewrites' in performative scripts. Other sponsors go so far as to require Javanese puppeteers (sometimes in collaboration with local artists) to adapt entirely new story material to *wayang kulit*. This has become increasingly the case over the last two decades or so, due less to a spirit of innovation as to ideologies of multiculturalism and cultural diversity: performative projects are effectively valued by how much they recognise and incorporate values and traditions of constituent cultures and subcultures of societies. Successful funding bids must do more than represent Java abroad, they must also pay heed to the dominant local culture as well as numerous ethnic minorities.

One of the more active Javanese puppeteers in what might be called multicultural *wayang kulit* has been Joko Susilo, a professional fifth generation Javanese puppeteer from Sragen, Central Java, and puppetry lecturer at Sekolah Tinggi Seni Indonesia Surakarta (STSI, one of Indonesia's most highly ranked artistic conservatories). Joko Susilo has a unique profile that has contributed to his worldwide marketability as an 'international puppeteer' (*dhalang internasional*).[16] He is a first-rate shadow puppeteer, but is also an experienced animator of rod puppets (which are featured in the concluding tableaux and Limbukan clown scenes in Sragen style *wayang kulit*); he is an equally well puppet maker, martial artist and a highly competent *gamelan* musician – in addition to possessing an affable personality and a professional work ethic. Joko Susilo has lived since 1992, in New Zealand, where he learned English, brought up two children and obtained a PhD in ethnomusicology at Otago University. Joko Susilo's initiation into intercultural theatre began much before his move to New Zealand, however. He participated in numerous 'experiments' in shadow puppetry at STSI, a hotbed for innovation in Javanese arts since the late 1970s, *inter alia* a multi-puppeteer experimental form of shadow puppet theatre telling Buddhist stories known as *wayang Budha* and a large-scale French-Indonesian co-production of the Gilgamesh epic with shadow puppets in 1987. It was this year that he began to teach foreign students of shadow puppetry at the conservatory as well. One of those students, Katherine Knox, became his wife; I was another (I refer to him thus as Mas Joko). Intimate contact with these foreign students and participation in theatrical productions with them and others stimulated Mas Joko to think seriously about how *wayang kulit* might be perceived and re-conceived in a foreign environment.

This work continued in New Zealand. While studying at Otago University, Mas Joko received, Creative New Zealand funding to create a theatre work combining the technical apparatus of Javanese shadow puppet with Maori tales and Maori icons known as *karetao*. These performing objects, articulated at the arms, were museum pieces and not in active use by members of the Maori community or others, though available historical sources indicate they were previously used to tell stories and accompany songs. Mas Joko recounts that he approached a Maori tribal elder whether it would be permissible for him as a non-Maori to use replicas of these objects in a theatrical performance and received a firm 'no' as a reply. 'But I took this no to mean yes', he says, and immediately began to put together a team to produce a sensational dance drama with large-scale shadow puppets and Maori performing objects. Subsequently, Mas Joko was invited by New York composer Barbara Benary to perform in her *Wayang Esther*, a shadow puppet operatic telling of the Biblical book of Megilat Esther. In the remainder of this essay, I would like to discuss one of Mas Joko's most recent project, carried out in residence in Glasgow, Scotland.

The completion of his dissertation at Otago University left Mas Joko available for more extensive foreign touring and Mas Joko and I, together wrote a successful grant proposal to the Leverhulme Trust under their artist-in-residence category to allow Mas Joko to come to Glasgow for the academic year 2001-2002. It was Mas Joko's idea to do a production of a Scottish saga that could be presented using puppets, masks and *gamelan* music. The funds from Leverhulme were not sufficient to cover all his living expenses though, and he supplemented the grant income with teaching at the Scottish Mask and Puppet Centre (SMPC), which runs a two-year HND course in puppet arts for Anniesland College.

Mas Joko found ready musical collaborators in Scotland, as well as support from the SMPC and the University of Glasgow. A community *gamelan* group called Naga Mas has been active in Glasgow since 1991, playing on a *pelog* set of instruments purchased by the regional council and the Scottish Chamber Orchestra and currently housed at the Tramway, Glasgow's major arts centre. The presence of a Javanese teacher energised old members and attracted new ones (including my wife and I); together we embarked on a series of English-language *wayang kulit* performances. I have described elsewhere performances we gave during March and April, 2002.[17] I would like now to deal with the academic year's culminating effort, *Wayang Cuchulain*, a collaboration between Gamelan Naga Mas with students from the SMPC and the Department of Theatre, Film and Television Studies at the University of Glasgow.

*Wayang Cuchulain* built directly on our earlier productions, incorporating music, puppets, texts and performers introduced over the previous months. It had been the suggestion of a lecturer in Celtic Literature at Glasgow University that we turn to the *Cuchulain* saga for a story source. This saga is better known in Ireland than in Scotland, but numerous Scottish *Cuchulain* manuscripts are known and the tales remain part of the oral tradition of people of the west coast and the islands. We focussed on the earliest episodes of the saga, from *Cuchulain's* birth in a fairy palace, his upbringing by the warriors of Ulster, his assumption of arms, his courting of the maiden Emer, his studies with Skatha, and the battle and love of Aoife. Our principal sources were the celebrated compilations by Lady Gregory and T.W. Rolleston, but we consulted other texts as well.[18] Much of the final script was in fact composed of direct citations from Lady Gregory and Rolleston, making for a slightly archaic linguistic texture not unlike *wayang kulit*.

The play began with a version of the musical overture for *gamelan* known as *talu* that ended with a jazz composition with flugelhorn solo. An onstage narration segued into a prologue depicting the abduction of *Cuchulain's* mother, Dechtire, on the night of her wedding to Lugh, when Dechtire and the maidens, who accompany her are transformed to birds, and mystically transported by Lugh of the Long Hand (the Celtic sun god) to the fairy world. Time passes and the kingdom of Ulster is inflicted by a plague of birds. Ulster's king, Conchubar, sends his troops to chase the birds (corresponding to the *budalan* scene of classical *wayang kulit*), arriving at a fairy mound, which is the portal to Lugh's world. They meet Dechtire, who then gives birth to Setanta (later known as Cuchulain). Cuchulain is brought up communally by the great warriors and sages of Ulster. His birth-name Setanta is replaced by 'Cuchulain' (meaning the hound of Culain), when he accidentally kills the watchdog of the smith Culain and vows to guard Culain's dun in its stead. (The fight between Setanta and the hound corresponds dramatically to the *perang gagal* of classical Solonese *wayang kulit*.)

The second part of the play begins with *Cuchulain's* courting of the maiden Emer. Emer rejects his overture, protesting that *Cuchulain* still needs to prove his mettle, and *Cuchulain* departs for the Land of Shadows (located in the island of Skye) to study feats of arm with the woman-warrior Skatha. Then followed an on-stage dialogue with light *gamelan* music featuring *Cuchulain's* driver Laeg and his Laeg's brother Id macRiangabra, who is the driver of *Cuchulain's* friend Ferdiad. This interlude, corresponding to the *gara-gara* or clown scene of *wayang kulit*, was devised and acted by two company members in kilts, and allowed a chance to refer to topical humour – the World Cup, intercultural theatre, the Ladyboys of Bangkok. It also featured gentle ribbing of the apparent absurdity of performing a Celtic epic in Indonesian style in Glasgow today. The play then returns to the shadow world, as *Cuchulain* leaps across the gulf that separates Skye from the mainland and demands that Skatha accept her as a student. Skatha agrees and a silent training sequence is depicted using human shadows. When Skatha wages war against the Scottish queen Aoife, *Cuchulain* fights on the side of his teacher. (The battle corresponds to the final chaotic battle, sometimes called *perang amuk-amukan*, of Solonese *wayang kulit*.) *Cuchulain* defeats Aoife and they become lovers. At the battle's conclusion, *Cuchulain* receives the gift of the fearsome belly-spear known as the Gae-Bolg from Skatha.

It was our intention that the production would allow the myths and ancient expressive traditions of two island nations (Britain and Indonesia) to reverberate and cast light upon each other, to revel in connections that exist at a deep substructural stratum and bring to the surface startling incongruities in a contemporary theatrical milieu. *Cuchulain*, the great culture hero of the Celtic world, is not an commonman, he is unique and heroically so. Yet his exploits and adventures, if not his personality, when explored through an

Indonesian aesthetic, speak to common experience. His deeds are used collectively, though he is not. There in was a paradox we hoped to bring to life theatrically.

The collective process of rehearsing and staging this piece of theatre and its reception in Glasgow and elsewhere provide lessons that are broadly applicable to 'multicultural' *wayang kulit* in the contemporary world. Even the pronunciation of the eponymous hero's name was a source of amusing confusion. *'Cuchulain'* after the Irish pronunciation recommended by W.B. Yeats (for example), in his dramatic adaptations of saga materials, is a close homophone for the Javanese word meaning pox or facial scars. Mas Joko consistently resisted this preferred pronunciation; he could not bring himself to refer to the culture hero with a word suggesting a deformity, calling the hero 'Kukulen' (as an Indonesian orthography would have it) instead.

The starting place for Joko Susilo were the puppets themselves, which were only visible as shadows projected onto an enormous cych. These puppets were carved from cardboard (water buffalo hide not being readily available in Glasgow) and spray-painted black (for sharper shadow effects). One of these puppets could take up to a week to design and carve, and Mas Joko consequently had to start carving even before the script had been finalised. The fragility of the material (card will break if bent) was a cause of regret for Mas Joko; the impermanence of the medium was offset only slightly by the possibility that his puppets *might* one day be used as models for more durable objects, *if* a *Cuchulain* piece were to be staged again.

The design of the puppets followed the basic conventions of Javanese puppetry, with three control rods and arms articulated at elbows and shoulders. Most of the male figures are depicted with kilts, closely resembling the *kain* skirts worn by some Javanese shadow puppets. Mas Joko was also initially tempted to give these puppets three-quarters pants as an undergarment, until it was explained to him that 'real men don't wear underpants' in Scotland. A few traditional Javanese puppets were appropriated for the demon army of Aoife, and the spade-shaped *kayon* (tree of life) puppet was also used (as was a Celtic tree of life puppet), but there were in all more than twenty original character designs executed by Joko Susilo. A number of these were directly inspired by comical puppets popularised in the 1970s and 1980s by Gondho Dharman, a comic Sragen-style puppeteer, in his highly innovative *wayang kulit* shows.

None of the puppeteers, aside from Joko Susilo and myself, had prior experience in manipulating Javanese shadow puppets, and all were greatly challenged to bring life to the puppets. A number of the actors were resistant to the text, finding the syntax used by Lady Gregory and Rolleston to be forced and unnatural to the tongue. One actor actually changed his lines to suit him. Another of the performers, brought in because of his skill in vocal impressions and Celtic wrestling, revealed in rehearsals that he could also play the Celtic drum or Bodhrán. He began by accompanying rehearsals attended by only actors and puppeteers, but ended up musically accompanying a sizeable part of the play's narrative sections, playing on stage adjacent to the narrators. Other opportunities were found to lighten a text which some of the performers found 'grim' in the in-front-of-the-screen live action. So intensely focussed were all performers on their tasks (dancing, miming, puppeteering, speaking dialogue, narrating, playing music) that nobody paid any heed to Michael McCann's backstage filming during our second performance.

Both performances at the Gilmorehill Centre Theatre at the University of Glasgow were effective sell-outs. Audience members came from many walks of life. Some had seen previous Naga Mas performances and were *gamelan* regulars. Others came due to personal connections with cast members. A large percentage though came out of interest in the *Cuchulain* saga, which had received little in the way of theatrical play in Scotland over the last decades. (The *Cuchulain* plays of W.B. Yeats are much more celebrated in his native Ireland.) A restaurant owner from the west coast of Scotland reported her delight and pride to see the tales, which she heard as a child being presented for the first time in her memory on stage: it was an opportunity for her to share her heritage with her family, and find value in her oral tradition. The Irish father of one cast member shared with him his own recollection of the *Cuchulain* story, and pointed out differences between our theatrical rendition and the tales he recalled from his youth, giving him pointers as well on the rendition of the heroic character.

There were other critical and reflective reactions as well. One theatre professional found the structure overly episodic, saying that we in fact performed two plays, *Cuchulain's* youth and the courtship of Emer, not one. (Such criticisms are also characteristic of Western reactions to *wayang kulit* and other oral traditions.) This same theatre worker was critical of the performance's dramaturgy. There are some

things that puppets should show, and some things that should be told,
he reported. You shouldn't try to do both. This charge of unnecessary
repetition is also a characteristic Western complaint against *wayang
kulit*. Others found the language to be difficult to understand and the
various names hard to keep track of. Yet there was also a three-year-old
child, who saw the play and spoke of it (and enacted parts of it) daily for
months: it was the first time she had set foot in a theatre and it was a
magical experience for her. My four-year-old daughter, who was
present at most of the rehearsals, was still singing the *gamelan* melodies
from the show, four months later.

Interestingly, there were no direct critiques of the use of
Javanese-inspired shadow puppets and *gamelan* to enact a Celtic saga.
This might be because there is little sense of ownership of the
*Cuchulain* tales in Glasgow; it is too far from the normal daily concerns
of people and has not been sanctified as the exclusive cultural property
of the Celtic world.

Reactions to the video, when it was shown at a symposium at STSI
Surakarta in September 2002 are also worth noting. *Wayang Cuchulain*
placed the *gamelan* orchestra in front of the screen, so that it was
directly visible to the audience. The spectacular gongs, chimes and
other percussion instruments constituted a major part of the
scenography. Spectators reported being more interested at times in
what the musicians were doing than the action depicted upon the
shadow screen or enacted by live actors. STSI faculty members admired
this creative placement of the gamelan. Less enjoyable was a bit in the
clown scene, when two *bonang* pots were transformed from musical
instruments into breasts – although *gamelan* instruments are not
universally treated with reverence in Java today, this crudely comic bit
was deemed to be a bit extreme. All admired the facility and ease with
which a Celtic saga could be conveyed using the dramaturgical
structure and technical apparatus of *wayang kulit*; the translation lost
few of the essentials of the Javanese form. Even with the kilts, Celtic
drumming, English language and overly crude clowning, this was still
recognisably a piece of Javanese theatre.

## Imparting Thought

This account of various international and global peregrinations of
*wayang kulit* is intended to provide perspective by incongruity on an
art form overly identified with a single ethnic group. *Wayang kulit* is

not a fixed essence, but is itself a contact zone where different people and groups can meet and work out what is important to them politically, linguistically, socially and culturally. It is at this level at which exchange becomes meaningful, imparting thought and structuring feeling.

This understanding of what *wayang kulit* is and how it means cannot be dissociated from the researcher's own perspective on this theatre. Research projects in theatre studies are typically conceived, funded, researched and written up as projects. My own involvement in *wayang kulit* operates according to a different temporal logic; I have been drawn into its complex field of play for nearly half of my life. I do not claim a particularly privileged position in this regard, but recognise that I follow in the well-laid tracks of Asian theatre practitioner-scholars including John Emigh, Phillip Zarrilli and Saskia Kersenboom, as well as generations of *gamelan* experts. All of us have trained in Asian theatre forms to the point where they are no longer foreign, but part of the self. I am not bi-theatrical; *wayang kulit* constitutes today (and for the last decade) my primary idiom of artistic expression. This essay's survey of *wayang kulit* as contact zone suggests that my practical-scholarly purchase is not a newly emergent possibility, but a response to aspects and tendencies always present in *wayang kulit* as a performatively poly- and ever-changing arts form.

[This essay is based in part upon research carried out while being a postdoctoral research fellow at the International Institute for Asian Studies (1998-2000) and also at the University of Glasgow (2001-2002) with the assistance of the Leverhulme Trust. Another version of this essay will be appearing in a Horniman Museum volume on objects in performance in Southeast Asia edited by Fiona Kerlogue. Kind thanks to Dr Kerlogue and the Horniman Museum for allowing the essay's inclusion in the current volume.]

## Notes

1. Alan Read, *Theatre and Everyday Life: An Ethics of Performance.* (London: Routledge, 1993), p. 3. For a recent review of global and intercultural performance, see Richard Schechner, *Performance Studies: An Introduction* (London: Routledge, 2002), pp. 226-272.

2. Richard Schechner, *Between Theater and Anthropology* (Philadelphia: University of Pennsylvania Press, 1985).

3. Clifford Geertz, *Available Light: Anthropological Reflections on Philosophical Topics.* (Princeton: Princeton University Press, 2000), p. 115.

4. Ward Keeler, *Javanese Shadow Plays, Javanese Selves* (Princeton: Princeton University Press, 1987).

5. A.L. Becker, 'The Journey through the Night: Some Reflections on Burmese Traditional Theatre', in Mohd. Taib Osman, ed., *Traditional Drama and Music of Southeast Asia* (Kuala Lumpur: Dewan Bahasa dan Pustaka, 1974).

6. See particularly Clifford Geertz, *The Religion of Java* (Chicago: University of Chicago Press, 1960).

7. James A. Boon, 'Folly, Bali, and Anthropology, or Satire Across Cultures', in E. Bruner, ed., *Text, Play, and Story.* (Prospect Heights, IL: Waveland, 1984).

8. This text, which has been titled *Hikayat Suhunan Gunung Jati* by its editor and translator, was collected by Sir Thomas Raffles in 1815, and possibly based on a Javanese original. See M. S. Pusposaputro, *Hikayat Suhunan Gunung Jati: A Hagiography of a Muslim Saint in Java* (unpublished thesis, School of Oriental and African Studies, 1976).

9. Mikhail Bakhtin, *The Dialogic Imagination* (Austin: University of Texas Press, 1981), pp. 358-362.

10. D.A. Rinkes, Pangeran Panggoeng, zijne honden en het wajangspel. *Tijdschrift voor Indische Taal-, Land- en Volkenkunde Uitgeven door het Bataviaasch Genootschap van Kunsten en Wetenschappen* 54 (1912), p. 150.

11. Darmabhakti, *Bumiloka* (Unpublished manuscript, 1994).

12. Basari and Langen Suara, *Rama Nitis.* (Jakarta: Dian Records, n.d.), Cassette 1b.

13. Basari, *Demon Abduction: A Wayang Ritual Drama from West Java*, ed. Matthew Isaac Cohen (Jakarta: Lontar Foundation, 1999) pp. 70, 204.

14. Claude Lévi-Strauss, *The Way of the Masks* (Seattle: University of Washington Press, 1988).

15. Richard Schechner, 'Wayang Kulit in the Colonial Margin', *TDR* 126 (1993), pp. 25-61.

16. The term *dhalang internasional* came into general currency in connection with performances by foreign puppeteers and expatriate Indonesian puppeteers at the 1999 Pekan Wayang Nasional, the National Wayang Festival, organised every five years in Jakarta. The category conflated both foreign performers of *wayang golek* and *wayang kulit* (including myself) and Indonesian puppeteers with extensive experience performing abroad (including Joko Susilo).

17. Matthew Isaac Cohen, 'Bima Meets Cuchulain and Other Stories', *Seleh Notes* 9, no. 3 (2002), pp. 14-15.

18. These texts are available on-line. For Lady Gregory's *Cuchulain of Muirthemne* see http://www.sacred-texts.com/neu/celt/cuchand for T.W. Rolleston's *Myths and Legends of the Celtic Race* see http://www.sacred-texts.com/neu/celt/mlcr/).

# 37

# Okinawan Drama

## Its Ethnicity and Identity Under Assimilation to Japan

**Shoko Yonaha**

Okinawa was reinstated as a prefecture of Japan quite recently, in 1972; excluding the American Military Occupation (1945-1972), she had been one prefecture of Japan since the abolition of the Kingdom of Ryukyu in 1879[1]. Nonetheless, despite the long history of the islands, it would not be an exaggeration to say that Okinawans are still struggling to find their identity as Okinawans, even if their geo-political identity is defined as being Japanese. This is perhaps because Okinawa was once an independent country whose cultural identity was strongly caught between two dominant countries, i.e., China and Japan. The Kingdom of Ryukyus' independence had flourished for more than four centuries under the sponsorship of China; Chinese investiture envoys were sent to crown the Ryukyu king 24 times, until the last Sho Dynasty. It lasted even after the unfortunate invasion by the domain of Satsuma (currently Kagoshima Prefecture) in 1609. Secretly hiding its submissive socio-economic stance being exploited from Satsuma, but facing China as her patron-the Kingdom of Ryukyu had to take a double standard on the surface of its policy. However, this did not extend to the performing arts, which in many ways kept the independent culture alive. The purpose of this paper is to discuss how a new form of drama, Okinawa *shibai*, was born and developed. This will be preceded by a short introduction of the *Ryukyuan kumi udui*. It also focuses on how Okinawan drama functioned as a device to preserve

Okinawans' past memories and express their ethnic identity under assimilation to Japan.

Even while being a colonial country of Satsuma, and eventually of the Tokugawa Shogunate,[2] the *Ryukyu* kingdom tried to make its system of policy and idea of cultural identity strongly *Ryukyuan*. Thus, *Ryukyuan* aesthetics in the performing arts were born and refined in a politically complex milieu. Tamagusuku Chokun (1687-1734)[3] first created a combined drama called *kumi udui*[4] and presented it to Chinese envoys in 1719. The presentation of those first five works of *kumi udui*-"*Nidou Tekiuchi*" (Revenge of the Two Boys), "*Shushin Kane Iri*" (Passion and the Bell) which is often compared to the noh play "*Dojoji*", "*Mekaru-shi*" (Master Mekarushi), "*Onna-mono-gurui*" (The Madwoman), and "*Koko no Maki*" (Filial Piety) was an epoch-making event for all *Ryukyuans*, and these works are all well-appreciated for their excellence even today. *Kumi udui* is a kind of multi-faceted crystal of the performing arts; based on *Ryukyu's* local celebratory dance form, *choja nu ufusu*, and taking some ideas of performance techniques from the Japanese noh, *kyogen*, and kabuki forms, it is built upon plots taken from original *Ryukyuan* legends or folk tales. *Kumi udui* is a composite drama in which chanted dialogue, classic music accompanied by a three-stringed musical instrument called *sanshin*, other musical instruments such as *kutu* (koto), *kuchoh* (Chinese fiddle), *fansoh* (flute), and *tehk* (drum), and dances are all combined to make one beautiful harmony. In the complexity of its artistic accomplishment, it is comparable to the highest performing arts anywhere. According to Teruo Yano, a Japanese scholar who has published three books about *kumi udui*, it is a composite art comprised of poems, music, and dances comparable to an opera of Wagner.[5]

The main characteristics of *Chokun's* five *kumi udui* are, first, the beauty of its lyrics both in dialogues and as chanted by musicians (called *jiyute*). Second, the rhythm of songs and dialogues mostly consist of 30 syllables, in four lines of eight, eight, eight and six, chanted in tones, which are as crucial as the costumes-colourful and very much stylized. Third, the style of acting has some similarity to *noh* plays, although generally masks are not used. Four, the plot doesn't look back, but rather moves only forward to its happy conclusions. Fifth, as it was originally called *ukanshin udui* (court dances) and appreciated by noble classes and Chinese high-ranking diplomats, those who performed were youth chosen from the nobility. Sixth, the words of those dialogues are a mixture of old classical usages of the Ryukyuan language as well as some old Japanese rhetorical words. Last, *kumi udui* includes some classical Ryukyu dances, both beautiful and entertaining to audience's eyes.

Those essential qualities of *kumi udui* simply symbolize the ethnicity of a very Ryukuan sense with which the kingdom's ideologies and morals were viewed. For instance, although Confucian ethics (loyalty, filial piety and chastity) form its backbone, folk customs and indigenous beliefs such as Okinawan animism and shamanism, ancestor worship and very strong maternal bonds are also merged into the whole. Above all, ritualistic songs (called *omoro*) and *ryuka* (eight-eight-eight-and-six-syllable short poems like Japanese *waka* or *haiku*) are taken into the form of *kumi udui*. To sum up, the birth of *kumi udui* was significant for the people of *Ryukyu*, as it has crystallized the core of *Ryukyuan* ethnicity and identity. Furthermore, it was its performances by the *Ryukyu* national theatre, which in many ways kept the culture alive.

## The Birth and Development of Okinawan Drama (*Shibai*) from 1879 to 1945 under Assimilation

When the Kingdom of *Ryukyu* existed, people of *Ryukyus* were called *Ryukyuan*, but after the kingdom was overthrown, *Ryukyu-han* was changed to Okinawa Prefecture, and the people came to be called Okinawan (or *uchinanchu*, as opposed to *yamatonchu* for the Japanese). Since that time, Okinawans have created a Japanese other against which to identify themselves.

Sociologist Milton Gordon's definition[6] of 'behavioural assimilation' (also known as 'acculturation') fits in the case of Okinawa from 1879 to the Second World War. During this period, Okinawans were obliged to absorb the-supposedly superior-Japanese cultural norms, beliefs, and behaviour patterns, and to adapt to them in order to become more Japanese. The process was forceful and it appeared to some extent like a colonization process; Japanese policy didn't mind eradicating Okinawan culture, languages and beliefs. Japan's colonial implementation was immediately implemented; the first governor of the newly created Okinawan prefecture successfully spearheaded a new educational system that would plant the Japanese identity into all Okinawans. Language played the main role for achieving this purpose. The *Ryukyu* languages were looked down upon; students who spoke in

*Ryukyu*an were punished by having a dialect placard (*fogen-fuda*) hung around their necks in schools.

Later, as we see in many Okinawa plays,[7] which depict subject matters taken from the period of *haihan chiken* (the abolition of *Ryukyu-han* and the establishment of Okinawa Prefecture), this historical incident was a difficult change for many Okinawans. Many had to find alternate means of living, especially government officials and others of the samurai-class who served the kingdom. Some of them moved to the villages and taught their songs and dances as well as *kumi udui* to the villagers. Ironically then, some 'court' performing arts were passed down and preserved by the efforts of local villagers; many of them began to be performed in the open-air theatres (*ashibina*) in the villages.[8] On the other hand, there were some others who stayed in the cities-Shuri and Naha-and held their performances in small open playhouses to earn a living for the first time in the history of Okinawa.

The first performance presented in 1882 was the beginning of commercial theatre in Okinawa. Among those performers, Tamagusuku Seijuu (1868-1945), Tokashiki Shuryo (1880-1953) and Arakaki Shogan (1880-1937) are well known. Though they were showing the court performing arts at first, as time passed by, audiences started to demand new dances and songs, and *kyougen* or *Chogin* (a short drama in Okinawan dialect). Audiences wanted their own tastes reflected on the stage. A short time later, Okinawan drama (Okinawa *shibai* or *uchina-shibai*) was born. New styles of dances called *zou udui* (miscellaneous dance) were created, and many commoners became fascinated with the new form of theatre in which they were the main characters along with samurai-class. The first significant opera, which was a 35-minute-long form of *shibai*, was "*Uyanma*" (Concubine); it is composed of one scene, in which a *zaiban* (a samurai sent to *Yaeyama* Island as its chief bureaucrat), leaves his concubine who served him for two or three years with a child. A boatman takes an initiative and the *zaiban* accepts the ritual of separation and the couple and the child dance with each other. It is a transitional form between *kumi udui* and *Ryukyu kageki* (an opera sung in *Ryukyu*an language with folk music, adding some classical songs) and called *hougen serifu-geki* (spoken drama in *Ryukyu*an, in which subjects are taken from history, legends and real incidents). The way the characters spoke was similar to those of *kumi udui* but with slight variation, and the dances were accompanied by songs (local folk songs from Yaeyama) and sanshin. The first appearance of "*Uyanma*"[9] is not recorded, but it is estimated at around 1893.

Later, a large permanent theatre was built and several performing companies in mainland Japan visited Okinawa and performed kabuki and *soshi shibai* (*kiwamono*, a form of drama based on real stories). Also, Okinawan actors traveled to Tokyo and Osaka to practice their sense of performance. Cultural exchanges began to take place and Okinawan actors absorbed the essence of both old and modern Japanese style of theatre. Even adapted versions of Shakespeare's plays, including "Othello", "Hamlet" and "The Merchant of Venice" were performed in Okinawan dialect in 1906.[10]

All this happened scarcely 30 years after the *Ryukyu*an annexation to Japan. Okinawa was even taking in western culture through Japan, and thus Japanese assimilation meant also a sort of westernization. Okinawans performing artists and their art form, Okinawa shibai, were in the process of learning and creating through cultural contact, and it was in this period, in 1907, that the first marvelous *Ryukyu kageki* (opera) debuted. The three authentic *kageki* (also called the three greatest Okinawan tragedies) were created from the late Meiji era to Taisyo era and many audiences, especially women, rushed into the theatre. These *kageki* were "*Tumaiaka*" (a tragic love story) in 1907, "*Okuyama no botan*" (a tragic story of a low-caste woman who bore a boy to a samurai, and eventually commits suicide for the sake of her son's happiness) in 1914, and "*Iejima Handuugwa*" (about a girl who falls in love with a married man she saves, but who is forsaken and commits suicide) in 1924. These *kageki*'s lines, songs, and dances cast a spell on the minds of Okinawans, and even now they are repeatedly performed every year. *Hougen serifu-geki* was also at its peak in 1907; "*Nakijin Yuraiki*" (a story of a prince of the castle of Nakijin), "*Ufu Aragusuku Chyuuden*" (a story of one high-ranking samurai's loyalty and filial piety in the Taisyo era) were also performed around this time. Obviously those *kageki* and *hogen serifu-geki* were greatly influenced by *kumi udui*. Without *kumi udui*, those great masterpieces of Okinwan *shibai* wouldn't have been produced. The details of *kumi udui* and Okinawa *shibai* are beyond the scope of this paper, so a lengthy discussion is not needed.

The popularity of Okinawa *shibai* among the common people was a new phenomenon of this period; accordingly, theatre became the centre of media and cultural dissemination. People gathered at the theatre to get a new sense of the era as well as to remind themselves of the history of the kingdom of *Ryukyu*s. Through these drama forms, audiences were unconsciously re-enforcing their cultural identity as *Ryukyu*ans, despite the severe Japanese assimilation policy. Nevertheless, it appears that even among the population, the general trend was toward being Japanese, which, combined with the strict education policy, made great progress towards the termination the *Ryukyu*an language and the discrediting of *Ryukyu*an customs.

Because of assimilation policies, it was also true that those who engaged in theatre performance were discriminated against by some establishments and those who highly appreciate Japanization, even if they were welcomed by many audiences. As already noted above, the *Ryukyuan* languages (also referred to as 'the Okinawan dialects') were pushed aside as accommodation to Japan was institutionalized through education. However, Okinawa *shibai* was spoken in *Ryukyu*an, using a mixture of Shuri and Naha dialects, and had a specific tone of speaking (*shibai-kucho*) For instance, samurai and commoners' way of speaking was strictly distinguished. Many plays were colloquially created; for example, there was a style called *kuchidate* in which a plot was first created and lines were added impromptu by each actor, to the accompaniment of folk music and dances.

What was going on in the society was so complicated that Okinawan performing artists and their audiences were trying, at the same time, to seek and sustain their old cultural memories, and to soak up the new influences of the era. It meant they simultaneously tried to reproduce the heritage their predecessors left behind and recreate new ones; this was done not strictly to sustain the communal cultural memories and assets, but rather to struggle with the big wave of assimilation itself.

In the 1930's, after a half-century had passed since the abolition of the Kingdom of *Ryukyu*s, Okinawa *shibai* entered its real golden age; Okinawans came to face-to-face with the tragic history of their country, in a history play written by Yamazato Eikichi (1902-1989). This was a story of the last struggle of the last king and his high-ranking officers. The moment of the fall of the kingdom was presented on stage. Each character's inner conflict and vision were articulated plainly for all to see. It is said that for one month many Okinawans thronged to see the theatre and shed tears. In addition to the newly written history plays, *Sangoza* (a theatre troupe) was established; it was led by Majikina

Yuko (1888-1982) and five other actors, Oyadomari Kosyo (1897-1986), Higa Seigi (1893-1976), Hachimine Kiji (1890-1971), Miyagi Nozo (1893-1987), and Shimabukuro Koyu (1893-1987), all highly-valued for their skill. It is said that more than a thousand *kageki* and quite a few *hogen serifu-geki* were performed by that time. However, the glory of *Sangoza* only lasted for 12 years, ending with the destruction of the theatre itself by a U.S. air raid in 1944.

It appears likely that, had the pacific war never occurred, Okinawan drama and its history would have been far more well developed and known today. Nevertheless, history shows that the unfortunate results of assimilation to Japan seemed to have been headed to eventual success, despite rampant and cruel discrimination against the Okinawans. This discrimination was made abundantly clear through the actions of Japanese troops stationed there; some Okinawans were killed because of allegations of being foreign spies due to speaking in their Okinawan dialect, and all were treated like secondary Japanese. Okinawans' identity crisis is perhaps most tragically exemplified by the mass-suicides during the US-Japanese land battles. Countless Okinawans were victimized by the war, and as many as 150.000-one out of every three-Okinawans were killed.

## Okinawan *shibai* from 1945 to the Present under Assimilation

After the pacific war, Okinawa was occupied by the U.S. military and remained under its control for twenty-seven years. The Japanese emperor's declaration that he wished Okinawa to be occupied by the U.S. in 1947 became yet another bitter memory for the population. Surprisingly, U.S. General MacArthur declared that the Okinawans are not Japanese and are discriminated against.[11] In effect, MacArthur determined Okinawa's fate, as it developed into a keystone of the U.S. presence in the Pacific, and remains so to this day. The U.S. occupation period was not a detrimental influence on Okinawa *shibai*, however The U.S. military policy tried to encourage Okinawa traditional values and even supported its development in order to entertain those devastated by the war; *shibai* troupes were urgently organized and given some official support. Within one year, there existed around forty commercial *shibai* troupes. Nevertheless, within a decade, Okinawans began to prefer new forms of entertainment like movies and TV shows. Furthermore, political demonstrations asking for a reversion and the reclamation of Japanese citizenship to overcome an unstable political-social status under the U.S. occupation led to the decline of the performance of domestic *shibai*; being Japanese and having Japanese values were highly appreciated again.

Several Okinawa shibai troupes experienced difficulties and most of them had to cease their theatre activities. Ironically, however, after reversion to Japan in 1972, Okinawans again tried to find their own cultural identity in the performing arts, as can be seen in the *Ryukyu* dances that have prevailed among women (these were forbidden before the war). *Shibai* was less accepted but has survived even though not many Okinawans speak *Ryukyu*an anymore. Nevertheless, the designation of *kumi udui* as a National Intangible Cultural Treasure in 1972, has preserved the form. *Shibai* actors had been the main unofficial custodians of *kumi udui* in the period prior to the war, but this ended when the Okinawan performing arts were divided into five categories: *Ryukyu* dance, *Ryukyu* classical music, *Ryukyu* folk music, Okinawa *shibai*, and *kumi udui*. The masters of Okinawa *shibai*, such as Majikina Yuko, Oyadomari Kosyo, and Miyagi Nozo, stopped practicing *shibai* performance, and instead opened their private *Ryukyu* dance *kenkyujo* (schools).

Ogimi Kotaro (1918-1994) and Makishi Kochu (1903-) are superb Okinawa *shibai* actors and playwrights who represent the post-World War II era in Okinawa, while Chinen Seishin emerged from the field of *shingeki* (new theatre). He created a striking play "*Jinruikan*"(Mad House), and won the 22nd Kishida Drama Award in 1977. The play is about Okinawa and Okinawans in modern history, and discrimination and assimilation in the name of the emperor are cynically observed with a sense of comedy.

Now looking back at more than a century of Okinawa Shibai history, it seems that the fate of *kumi udui* and Okinawa *shibai* will be decided in relation to the survival of the Ryukuan language in which they are performed. Today, fortunately, there are a number of young people who not only belong to *kumi udui* and *kageki* preservation organizations, but who also make their own theatre groups and are interested in performing Okinawa *shibai*; they are proud to perform as advocates of Okinawan culture.[12] It is certain that they recognize Okinawa *shibai* as centred in their communal cultural memory.

In 2004, the fourth national theatre "Kokuritu Gekijyo Okinawa" will open in Okinawa. It is expected that the new national theatre, mainly focussed on kumi udui, will bring Okinawans some new aspects for the future of traditional Okinawan performing arts.

Nevertheless, Okinawans as a whole don't appear to be overly excited about the project. The reason is not clear, but it could be that the theatre is overshadowed by Okinawa's geopolitical position between Japan and the U.S.; after 27 years of U.S occupation, the reversion to Japan in 1972, and the current continued presence of bases, the role of being the U.S.'s military keystone in the Pacific has never changed, and the Japanese government continues to dominate and influence Okinawa with large amounts of money to keep the bilateral security treaty with the U.S. As some say, for Japan's dependence on U.S. defense, Okinawa's self-autonomy and economic independence have been hindered ever since. Obviously, the U.S and Japan are exercising political and economic control and they take advantage by keeping the present situation of Okinawa as it is.

In this socio-political climate, what the national theatre can bring to Okinawans is not very clear. The national theatre could be used as a symbol of Japan's dominant power over Okinawans, or could be used as the strategic centre as a measure to win Asians over to Japan's side; or, as some Okinawans genuinely wished to have a specific theatre for preserving their traditional performing arts, it might serve as they wished as a place for their minds to reside.

## Identity Crisis and the New Sphere of Assimilation and Possibility of the Okinawan Drama

Tatsuhiro Oshiro, a well-known writer and playwright from Okinawa, has created new Okinawan *shibai* scripts, and recently published a collection of opera plays called *"Madama-michi"* (2001), and which consist of five new works of *kumi udui* and a new *kageki*-certainly a valiant effort to keep Okinawan culture alive. Oshiro, a winner of Japan's highest literary honour, the *Akutagawa* prize, for his 1969 novel "Cocktail Party", was quoted in 2002 in an interview with the Asahi Shimbun newspaper as saying that "Okinawa was once an independent kingdom and now is an internal colony of Japan, and unless some changes occur in both the U.S. and Japan, Okinawa won't be given any opportunity to change." He stressed that it is the Japanese government's policy toward the U.S that should be urgently changed.[13]

Oshiro's remark is pessimistic regarding the present situation of Okinawa. Yet, in creating five new works of *Kumi-Udui*, he has worked to maintain Okinawa's cultural identity. This identity, however, is ambiguous; as Johan Michael Purves points out, "

Assimilation to Japan, which had previously been welcomed by the Okinawans themselves, has slowed since the later part of the 1980's and into the 1990's, and is now seen to be eroding the foundations of traditional Okinawan culture of 'Okinawa-ness'.[14] Shun Medoruma, a 41-year-old writer who won the *Akutagawa* prize in 1997 says, "Now, we're neither completely Okinawan nor completely Japanese. We have to find out who we are."[15]

As is represented by the notions of Oshiro and Medoruma, Okinawans continue to struggle in their quest to find their true identity. Problems such as war, U.S military occupation and Japan's assimilation have made this difficult over the past century. The future of Okinawa's identity will also be affected further by globalization, although it remains to be seen whether this influence will be good or bad.

In fact, Okinawa's socio-political climate could be said to have been very much global from the beginning of the U.S. military occupation in 1945, since Okinawans were completely under the influence of the U.S.' strategic decisions during this period. Inevitably, Okinawans have had to face America, Japan, and other Asian countries while struggling herself to find her own direction. The best choice in the past was to return to Japan again. Okinawans wished to be protected by Japan's peaceful constitution. However, since the reversion to Japan, many Okinawans have come to question their decision. One of reasons stemmed from the disillusionment that, even after the occupation, the U.S. military presence has remained essentially the same. As well, as John Purves notes, the idea of assimilation itself has undergone a revision. Okinawans have begun to build their self-confidence and their inferiority complex has decreased. The background of this change in perspectives has several reasons; one of these is the rigidity of the Japanese national identity; another is a gradual economic improvement over the years in Okinawa-although Okinawa's per capita income levels remain the lowest in Japan. Finally, there is the concept of, as Milton Gordon defines it, cultural pluralism;[16] Okinawans have begun to recognize that Okinawa's unique cultural norms, traditions and behaviours are not always in conflict with shared common national values, goals and institutions.

Cultural pluralism is occurring in Okinawa. As Okinawans' cultural differences are seen to be an asset rather than a defect, and as "Okinawa-ness" has begun to gain acceptance throughout the world,

Okinawan ethnic music has become very popular in Japan. Certainly, this is one bright side to Okinawa in the beginning of the 21st century. As for Japan, which is supposed to be known as a homogeneous country, it could be a good exercise to take a deeper look at Okinawa's different cultures and customs in order to meet the requirements of globalization and the multicultural trends of this century.

Not many Okinawans speak in Okinawan dialect anymore. Nonetheless, almost all Okinawan performing arts are written and performed in *Ryukyu*an; it is in these dialects, and the rhythm of *ryuka*, that the true sense of 'Okinawa-ness' is implanted. No matter what changes time will bring, it is certain that the classic Okinawan performing arts, especially Okinawan *kumi udui* and *shibai*, will remain centre-stage for Okinawa's ethnic identity.

## Notes

1. King Satto is known for establishing tributary relationships with China in 1372, but the first *Sho* Dynasty (1406-1469) achieved the political unification of Okinawa in 1422. The second *Sho* Dynasty (1470-1879) lasted longer than any dynasty and those two *Sho* Dynasties represent the kingdom of *Ryukyu*.

2. The *Tokugawa Shogunate* was the government of the *Tokugawa* families who were *Sho*guns, and dominated Japan during the *Edo* period (1603-1868).

3. *Tamagusuku Chokun* was the magistrate in charge of entertainments for the most important events in the *Ryukyuan* royal court, the banquets for the Chinese envoys. He visited *Satsuma* and *Edo* several times as a represent of the national mission. It is said that he absorbed Japan's traditional theatre forms, noh and kabuki, on that occasion.

4. Now, 75 *Kumi Udui*(Odori) scripts are found, but not all of them have been performed yet. Along with Tamagusuku Chokun, Heshikiya Chobin (1700-1734), and Tasato Cyocyoku (1714-1775) are well known Kumi Udui writers.

5. Yano, Teruo, *kumiodori wo kiku*, Mizuki-*Sho*bou, 2003, p. 4.

6. Milton Gordon is an author of Assimilation in American Life: The Role of Race, Religion and National Origins, Oxford Univ. Press on Demond, 1964. His definition of assimilation is viewed in the web site such as Douglas Massey "What is Assimilation and has it a Spatial Dimension?" (1985) Essay Bank Co.UK. http://www.essaybank.co.uk/free_coursework/290.html.

7. For instance, *Shuri Jyo Akewatashi* (surrender of shuri castle), *Naha-Yumachi-Mukashi-Katagi* (old fashioned gentlemen in Naha), *Giwan Cyoho no Shi* (a death of Giwan Cyoho) by Yamazato Eikichi; *Haihan no Ayaame* (a wife of samurai in the abolition of the kingdom of *Ryukyus*) by Ogimi Kotaro; *Chinsagu nu Hana* (a love story of an outlaw), *Aku wo Moteasobumono* (a wicked man) by Makishi Kochu, and *Yogawariya Yogawariya* (a change of the time) by Oshiro Tatsuhiro.

8. Even today, the village festival called *Mura-Udui*, or *Mura-Shibai* is occasionally performed during the harvest season, and usually *Kumi-Udui* is performed at the end of the programs. *Hachigatu-Udui* in *Tarama* island (village) is well known for its specific forms of dances and *Kumi-Udui*, held for three days every year.

9. Its way of chanting is called *Wandon-Tari-Cho*: Wan means I, and it is a style of giving one's name at the opening of the *Show*.

10. Most of those Shakespearean plays were adaptation from the production done by Kawakami Otojiro in Japanese in Tokyo or Osaka. Those days, Okinawa theatre, and *Kyu-yo* theatre had a competition of performing new adapted plays from mainland Japan.

11. Nomura Hiroya, "Okinawa and Post-colonialism." p.156-158 in Post-Colonialism, ed., by Kan Sanjun, sakuhin-sya, 2001.

12. *Shochiku-kageki-Dan* led by Tamaki Mituru, and *Gekidan 58 gou sen* led by Fukuhara Akira are the main of those theatre groups.

13. From an interview of Oshiro Tatsuhiro reported in MY TOWN OKINAWA, asahi. com. < http://mytown.asahi.com/okinawa/news01.asp?c=18&kiji=99>

14. John M. Purves, "Postwar Okinawan Politics and Political Culture", Contemporary Okinawa Website 1955-2002. < http://www. niraikanai. wwma.net/pages/base/chap3-1.html>

15. From an interview of *Medoruma Shun* reported by Tim Larimer, "Identity Crisis," TIME ASIA July 24.2000 Vol 156 No.3. < http://www.time.com.time/asia/magazine/2000/0724/japan/okinawa.html. >

16. Milton Gordon, see the web site "Assimilation and Ethic Identity, Egoldwish. http://www.egoldwish.com/aboutus.htm

# Contributors

**Amelia Howekritzer** is Associate Professor of Theater and Chairperson of the Department of Theater of University of St. Thomas in St. Paul, Minnesota. She is author of *The Plays of Caryl Churchill: Theatre of Empowerment* (1991). Her essays have appeared in a wide range of journals and edited collections, and she also edited *Plays by Early American Women, 1775-1850* (University of Michigan Press, 1995).

**Asma Mundrawala** is an artist/performer from Karachi (Pakistan), and have recently completed MA in Art and Performance Theory at Wimbledon. Her dissertation advocated the efficacy of participatory theatre, using a theatre group from Karachi, the *Tehrik-e-Niswan* (the Women's Movement) as a case study. She has been a regular performer with the group.

**B. Ananthakrishnan** is Professor in Theatre Discipline in Sarojini Naidu School of Performing Arts at Hyderabad Central University. He is actively related with theatre research and practice. He is a recognized actor, director and critic.

**Bett Pacey** is a Lecturer at the Drama Department of Technikon, Pretoria where she teaches Scene Studies, Voice Animation, Dialects and Puppetry. She also supervises post-graduate programmes. She has written children's plays, Puppetry and Street Theatre scripts, a musical and several cabarets. She performs as a stage and television actress and voice artist.

**Catherine Diamond** teaches theatre at Soochow University, Taiwan. She is the director of Phoenix Theatre – an English-language troupe that performs contemporary dramas. She has written extensively on the contemporary theatre in Southeast Asia.

**Chia-Hsin Chou** is young research scholar earlier associated with Washington University. She now teaches in the Department of Applied Languages for Translation and Interpretation in the Chang Jung University of Taiwan besides carrying out her research work.

**Christina Nygren** is Associate Professor in the Department of Theatre Studies at Stockholm University. She is also a Research Fellow of the Swedish Council for Research in the Humanities and Social Sciences. She has authored several scholarly papers in reputed journals.

**Christopher Innes,** Fellow of the Royal Society of Canada and Fellow of the Royal Society of Arts (England), is a Research Professor at the York University and holds the Canada Research Chair in Performance and Culture. He is also the author of books on *Modern Theatre, Avant Garde Theatre: 1892-1992, The Theatre of Gordon Craig, A Sourcebook on Naturalist Theatre* and *Modern British Drama: The Twentieth Century.* He is also the Editor of *The Cambridge Companion to Bernard Shaw* and General Editor for several series of monographs, including the Cambridge *Directors in Perspective.*

**Ciane Fernandes** is a tenured Professor at the Graduate Program for Performing Arts and at the School of the Federal University of Bahia. Honoured with several academic and artistic awards and prizes, including the Brazilian National Prize for Art at Universities, she has studied Bharatnatyam also with Rajyashri Ramesh. She is author of several important books on body aesthetics and movement.

**David G. John** studied at the Universities of Toronto (Ph.D. German, 1975) and Vienna. Since then, he has been a Professor of German in the Department of Germanic and Slavic Studies at the University of Waterloo, Canada, and a Visiting Professor at McGill University, Montreal. His research focuses on the enlightenment and classical periods of German literature (Lessing, Goethe, Schiller), especially theatre and its international performance and reception. His major publications include books on Johann Christian Krüger, the German *Nachspiel*, and Goethe.

**David Whitton** teaches theatre, film and literature at Lancaster University (England), where he is Professor of European Languages & Cultures and also Dean of Arts & Humanities. His research interests include theory and practice of staging; production studies; the avant-garde; Molière. He is currently researching/writing a history of French theatre. He is Joint Secretary General of IFTR.

**Diane Smith-Sadak** is the Head of the Performance Programme in the Department of Theatre Arts at Towson University, USA. She has a wide academic experience also. She is member of the IFTR's Theory & Practice Performing Group. She is an AEA actor and professional director.

**Elizabeth Bonjean** is a Ph.D. student at the University of Washington School of Drama. She was the recipient of the School of Drama's Muichale Quinn Writing Award (2002) for her paper, "The Commodification of the Female Body and Breast Cancer Culture".

**Elzabieta Koldrzak** is working with the Department of Drama and Theatre, University of Lödz. She holds a specialization in Indian Theatre and interestingly has also studied Sanskrit Theatre in global pretext. She has undertaken several courses in different performing genres. As a theatre activist, she has worked in India and abroad.

**Erik Rynell** is a scholar of history, art, philosophy, drama and music. He has had experience as musician, journalist, playwright, dramaturge and teacher of Theatre Theory. As the vice-head of the course on Dramatic Writing, he is presently at the Malmo Theatre Academy, Lund University.

**Ewa Wachocka** is the Manager at the Department of Theatre Studies in the University of Silesia. Her publications include several books as well as articles in many collective works. She co-operates with ·Polish and German journals like *Dialog*, *Pamietnik Literacki* and *Balagan*, *Slavisches Drama*, *Theater and Kino*.

**Glen McGillivray** currently lectures in Theatremaking in the School of Contemporary Arts at the University of Western Sydney. He has worked extensively as a director, performance maker and dramaturg.

In 2002, he was an Australia Council-funded dramaturge-in-residence at the Banff Playwrights colony in Alberta, Canada.

**Jelena Rajak** is a Ph. D. student in the Contemporary Dance Studies at the University Paris-8 (Saint-Denis) where she earned her Master of Arts Degree in Theatre and a First Degree in Contemporary Dance, after graduating in French and Comparative Literature at the Faculty of Philosophy of Zagreb (Croatia). Her fields of study are cognitive and anthropological aspects of actor's and dancer's training, as well as autoreflexivity in contemporary dance performance as critical metapraxis.

**John Warrick** is a Ph.D. student in Theatre at the University of Washington in Seattle, where he is currently working on a dissertation concerning the iconography of the medieval Hell-mouth within its cultural semiotic system.

**Li, Ruru**, Workshop Theatre at Leeds University. Her major publications include: *Shashibiya: Staging Shakespeare in China* (Hong Kong University Press, 2003), *Mao's Chair: Revolutionizing Chinese Theatre*, (TRI, March 2002), *Sino the Times: Three Spoken Drama Productions on the Beijing Stage* (TDR, Summer 2001), *Conventionalization: The Soul of Jingju, Performing Processes - creating live performance*, edited by Roberta Mock, (Bristol: Intellect, 2000), 'Shakespeare on the Chinese Stage in the 1990s' (*Shakespeare Quarterly*, Fall 1999).

**Matthew Issac Cohen**, is a Lecturer in Theatre Studies at the University of Glasgow. He studied Psychology at Harvard University as an undergraduate and completed Ph.D. at Yale University in Anthropology in 1997. He was a post-doctoral research fellow in the performing arts at the International Institute for Asian Studies, The Netherlands, from 1998-2000, and has held two Fulbright grants to study Javanese shadow puppet theatre. He has published extensively in the fields of Southeast Asian performance, theatre ethnography, children's play, and interculturalism, and is a practising shadow puppeteer.

**Matthijs Engelberts** currently conducts research and teaches at the University of Amsterdam. After having studied in Amsterdam, he spent a year at Tulane University (New Orleans, USA) and received a (post-doctoral) DEA at the Université de Paris III (comparative literature) and X (theatre), and defended his thesis at the University of Amsterdam.

**Nicholas Till** is Senior Lecturer in Theatre at Wimbledon School of Art, London. He has worked as a writer and director of new opera and music theatre works for the English National Opera Studio and the Royal Opera Garden Venture, and is co-artistic director of the experimental music theatre company Post-Operative Productions. His previous publications include *Mozart and the Enlightenment* (Faber & Faber/WW Norton, 1992). He is currently editing the *Cambridge Companion to Opera* (CUP).

**Nigel Stewart** is Lecturer in Theatre Studies at Lancaster University, UK. He has worked extensively as a director, choreographer and dancer, and his research concerns the relationship between movement analysis, notation and aesthetics. He has published in *New Theatre Quarterly*, *Performance Research* and *Total Theatre*; he has contributed to *Negotiating Cultures: Eugenio Barba and The Intercultural Debate* (MUP, 2002) and to *Dance Theatre: An International Investigation* (MMU, 2002); and he is currently co-editing *Performing Nature: Explorations in Ecology and the Arts* (Peter Lang, 2005).

**Peter G.F. Eversmann** is currently Associate Professor at the Department of Theatre Studies, University of Amsterdam and Vice-President of the IFTR. His research interests include the history and theory of the theatrical environment and audience and reception research.

**Poh Sim Plowright** is a Lecturer at Royal Holloway specializing Oriental Drama and has also studied extensively about East-West Theatre Connections and has done her research in the same subject. She became the Director of Europe's first centre of study of Noh Drama in 1991.

**Poonam Trivedi,** Reader in English, Indraprastha College, University of Delhi, received her Ph. D. from The Shakespeare Institute, University of Birmingham, UK. She has published articles on women in Shakespeare, the performance of Shakespeare in India, and on Indian theatre traditions.

**Radha Ramaswamy** is a Lecturer of English at Mount Carmel College, Bangalore, India. She has taught English language and literature in Mumbai, Cambridge and Bangalore. She has been a keen student of theatre, trying to combine an academic/literary interest with an interest in the socio-cultural aspects of theatre practices.

**Ranbir Sinh**, a senior actor, director, playwright and researcher, is the member of the executive committee for Cultural Identity and Development (CIDC) of ITI, UNESCO. He is a Fellow of Royal Asiatic Society of Great Britain and Rajasthan State Academy of Drama and Music. His important publications include books on *Parsi Theatre: History; Indra Sabha: Critical Assessment; Wazid Ali Shah: The Tragic King*; and ten full-length plays.

**Rebecca Caines** is a community arts practitioner, who has been working on the North Coast of NSW, Australia, directing, writing and event managing for community theatre and arts festivals for over six years. She is currently studying for her Ph.D. with the School of Theatre, Film and Dance at the University of New South Wales in Sydney.

**Robyn Marie Campbell** is a graduate of Laban Centre, having earned her Master of Arts Dance Studies and Professional Diploma in Community Dance Studies. She has worked in England, Canada and Germany as a dance artist, performance scholar, community dance facilitator and art administrator. She is currently employed at Laban Centre as Guest Lecturer and Scheduling Coordinator.

**Seth L. Wolitz** is Professor of Comparative Literature, French and Slavic and holds the Gale Chair of Jewish Studies at the University of Texas at Austin, USA. He is also a member of the Theater Group at the University. He has published books on Proust, and I. B. Singer and many articles on theatre and opera libretti ranging from the francophone theatre of Aime Cesaire, Il Trovatore of Verdi to the Yiddish musical theatre of Abraham Goldfaden. He is at present writing a book on the development of modern Jewish theatre.

**Shoko Yonaha** is a drama critic in Okinawa.

**Tiina Rosenberg** is Associate Professor in Theatre Studies and Gender Studies at Stockholm University, Sweden. She has written extensively on queer theory and feminism. She is currently working on a project on heteronormativity in Swedish 20th Century Performance and working on two new books.

**Tim Prentki**, Professor in Worchester College, is the Course Director of the MA Programme in Theatre for Development and has published in *New Theatre Quarterly*, published by the National Association for Drama in Education and in Research in Drama Education. He has run numerous 'Theatre for Development' workshops, in Nigeria and Zambia, and has also led the British Council's HIV/AIDS awareness drama programme in Cameroon.

**Vibha Sharma**, a Gold Medalist in English, is a Ph. D. scholar in Aligarh Muslim University and also teaching in the university. She has presented several papers on literature at university and various national level seminars. She has also published several articles in reputed journals.

**Yael Feiler** is a Ph.D. candidate working at the Department of Theatre Studies, Stockholm University, Sweden. During the early 1980s, she was active as an actress, theatre director and a playwright. Since the 1990s, she has been combining theatre research and literary translation. She is interested in the relations between feminism and postcolonial theory and is also involved in the debate concerning migration and identity politics in Sweden.